Discourse Studies and Biblical Interpretation

Discourse Studies
& Biblical Interpretation

A Festschrift in Honor of Stephen H. Levinsohn

Steven E. Runge
Editor

LEXHAM PRESS

Discourse Studies and Biblical Interpretation: A Festschrift in Honor of Stephen H. Levinsohn

Lexham Press, 1313 Commercial St., Bellingham, WA 98225
http://www.lexhampress.com

ISBN 9781577995203

Editor: Steven E. Runge
Contributors: Nicholas A. Bailey, Regina Blass, Rick Brannan, Randall Buth, Constantine R. Campbell, Robert A. Dooley, Buist Fanning, Jenny Read-Heimerdinger, Iver Larsen, Stanley E. Porter, Steven E. Runge, Margaret G. Sim, R. J. Sim, Lindsay J. Whaley
Copy Editor: Micah Wierenga
Cover Design: Sean Fields
Typesetting: projectluz.com
Project Support: Jessi Gering
Publisher: John D. Barry

Table of Contents

Pragmatics

Appendix

Introduction

Why We're Honoring Stephen H. Levinsohn

Steven E. Runge

Stephen Levinsohn's career with Wycliffe Bible Translators and its sister organization SIL International has combined Bible translation with academic scholarship. After completing a B.Sc. in mathematics from the University of Manchester and a Diploma in Theology from the University of London, Stephen and his wife, Nessie, were accepted as members to SIL International. In 1968, after Jungle Camp and other training, they started working with the Inga people of Columbia. From 1970–98, Stephen served as a Linguistic Consultant for the Columbia branch of SIL International. He also served as Director of Linguistic Workshops for SIL International Panama from 1973–76. Training national and expatriate translators became his passion. SIL International recognized his expertise in equipping others by making him an International Linguistic Consultant in 1976, and he still holds this position. During his tenure as International Linguistic Consultant, Stephen also served as Director of Linguistic Workshops in twenty different contexts in Mexico, India, Africa, and Southeast Asia. During the 1970s he also worked on degrees in linguistic sciences from the University of Reading, England, completing both a master's degree and a Ph.D.

Language typologists have found that all languages, despite their diversity, need to accomplish the same basic communication tasks. Levinsohn's linguistic training provided the foundation he needed for equipping translators to describe the various language features they encountered. The workshop format that Levinsohn used for his training constantly tested his linguistic framework. With each new set of language data he encountered, Levinsohn continually refined his conceptualization of different typological features. His passion for ongoing refinement can be seen in his publications. He was not afraid to revise his claims if some new innovation allowed greater precision and clarity. The publication of Knud Lambrecht's *Information Structure and Sentence Form* is a case in point.[1] Lambrecht's cognitively based Construction Grammar model of word-order analysis (i.e. information structure) overcame weaknesses of the model Levinsohn had been using. Innovations like this led Levinsohn to completely revise his 1992 edition of *Discourse Features of New Testament Greek* into its current version.[2] We find similar growth in his other publications as he constantly improved the precision and clarity of his descriptions.

The sheer volume of workshops Stephen has conducted in the past forty years has provided him with unparalleled opportunities to see discourse features in action. I remember discussing a particular feature of Hebrew from the Exodus narrative with him during a workshop in 2003. "Oh yes, I recall having seen something similar before," he said, and then he went on to rattle off languages from the Philippines and Africa that used a similar strategy to accomplish the same discourse task. His encyclopedic retention of such data is astounding.

This wide exposure to language has also made Levinsohn a sought-after sounding board by researchers. He learned not only how languages work but also how languages *don't* work. When an ill–formed proposal was presented, he would firmly, but respectfully, redirect the scholar in a more productive direction. On countless occasions he has offered feedback on theses and dissertations focused on biblical languages. Due to his service with SIL International, rather than as a formal faculty member of an institution, much of his academic advising has been informal, or as an external reader. As I first began reading my way into discourse studies, I

---

[1] Knud Lambrecht, *Information Structure and Sentence Form: Topic, Focus, and the Mental Representations of Discourse Referents* (Cambridge; New York: Cambridge University Press, 1996).

[2] Stephen H. Levinsohn, *Discourse Features of New Testament Greek: A Coursebook on the Information Structure of New Testament Greek*, 2nd ed. (Dallas: SIL International, 2000). Levinsohn continues to update this text in preparation for another version—further evidence of his continuing quest for improvement.

came across one acknowledgement after another from authors thanking him for his influential feedback.

My own relationship with Stephen began in late 2000 through a serendipitous internet search result as I was trying to discover what to even call the kind of research in which I was interested.[3] His paper was exactly the kind of research I had wanted to do myself. In response to my initial inquiry, I received an encouraging note along with a reading list. So began a mentoring process that continues to this day. My questions would expose holes in my thinking, and Levinsohn would help me fill them in by sending lecture notes, papers, or other reading lists to help me acquire the requisite background. My story is not unique, as I have heard of the same from others who have interacted with him.

If all of these claims about Levinsohn's expertise are valid, why it is that his work has not gained greater notoriety within biblical studies? Why isn't his work cited alongside Wallace, Robertson, Porter and other Greek grammarians? There are two possible reasons for this. First, Levinsohn has focused on translation. He writes as a translator/linguist for other translators and linguists. Despite the fact that his ideas have significant consequences for exegesis and interpretation, he has nevertheless remained focused on his core objective of equipping translators. In the last decade, he has become noticeably more involved within the guild of biblical studies by regularly presenting papers at the Society of Biblical Literature meetings. This shift is due in part to the recognition that most Bible translators acquire their knowledge of Greek and Hebrew through traditional graduate theological programs. Translators in such programs often feel as though the traditional approach to describing the biblical languages runs counter to what they have learned in the their linguistic training. Despite this shift, most of Levinsohn's publications have focused more on translation than exegesis. Any application to the latter requires the reader to make the necessary adaptations themselves. Thus, Levinsohn's work has primarily benefited those willing to make the investment needed to apply his principles to exegesis.

[3] Stephen H. Levinsohn, "NP References to Active Participants and Story Development in Ancient Hebrew," *Work Papers of the Summer Institute of Linguistics, University of North Dakota Session* 44 (2000): 1-13.

There is another factor which has limited Levinsohn's influence—it has affected translators and exegetes alike. Levinsohn places an extremely high value on precision. In other words, unless his description can account for 90–95% of the data, he considers it inadequate. Generally speaking, well-formulated principles can typically explain 75–85% of language data. However, as we move beyond basic principles to account for the remaining data, matters become significantly more complex.

Within Greek there are basic principles that account for much of the variation in word order and usage of verb tenses. Describing the remainder of the data requires us to take into account other factors such as genre, presence of other discourse devices, and stylistic preferences of specific authors. The more specific the explanation, the more complex it tends to be.

Outside of Greek, there are other factors that can affect language usage and thus language description. Since Levinsohn's research focuses on equipping others to translate Scripture into diverse languages, simply describing a feature within the Greek language context is often insufficient. Many languages use other means to accomplish discourse tasks than those used in Greek or English; this is called a mismatch in the languages. A translator's description must take into account potential mismatches, even though they are a non-issue for the English-speaking Greek student. For example, the function of adverbial participles in Greek matches quite closely with the usage in English. The adverbial participles that precede the main verb typically provide circumstantial information with respect to the main verbal clause. In contrast, the participles that follow the verb tend to elaborate on some aspect of the main verbal action. So while the circumstantial participles convey actions that occur independent of the main action, the elaborating participles directly modify the main action. Such is not the case in Object-Verb (OV) languages of the Philippines. In OV languages, circumstantial clauses tend to *follow* the main verb rather than *precede* it. Thus while this detail about participles might be of little value to the English speaker because of its continuity with English, it would be of critical importance to a translator working in a mismatched language.

Levinsohn's service as an International Linguistic Consultant has required significant sacrifice. Each new language that he has encountered has effectively raised the bar on the requirements for his linguistic descriptions.

Each new workshop has also typically required significant time away from family and loved ones, often in less-than-comfortable living conditions. The honor and recognition normally associated with serving at an academic institution has been traded for the privilege of equipping disadvantaged translation teams using only minimum resources. To address this need, Levinsohn has shifted his focus in recent years from traveling and teaching to preparing materials that can be studied independently.[4] He continues to contribute feedback on research projects and theses in addition to offering a limited number of workshops.

Levinsohn is by no means the only SIL International member deserving recognition for significant contributions to the field of biblical studies; all too frequently such work goes unrecognized, even if it is appreciated in some quarters. The goal of this volume is to see that at least in Stephen's case, his work receives the commendation that it deserves. Each of the contributors to this volume has had their ideas challenged or influenced by Levinsohn's work, and each counts it an honor to contribute to a volume honoring him. The caliber of these scholars should dispel any doubts about why we're honoring Stephen's work in this Festschrift; the list of contributors speaks for itself. If you have been wondering exactly what discourse studies has to offer to biblical interpretation, I commend these articles to you as evidence of the dividends that are in store for those who invest the time and effort to enter this field.

---

[4] Stephen H. Levinsohn, *Self-Instruction Materials on Non-Narrative Discourse Analysis.* (Self-published, 2008), http://www.sil.org/~levinsohns/NonNarr.pdf; Stephen H. Levinsohn, *Self-Instruction Materials on Narrative Discourse Analysis.* (Self-published, 2008), http://www.sil.org/~levinsohns/narr.pdf.

Practice

Discourse Analysis as an Aid to Bible Translation

Iver Larsen

Introduction

In this paper I shall discuss and give an overview of the function of the Greek particles δέ, καί, τέ, γάρ and οὖν from the perspective of discourse linguistics. These particles have not been adequately described within the parameters of traditional Greek grammar. They are better handled from the standpoint of discourse linguistics. Even the latest edition of the standard New Testament Greek lexicon (BDAG)[1] has not adequately explained their use and function.

My interest in discourse studies started long before I knew what it was. I remember reading a book that was translated from English into my mother tongue, Danish. Quite often the book would have a sentence like, "When he arrived at his house, John noticed that the door was open." In Danish, the initial "he" is always anaphoric, so I would search the preceding sentence for a clue as to who the "he" referred to. Failing to find such a clue I realized that this mystical "he" was actually John. How odd. Mother tongue speakers will often have a feeling that something is wrong when the discourse patterns are wrong because of too literal a translation, but often we cannot figure out what exactly *is* wrong.

[1] William F. Arndt, Frederick W. Danker, and Walter Bauer, *A Greek-English Lexicon of the New Testament and Other Early Christian Literature* (3rd ed.; Chicago: University of Chicago Press, 2000).

When I attended my first course in practical linguistics at the SIL International school in the UK in 1972, Stephen Levinsohn was one of my teachers. I am very grateful for his pioneering work in discourse analysis in addition to another pioneer, Dr. Robert Longacre. The need for discourse analysis was felt early on by SIL International linguists, because they came across features in non-Indo-European languages that just could not be explained in terms of Greek, Latin or English grammatical tradition. In this paper the term "discourse analysis" refers to a discipline within descriptive linguistics, not the sociolinguistic or political discourse analysis. SIL International linguists used to talk about "pesky little particles," referring to certain words whose meaning and function was often difficult to pin down. Mother tongue speakers would instinctively know how and when to use them, but most of them would be unable to describe either their meaning or their function. In the following I shall discuss some discourse topics that I have enjoyed studying because an understanding of their function is crucial for me as a Bible translator who is committed to produce translations that use natural and clear language.

Pesky little particles in Danish and Greek

A former general secretary of the Danish Bible Society many years ago wrote that in a Bible translation into Danish the small "superfluous" words should be eliminated. They were simply filling up the page without having any meaning. Many theologians have expressed similar ideas, suggesting that these "superfluous small words" have no place in a Bible translation.[2],[3] They might be used in spoken language, but had no place in the written language. This was before discourse studies came into vogue. Many did not realize that when we remove these discourse particles from the language, we not only suck the life and soul out of the translation but also obscure the flow and coherence of the text; this has a negative impact on translation.

People are used to temporal and logical conjunctions between clauses, but discourse particles operate above the sentence level and are usually neither

[2] *Det Danske Bibelselskabs Årbog* (København: Det Danske Bibelselskab,1987), 25.

[3] Robert W. Funk called them function words without meaning apart from being a signal. Robert W. Funk, *Beginning-Intermediate Grammar of Hellenistic Greek* (Missoula, MT: Scholar's Press, 1973), 475.

temporal nor logical. A common discourse particle in Danish is "jo." It either indicates that the speaker thinks that the statement that contains the particle (or the statement that the particle refers to) is obvious to everyone, or it may indicate a concession. The closest English equivalent is "after all," but there is no one-to-one correspondence between the two, as there rarely is when we cross language barriers, even related languages like English and Danish. Another common one is "nemlig," which indicates that what follows is a further elaboration of or background for what has just been mentioned. The particle "for" is similar, but more restricted in usage.

In the following I shall briefly note the basic functions of some Greek "pesky little particles." It is worth noting that Levinsohn has shown how inadequate traditional Greek grammar is when it comes to describing the function of particles like καί and δέ. In chapter 5.1 he says:

> Some New Testament grammarians take the position that δέ is "usually . . . indistinguishable from καί" (Turner 1963:331, see also Thrall 1962:51). The problem is captured nicely by a comparison of Porter's list of "senses" for the two conjunctions:
>
> "δέ (. . . Adversative or Connective or Emphatic . . .)" (1992:208)
>
> "καί (. . . Connective or Adversative or Emphatic)" (211)!

Levinsohn then proceeds to give a better description: "My research into the distribution of καί and δέ in Acts determined that, for δέ to be used, a factor of distinctiveness (a change of spatio-temporal setting or circumstances, a change in the underlying subject, or a change to or from background material) had to be present."[4]

This description does not necessarily apply when the Greek text follows underlying Hebrew connectives, because here we often find a so-called Semitic καί where another Greek connective would have been better Greek. This is common in Matthew and parts of Luke.

---

[4] Stephen H. Levinsohn, *Discourse Features of New Testament Greek: A Coursebook on the Information Structure of New Testament Greek* (2nd ed.; Dallas: SIL International, 2000), 71-2.

Levinsohn then proposes that for δέ to be used, a new step or development in the author's story or argument needs to be present. I find it simpler to say that δέ can indicate a change from one theme (or paragraph) to another. He also talks about an "event cluster" where individual events within the cluster are normally linked by καί whereas different clusters are separated by δέ.[5]

The particle δέ

The most common Greek sentence connector is δέ. In Matthew there are 494 occurrences, in Mark 163, in Luke 542, in John 213, in Acts 554, in Romans 148, in 1 Corinthians 211 (!), in 2 Corinthians 73, in Galatians 58 (!), in Ephesians 20, in 1 John 11, and in Jude 13.[6]

We see, then, that Matthew, Luke, and Paul use δέ frequently. John uses it sparingly. (Some of the functions that δέ has in the other books have been taken over by οὖν in John's writing.) It is noteworthy that the small letter of Jude has more δέ's than the whole of 1 John. It is also interesting that 1 Corinthians has many more δέ's than Romans although it is shorter, and that Galatians has almost three times as many δέ's as Ephesians, although it is shorter. Both 1 Corinthians and Galatians are high-tension letters with lots of contrast between how the readers behave and how they ought to behave. Mark and especially John often use asyndeton (the absence of a connecting particle) instead of δέ. In addition, Mark uses καί quite frequently, often where Luke would use δέ (probably due to Semitic influence).[7]

To pin down the various uses of δέ by different NT authors is not easy. BDAG describes it as "one of the most common Gk. particles, used to connect one clause to another, either to express contrast or simple continuation. When it is felt that there is some contrast betw. clauses—though the contrast is oft. scarcely discernible—the most common translation is 'but'. When a simple connective is desired, without contrast being clearly implied, 'and' will suffice, and in certain occurrences the marker may be left untranslated."[8] The first

[5] Ibid., 75.

[6] These numbers are from the SIL International program BART, version 5.3.

[7] See Randall Buth, "Semitic καί and Greek δέ," *Selected Technical Articles Related to Translation* 3 (1981): 17.

[8] BDAG, 213.

problem with such an entry is that it does not properly describe the function of the particle. The second problem is that it tries to explain the function in terms of English, even though English has no comparable particle.

I think it is safe to say that δέ is an adversative particle. It signals change.[9] Its various functions should correlate with this basic idea. Therefore a change of participants is acceptable, but *introduction* of new participants is not. It may indicate a change of scene, and that may mean that new participants come onto the scene, but strictly speaking δέ does not introduce these participants. A change from event-line to background or from background to event-line is also acceptable. That it may introduce a response in general as suggested by Levinsohn[10] is questionable, but it may well introduce an adversative, uncooperative, or hostile response. A co-operative, expected response would be introduced by καί or asyndeton. However, it often introduces a change of speaker.

The particle καί

When καί connects words, phrases or sometimes clauses, it does not present any problems. It simply joins and coordinates the items and means "and." It does not here function as a discourse particle. However, when it connects sentences, it is a discourse particle and should normally not be translated "and" in English. Still, its basic meaning remains. It is a conjoining particle that refers to some kind of *addition*. It shows that somehow there is a coordinate or close sequential connection between the sentences it links.

Levinsohn[11] has shown that in Luke and Acts καί often works in harmony with δέ. The δέ particle often separates or starts off what he calls "development units," while καί binds together the sentences within such a unit.

---

9 Buth, "Semitic καί and Greek δέ," 17.

10 Stephen H. Levinsohn, "The Function of De in the Narrative of Mark 14.1–16.8," *Notes on Translation* 67 (1977): 3; idem., *Discourse Features of New Testament Greek: A Coursebook on the Information Structure of New Testament Greek* (2nd ed. Dallas: SIL International, 2000), 74.

11 Stephen H. Levinsohn, "Sentence Conjunctions and Development Units in the Narrative of Acts," *Selected Technical Articles Related to Translation* 5 (1981): 2–39; idem., "Notes on the Distribution of δέ and καί in the Narrative Framework of

As with most other sentence-linking discourse particles, καί may have more than one function. However, the function ascribed to καί has to correlate with its basic meaning of conjoining or adding something rather than separating or contrasting something.

A special problem with καί in the NT, especially the synoptic Gospels, is that Hebrew does not have two paired particles like δέ and καί. It has only one general linking word (waw) which is literally translated by καί into Greek. Therefore, a literal translation from Hebrew will have more καί's in it than normal Greek discourse structure allows. (Similarly, the KJV has an inordinate number of sentence-initial "and's.")[12]

Although καί is a conjoining and not a contrastive particle, it is best translated by a contrastive connector in English (but or yet) in those cases where the two conjoined clauses or sentences have contrastive content (for example, 1 John 1:6 and 2:1). Or one could keep the "and" and show the contrast by adding a word like "yet" as in the NET Bible at 1 John 1:6.

The particle τέ

The particle τέ is a cousin of καί. If the two occur together they are similar in function to two καί's; that is, they mean "both . . . and." When τέ occurs alone (τέ solitarium[13]) it functions similarly to καί, but it seems to have a stronger conjoining function, often as an afterthought which was really part of the first thing mentioned. When τέ conjoins two clauses or sentences, the second event is considered to overlap with or be a close continuation of the first event. Levinsohn[14] describes it as follows: "they refer to different aspects of the same event, the same occasion, or the same pragmatic unit."

Luke's Gospel," *Selected Technical Articles Related to Translation* 5 (1981): 39–53; idem., *Discourse Features*.

[12] For further information, see Buth, "Semitic καί and Greek δέ"; idem., "Some Notes on Sentence Level καί in the Martyrdom of Polycarp," *Selected Technical Articles Related to Translation* 3 (1981): 19–21; idem., "On Levinsohn's Development Units," *Selected Technical Articles Related to Translation* 5 (1981): 53–56.

[13] Levinsohn, *Discourse Features*, 94.

[14] Ibid.

The τέ particle is very common in Acts; it is often helpful to look at the word immediately preceding the τέ particle. This word may indicate the hinge on which the afterthought or close continuation swings as in the following examples:

> Matt 28:12: καί συναχθέντες μετὰ τῶν πρεσβυτέρων συμβούλιόν τε λαβόντες ἀργύρια ἱκανὰ ἔδωκαν τοῖς στρατιώταις
> And they (chief priests) met with the elders and (while meeting) (τέ) they took counsel together and gave a considerable sum of money to the soldiers[15]
>
> John 4:41–42: καί πολλῷ πλείους ἐπίστευσαν διὰ τὸν λόγον αὐτοῦ, (v. 42) τῇ τε γυναικὶ ἔλεγον ὅτι Οὐκέτι διὰ τὴν σὴν λαλιὰν πιστεύομεν, αὐτοὶ γὰρ ἀκηκόαμεν.
> And many people came to believe because of his words (v. 42) and (τέ) they said to the woman: "Now it is no longer just because of what you said that we believe, for we ourselves have heard him." (When NIV puts a paragraph break before John 4:42, it violates the Greek structure; compare GNB.)
>
> Acts 6:11–13: τότε ὑπέβαλον ἄνδρας λέγοντας ὅτι . . . συνεκίνησάν τε τὸν λαὸν καί τοὺς πρεσβυτέρους καί τοὺς γραμματεῖς καί ἐπιστάντες συνήρπασαν αὐτὸν καί ἤγαγον εἰς τὸ συνέδριον, (v. 13) ἔστησάν τε μάρτυρας ψευδεῖς
> Then (τότε) they secretly persuaded some men to say . . . they stirred up (τέ) the people, elders and scribes and brought Jesus before the Council . . . they produced (τέ) false witnesses

The three events conjoined by τέ are close-knit overlapping events which all have the same purpose (and the same subject). The second event has two parts conjoined by καί: stirring up the people and bringing Jesus before the Council.

In Acts 9:3 τέ functions to knit together the event of the light and voice to the fact that Paul had almost reached his goal of eradicating the church in Damascus.

---

[15] All translations my own unless otherwise noted.

> Acts 9:3: ἐν δέ τῷ πορεύεσθαι ἐγένετο αὐτὸν ἐγγίζειν τῇ Δαμασκῷ, ἐξαίφνης τε αὐτὸν περιήστραψεν φῶς ἐκ τοῦ οὐρανοῦ καί πεσὼν ἐπὶ τὴν γῆν ἤκουσεν φωνὴν
> In his travelling it happened that he was approaching Damascus and (τέ) a light from heaven shone around him. And (καί) as he fell down he heard a voice.

The phrase "it happened" in the above rendering has a highlighting function. A more free translation might read: "As Paul was travelling along he had almost reached Damascus, when suddenly a light from heaven . . ."

> Acts 12:17: διηγήσατο [αὐτοῖς] πῶς ὁ κύριος αὐτὸν ἐξήγαγεν ἐκ τῆς φυλακῆς εἶπέν τε, Ἀπαγγείλατε Ἰακώβῳ καί τοῖς ἀδελφοῖς ταῦτα. καί ἐξελθὼν ἐπορεύθη εἰς ἕτερον τόπον.
> He told them how the Lord had led him out of the prison and (τέ) he added: "Tell this to James and the brothers." And he left to go to a different place.

The translation "he added" rather than "he said" is chosen because of τέ. He was in a hurry to get away, and therefore could not himself tell the story to James and the brothers. The use of direct speech makes the command prominent.

In Acts 21:27–32 we find an interesting array of τέ's and καί's:

> v. 27 . . . some Jews having seen him (Paul) at the temple were stirring up the whole crowd καί they seized him
> v. 28 shouting: "Help! (We have caught this criminal)"
> v. 29 for (γάρ) (they thought Paul had taken a Gentile into the temple)
> v. 30 and (τέ) was aroused the whole city καί there was a commotion of all the people καί having seized Paul they dragged him out of the temple καί immediately the doors were shut
> v. 31 and (τέ) as they were trying to kill him, it was reported to the commander who hastily gathered some soldiers and ran to the place.

The καί in v. 27 indicates that the two clauses describe consecutive events: stirring up the crowd who then seized him. The καί's in v. 30 again connect consecutive events: the city was aroused and this resulted in a commotion which again led to dragging him out of the temple after which the doors were shut.

When we have a τέ, the events overlap as can be seen by the thematically connected verbs "stirring up," "arouse" and "try to kill." The purpose of stirring up the crowd was to kill him and the means was to arouse the crowd. These verses ought to be translated in the breathtaking style Luke is using without a single δέ. (GNB is better than NIV here.) An understanding of the function of the discourse connectors enables the translators to catch and represent the "soul" and drama of the text.

A similar passage follows a little later in Acts 21:35–37. Notice the overlap between "being carried on the steps" and "about to be brought into the barracks":

> v. 35 ὅτε δέ ἐγένετο ἐπὶ τοὺς ἀναβαθμούς, συνέβη βαστάζεσθαι αὐτὸν ὑπὸ τῶν στρατιωτῶν διὰ τὴν βίαν τοῦ ὄχλου,
> v. 36 ἠκολούθει γὰρ τὸ πλῆθος τοῦ λαοῦ κράζοντες, Αἶρε αὐτόν.
> v. 37 Μέλλων τε εἰσάγεσθαι εἰς τὴν παρεμβολὴν ὁ Παῦλος λέγει τῷ χιλιάρχῳ, Εἰ ἔξεστίν μοι εἰπεῖν τι πρὸς σέ;
> v. 35 But (δέ) when he reached the steps, the crowd was so violent that the soldiers had to carry him,
> v. 36 for (γάρ) a big group of people were chasing him, crying out: "Get rid of him!"
> v. 37 And (τέ) just as Paul was about to be carried into the barracks, he asked the commander: "Can I say something?"

Levinsohn[16] notes that the conjoining force of τέ precludes a paragraph break before v. 37 as the UBS text wrongly suggests. If anything, the δέ of v. 35 as well as ἐγένετο points to a possible paragraph break before v. 35.

The γάρ particle

According to BAGD[17] γάρ is a "conjunction used to express cause, inference,

[16] "Sentence Conjunctions," 26.

[17] Arndt, William F., F. Wilbur Gingrich, Frederick W. Danker and Walter Bauer, *A Greek-English Lexicon of the New Testament and Other Early Christian Literature: A Translation and Adaptation of the Fourth Revised and Augmented Edition of Walter Bauer's Griechisch-deutsches Wörterbuch zu den Schriften des Neuen Testaments und der übrigen urchristlichen Literatur* (2nd ed.; Chicago: University of Chicago Press,

continuation, or to explain." This was adjusted in BDAG[18] to "express cause, clarification, or inference."

The King James version consistently translated it "for," but modern translations have realized that γάρ in Greek certainly does not always function as the English "for." David Lithgow[19] pointed out that it is often wrong to suppose that γάρ indicates a reason relationship. Harbeck[20] was the first, as far as I know, to suggest that γάρ is used to introduce background information in narrative texts.

I am suggesting that the BAGD and BDAG lexicons are assigning too many varied meanings to γάρ. The particle γάρ is simply explanatory and introduces additional information which the author/speaker wishes to give to his readers/hearers so that they can better understand some word or aspect of the previous sentence or clause. In some cases, there may be a causal relationship between the explanatory new information and the previous statement. But if that is so, it is not signaled primarily by γάρ, but shown by the context. Runge says, "Robertson advocates that it is best viewed as explanatory in nature, before making an appeal for other senses. Robertson's 'explanatory' assertion has largely been confirmed as the core constraint of γάρ in modern linguistic treatments."[21]

Throughout the NT γάρ is used in both narrative and non-narrative texts. In narrative texts, γάρ takes the reader off the main event-line into the background. In non-narrative texts there is not always a clear distinction between the main theme-line and background information, but γάρ still maintains its basic explanatory function. This explanatory function is also called "supportive" or "strengthening" by some linguists.[22]

1979), 151 (hereafter BAGD).

[18] BDAG, 189.

[19] David Lithgow, "New Testament Usage of the Function Words Gar and Ei," *Notes on Translation* 47 (1973): 16–18.

[20] Warren A. Harbeck, "Mark's Use of Gar in Narration," *Notes on Translation* 38 (1970): 10–15.

[21] Steven E. Runge, *A Discourse Grammar of the Greek New Testament: A Practical Introduction for Teaching and Exegesis* (Bellingham, Wash.: Lexham Press, 2010).

[22] E.g., Levinsohn, *Discourse Features*, 91.

I shall give a few examples to illustrate its use:

> Matt 9:12–13: Οὐ χρείαν ἔχουσιν οἱ ἰσχύοντες ἰατροῦ ἀλλ᾽ οἱ κακῶς ἔχοντες. (v. 13) πορευθέντες δέ μάθετε τί ἐστιν, Ἔλεος θέλω καί οὐ θυσίαν· οὐ γὰρ ἦλθον καλέσαι δικαίους ἀλλὰ ἁμαρτωλούς.
> The healthy don't have a need for a doctor, however the sick have. (v. 13) But go and learn what this saying means: Mercy is what I want, not sacrifice. Γάρ (After all), I have not come to call "righteous people" but "sinners."

The γάρ not only explains why Jesus showed and wanted others to show mercy, but also that those who consider themselves righteous don't see their own need for mercy or forgiveness.

> Matt 9:20–21: γυνὴ . . . προσελθοῦσα ὄπισθεν ἥψατο τοῦ κρασπέδου τοῦ ἱματίου αὐτοῦ· (v. 21) ἔλεγεν γὰρ ἐν ἑαυτῇ, Ἐὰν μόνον ἅψωμαι τοῦ ἱματίου αὐτοῦ σωθήσομαι.
> a woman came from behind and touched the tassel of his cloak. (v. 21) Γάρ she was thinking: If only I get to touch his cloak, I'll be healed.

The author explains the somewhat strange action of touching Jesus' cloak from behind.

> Mark 16:2–4: ἔρχονται ἐπὶ τὸ μνημεῖον . . . (v. 3) καί ἔλεγον πρὸς ἑαυτάς, Τίς ἀποκυλίσει ἡμῖν τὸν λίθον ἐκ τῆς θύρας τοῦ μνημείου; (v. 4) καί ἀναβλέψασαι θεωροῦσιν ὅτι ἀποκεκύλισται ὁ λίθος· ἦν γὰρ μέγας σφόδρα.
> they arrived at the tomb. (v. 3) (And) they had been saying to one another, "Who will roll away for us the stone from the tomb's entrance?" (v. 4) (And) when they looked up, they saw that the stone had already been rolled back. Γάρ it was very large.

This example is interesting in that the γάρ-clause at the end of v. 4 does not explain anything in the sentence immediately preceding it. (That sentence is on the event-line and connected back, with καί, to the previous event of arriving at the tomb.) Instead, the γάρ-clause explains the previous background comment in v. 3 about the impossibility of two women removing the enormous stone.

A similar instance is found in

> John 21:7–8: καί ἔβαλεν ἑαυτὸν εἰς τὴν θάλασσαν, (v. 8) οἱ δέ ἄλλοι μαθηταὶ τῷ πλοιαρίῳ ἦλθον, οὐ γὰρ ἦσαν μακρὰν ἀπὸ τῆς γῆς . . . σύροντες τὸ δίκτυον τῶν ἰχθύων.
> and he jumped into the lake, (v. 8) while the other disciples came in the boat, γάρ they were not far from land . . . dragging the net with fish.

Here the γάρ-clause does not explain why the other disciples stayed in the boat, but it explains the previous clause about Peter jumping into the lake. In Greek, the whole thing is one long sentence. I have argued elsewhere[23] that Peter did not swim to the shore before the others, but that John is describing the somewhat complex idea of getting the whole catch of fish safely to shore, which they managed to do because Peter was wading behind or beside the boat holding the net to prevent it being torn against any sharp objects on the bottom of the lake.

Paul uses the γάρ particle frequently, especially in his more argumentative sections. He is very associative in his thinking, often picking one concept from a sentence and further explaining or developing that concept in the following sentence. An example from Rom 1:15–20:

> v. 15 being eager to evangelize you in Rome, too,
> v. 16a γάρ I am not ashamed of the gospel (explains "eager")
> v. 16b γάρ it is the power of God to salvation for everyone who believes, Jews as well as Greeks (explains "not ashamed")
> v. 17 γάρ a righteousness from God is revealed in it [the gospel] based on faith and proceeding in faith as it is written: "The just shall live by faith." (explains "salvation for everyone who believes")
> v. 18 γάρ the wrath of God is on the unrighteous people (explains "righteousness from God" to believers by contrasting it to "wrath/punishment from God" on the "unrighteous people")
> v. 19a because (διότι) the knowledge of God is revealed to them,
> v. 19b γάρ God revealed it to them (explains who revealed it)

---

[23] Iver Larsen, "Did Peter Enter the Boat?" *Notes on Translation* 2/2 (1988): 34–41.

v. 20 γάρ God's power and divine nature is shown through creation (explains how it was revealed)

If we compare the KJV, NIV, and GNB renderings of this passage, we first notice that KJV uses the word "because" once, but it translates διότι, not γάρ. KJV translates each of the six γάρ's with "for." NIV and GNB translate these six γάρ's as follows: NIV translates 16b "because," 17 "for," 19b "because," 20 "for," and does not translate the word in 16a and 18. GNB translates the word in 17 and 19b as "for" and does not translate it in 16, 18, and 20.

Now, to sum up the use of γάρ, we can say that its basic function is explanatory. In narrative, it introduces a background comment which may be of various types.[24] In non-narratives, it gives a further explanation or comment on some aspect of the previous context. This may involve a reason relationship, but not necessarily so. In English it may be translated "since" (because), "for," "you see," "after all" or it may be left untranslated. It all depends on the context.

The particle οὖν

Many writers have pointed out that John is particularly fond of using the particle οὖν. However, it does occur fairly commonly in most NT books. (Mark is characteristic in his almost complete non-use of οὖν; he uses καί instead. In Matthew there are 56 occurrences, in Mark 6, in Luke 33, in John 200, in Acts 61, and in Romans 48.[25]

BDAG[26] says, "it is an inferential and then mainly a transitional conjunction." Not a very helpful description.

The basic relationship expressed by οὖν is consequence. However, in classical Greek οὖν signified continuation.[27] Moulton et al.[28] suggest eight functions for οὖν:

---

24 Harbeck, "Mark's Use of Gar in Narration."

25 The numbers are from BART, but are approximate, since some of the occurrences are textually disputed, including at least two in Mark.

26 BDAG, 736.

27 See Levinsohn, "Sentence Conjunctions," 28; and idem., *Discourse Features*, 126–32.

28 W. Moulton and A. S. Geden, *A Concordance to the Greek New Testament* (5th ed.; rev. by H. K. Moulton; Edinburgh: T. & T. Clark, 1978), 1104.

1. Inference (logical consequence)
2. Consequent command or exhortation
3. Consequent effect or response
4. Inferential question
5. Summary (a final inference, a conclusive statement)
6. Adversative
7. Continuation or resumption of narrative
8. Continuation of discussion

In this concordance a number is assigned (occasionally two numbers) to each occurrence of οὖν. Numbers 7 and 8 occur frequently in John, but never in Matthew or Mark proper (once in 16:19), and rarely in other authors. As can be seen from the description above, the meaning correlates with the classical usage (continuation). The first four functions (numbers 1–4) occur evenly spread throughout the NT (number 3 in narratives, and 1, 2, and 4 mainly in non-narrative texts and speeches). The summary function (number 5) is very rare (less than 1%). All of the above listed meanings except 6 can be closely related to the basic meaning of consequence or continuation. But number 6 is suspect in this regard, because there is no close connection between adversative and consequence. Only ten instances of οὖν (about 2% of the occurrences) are 6, and I am convinced that the adversative aspect is carried by something other than οὖν, so that these ten instances (Matt 26:54; John 8:38; 9:18; 12:7; Acts 23:21; 25:4; 26:22; 28:5; Rom 10:14; 11:19) should be reclassified. Levinsohn[29] discusses some of these and agrees that they are better analyzed as resumptive or inferential rather than adversative.

Reimer[30] suggests that one of the functions of οὖν in John's Gospel is to move "the story-line along by introducing "distinctive information" which furthers the author's purpose." In addition, she suggests that οὖν has the thematic function of "monitoring the tension of the developing theme according to the author's purpose." I am a bit skeptical about these two hypotheses, but it does seem that the occurrence of οὖν in John's Gospel is often connected with conflict between Jesus and his opponents, "the Jews,"

---

[29] Levinsohn, *Discourse Features*, 126–32.

[30] Martha Reimer, "The Functions of Oun in the Gospel of John," *Selected Technical Articles Related to Translation* 13 (1985): 35.

and between faith and lack of faith. That is an important and recurrent theme in the book. I would prefer, however, to keep tension connected to John's use of the historic present. I do agree, though, that οὖν is often used at places where the local theme is supporting the overall theme of the need to believe in Jesus and be saved.

The following chart gives a brief overview of the usage of these particles in the Gospels and Acts. The symbol ø refers to asyndeton:

Matthew	Mark	Luke/Acts	John	
change of scene or theme	δέ, τότε	Sem. καί,	δέ, Sem. καί	Sem. καί
Sem. καί	δέ	(esp. Luke)		ø, δέ
change to backgr. comment	δέ	δέ, ø	δέ	δέ, ø
change of (underlying) subject	δέ	δέ	δέ	δέ
change to backgr. explanation	γάρ	γάρ	γάρ	γάρ
return to (or start) foreground	δέ, καί	καί, ø	δέ, καί	οὖν, ø
continuative response	καί	καί	καί	οὖν, ø
contrastive response	δέ	δέ	δέ	ø, (h. pres.)
conjoining sentences within the same theme (incl. setting)	καί	καί	καί, τέ (Acts)	ø, καί
close temporal/	καί,	καί	καί,	οὖν,
consequential	τότε		οὖν,	καί,
sequence			τέ, τότε	τότε

Participant reference

Levinsohn devotes two chapters (8 and 9) to the topic of participant reference.[31] It is vitally important to study and understand the rules that govern participant reference in different languages in order to correctly

31 Levinsohn, *Discourse Features.*

understand and translate a text. Certain aspects are fairly universal, others are language- and culture-specific.

There are several different parameters to look at. One is the study of how participants are first introduced into the story, either at the very beginning or later. There is often a difference between major or global participants on one hand and minor or local participants on the other. Major participants are on stage throughout most of the discourse, while minor ones only appear in a small section. Another parameter is the relative status of the participants. Who has the upper hand in the dialogue or conflict?

For both of these parameters, we need to look at the status hierarchy.[32] If a person is referred to by name, it puts him or her at the top of the hierarchy. Minor participants are rarely named, but if they are, the meaning of the name is significant. The status assigned is from the perspective of the speaker and/or author. For instance, in the parable about the rich man and Lazarus (Luke 16:19–31), the rich man is not named. He would have had a high status in society, but not in this parable. But the poor man is named. This indicates that he has the upper hand in the end when it really counts. It is likely that the Greek Lazaros comes from Hebrew Eleazar which means "My God has helped," a fitting name for this character.

The next rung in the status hierarchy is a noun phrase. This is commonly used when participants are first introduced, but it may also be used when a participant is later referred to in order to clarify the reference. The third rung is a personal or demonstrative pronoun. The lowest rung is a verbal affix or simply nothing at all, often signified by Ø.

This status hierarchy may be more or less universal. I remember how it struck me when I looked at a story in the Sabaot language[33] that described a conflict between two friends. Both were named when first introduced. In the first section, one of them tricked the other, and in this section the one who had the upper hand was referred to by name. In the second section, the tables were turned, and the second person got his revenge by tricking the first person. In this second section, the second person who now had the upper hand was

[32] See also ibid., 135–41.

[33] A Southern Nilotic language spoken by about 250,000 people in Western Kenya.

referred to by name. The person who was being tricked, the underdog, was referred to by a demonstrative pronoun ("the other one") in both sections.

An aspect that is specific to Greek is that a major participant is often referred to by a pronoun alone. This is a principle of economy and is probably related to the common use of ellipsis in Greek. It is expected that the hearer remembers what has been said previously and uses this information to understand the current text. Since major participants are always on stage, they only need to be named in the introduction, not when later referred to. In the Gospels, Jesus is the major participant, so he is often referred to by a simple pronoun. This is not the case for English, and that is why modern English translations of the Bible often insert the name "Jesus" where the Greek text only has a pronoun.

Another aspect specific to Greek is that even personal names may take a definite article. Levinsohn describes a default rule for the use of the definite article with names: "When a participant is [made] active (introduced for the first time), reference to him or her by name typically is anarthrous. However, once he or she has been active, subsequent references to him or her by name within the same episode are articular."[34]

When this default rule is not adhered to, it indicates that the participant is given higher prominence. Levinsohn discusses this in chapter 9.2.3: "According to the principle of sec. 9.2.1, further references to active participants are normally articular. Anarthrous references to active participants are therefore of particular significance. In particular, they make the participant and/or his or her initiative or speech prominent, because it is of particular importance."[35]

I would like to illustrate this with reference to John 8:12–59, a section with a lot of conflict between two opposing sides. Jesus is a global participant while a group of Pharisees is also a global participant. These two participants repeatedly oppose one another. The verbal conflict takes place in the temple precincts (John 8:20) and there is a crowd of common Jews listening to Jesus speaking, but they do not take part in the conversation. In a sense the crowd is also a global participant, since Jesus preached many times in public to the

---

[34] *Discourse Features*, 150–51.

[35] Ibid., 155–61.

crowds, and it was common to find people listening to him in the Temple compound, but they are less important in this section.

The section starts at 8:12:

> Πάλιν οὖν αὐτοῖς ἐλάλησεν ὁ Ἰησοῦς λέγων
> Once again Jesus spoke to them.

Πάλιν indicates that Jesus resumes his teaching of the crowd in the Temple. The οὖν may suggest that the following scene is important for John's overall theme, but it could also be just resumptive. Jesus is re-introduced with an articular name. In English we prefer a clearer reference to the audience than simply "them," so GNB explicates "to the Pharisees," while NIV and CEV explicates "to the people." NET sits on the fence and removes the pronoun: "Then Jesus spoke out again." If we look back to verse 8:2 or further back to 7:37 or 40, it is most likely that the intended audience is the crowd but a group of Pharisees would be present and would have taken a position close to Jesus. The content of Jesus' speech in v. 12 also suggests that a general crowd is intended. ("I am the light of the world. Whoever follows me will never walk in darkness, but will have the light of life.")

The Pharisees do not allow Jesus to continue his speech, but break in to oppose him. The intrusion is indicated as follows:

> 8:13 εἶπον οὖν αὐτῷ οἱ Φαρισαῖοι
> The Pharisees said to him.

The Pharisees are re-introduced by a noun phrase, since a plural pronoun (they) could have been misunderstood as a reference to the crowd. Jesus is referred to by a pronoun which may indicate that at this point the Pharisees are attacking Jesus and show a lack of respect. If τῷ Ἰησοῦ had occurred instead of just αὐτῷ, he would have had a higher prominence.

Jesus responds:

> 8:14 ἀπεκρίθη Ἰησοῦς καί εἶπεν αὐτοῖς
> Jesus responded and said to them.

Here the Pharisees are downgraded to the third rung and Jesus is made prominent not only by the name being used, but by the lack of the definite article. It is clear whose side the author is on. It is fairly impossible to get this aspect across in translation.

The Pharisees respond with an apparently innocent question:

> 8:19a ἔλεγον οὖν αὐτῷ, Ποῦ ἐστιν ὁ πατήρ σου;
> They were saying to him, "Where is your father?"

Now the Pharisees are down at the bottom rung with a Ø reference (verbal suffix). Some might say that this is the default encoding, but the point is that the author had a choice of three levels, and he chose the lowest.

Jesus responds:

> 8:19b ἀπεκρίθη Ἰησοῦς
> Jesus responded.

Now the Pharisees are not even given a pronoun, but Jesus is mentioned by name without the article. This is the biggest possible difference between the top and bottom rung, between the upper hand and the underdog. Jesus is rebuking the Pharisees, because they do not believe that he has come from God, his Father in Heaven.

Verse 20 is a side comment by John, but then the dialogue resumes in

> v. 21 Εἶπεν οὖν πάλιν αὐτοῖς
> He continued speaking to them.

Since Jesus is the major and global participant, a Ø reference is adequate. Likewise the plural pronoun refers to the group of Pharisees who are also major participants. οὖν may indicate resumption as mentioned above, but πάλιν shows the same, so it is possible that οὖν is used by John to highlight an important speech content that relates to the overall theme of the Gospel as suggested by Reimer.[36] Jesus is not here rebuking the Pharisees, but giving a general statement that applies beyond the Pharisees to other unbelievers. NIV translates the speech as follows: "I am going away, and you will look for me, and you will die in your sin. Where I go, you cannot come."

> v. 22 ἔλεγον οὖν οἱ Ἰουδαῖοι
> The "Jews" then continued

[36] "The Functions of Oun," 28–36.

The use of a noun phrase indicates that the Pharisees are trying to get an upper hand. Their words show a lack of respect. (They ask, "Is he going to commit suicide?") When John calls the Pharisees οἱ Ἰουδαῖοι, it is clear that he refers to the Pharisees rather than the crowd of Jews, contra some translations like NLT (2004) and CEV who use "people." NLT (1996) had "Jewish leaders" as does NET. It is a group of hostile pharisaic Jewish leaders who oppose Jesus in this confrontational dialogue, not the Jews in general.

> v. 23 καί ἔλεγεν αὐτοῖς
> And he said to them.

Again a minimum participant reference. The dialogue continues without Jesus asserting himself, but giving a less confrontational explanation.

> v. 25a ἔλεγον οὖν αὐτῷ, Σὺ τίς εἶ;
> Then they said to him, "Who are you?"

Minimal participant reference. It sounds almost like an honest question. It does not appear to be a hostile response.

> v. 25b εἶπεν αὐτοῖς ὁ Ἰησοῦς, Τὴν ἀρχὴν ὅ τι καί λαλῶ ὑμῖν
> The Jesus said to them, "(I am) what I have been telling you all along."

Here John makes Jesus assert himself through a noun phrase. He seems to be getting impatient with them. He has told them who he is, but they refuse to believe, so it sounds like Jesus is taking their question as one of unbelief rather than an honest willingness to listen.

John makes one of his common authorial comments in v. 27: "They did not understand/realize that he was telling them about his Father." John uses asyndeton here as he often does rather than a δέ to indicate a shift to background or a γάρ to indicate an explanatory comment.

> v. 28 εἶπεν οὖν [αὐτοῖς] ὁ Ἰησοῦς
> The Jesus said to them

There was no response from the Pharisees this time, and Jesus continues to assert himself and explains once more who he is. He adds that when they [Jewish leaders/Pharisees] have gotten him crucified, they have another chance to realize who he is. This is the end of the first round of discussion/

confrontation with the Pharisees, and John turns to another of his interspersed comments, now about the crowd who had been listening in:

> v. 30 Ταῦτα αὐτοῦ λαλοῦντος πολλοὶ ἐπίστευσαν εἰς αὐτόν.
> As he was speaking like this many [in the crowd] came to faith in him.
>
> v. 31 Ἔλεγεν οὖν ὁ Ἰησοῦς πρὸς τοὺς πεπιστευκότας αὐτῷ Ἰουδαίους
> Then Jesus spoke to those Jews who had come to believe in him, "If you hold to my teaching, you are really my disciples. Then you will know the truth, and the truth will set you free." (NIV)

Whether the οὖν is only resumptive of Jesus's speech or whether John intends to highlight another important thematic concept is not clear to me. I suspect the thematic option is more likely, since it is not a resumption of speaking to the Pharisees, but now speaking to a different group. Jesus is made prominent and the hearers are described in terms of John's previous comment about having come to believe in him. In this case "Jews" does not refer to the Pharisaic leaders. There is no indication that they came to believe in him. Instead they quickly break in with their usual antagonistic comments:

> v. 33 ἀπεκρίθησαν πρὸς αὐτόν, Σπέρμα Ἀβραάμ ἐσμεν καί οὐδενὶ δεδουλεύκαμεν πώποτε· πῶς σὺ λέγεις ὅτι Ἐλεύθεροι γενήσεσθε;
> They responded to him, "We are the seed of Abraham and we have never been slaves of anybody! How dare you say: 'You shall be set free'?"

Since both the Pharisees and Jesus are still on stage having their discussion, these two major participants can be referred to at the lowest rank of the hierarchy. It would have been helpful if John had used a noun phase for the Pharisees, but these discourse patterns are not fixed rules. They are more like tendencies. Apparently, John thought that the default usage of ø reference to the major participant, the Pharisees, was enough to indicate the reference. English translations are often misleading, when they do not recognize the different strategies for participant reference in Greek and English. According to English patterns, the "they" in v. 33 would be interpreted as those who had come to believe in Jesus, since these are the last people referred to. But these people are not participants in the dialogue. Although Jesus addresses them, they never respond. The content of the response makes it clear that it is the Pharisees who say these words, and a Greek reader would understand this with fewer problems than an English reader is faced with when reading English translations. It would also have been helpful to have a new section start at v. 33, where the second and last round of confrontation is initiated by the Pharisees, but no English version (or Greek edition) does that. Many translations have a paragraph or even a section break before v. 31, which adds to the confusion for the readers of the translations.

> v. 34 ἀπεκρίθη αὐτοῖς ὁ Ἰησοῦς, Ἀμὴν ἀμὴν λέγω ὑμῖν ὅτι πᾶς ὁ ποιῶν τὴν ἁμαρτίαν δοῦλός ἐστιν τῆς ἁμαρτίας.
> The Jesus responded to them: "Surely, I am telling you that every person who lives in/habitually does sin is a slave of sin."

John lets Jesus get the upper hand again by using a name and referring to the Pharisees with a pronoun. The speech ends with:

> v. 38 ἃ ἐγὼ ἑώρακα παρὰ τῷ πατρὶ λαλῶ· καί ὑμεῖς οὖν ἃ ἠκούσατε παρὰ τοῦ πατρὸς [ὑμῶν] ποιεῖτε.
> What *I* speak about is what I have heard while being with the Father, but *you* are doing/following what you have heard from (your) father.

The use of οὖν here does not follow the normal pattern, and it is not reflected in any translation, not even the KJV. Does it resume the theme from v. 34—"You are slaves of sin"—or does it highlight the final punch line—"You obey your father (Satan)"? I think it is likely that it highlights a theme that is crucial to John's overall theme of having faith in Jesus: listening/obeying Satan rather than Jesus is the opposite of belief and leads to destruction, not salvation. In any case, this final accusation has to be countered by the Pharisees:

> v. 39a Ἀπεκρίθησαν καί εἶπαν αὐτῷ, Ὁ πατὴρ ἡμῶν Ἀβραάμ ἐστιν.
> They responded and said, "Our father is Abraham!"

Again a minimal participant reference. John apparently wants to keep the Pharisees at a low position. They are trying to defend themselves without success. Sometimes the choice of hierarchical reference seems to follow how the writer sees them, sometimes how the speakers see themselves. It appears that the beginning of the dialogue indicates how they see themselves, but the end (from v. 33) indicates how John sees them.

> v. 39b λέγει αὐτοῖς ὁ Ἰησοῦς, Εἰ τέκνα τοῦ Ἀβραάμ ἐστε, τὰ ἔργα τοῦ Ἀβραὰμ ἐποιεῖτε·
> The Jesus says to them, "If you were children of Abraham, you would have been doing the deeds of Abraham."

Jesus is shown to have the upper hand by the use of his name. The present tense "says" has a highlighting function: Sit up and listen, what follows is an important principle. A "child of Abraham" in the spiritual sense is a true believer. The Pharisees and other Jews may well be physical children/descendants of Abraham, but that does not make them true believers.

> v. 41 εἶπαν [οὖν] αὐτῷ, Ἡμεῖς ἐκ πορνείας οὐ γεγεννήμεθα· ἕνα πατέρα ἔχομεν τὸν θεόν.
> Then they said, "Us, we are not illegitimate children. We have only one father, God."

Minimal participant reference. The Pharisees are still kept low by John.

> v. 42 εἶπεν αὐτοῖς ὁ Ἰησοῦς, Εἰ ὁ θεὸς πατὴρ ὑμῶν ἦν ἠγαπᾶτε ἂν ἐμέ
> The Jesus said to them, "If God had been your father, you would have loved me"

Again the use of the name gives Jesus the upper hand in the discussion. The denunciation of the Pharisees continues to v. 47.

> v. 48 Ἀπεκρίθησαν οἱ Ἰουδαῖοι καί εἶπαν αὐτῷ
> The "Jews" responded and said to him

Here John shows by the noun phrase that the Pharisees try to assert themselves over Jesus and they come with a very strong accusation: "You must be demon-possessed!" No arguments any longer, only an accusation. The reference "the Jews" indicates hostility.

> v. 49 ἀπεκρίθη Ἰησοῦς, Ἐγὼ δαιμόνιον οὐκ ἔχω
> Jesus responded, "Me, I am not demon-possessed."

Now we have the greatest contrast again between Jesus without an article and zero reference to his opponents. It is clear that Jesus is shooting them down.

> v. 52 εἶπον [οὖν] αὐτῷ οἱ Ἰουδαῖοι, Νῦν ἐγνώκαμεν ὅτι δαιμόνιον ἔχεις.
> Then the "Jews" said to him, "Now we know for sure that you are demon-possessed!"

The repeated usage of "the Jews" as a reference indicates the increasing hostility.

> v. 54 ἀπεκρίθη Ἰησοῦς
> Jesus responded.

Similar to v. 49 we see the highest possible contrast in reference between an anarthrous Jesus and not even a pronoun for the Pharisees.

> v. 57 εἶπον οὖν οἱ Ἰουδαῖοι πρὸς αὐτόν, Πεντήκοντα ἔτη οὔπω ἔχεις καί Ἀβραὰμ ἑώρακας;
> Then the Jews said to him, "You are not yet fifty years old and you have seen Abraham?!"

The hostility level is maintained with "the Jews."

> v. 58 εἶπεν αὐτοῖς Ἰησοῦς, Ἀμὴν ἀμὴν λέγω ὑμῖν, πρὶν Ἀβραὰμ γενέσθαι ἐγὼ εἰμί.
> Jesus said to them, "Surely I am telling you: I have been in existence from long before Abraham."

Jesus is still anarthrous. The pronoun reference to the Pharisees may indicate that this is the end of the dialogue, and in John's view they have lost the battle. At this point the Pharisees try to stone Jesus.

Conclusion

The main reason that Bob Longacre, Stephen Levinsohn and other SIL International linguists are so interested in studying the discourse features of Hebrew, Greek and local languages is our common goal to produce faithful translations of the Bible. By faithful I mean translations that are based on a thorough analysis of the original texts of the Bible, an analysis that helps to understand and appreciate what the original authors intended to communicate. But for a translation to be a faithful representation of that intended meaning, I believe it is also important to study and analyze the discourse features of the language receiving the translation. It is no mean task, but a fascinating one.

Bibliography

Arndt, William F., F. Wilbur Gingrich, Frederick W. Danker and Walter Bauer. *A Greek-English Lexicon of the New Testament and Other Early Christian Literature: A Translation and Adaptation of the Fourth Revised and Augmented Edition of Walter Bauer's Griechisch-deutsches Wörterbuch zu den Schriften des Neuen Testaments und der übrigen urchristlichen Literatur*. 2nd ed. Chicago: University of Chicago Press, 1979.

———. *A Greek-English Lexicon of the New Testament and Other Early Christian Literature*. 3rd ed. Chicago: University of Chicago Press, 2000.

Buth, Randall. "Semitic καί and Greek δέ." *Selected Technical Articles Related to Translation* 3 (1981): 12–19.

———. "Some Notes on Sentence Level καί in the Martyrdom of Polycarp." *Selected Technical Articles Related to Translation* 3 (1981): 19–21.

———. "On Levinsohn's Development Units." *Selected Technical Articles Related to Translation* 5 (1981): 53–56.

Harbeck, Warren A. "Mark's Use of Gar in Narration." *Notes on Translation* 38 (1970): 10–15.

Larsen, Iver. "Did Peter Enter the Boat?" *Notes on Translation* 2/2 (1988): 34–41.

Levinsohn, Stephen H. "The Function of De in the Narrative of Mark 14.1–16.8." *Notes on Translation* 67 (1977): 2–9.

———. "Sentence Conjunctions and Development Units in the Narrative of Acts." *Selected Technical Articles Related to Translation* 5 (1981): 2–39.

———. "Notes on the Distribution of δέ and καί in the Narrative Framework of Luke's Gospel." *Selected Technical Articles Related to Translation* 5 (1981): 39–53.

———. *Discourse Features of New Testament Greek: A Coursebook on the Information Structure of New Testament Greek*. 2nd ed. Dallas: SIL International, 2000.

Lithgow, David. "New Testament Usage of the Function Words Gar and Ei." *Notes on Translation* 47 (1973): 16–18.

Longacre, Robert E. *The Grammar of Discourse*. 2nd ed. Topics in Language and Linguistics. New York: Plenum Press, 1996.

Manton, Margaret. "The Semitic Kai." *Selected Technical Articles Related to Translation* 16 (1986): 1–12.

Moulton, W., and A. S. Geden. *A Concordance to the Greek New Testament.* 5th ed., rev. by H. K. Moulton. Edinburgh: T. & T. Clark, 1978.

Porter, Stanley E. *Idioms of the Greek New Testament.* Sheffield: Sheffield University Press, 1992.

Reimer, Martha. "The Functions of Oun in the Gospel of John." *Selected Technical Articles Related to Translation* 13 (1985): 28–36.

Runge, S. E. *A Discourse Grammar of the Greek New Testament: A Practical Introduction for Teaching and Exegesis.* Bellingham, Wash.: Lexham Press, 2010.

Thrall, Margaret E. *Greek Particles in the New Testament: Linguistic and Exegetical Studies.* Leiden: Brill, 1962.

Turner, Nigel. *Syntax.* A Grammar of New Testament Greek 3. Edinburgh: T. & T. Clark, 1963.

Why Hasn't Literary Stylistics Caught on in New Testament Studies?

Stanley E. Porter

Introduction

I consider it an honor to have been asked to contribute to this festschrift dedicated to Stephen Levinsohn. I have known Stephen for over twenty-five years, our first meeting dating back to when I was working on my PhD and he was already a well-respected linguist with particular interests in the Bible. Since that time, we have participated in various ways in society presentations and publications that have advanced what might be called biblical linguistics. Like so many others, I have also benefited especially from his significant work on discourse analysis, *Discourse Features of New Testament Greek*, now in its second edition.[1] In this volume, and even more so in the revised edition, Stephen has made significant strides to advance a model of discourse analysis that pays attention to the specific linguistic phenomena of the Greek of the New Testament within the context of larger linguistic and especially discourse considerations. It is in the spirit of this communal and combined effort—which this Festschrift no doubt bears witness to—that I offer this paper as one more contribution to the furtherance of this discussion.

This paper is not concerned with a particular linguistic problem but with the more general linguistic question of why it is that what has been called literary

[1] Stephen H. Levinsohn, *Discourse Features of New Testament Greek: A Coursebook on the Information Structure of New Testament Greek* (2nd ed.; Dallas: SIL International, 2000).

stylistics has not been used in New Testament studies. In the following sections, I will first define what literary stylistics is and describe its major concerns; then I will offer possible reasons for the lack of its use in New Testament studies; and finally, I will briefly offer an example of linguistic stylistics as an indicator of a possible way forward, before offering a conclusion.[2]

What is literary stylistics?

Many New Testament scholars, and even some linguists, will be unfamiliar with what I am referring to here as literary stylistics. Literary stylistics (as opposed to non-literary stylistics)[3] can be characterized as an attempt to bring the insights and mechanisms of linguistics to bear on the analysis of literature (as opposed to stylistics of any type of text).[4] Literary stylistics had its roots in concepts developed by the Russian Formalists and the Prague School linguists, who developed the notion of "foregrounding" as a way to account for how the kind of emphasis found in non-literary texts can be quantified.[5] Notions from the Prague School of linguistics made its way into various forms of literary criticism by way of such scholars as René Wellek,[6] who was a Prague student who emigrated to the US and became a leader in the literary movement known

---

[2] This question arose out of my MA/PhD course in Linguistic Modeling taught at McMaster Divinity College (Fall 2010), and specifically the questions raised by students and one student in particular who was grappling with related questions. I am thankful to these students for discussion that led to this paper.

[3] Michael Halliday labels the integration of linguistics and stylistics "linguistic stylistics." See Michael A. K. Halliday, "The Linguistic Study of Literary Texts," in *Proceedings of the Ninth International Congress of Linguists* (ed. Horace G. Lunt; The Hague: Mouton, 1964), 302–07, esp. 302.

[4] For a history of stylistics, and followed in part below, see Kirsten Malmkjaer, "Stylistics," in *The Linguistics Encyclopedia* (ed. Kirsten Malmkjaer; London: Routledge, 1991), 438–47. Cf. also Roger Fowler, with contributions by Peter Mercer and F. W. Bateson, *The Languages of Literature: Some Linguistic Contributions to Criticism* (London: Routledge & Kegan Paul, 1971), 1–31.

[5] Malmkjaer, "Stylistics," 440, notes that the use of statistics in language study originated in the nineteenth century to study Paul's letters, according to Anthony Kenny, *The Computation of Style: An Introduction to Statistics for Students of Literature and Humanities* (Oxford: Pergamon Press, 1982), 1.

[6] René Wellek and Austin Warren, *Theory of Literature* (New York: Harcourt, Brace, Jovanovich, 1963 [1949]).

as the New Criticism (the movement at the heart of much so-called narrative criticism in current New Testament studies).[7] Literary stylistics developed into a discipline in its own right as various scholars attempted to bring insights from linguistics to bear upon a variety of literary texts to be able to appreciate their distinctive literary features. Precursors of literary stylistics include I. A. Richards and early practitioners such as Leo Spitzer.[8] Their work gave way to major symposia on literary stylistics. Two of these symposia are the collection edited by Thomas Sebeok from a conference in 1958 that includes pertinent essays by Richards, Dell Hymes, Seymour Chatman, and the classic essay on poetics by Roman Jakobson;[9] and one edited by Chatman from a conference in 1969 that includes papers by Roland Barthes, Tzvetan Todorov, Wellek, Stephen Ullmann, W. K. Wimsatt, Harald Weinreich, Richard Ohmann, Jean Starobinski, Ruqaiya Hasan, and Michael Halliday, among others.[10] The heyday of literary stylistics was in the 1960s and 1970s, which resulted in significant and sustained work by a number of scholars, several of the best known being Samuel Levin, Nils Erik Enkvist, Ohmann, Halliday, Chatman, Roger Fowler, Geoffrey Leech, and Ronald Carter,[11] besides some of those

---

[7] See Stanley E. Porter, "Literary Approaches to the New Testament: From Formalism to Deconstruction and Back," in *Approaches to New Testament Study* (ed. Stanley E. Porter and David Tombs; JSNTSup 120; Sheffield: Sheffield Academic Press, 1995), 77–128, esp. 103–4.

[8] I. A. Richards, *Principles of Literary Criticism* (London: Routledge & Kegan Paul, 1924); Leo Spitzer, *Linguistics and Literary History: Essays in Stylistics* (Princeton: Princeton University Press, 1948).

[9] Thomas A. Sebeok, ed., *Style in Language* (Cambridge, Mass.: MIT Press, 1960). The essay by Roman Jakobson is his concluding statement, entitled "Linguistics and Poetics," 350–77.

[10] Seymour Chatman, ed., *Literary Style: A Symposium* (London: Oxford University Press, 1971).

[11] Samuel R. Levin, *Linguistic Structures in Poetry* (The Hague: Mouton, 1962); Nils Erik Enkvist, "On Defining Style: An Essay in Applied Linguistics," in *Linguistics and Style* (ed. Nils Erik Enkvist, John Spencer and Michael J. Gregory; Oxford: Oxford University Press, 1964), 1–56; Richard Ohmann, "Generative Grammars and the Concept of Literary Style," *Word* 20 (1964): 423–39; idem., "Poetry and Grammaticalness," in *Proceedings of the Ninth International Congress of Linguists* (ed. Horace G. Lunt; The Hague: Mouton, 1964), 308–14; M. A. K. Halliday, "Linguistic Study of Literary Texts," along with other of his essays collected in his *Linguistic Studies of Text and Discourse* (ed. Jonathan Webster; London: Continuum,

mentioned above. Others who addressed major questions in literary stylistics include Stephen Ullmann, George Steiner, and Michael Short.[12] Several important textbooks on literary stylistics have been written,[13] and some significant work has continued in the field.[14] However, in many ways, literary stylistics did not fulfill its initial promise. This is seen in several ways. At the relative outset, there was a noteworthy and sometimes acerbic dispute between Fowler and the literary scholar Frederic Bateson over the merits and methods of literary stylistics.[15] Fowler advocates for the method, while Bateson soundly refutes its significance and the sophistication of its findings. What may have been a welcome liaison between language-oriented methods was apparently stymied almost from the outset by such a set of recriminating responses. Furthermore, many of the early proponents seemed to drift naturally and quickly from literary stylistics to various forms of discourse analysis.[16] The reasons are obvious, with stylistics being concerned with several of the same

---

2002); Seymour Chatman, *A Theory of Meter* (The Hague: Mouton, 1964); Roger Fowler, ed., *Languages of Literature*; idem, ed., *Essays on Style and Language: Linguistic and Critical Approaches to Literary Style* (London: Routledge & Kegan Paul, 1966); idem., ed., *Style and Structure in Literature: Essays in the New Stylistics* (Oxford: Blackwell, 1975); idem., *Linguistics and the Novel* (London: Methuen, 1977); Geoffrey N. Leech, *A Linguistic Guide to English Poetry* (London: Longmans, 1969); Leech and Michael H. Short, *Style in Fiction: A Linguistic Introduction to English Fictional Prose* (London: Longman, 1981); Ronald Carter, ed., *Language and Literature: An Introductory Reader in Stylistics* (London: Allen & Unwin, 1982).

[12] Stephen Ullmann, *Language and Style: Collected Papers* (Oxford: Blackwell, 1966); George Steiner, "Linguistics and Literature," in *Linguistics at Large* (ed. Noel Minnis; London: Paladin, 1971), 111–36; and Mick Short, *Exploring the Language of Poems, Plays and Prose* (London: Longmans, 1996).

[13] See, e.g., G. W. Turner, *Stylistics* (Harmondsworth: Penguin, 1973); Raymond Chapman, *Linguistics and Literature: An Introduction to Literary Stylistics* (London: Edward Arnold, 1973); Anne Clysenaar, *Introduction to Literary Stylistics* (London: Batsford, 1976); E. L. Epstein, *Language and Style* (London: Methuen, 1978);

[14] For example, a recent work with similar concerns is Nigel Fabb, *Language and Literary Structure: The Linguistic Analysis of Form in Verse and Narrative* (Cambridge: Cambridge University Press, 2002).

[15] Reprinted in Fowler, *Languages of Literature*, 43–74.

[16] As seen in Ronald Carter and Paul Simpson, eds., *Language, Discourse, and Literature: An Introductory Reader in Discourse Stylistics* (London: Unwin Hyman, 1989).

types of phenomena as have become hallmarks of discourse analysis, such as prominence/foregrounding and cohesion, among others.[17] Several essays written after the heyday of the movement indicate the influence of discourse analysis upon the movement, and most of those who have followed such scholars as Halliday have turned toward forms of discourse analysis, such as critical discourse analysis.[18] Fowler himself came to call his type of analysis linguistic criticism, and was apparently concerned with more than simply literary stylistics.[19]

The major tenets of literary stylistics, besides adequate general linguistic knowledge, are as follows. (1) Analysis of the language of literature demands that we develop methods of linguistic analysis that move beyond the sentence.[20] Various types of structuralism, especially in North America, restricted analysis to the sentence as the largest unit of grammatical structure. This type of Bloomfieldian inspired analysis was unable to address literary questions. Despite some early attempts, subsequent structuralist and Chomskyan motivated forms of linguistics did not play a significant part in literary stylistics. Instead, literary stylistics appealed to functionalist linguistic perspectives that have tended to be concerned with usage beyond the sentence. (2) Literary stylistics appreciates the literary dimension of texts by accounting for both "habitualization" and "defamiliarization."[21] In other words, it accounts for basic characteristics of what makes people respond to literature—that which is out of the ordinary in relation to the expected.

---

17 For an overview of discourse analysis, see Deborah Schiffrin, Deborah Tannen, and Heidi E. Hamilton, eds., *The Handbook of Discourse Analysis* (Oxford: Blackwell, 2003).

18 On critical discourse analysis, see Stanley E. Porter, "Is Critical Discourse Analysis Critical? An Evaluation Using Philemon as a Test Case," in *Discourse Analysis and the New Testament: Approaches and Results* (ed. Stanley E. Porter and Jeffrey T. Reed; JSNTSup 170; SNTRG 4; Sheffield: Sheffield Academic Press, 1999), 47–70.

19 Roger Fowler, *Literature as Social Discourse: The Practice of Linguistic Criticism* (Bloomington: Indiana University Press, 1981); idem., *Linguistic Criticism* (Oxford: Oxford University Press, 1986), although he had already suggested such a label in his *Languages of Literature*, 10.

20 Karl D. Uitti, *Linguistics and Literary Theory* (Englewood Cliffs, New Jersey: Prentice-Hall, 1969), 194–96.

21 Fowler, *Linguistic Criticism*, 8; Malmkjaer, "Stylistics," 441.

(3) Literary stylistics is concerned with being able to describe and quantify the kinds of observations made in literary studies. I have noted above how the concept of foregrounding was important in the development of literary stylistics. Foregrounding is a way of describing the kinds of prominent structures that are found in literature but that are not so obviously marked as they are in non-literary texts.[22] (4) Quantification of linguistic features is an important part of literary stylistics (as well as non-literary stylistics). Significance of linguistic phenomena is seen to be important in relation to the frequency and expectation of such phenomena being used, as opposed to the other possible choices available to the author. (5) Various conventions and patterns of literature, such as meter, rhyme, and even genre, are held to be susceptible to literary stylistic analysis.[23] A number of essays written from a literary stylistic perspective investigate patterns of structure in literature and attempt to account for these on a linguistic rather than on an aesthetic basis. (6) For literary stylistics, literary language becomes a part of language in the broad sense, rather than being distinguished from language as non-literary or the type of language typically studied by linguists.[24] (7) Literary stylistics attempts to go beyond simple description to criticism and evaluation, unlike many other linguistically based approaches.[25] (8) The aim of literary stylistics is to be able to account for the style of individual texts and the style of an author.[26] In this way, literary stylistics supplements linguistic description not only through interpretation but in its focus upon the author's style. (9) Literary stylistics for many was oriented toward the meaning of the text, and attempted to describe this meaning using linguistics. For some literary scholars, meaning is not translatable, and for some linguists meaning is not relevant. Literary stylistics attempts to bring the two together in a describable way.[27] (10) The study of literature can benefit from the kinds of analyses that

---

[22] Malmkjaer, "Stylistics," 441.

[23] Uitti, *Linguistics*, 208–9.

[24] Ibid., 210–11.

[25] Fowler, *Literature*, 11.

[26] Michael Hoey, "Discourse-Centred Stylistics: A Way Forward?" in *Language, Discourse and Literature* (ed. Ronald Carter and Paul Simpson; London: Unwin Hyman, 1989), 123–38, esp. 123.

[27] Fowler, *Literature*, 20.

are performed by literary stylists.[28] The understanding of literature, though often treated as something of a mystery, can be bolstered and emboldened by various means of describing how the literary text is structured and achieves meaning. (11) Literary stylistics allows observations made for a single literary text to be transferred to observation of other texts.[29] In this way, aesthetic judgments are not allowed simply to stand alone, but show similarities and differences among other works of literature.

Literary stylistics, though associated with many significant linguists, had a relatively short lifespan, before the movement seemed to dissolve and pursue interests in a variety of other areas. Nevertheless, there are a number of interesting principles that define literary stylistics that are worth considering in their relationship to New Testament studies.

Literary stylistics and New Testament Studies

From the description above, it would appear sensible that there are any number of reasons for literary stylistics to become something of use and importance in New Testament study and exegesis. For example, the desire of literary stylistics to move beyond description to criticism or evaluation would seem very compatible with the desire of New Testament scholars to provide explanations for their exegetical observations. Although there are occasional comments made in various interpretation, hermeneutics, and exegesis books about "style" or "stylistics," there is none that I know of that actually incorporates what I have described above as literary stylistics into their methodological discussion. The simplest answer may simply be that biblical scholars are completely ignorant of this movement and its possible potential for interpretation. This is entirely possible. However, a number of the scholars who are mentioned above, while not being biblical scholars or writing in the area of biblical scholarship, are nevertheless known in biblical interpretive circles.

There may be other reasons for this neglect. One of these might be that, as observed above, to my knowledge there are very few treatments of style in

28 Ibid., 11–12.

29 Ibid., 17.

New Testament studies, and even fewer of literary stylistics, and hence no interpretive momentum to pursue such an approach. Nigel Turner's treatment of style, the fourth volume in James Hope Moulton's *A Grammar of New Testament Greek*, is clearly not an example of literary stylistics, even though it contains a wealth of interesting and potentially informative information.[30] Turner's treatment lacks the linguistic foundation of literary stylistics, and is instead an accumulation (sometimes questionable) of data, without an apparent overriding framework. The only literary stylistic treatment of the New Testament that I am aware of is Aída Besançon Spencer's treatment of Paul and his literary style.[31] This treatment of three major Pauline passages—2 Cor 11:16—12:13, Rom 8:9–39, and Phil 3:2–4:13—utilizes the stylistics of Mitchell Leaska along with Leo Spitzer.[32] This may point to another reason that literary stylistics has not been employed widely in New Testament studies. As I pointed out in my review of Spencer's work, much of her approach is based primarily upon stylistic tests developed for English, without sufficient justification of their applicability or adaptability to Greek.[33] Thus, when she says that Greek word order is the same as English word order, and proceeds along those lines, she immediately skews her results. The burden of developing stylistic criteria for Greek, when primarily English criteria are available, may have a stultifying effect upon the use of literary stylistics.

A further contributing factor may be that, by the time New Testament studies became aware of the interpretive potential of literary stylistics, the field itself had, to a large extent, moved into other areas of development, such as discourse analysis, linguistic criticism, critical discourse analysis, and non-literary stylistics, among other possible areas. Only discourse analysis has shown any signs of becoming even minimally used in New Testament

---

[30] Nigel Turner, *Style* (vol. 4 of *A Grammar of New Testament Greek*; ed. James Hope Moulton; Edinburgh: T. & T. Clark, 1976).

[31] Aída Besançon Spencer, *Paul's Literary Style: A Stylistic and Historical Comparison of II Corinthians 11:16–12:13, Romans 8:9–39, and Philippians 3:2–4:13* (Jackson, MS: Evangelical Theological Society, 1984; repr. Lanham, Md.: University Press of America, 1998).

[32] Mitchell A. Leaska, *Virginia Woolf's Lighthouse: A Study in Critical Method* (New York: Columbia University, 1970); and Spitzer, *Linguistics*.

[33] Stanley E. Porter, "Review of *Paul's Literary Style*," *JETS* 28 (1985): 502–4, esp. 503.

studies. This is somewhat surprising—and also disappointing—because it strongly signals how lacking contemporary New Testament studies is in its use of linguistically-based interpretive models, and it has missed out on any number of opportunities to utilize potentially helpful interpretive approaches. I am still astonished at how basic, and even confused, many attempts to introduce linguistics are in basic exegetical and interpretive tools for New Testament study, and how shockingly absent the use of linguistic research is in monographs and even commentaries that purport to be written on the basis of the Greek text. Much more could be done to appreciate the rigorous analytical techniques found in various types of discourse analysis, and how these linguistic frameworks can help to analyze, interpret, and even explain the meanings and functions of texts. Missed interpretive opportunities also include the failure to appropriate linguistic criticism or critical discourse analysis in support of a variety of interpretive methods, including those that are ideological in nature. Even if literary stylistics is rejected as an interpretive method, one might expect non-literary stylistics to find a potential place, as scholars explore the stylistic character of the non-literary New Testament books.

In light of this situation, the question must be asked whether there is a way forward in this discussion. Perhaps the time has come and gone for literary stylistics, as it apparently has in linguistics as a whole. That may be the case. However, there are various interpretive and comparative features of literary stylistics that may still prove useful for study of the Greek New Testament.

Possible ways forward with literary stylistics in New Testament Studies

The fact is that literary stylistics, despite a few efforts, has not apparently caught on in New Testament studies. However, that does not mean that there is not room for its use in those circles that could benefit from such interpretive aid. There are those who, no matter how much explanation and justification, will never undertake what is necessary to become linguistic critics in the full extent of the term. Such an aspiration is simply beyond them, either by inclination or even by ability. Many are thus potentially excluded from using discourse analysis or critical discourse analysis because they are simply unable to. That does not mean that these linguistic models are not beneficial and would not be of benefit to a variety of biblical interpreters. They no doubt would be and have been and, I hope, will continue to be. In fact, I would like to encourage them for those who are able—those willing to master the sources and vocabulary and willing to discipline their learning of a new academic field. However, for others, something like literary stylistics may also prove useful, because of its less formal or apparently rigorous approach to linguistics and its attempt to incorporate an aesthetic or literary dimension into the interpretive model. Such a literary component may well find resonance in the current state of New Testament studies, where literary readings are becoming too predictable and even redundant, and seem to need a theoretical overhaul and an ability to generate transferable results.

In this section, I wish to demonstrate some of these potential results by briefly examining a passage from the Gospels, the account of the healing of Jairus's daughter and the story of the hemorrhaging woman. This is not meant as a complete literary stylistic treatment, but suggestive of the kinds of comparative results that could prove insightful.

Matt 9:18–26, Mark 5:21–43, and Luke 8:40–56

In this comparative analysis, I wish to examine the means by which the various Gospel authors introduce the characters in this complex episode, and evaluate and interpret the ways in which they do so. I have intentionally chosen this episode because it involves the introduction of two sets of characters, those from the frametale involving Jesus and Jairus and his daughter, and those from the embedded tale involving the hemorrhaging woman. The material, though relatively brief, allows for internal and external comparison and evaluation.

The Matthean account is the shortest, with 187 words, the Lukan account the next longest with 287 words, and the Markan account the longest with 370 words.[34] There are many different dimensions to the account that could

[34] This finding alone is interesting in that it confirms—if Markan priority is correct—the findings of E. P. Sanders that tendencies in the synoptic tradition are not easily established, and certainly do not move simply from small to large or simple to complex, as many form critics had earlier posited. See E. P. Sanders, *The Tendencies of the Synoptic Tradition* (SNTSMS 9; Cambridge: Cambridge University Press, 1969).

be analyzed, but I am choosing to emphasize the means by which characters are introduced as a means of examining the style of each of the authors and then comparing their accounts. Jesus is the first character introduced in each account. In Matthew, Jesus is introduced simply with the genitive singular intensive pronoun (αὐτοῦ) as part of a genitive absolute. Mark similarly employs a genitive absolute, but with a proper name and anaphoric article (τοῦ Ἰησοῦ).[35] Luke uses an accusative form of the proper name with anaphoric article as part of a temporal infinitival construction (τὸν Ἰησοῦν). Since Jesus is the major figure of each Gospel, and has been the major figure and explicitly referred to in the previous episode for each of the Gospels (note Matt 9:15, where Jesus speaks what follows; Mark 5:20, where Jesus does things that all marvel over; and Luke 8:39, which ends with specific mention of Jesus), these types of transitional introductions are not unusual, that is, with either a genitive absolute construction or temporal infinitive construction, along with either a pronoun or anaphoric use of the proper noun. These serve as important cohesive devices in making the transition from a previous episode into this one. Luke's transitional ἐν τῷ construction—though far more frequently found in Luke's Gospel than in the other Gospels (32x and usually as part of an ἐγένετο construction vs. 3x in Matthew and 2x in Mark), is nevertheless far less frequent than the use of the genitive absolute. Luke's account, with this construction, indicates most clearly the transition to the new account, a construction he uses again in 8:42b at the transition to the embedded tale of the woman. Mark's and Luke's accounts also introduce the presence of the crowd, something Matthew does not note. Mark does so with the simple noun, while Luke uses the article and noun.

The major protagonist of the frametale is Jairus. He is introduced in Matthew 9:18 as simply ἄρχων εἷς, without his name ever being mentioned, while he is more fully described in a complex word group by Mark 5:22 as εἷς τῶν ἀρχισυναγώγων, ὀνόματι Ἰάϊρος, and yet more fully in Luke 8:41 with the appellative and the following clause used to define him more specifically:

---

[35] I use the term "anaphoric article" for the use of the article to invoke known or given information, as does a relative pronoun referring to its antecedent, one of the common uses of the article as a cohesive device. See Stanley E. Porter, *Idioms of the Greek New Testament* (2nd ed.; Sheffield: Sheffield Academic Press; London: Continuum, 1994), 106.

ἀνὴρ ᾧ ὄνομα Ἰάϊρος, καὶ οὗτος ἄρχων τῆς συναγωγῆς ὑπῆρχεν. The lack of the use of the name is unusual for Matthew (a point to which I will return below), but emphasized further by the other two Gospels by their use of the name and other descriptors. Whereas Matthew provides a concise account of Jairus's coming (aorist participle) and worshipping (imperfect) Jesus, Luke and especially Mark are more explicit.[36] Luke says that he came (aorist), and, falling (aorist participle) at his feet, pleaded (imperfect) with him, expanding the number of processes (not counting the clause of explication of Jairus). Mark says that he came (narrative present) and, seeing (aorist participle) Jesus, fell (narrative present) at his feet and pleaded (narrative present) with him—with three narrative uses of the present tense-form.[37] All three accounts use aorist participles (perfective aspect) to provide background for the foregrounded main actions (imperfective aspects). Luke expands the number of processes, while Mark expands the processes and marks them by use of the narrative present. In both Luke's and Mark's accounts, the more explicit introduction of Jairus as the protagonist of the frametale is supported by the surrounding syntax so that he is foregrounded. Jairus comes to Jesus about his daughter. The daughter, however, is introduced simply as the content of a verb of saying in Matthew (9:18) and Mark (5:23) and as part of a narrative aside in Luke (8:42). Each uses an article + noun + pronoun or adjective. In Matthew and Mark the daughter is the object of the process (complement), while in Luke she is the subject but in a content clause. The frametale then progresses by mentioning Jesus going on his way to Jairus's house. Matthew explicitly states that Jesus (ὁ Ἰησοῦς) is accompanied by his disciples (οἱ μαθηταὶ αὐτοῦ), while Luke only mentions explicitly the crowd (οἱ ὄχλοι), and Mark the great crowd (ὄχλος πολύς). Matthew depicts Jesus and his disciples as following after the ruler (Jairus), while Mark and Luke draw attention to the crowds and their crushing Jesus (αὐτόν).

---

[36] On the use of the tense-forms to indicate verbal aspect, and their various functions, see Stanley E. Porter, *Verbal Aspect in the Greek of the New Testament, with Reference to Tense and Mood* (SBG 1; New York: Peter Lang, 1989), passim; idem., *Idioms*, 20–45 and passim.

[37] On the narrative (or historical) present, see Porter, *Verbal Aspect*, 189–98; idem., *Idioms*, 30–31.

The embedded tale is insinuated into the frametale in each of the Gospel accounts by the introduction of another character, the protagonist of the embedded story. The conjunction for Matthew and Mark is simply the use of καὶ, with Matthew also using the attention marker ἰδοὺ, while Luke uses a second transitional ἐν τῷ construction. The hemorrhaging woman is introduced with a descriptive expression in each Gospel. Matthew (9:20) has γυνὴ αἱμορροοῦσα δώδεκα ἔτη, while Mark (5:25) has γυνὴ οὖσα ἐν ῥύσει αἵματος δώδεκα ἔτη, and Luke (8:43) has γυνὴ οὖσα ἐν ῥύσει αἵματος ἀπὸ ἐτῶν δώδεκα. Matthew's account is the most compact, using the single participle where the other two Gospels use the participle and prepositional word group (one word instead of four words). However, the use of the participle is also an important stylistic feature of Matthew's account. The more analytic and probably rougher syntax of the lengthier construction used in Mark and Luke is syntactically compressed and semantically widened by the use of the New Testament *hapax legomenon* (and generally infrequent biblical word), which is a medical term describing bleeding in general (used by Hippocrates in the fifth/fourth century B.C.E.).[38] This stylistic pattern is found elsewhere in Matthew, such as 8:28, where Matthew uses a participle for Mark's (5:1) nominal word group.[39] Both Matthew and Mark refer to the length of time of the woman's affliction using the accusative of time, whereas Luke uses a genitive expression to indicate the point from which she began to suffer. The result is that both Matthew and Luke foreground elements of their account—Matthew the issue of the flow of blood and Luke the matter of the time from when the woman was afflicted.

With these major participants introduced, the stories both unfold. Matthew's account is noticeably shorter than the other two accounts, not detailing either the frustration of the woman over not being able to be healed by

---

[38] W. D. Davies and Dale C. Allison, Jr., *A Critical and Exegetical Commentary on the Gospel According to Saint Matthew* (ICC; 3 vols.; Edinburgh: T. & T. Clark, 1991–1997), 1:128. Other phrases regarding the "flow of blood" may be narrower in scope. See Johannes P. Louw and Eugene A. Nida, eds., *Greek-English Lexicon of the New Testament Based on Semantic Domains* (2 vols.; New York: United Bible Societies, 1988), domain 23.181 n. 21 (abbreviated as LN).

[39] See Willoughby C. Allen, *A Critical and Exegetical Commentary on the Gospel According to S. Matthew* (ICC; Edinburgh: T. & T. Clark, 1907), 84, 95.

doctors (found in Mark 5:26 and, with variants indicated, in Luke 8:43) or the details of her healing and Jesus's enquiry about what has happened (Luke does not include Jesus's question regarding his power). In the other two Gospels, major characters are not introduced, but the ways in which minor characters or previous characters are depicted is worth noting. In Mark, Jesus is mentioned two times without parallel in either Matthew or Luke (Mark 5:27, 30). Each time he is referred to with the articular form, the first time in the genitive and the second time in the nominative case. The first parallel characters mentioned in the Markan and Lukan accounts at this place in the episode are the disciples (Mark 5:31) and Peter (Luke 8:45). Mark has Jesus's disciples, referred to with a nominal word group (οἱ μαθηταὶ αὐτοῦ), speak to him after he enquires after who has touched him. Luke has Peter answer the similar query (ὁ Πέτρος). This is only the second time in Mark's Gospel that "his disciples" have been introduced in the nominative case, the other instance being in 2:23, when they are the major participants in the plucking episode. However, after this episode, the disciples are introduced in this way relatively frequently (e.g., 6:1, 29, 35; 7:17; 8:4, 27; 9:28; 11:14; 14:4, 12; cf. 7:5; 10:10; 14:16). Somewhat similarly, Luke's use of Peter's name with the anaphoric article is the first time that this construction has been used in the Gospel (the first two episodes involve Peter's following Jesus in 5:8 and his naming as Peter in 6:14). Subsequent uses are similar (9:32, 33; 12:41; 18:28; 22:54, 55, 58, 60; 24:12; except for 9:20). The answer of the disciples or Peter concerns the pressing crowd, both referred to with the articular form. Mark cites the disciples' observation about the crowd with the crowd in the accusative case, while Luke has Peter invoke them in the nominative case. The Markan citation demotes their status to the objects of observation, while Luke elevates them to agents in the crushing action that obscures indication of the one who touches Jesus. In Luke 8:46, Luke includes references to Jesus (ὁ Ἰησοῦς), whereas Mark includes reference to Jesus within the second person singular verb of the disciples' speech. Both Mark and then Luke have the woman come forward, with the same phrase used to refer to her (ἡ γυνὴ). What are we to make of this small interchange within each of these Gospel accounts? The Markan account uses the articular reference to Jesus twice, and otherwise only refers to the disciples, crowd and woman. Luke's Gospel has a more personalized interplay between Peter and Jesus, each of whom is specifically referred to, with Peter mentioned before Jesus in this episode. The Markan account is stylistically oriented toward Jesus and reflects a Markan characteristic of downplaying others with whom he comes into contact, while Luke takes a more personal approach that emphasizes individuality and pairs them off against each other. These stylistic characteristics in this episode are not necessarily stylistically characteristic of the individual Gospels. Mark's Gospel often does not specify its major participants with full or expanded nominal group references, but anaphorically refers to previous participants through minimal forms, such as verbal forms. Luke's Gospel, however, stylistically includes many accounts where lesser characters (other than Jesus) are brought into episodes (e.g., the widow of Nain and her son in Luke 7:11–17; the sinful woman in Luke 7:36–50; the women who accompany Jesus, given by name, in 8:1–3).

The narrative closes the embedded portion with Jesus addressing the formerly hemorrhaging and now healed woman. Matthew uses the articular noun (ὁ Ἰησοῦς) and addresses the woman in the vocative (θύγατερ), while Mark and Luke use the simple article and conjunction (ὁ δὲ) and address her in the nominative. The Matthean use of the vocative is preceded by the present-tense imperative, whereas the nominative of direct address in Mark and Luke is not. All three Gospels record Jesus's words to her identically, with the subject-predicator-complement structure with the explicit subject and perfect tense-form with stative aspect (ἡ πίστις σου σέσωκέν σε). Matthew's account is foregrounded in comparison with the other accounts, with the use of the articular noun, present imperative and perfect-based clause. The Markan and Lukan accounts have the perfect-based clause, but do not have the same foregrounding features in the other elements of the sentence.

When we return to the frametale, Matthew does not have the material found in both Mark and Luke about someone from the ruler's household informing Jesus and his followers of the death of the daughter. Mark and Luke both have this account. Here the interplay is set up between the daughter and Jesus. Whereas above all three Gospels downplay the significance of the daughter in relation to the introduction of Jairus, here Mark and Luke foreground what has happened to her without regard for the one who brings the message, even though the message about her is contained within a subordinate clause. Mark and Luke both use the articular noun with modifying possessive pronoun (ἡ θυγάτηρ σου), with Luke also using the perfect tense-form (τέθνηκεν) rather than Mark's aorist. They do this by not explicitly introducing any other participant by name or extended descriptor, even the messenger who brings word of the girl's death. Mark (5:35) simply uses the third person plural verb, while Luke (8:49) has the indefinite pronoun (τις). Jesus (ὁ Ἰησοῦς) responds in both Mark and Luke, encouraging his hearers and taking with him a number of disciples and others. Mark (5:37) states that the three disciples went with him (τὸν Πέτρον καὶ Ἰάκωβον καὶ Ἰωάννην τὸν ἀδελφὸν Ἰακώβου), while Luke (8:51) includes them and the father and mother of the child (Πέτρον καὶ Ἰωάννην καὶ Ἰάκωβον καὶ τὸν πατέρα τῆς παιδὸς καὶ τὴν μητέρα). Later on in the account, Mark (5:40) mentions the father and mother and those with him, presumably including the disciples (τὸν πατέρα τοῦ παιδίου καὶ τὴν μητέρα καὶ τοὺς μετ' αὐτοῦ). It is interesting to note that Mark uses the article with the proper names, even though in this episode there is no previous mention of these characters by name, while Luke does not use the article, even though Peter has been explicitly mentioned above (Luke 8:45). This may be because Mark is using the article anaphorically with reference back to "the disciples" in Mark 5:31, while Luke does not include the article because these are new participants as a group. The parents, however, introduced by means of Jairus and expected in such a story, have the anaphoric article in both Mark and Luke (as well as those accompanying Jesus, known from the above in Mark).

The last participant in the story to be noted is the daughter who is healed.[40] Matthew mentions her twice in the closing part of the episode. Whereas in Matt 9:18 the daughter is referred to (by the father) as ἡ θυγάτηρ μου, later in the account, when Jesus refers to her and heals her, she is referred to as τὸ κοράσιον (Matt 9:24, 25). Whereas Mark refers to the daughter initially using the diminutive form (τὸ θυγάτριόν μου), in the latter part of his account he refers to her as "the child" (τὸ παιδίον in Mark 5:39; τοῦ παιδίου and τὸ παιδίον in 5:40; τοῦ παιδίου in 5:41) and as τὸ κοράσιον (5:41, 42). Whereas in Luke 8:42 the fullest nominal word group is used to

[40] I will pass over reference to the house being that of the ruler (Matt 9:23) or chief of the synagogue (Mark 5:38), the crowd (Matt 9:24), and the mourners (Mark 5:38). Discussion above makes these uses understandable as part of the flow of the narrative.

refer to the daughter (θυγάτηρ μονογενὴς), Luke uses the articular noun τῆς παιδὸς in 8:51 and ἡ παῖς in 8:54. All of the instances appear to be using the anaphoric article. The more extensive Markan account has the largest number of references to the daughter/child. This is perhaps understandable because the account is longer than the other Gospel versions. However, there are several other considerations to take into account. In Matthew's version, Jesus refers to the girl as not being dead, and then it is this same girl (the article with possibly demonstrative force) who is raised. In Mark's account, Jesus, using the articular form with reference to the daughter says the child is not dead, and then goes into the place where the child (anaphoric or possibly demonstrative use of the article) is, grasps the hand of the child and then speaks to her. He uses the nominative of address to the girl, and this girl then gets up. Luke's use of the articular noun in 8:51 occurs as a genitive modifier in a nominal word group, followed by Jesus's nominative address to the girl to rise in v. 54.

In some ways, it would be easiest simply to perform a source-critical analysis of the relationship between the Gospel accounts and their reference to the daughter/child. In such an analysis, Mark provides the common wording that the other Gospel authors take over and adapt. Matthew uses the word κοράσιον, while Luke uses the related form παῖς. From a stylistic standpoint, however, more might be said of the Gospel usage. All of the Gospel writers share the common stylistic feature of using the article as a cohesive device that links reference within their literary units. Luke is probably the account that focuses the least upon the daughter, with his initial use, found as a modifying genitive in a serial nominal group being picked up one further time in the close of the episode. Matthew uses a word that only appears elsewhere in the Gospel at 14:11. This is an infrequent word for him, as he had other words available, including παῖς and παιδίον. Even if he got the word from Mark, he could have used one of his more frequent words. Instead, he chooses to use κοράσιον, which he uses of Herod's daughter. His use is appropriate for a girl of pubescent age, with possible implications for the story of Herod and his daughter (cf. Mark 5:41, where the daughter is said to be twelve).[41] The Markan account is noun-intensive. Whereas in some instances it is appropriate

[41] See LN 9.40 with comparison of other words for females.

to use a noun to ensure that participant reference is clear,[42] Mark does not seem to use the nouns for that reason here in his account, even though this usage could be justified in a few places. The effect instead is an explicitness and even redundancy not found in the other accounts. One cannot account for Markan usage on the basis of lexical alteration either, as he uses forms of τὸ παιδίον four times in a row in Mark 5:39-41, before switching to two uses of κοράσιον. Both words are found elsewhere in Mark's Gospel, with κοράσιον found three times in the Herod account (Mark 6:22, 28 twice) and παιδίον another eight times. The inevitable explanation must be that Mark wishes to conclude this account by foregrounding the episode with the daughter of Jairus.

Summary

I summarize by noting several of the stylistic features that this literary stylistic treatment of the characters in this episode reveal.

One observation is that all three Gospel authors share a number of common stylistic features. Perhaps the most obvious and important is the introduction of major new characters in the account by means of developed and complex nominal word groups, or more. The two major new characters in this episode are Jairus (or the ruler) and the hemorrhaging woman. For each, at their initial entrances, they are articulated using full descriptive expressions. The introduction of such new characters, though foregrounded by their nominal word groups and related structures, are often further reinforced (further foregrounded?) by other features that are used to signal the presence of a new character. By contrast, lesser characters, even if new to this particular scene, are introduced in less well-developed forms. This includes the use of smaller nominal groups, sometimes including nothing more than a noun. Known or expected characters from the previous narrative are introduced in a variety of ways, but usually in minimal structures, often with the article serving its anaphoric function.

---

[42] One could argue that the noun is necessary in Matt 9:25, because of the intervening of reference to "the crowd" and because the previous reference to the "child" is with a feminine pronoun (αὐτῆς).

A second common stylistic feature to observe is that all of the Gospel accounts have means of creating cohesion for their individual literary units. These features differ in their specific use, but can include such elements as the use of the article, the repetition of lexical items or the use of related lexical items (even if not in the same semantic domain), and the repeated use of a tense-form.

A third feature is the use of indicators for parts within the individual literary unit. This unit was selected because of its bipartite structure, including a frametale and embedded tale. For all three Gospels, the introduction of a major new character marked the beginning of a new segment of the literary unit, such as the introduction of Jairus or of the hemorrhaging woman. However, the individual Gospel accounts also have their own stylistic traits. Matthew's Gospel uses ὁ Ἰησοῦς as an indicator of sub-segments within the literary unit. Jesus first confronts the ruler and follows him, he then turns and addresses the healed hemorrhaging woman, and he finally comes into the house of the ruler to heal his daughter. Mark uses reference to Jesus and other figures as a way of contrasting Jesus with these other characters in the episode. However, he uses the figure of the child as the unifying and foregrounded feature of the closing part of the episode by saturation of the account with full nominal group reference to the girl and her healing. Luke probably does less to mark divisions within his account. This is not only because his narrative is not as long as Mark's, but because he seems to wish to hold individual participants on a more equal level of interaction throughout the episode, a feature that appears to be maintained elsewhere in the Gospel when he introduces a range of other participants into his account.

Conclusion

This instance and exemplification of literary stylistics is designed to provide an entrance into a neglected area of linguistic study. Literary stylistics has already apparently passed from the forefront of linguistic study, without having had much of an impact upon New Testament studies. In several ways, this is understandable, as we have seen that some of the topics and categories of thought in literary stylistics have been picked up and further developed in other areas of linguistic investigation, including some that have been used in biblical studies. However, there are those who believe that the kind of treatment often found in discourse analysis has not proved sensitive enough to the literary dimensions of the linguistic treatment, have not been sufficiently comparative in their approach, and have not arrived at the kinds of findings that are accessible to those who wish to read the New Testament with sensitivity to its linguistic character *and* literary dimensions. This reading of one synoptic passage, the healings of Jairus's daughter and the hemorrhaging woman, has attempted to provide a forum for further discussion of literary stylistics. The above interpretation is in no way meant as a definitive reading, but has focused upon a couple of areas of potential insight, especially the introduction of character and the resulting implications for the structure and development of literary units. The double account of this episode has provided a suitable vehicle for such an attempt. The temptation has been to slide easily into the kinds of analysis found within different forms of discourse analysis. I have tried to resist such efforts by maintaining language consistent with stylistic analysis, especially the comparative dimension that is so important in synoptic studies. It is not possible for me to say whether there is a future for literary stylistics, but I believe that it is worth considering whether such comparative interpretation—which moves beyond simple accumulation of data and descriptive analysis and engages in explanation of the text—does not offer a way forward in attempting to appreciate the literary features of the text within the framework of linguistic analysis.

Bibliography

Allen, Willoughby C. *A Critical and Exegetical Commentary on the Gospel According to S. Matthew*. International Critical Commentary. Edinburgh: T. & T. Clark, 1907.

Carter, Ronald, ed. *Language and Literature: An Introductory Reader in Stylistics*. London: Allen & Unwin, 1982.

Carter, Ronald, and Paul Simpson, eds. *Language, Discourse, and Literature: An Introductory Reader in Discourse Stylistics*. London: Unwin Hyman, 1989.

Chapman, Raymond. *Linguistics and Literature: An Introduction to Literary Stylistics*. London: Edward Arnold, 1973.

Chatman, Seymour. *A Theory of Meter*. The Hague: Mouton, 1964.

———, ed. *Literary Style: A Symposium*. London: Oxford University Press, 1971.

Clysenaar, Anne. *Introduction to Literary Stylistics*. London: Batsford, 1976.

Davies, W. D., and Dale C. Allison, Jr. *A Critical and Exegetical Commentary on the Gospel According to Saint Matthew*. International Critical Commentary. 3 vols. Edinburgh: T. & T. Clark, 1991–1997.

Enkvist, Nils Erik. "On Defining Style: An Essay in Applied Linguistics." Pages 1–56 in *Linguistics and Style*. Edited by Nils Erik Enkvist, John Spencer and Michael J. Gregory. Oxford: Oxford University Press, 1964.

Epstein, E. L. *Language and Style*. London: Methuen, 1978.

Fabb, Nigel. *Language and Literary Structure: The Linguistic Analysis of Form in Verse and Narrative*. Cambridge: Cambridge University Press, 2002.

Fowler, Roger, ed., *Essays on Style and Language: Linguistic and Critical Approaches to Literary Style*. London: Routledge & Kegan Paul, 1966.

———. *Linguistic Criticism*. Oxford: Oxford University Press, 1986.

———. *Linguistics and the Novel*. London: Methuen, 1977.

———. *Literature as Social Discourse: The Practice of Linguistic Criticism*. Bloomington: Indiana University Press, 1981.

———, ed., *Style and Structure in Literature: Essays in the New Stylistics*. Oxford: Blackwell, 1975.

Fowler, Roger, with contributions by Peter Mercer and F. W. Bateson. *The Languages of Literature: Some Linguistic Contributions to Criticism*. London: Routledge & Kegan Paul, 1971.

Halliday, Michael A. K. *Linguistic Studies of Text and Discourse*. Edited by Jonathan Webster. London: Continuum, 2002.

———. "The Linguistic Study of Literary Texts." Pages 302–7 in *Proceedings of the Ninth International Congress of Linguists*. Edited by Horace G. Lunt. The Hague: Mouton, 1964.

Hoey, Michael. "Discourse-Centred Stylistics: A Way Forward?" Pages 123–38 in *Language, Discourse, and Literature: An Introductory Reader in Discourse Stylistics*. Edited by Ronald Carter and Paul Simpson. London: Unwin Hyman, 1989.

Kenny, Anthony. *The Computation of Style: An Introduction to Statistics for Students of Literature and Humanities*. Oxford: Pergamon Press, 1982.

Leaska, Mitchell A. *Virginia Woolf's Lighthouse: A Study in Critical Method*. New York: Columbia University, 1970.

Leech, Geoffrey N. *A Linguistic Guide to English Poetry*. London: Longmans, 1969.

Leech, Geoffrey N. and Michael H. Short. *Style in Fiction: A Linguistic Introduction to English Fictional Prose*. London: Longman, 1981.

Levin, Samuel R., *Linguistic Structures in Poetry*. The Hague: Mouton, 1962.

Levinsohn, Stephen H. *Discourse Features of New Testament Greek: A Coursebook on the Information Structure of New Testament Greek*. 2nd ed. Dallas: SIL International, 2000.

Louw, Johannes P., and Eugene A. Nida, eds. *Greek-English Lexicon of the New Testament based on Semantic Domains.* 2 vols. New York: United Bible Societies, 1988.

Malmkjaer, Kirsten. "Stylistics." Pages 438–47 in *The Linguistics Encyclopedia.* Edited by Kirsten Malmkjaer. London: Routledge, 1991.

Ohmann, Richard. "Generative Grammars and the Concept of Literary Style." *Word* 20 (1964): 423–39.

———. "Poetry and Grammaticalness." Pages 308–14 in *Proceedings of the Ninth International Congress of Linguists.* Edited by Horace G. Lunt. The Hague: Mouton, 1964.

Porter, Stanley E. *Idioms of the Greek New Testament.* 2nd ed. Sheffield: Sheffield Academic Press; London: Continuum, 1994.

———. "Is Critical Discourse Analysis Critical? An Evaluation Using Philemon as a Test Case." Pages 47–70 in *Discourse Analysis and the New Testament: Approaches and Results.* Edited by Stanley E. Porter and Jeffrey T. Reed. Journal for the Study of the New Testament: Supplement Series 170. Studies in New Testament Greek 4. Sheffield: Sheffield Academic Press, 1999.

———. "Literary Approaches to the New Testament: From Formalism to Deconstruction and Back." Pages 77–128 in *Approaches to New Testament Study.* Edited by Stanley E. Porter and David Tombs. Journal for the Study of the New Testament: Supplement Series 120. Sheffield: Sheffield Academic Press, 1995.

———. "Review of *Paul's Literary Style.*" *Journal of the Evangelical Theological Society* 28 (1985): 502–4.

———. *Verbal Aspect in the Greek of the New Testament, with Reference to Tense and Mood.* Studies in Biblical Greek 1. New York: Peter Lang, 1989.

Richards, I. A. *Principles of Literary Criticism.* London: Routledge & Kegan Paul, 1924.

Sanders, E. P. *The Tendencies of the Synoptic Tradition.* Society for New Testament Studies Monograph Series 9; Cambridge: Cambridge University Press, 1969.

Schiffrin, Deborah, Deborah Tannen and Heidi E. Hamilton, eds. *The Handbook of Discourse Analysis.* Oxford: Blackwell, 2003.

Sebeok, Thomas A., ed. *Style in Language.* Cambridge, Mass.: MIT Press, 1960.

Short, Mick. *Exploring the Language of Poems, Plays and Prose.* London: Longmans, 1996.

Spencer, Aída Besançon. *Paul's Literary Style: A Stylistic and Historical Comparison of II Corinthians 11:16—12:13, Romans 8:9–39, and Philippians 3:2–4:13.* Jackson, MS: Evangelical Theological Society, 1984; repr. Lanham, Md.: University Press of America, 1998.

Spitzer, Leo. *Linguistics and Literary History: Essays in Stylistics*. Princeton: Princeton University Press, 1948.

Steiner, George. "Linguistics and Literature" Pages 111–36 in *Linguistics at Large*. Edited by Noel Minnis. London: Paladin, 1971.

Turner, G. W. *Stylistics*. Harmondsworth: Penguin, 1973.

Turner, Nigel. *Style*. Vol. 4 of *A Grammar of New Testament Greek*. Edited by James Hope Moulton. Edinburgh: T. & T. Clark, 1976.

Uitti, Karl D. *Linguistics and Literary Theory*. Englewood Cliffs, NJ: Prentice-Hall, 1969.

Ullmann, Stephen. *Language and Style: Collected Papers*. Oxford: Blackwell, 1966.

Wellek, René, and Austin Warren. *Theory of Literature*. New York: Harcourt, Brace, Jovanovich, 1963.

Let Me Direct Your Attention
Attention Management and Translation

Robert A. Dooley

Abstract: *Discourse in all languages uses knowledge management and attention management to communicate the message. The distinction between the two is essentially between communicating the facts and organizing the message around one particular salient concept, directing the reader's attention to something in which the author has a particular interest at that point. Whereas most treatments of translation issues deal with knowledge management, this paper deals with attention management, discussing five signals from the Koiné Greek of the New Testament: the development marker δέ, ἰδού "lo, behold," the historical present, special-purpose information structures, and signals of central participants. Attention management in the Greek is sometimes reflected in translation and sometimes not. The omission may be unintentional, through failure to recognize the function of Greek signals, or it may be by design since translation cannot hope to furnish exact equivalents for all language differences; when it attempts to do so, the effect may appear unnatural and distracting.*

Introduction

Authors consciously or subconsciously organize their material to facilitate comprehension by their readers. (In this paper I focus on written texts, hence speak of authors and readers instead of using the more general categories of text-producer and audience.) Two of the major ways they do this can be called knowledge management and attention management. This paper deals specifically with attention management, illustrating it with five linguistic patterns that are specific to the Greek New Testament. All of these have been elucidated in the work of Stephen Levinsohn in a much more thorough way than is possible to undertake here. This paper calls attention to attention management as a distinct dimension of text organization, one which shows up in a variety of ways.

What the New Testament authors did in attention management is sometimes reflected in translation and sometimes not. This omission may be unintentional, through failure to recognize the function of the signals found in the Greek text, or it may be by design, since translation cannot hope to furnish exact equivalents for all language differences. For each of the five attention management phenomena I discuss, I mention translation issues that are commonly involved.

Knowledge Management and Attention Management

The distinction between knowledge management and attention management is basically between what the the author wants to get across—the content of what he has to say—and how he organizes his message around a particular salient concept—what he is interested in talking about.[1] Knowledge management and attention management, then, represent different ways to organize discourse. They often interact in complex ways and show up together on different levels: the "global" level of the overall text, intermediate-size discourse units and the local level.

Here, "knowledge" means semantic or propositional content, and in knowledge management the author seeks to present this content in what we sometimes describe as "an orderly and organized way." On the local level, knowledge management signals the status of particular concepts in one's

[1] For similar distinctions, see Russell S. Tomlin, Linda Forrest, Ming Ming Pu and Myung Kim Hee, "Discourse Semantics" in *Discourse Studies: A Multidisciplinary Introduction* (vol. 1 of *Discourse as Structure and Process*; ed. Teun A. van Dijk; London: Sage Publications, 1997), 63–111, esp. 65; and Ronald W. Langacker, "Discourse in Cognitive Grammar," *Cognitive Linguistics* 12 (2001): 143–88, esp. 145, 154. There are other dimensions of discourse organization as well; managing audience empathy, for example, relates to both knowledge and attention management.

mental representation—whether concepts are referential, specific, identifiable ("definite"), and so forth. Local cognitive statuses can be ephemeral, changing from one utterance to the next. At a slightly higher level, knowledge management involves semantic relations which hold within a proposition (who did what to whom), as well as semantic relations between adjacent propositions or larger parts of the text (P, therefore Q).[2] For discourse units on intermediate and global levels, knowledge management uses discourse schemas. These are conceptual patterns of discourse organization which speakers use and readers generally perceive. Each schema typically contains individual "steps."[3] For example, the narrative of Christ's crucifixion contains several major steps: arrest, trial, crucifixion/death, removal/burial. Each one is a schema in its own right, with lower-level steps. Steps are related to their schema via conceptual roles. In narrative, these roles are often sequential or causal or, frequently, both; each step (such as the trial), besides conveying its own information, may in addition set up conditions under which the subsequent step (the crucifixion) is coherent, that is, "makes sense."[4] Making sequential and causal information clear is one job of knowledge management in narrative.

Discourse schemas are generally reflected in structural units of discourse. These discourse unites can be paragraphs (as structural units, not merely the graphical units which are indicated by indentation), episodes, or entire texts. Just as for schemas, smaller discourse units are typically embedded in larger ones. The paragraph is the minimal full discourse unit, but still has component parts called segments, which generally correspond to steps in the paragraph's schema.[5]

---

[2] See, for example, William C. Mann and Sandra A. Thompson, "Rhetorical Structure Theory: Toward a Functional Theory of Text Organization," *Text* 8/3 (1988): 243–81.

[3] John Hinds, "Organizational Patterns in Discourse" in *Syntax and Semantics* (vol. 12 of *Discourse and Syntax*; ed. Talmy Givón; New York: Academic Press, 1979), 135–57, esp. 150.

[4] Roger C. Schank, "The Structure of Episodes in Memory" in *Representation and Understanding: Studies in Cognitive Science* (eds. Daniel G. Bobrow and Allan Collins; New York: Academic Press, 1975), 237–72, esp. 243.

[5] Hinds, "Organizational Patterns," 137.

In the story of Peter's release from jail in Acts 12:1–11, there are two paragraphs: vv. 1–5 sets up the situation, including preparatory events, while vv. 6–11 relates the narrative events of Peter's release. (The story has sequels in vv. 12–19a, which we will not examine here.)

Acts 12:1–11[6]

v. 1 Now about that time Herod the king laid hands on some who belonged to the church, in order to mistreat them. (v. 2) And he had James the brother of John put to death with a sword. (v. 3) And when he saw that it pleased the Jews, he proceeded to arrest Peter also. Now it was during the days of Unleavened Bread. (v. 4) And when he had seized him, he put him in prison, delivering him to four squads of soldiers to guard him, intending after the Passover to bring him out before the people. (v. 5) So Peter was kept in the prison, but prayer for him was being made fervently by the church to God.

(v. 6) And on the very night when Herod was about to bring him forward, Peter was sleeping between two soldiers, bound with two chains; and guards in front of the door were watching over the prison. (v. 7) And behold, an angel of the Lord suddenly appeared, and a light shone in the cell; and he struck Peter's side and roused him, saying, "Get up quickly." And his chains fell off his hands. (v. 8) And the angel said to him, "Gird yourself and put on your sandals." And he did so. And he said to him, "Wrap your cloak around you and follow me." (v. 9) And he went out and continued to follow, and he did not know that what was being done by the angel was real, but thought he was seeing a vision. (v. 10) And when they had passed the first and second guard, they came to the iron gate that leads into the city, which opened for them by itself; and they went out and went along one street; and immediately the angel departed from him. (v. 11) And when Peter came to himself, he said, "Now I know

[6] In this paper, unless otherwise noted, all Scripture quotations come from the first edition of the *New American Standard Bible* (La Habra, CA: The Lockman Foundation, 1971).

> for sure that the Lord has sent forth His angel and rescued me from the hand of Herod and from all that the Jewish people were expecting."

These two paragraphs are signaled and delineated in ways that are common in narrative:[7] they use initial time expressions (v. 1: "Now about that time"; v. 6: "On the very night when Herod was about to bring him forward") and final summaries or "stock-taking" (v. 5: "So Peter was kept in the prison, but prayer for him was being made fervently by the church to God"; v. 11: "When Peter came to himself, he said, 'Now I know for sure that the Lord has sent forth His angel and rescued me' "). The schema of the first paragraph is transparent: Herod laid hands on "some"—first James, then Peter—followed by a final step of stock-taking:

Paragraph schema for Acts 12:1–5:
- Preparatory events: Herod laid hands on some (v. 1):
  - He killed James (v. 2)
  - He arrested Peter and took careful precautions with him (vv. 3–4)
- Stock-taking: Peter was being kept in prison, but the church was praying for him (v. 5)

This initial paragraph (vv. 1–5) functions as a step in the schema of the larger narrative, providing orientation or setting for the mainline narrative events of vv. 6–11. Orientation (often including preparatory events, as here) is a type of background information, which renders the foreground events of mainline narrative coherent. Thus, when we examine the conceptual roles that Acts 12:1–5 has in relation to the larger narrative, we discover roles of two kinds: besides the sequentiality and causality which, as we saw above, function within knowledge management, we also find orientation, a role of a different kind. As background which prepares for and highlights the following mainline (foreground) events, it is part of attention management.

The contribution of attention management to discourse coherence has to do, not with the facts per se, but with a particular construal of the facts, organizing

[7] Stephen H. Levinsohn, *Discourse Features of New Testament Greek* (2nd ed.; Dallas: SIL International, 2000), ch. 1–2.

the message around one particular salient concept: the author directs the readers' attention to what he is interested in talking about at that point. This focus of interest or attention can be local, intermediate, or global.

Local attention management can be seen in what is called "information structure."[8] This is exemplified in Acts 12:5, which presents two contrastive assertions:

> Peter (on the one hand) was being securely kept in prison.
> Prayer (on the other hand) was being made earnestly to God on his behalf.

The contrast is signaled in the Greek both by word order ("Peter" and "prayer" are fronted in their respective clauses) and by the use of the particles *μέν* "on one hand" and *δέ* "on the other hand." That is, at this point Peter and prayer are construed as balanced foci of interest, apparently to match up the brute reality of Peter's situation against the other-world possibilities of prayer. This contrastive construal is not dictated by the facts themselves, but shows the author's choice to present the facts in relation to a particular focus of interest. The same facts could have been presented in a different way: Luke could have said that Herod (on one hand) was doing all he could to secure Peter but God (on the other hand) was being earnestly entreated by the church to release him. Or again, these facts could have been presented with no particular contrast at all.

On intermediate and global levels, attention management is used to direct and sustain attention on longer-term foci of interest, called discourse topics or discourse themes.[9] Thematic or topical construal uses a large variety of signals, both linguistic and conceptual. Herod is discourse topic in the orientation paragraph of Acts 12:1–5, but Peter is discourse topic in the

---

[8] Knud Lambrecht, *Information Structure and Sentence Form: Topic, Focus, and the Mental Representation of Discourse Referents* (Cambridge Studies in Linguistics; Cambridge: Cambridge University Press, 1994), 3, 5.

[9] Discourse topics are here treated as referential discourse themes. For further discussion, see See Robert A. Dooley, "Explorations in Discourse Topicality," *SIL International Electronic Working Papers* 2007-010. Cited 12 October 2007. Online: http://www.sil.org/silewp/2007/silewp2007-010.pdf.

mainline narrative of vv. 6–11, as well as in the larger narrative of which this episode is part.

Herod's status as discourse topic in vv. 1–5 is signaled by such means as the following:

- He is named at the onset of this section (v. 1: "Herod the king laid hands on some") and continues active ("on stage") thereafter via minimal referential signals (in Greek, this is verbal inflection).
- He is the prime volitional agent in the paragraph; he *does things* that affect the story.
- His thought processes are portrayed: v. 1: "in order to mistreat them"; v. 3: "When he saw that it pleased the Jews"; v. 4: "intending after the Passover to bring him out before the people."
- His actions and their consequences are the subject of the entire paragraph.

In vv. 6–11, Peter is discourse topic, even though his role is undergoer rather than agent (as is the angel).

- Peter is active ("on stage") for the entire paragraph, whereas the angel enters after it begins and leaves before it ends.
- Peter is named at the onset (v. 6: "Peter was sleeping") and thereafter uses minimal referential signals, with the exception of v. 7 ("he struck Peter's side"—the name is needed for semantic clarity) and v. 11 ("When Peter came to himself, he said"—introducing the stock-taking closure). The angel, after being introduced, is referred to more fully (see vv. 8, 9, 10).
- Peter's thought processes are portrayed, but not the angel's: v. 9: "he did not know that what was being done by the angel was real, but thought he was seeing a vision"; v. 11: " When Peter came to himself, he said, 'Now I know for sure.' "
- Although the angel is a volitional agent, in favor of Peter's topic status is the fact that he is human and familiar to the readers, with a fully developed character delineation from earlier passages.

Thus, through a mix of linguistic and conceptual signals, including facts of the story, the author can establish and maintain discourse topics; these are entities which he is most interested in talking about at that point. Thus, this story is about the question "What happened to Peter?" rather than "What did the angel do?" or even "What did Herod do?" (except in relation to the orientational section vv. 1–6). Discourse topicality is broad-scope attention management, organizing discourse units of intermediate or global size around one salient entity.

In principle, then, it is fairly simple to state the distinction between attention management and knowledge management. In practice, however, the two domains of text organization interact in complex ways. For one thing, certain units of language can function in both domains. As we have seen, the paragraph Acts 12:1–5 relates to the larger narrative both in knowledge management (via the roles of sequentiality and causality) and in attention management (as background orientation). For another thing, attention management often makes use of the results of knowledge management. The fact that the author had earlier told many things about Peter (knowledge management) predisposes readers of Acts 12:1–11 to think of him as a likely discourse topic (attention management). The fact that the author cites the thought processes of first Herod (vv. 1–5) and then Peter (vv. 6–11), rather than, say, those of the Jewish leaders or the angel—a choice of content that is thus within knowledge management—also contributes to their identification as topics for their respective discourse units—a choice within attention management.

We now look at five ways attention management is used, and explicitly signaled, in the Koiné Greek of the New Testament. We will also mention certain translation issues which these phenomena raise.

Development markers

In transitioning from one sentence to another, languages often use sentential connectives such as "therefore" or "afterwards" in English. These two connectives primarily function in knowledge management, helping to establish semantic relations between propositions, causal in one case and temporal in the other. Some connectives, however, function in "text-forming" ways. In English, "anyway" and "now" often function in this way, serving to indicate how the text is being formed: "anyway" to resume the main line of communication after a digression, "now" to transition to a new point. But these text-forming connectives still remain largely within knowledge management, indicating what might be called the "logical structure" of the discourse.

Other "text-forming" connectives, however, function in attention management instead of, or as well as, knowledge management. In New Testament Greek narrative, the development marker *δέ* functions simultaneously in knowledge management and attention management. In knowledge management, *δέ* occurs with "a change of spatio-temporal setting or circumstances, a change in the underlying subject, or a change to or from background material"; at the same time, in attention management it signals something of "the author's purpose in presenting his material . . . a new step or development in the author's story or argument."[10] That is, *δέ* indicates that a particular change in the knowledge dimension is significant for attention management as well, indicating something of the author's interest in telling the story.

Levinsohn illustrates this with Matt 4:1–4:

> v. 1 Then (τότε) Jesus was led up by the Spirit into the wilderness to be tempted by the devil. (v. 2) And (καί) after He had fasted forty days and forty nights, He then became hungry. (v. 3) And (καί) the tempter came and said to Him, "If You are the Son of God, command that these stones become bread." (v. 4) But (δέ) He answered and said, "It is written, Man shall not live by bread alone."

As is common in Koiné Greek, each of these sentences begins with a connective: *τότε* "then" in v. 1, *καί* "and" in vv. 2 and 3, and *δέ*—here, translated "but"—in v. 4. Greek routinely uses sentential connectives whereas many languages, such as English, use them quite sparingly. This difference makes for a common translation issue, but one which we will not pursue. What we notice here is that in v. 4 *δέ* replaces the more common *καί*. According to Levinsohn, *δέ* highlights Jesus's reply, indicating it as the most salient event of the encounter, more salient than his hunger in v. 2 or the arrival and proposition of the tempter in v. 3, although of course in a logical sense (knowledge management) those earlier steps are necessary for the subsequent

[10] Levinsohn, *Discourse Features*, 72.

events.[11] Thus δέ signals, "This is why I am telling you this story—just listen to Jesus's reply." This effect is in attention management.

As a translation issue, many languages have no marker with the function of δέ. How then can readers know that the author considers Matt 4:4—and other verses marked by δέ—as especially noteworthy? Here the NASB uses *but*, a connective which, in itself, need not imply anything beyond the fact that Jesus's reply contrasts with the tempter's proposition: Tempter said X but Jesus said Y. If the English reader sees special salience in Jesus's reply, it may have to be from context or general Bible knowledge. In a language with no equivalent to δέ, or no other clear way to mark salience in developmental steps, readers must infer as best they can the importance of the event for the author.

"Lo" and "behold"

In the Greek New Testament, there are 237 occurrences of the particle ἰδού "lo, behold" (or, in certain places, the related form ἴδε). According to Van Otterloo, this particle is used to call attention to particular participants/entities or events.[12]

- It commonly occurs at the introduction of a major thematic participant, as in Matt 2:1: "Now after Jesus was born in Bethlehem of Judea in the days of Herod the king, behold, magi from the east arrived in Jerusalem."
- It can also draw attention to a surprising or noteworthy event, as in Matt 9:2: "And behold, they were bringing to Him a paralytic, lying on a bed."

Levinsohn notes that in the first use above ἰδού generally precedes a participant reference, whereas in the second it precedes a verb; that is, ἰδού directs attention to what follows it, functioning as a signal in attention management.[13]

[11] Ibid., 73.

[12] Roger Van Otterloo, "Towards an Understanding of 'Lo' and 'Behold': Functions of ιδού and ιδύ in the Greek New Testament ," *OPTAT* 2/1 (1988): 34–64, esp. 34.

[13] Levinsohn, *Discourse Features*, 197.

Van Otterloo notes that older or more literal translations translate ἰδού by using archaic words, usually "lo" or "behold," which are no longer common in the target language.[14] More modern translations either do not translate it at all or translate it in diverse ways. In the NIV (1984 version), for example, ἰδού is translated "at that moment," "without warning," "then," "at this," "just then," "here is," "look," "now," "see," "with that," "suddenly," "surely," "long," "on one occasion." "Without warning," for example, translates ἰδού in Matt 8:24 (NIV): *"Without warning, a furious storm came up on the lake." Now,* ἰδού itself does not mean "without warning," nor does anything else in the Greek text here have this meaning, but in English at least, initial expressions of suddenness do function as "attention-grabbers," whatever else they do in knowledge management. The issue with ἰδού, then, is that the target language may have no simple, consistent way to translate it, and certain ways of conveying its attention-directing function may result in extra meaning which is not in the original.

The historical present

In Matt 26:45–47, Jesus had just finished praying in Gethsemane and rejoined his disciples. In the passage below, the first two verbs (in bold print) are in present tense in the original:

> v. 45 Then He *comes* to the disciples, and *says* to them, "Are you still sleeping and taking your rest? Behold, the hour is at hand and the Son of Man is being betrayed into the hands of sinners. (v. 46) Arise, let us be going; behold, the one who betrays Me is at hand!" (v. 47) And while He was still speaking, behold, Judas, one of the twelve, came up (NASB has *came* and *said*).

The present tense of these two verbs is commonly called "historical present," a name "given to the use of the present tense in a narrative when the verb would be expected to have been in the past tense or perfective aspect. In Greek, this means that the verb would normally have been in the aorist."[15] In the New Testament, historical present occurs in specific discourse situations, the

[14] Van Otterloo, "Towards an Understanding."

[15] Levinsohn, *Discourse Features*, 201.

details of which I will not try to describe here. In regard to the passage above, Levinsohn says that the present-tense verbs "comes" and "says" in v. 45 "point forward to the arrival of the armed band led by Judas (v. 47)."[16] The following is a possible explanation of how present tense events can be forward-pointing: since the tense is not the typical narrative aorist, backgrounding is suggested, and background events are typically preparatory (i.e., forward-pointing).

Be that as it may, historical present in Greek functions in attention management. As Levinsohn states, "the primary motivation for using the historical present . . . is to highlight . . . the event(s) that follow . . . the H[istorical] P[resent] usually occurs prior to the event or group of events that are of particular significance."[17] That is, by signaling a background-foreground distinction, historical present is a signal of attention management.

Historical present is a useful device in languages which have it. But in some languages there is no tense at all, or the present tense is marked the same as the past, or, as in English, historical present is possible but would rarely be seen as appropriate for Scripture. One way English historical present is used is in headlines or titles of news articles: "Local man robs bank." Why is the present-tense verb *robs* used for a past act? As in Greek, to distinguish it from the usual past-tense narrative form: after all, a headline is not part of the story, only its title. Another usage of the historical present in English is in jokes: "One day *I'm sitting* at a bar and this guy *comes* up to me and *pulls* out a cat." Perhaps here as in Greek it indicates preparatory background events, but the association with jokes limits its appropriateness for other genres. A further use in English is in real-time sports reporting: "Messi *gets* a shot off, threading the ball through Boateng's legs, but *it's* pretty weak and Neuer *scoops* it up with contemptuous ease." There are literary uses as well, such as in "stream of consciousness" in fiction: "What *is happening* outside? Someone *is trying* to get in!" It would, however, be a rare occasion in English Scripture that historical present could be used without being perceived as a genre mismatch.

Some languages, including Greek itself, use an imperfective aspect for preparatory events, in a way that is similar to historical present.[18] But this

---

[16] Ibid., 204.

[17] Ibid., 200.

[18] "Thus, in narrative, the imperfect tends to correlate with background information

does not work for all languages. English, for example, only uses imperfective aspect for truly durative actions, so it would sound strange in Matt 25:45: "Then He *was coming* to the disciples, and *was saying* to them." All of the modern English versions I have seen—including the NASB—translate the historical present as simple past tense, canceling the pre-highlighting signal of the original. Other devices are sometimes used, but they may introduce other difficulties. The NASB of Matt 26:47 uses "behold," but as we have seen, that solution has problems of its own.

Special-purpose information structure

Information structure has to do with different possibilities for "packaging" the content of a sentence or of an independent clause using intonation, word order, special morphemes and special constructions.[19] Commonly, new information is signaled and presented in a framework of other information that is already known or given. It typically has constituent expressions which do one of the following:

- link the clause to preceding material (Connectives),
- supply information about the setting to orient the readers to the state of affairs at hand (Orientation expressions),
- provide a framework of given information to which to connect the new information (Topics or Presupposition expressions; these "sentence topics" may or may not be discourse topics),
- state essential new information (Focus expressions).

In Acts 12:1, cited previously, all four types of expressions occur:

Connective: *now*
Orientation: *about that time*
Topic: *Herod the king*
Focus: *laid hands on some who belonged to the church*

---

and the aorist with foreground events, because of their inherent nature" (Levinsohn, *Discourse Features*,174).

[19] Lambrecht, *Information Structure.*

In this clause, one signal of Herod's status as sentence topic is the fact that he is grammatical subject. For all languages, the following defaults have been posited:[20]

- the clause contains a particular concept—a nominal sentence topic—which it is primarily the author's intent to talk about and use as a basis for presenting new material;
- the sentence topic is the grammatical subject of the clause.

These are only defaults; there are times when they are overridden. When that happens, the information structure of the sentence or clause is special-purpose (also called "marked," whereas default choices are called "unmarked").[21]

Every utterance has a focus, which is the piece of essential new content that the author aims to communicate.[22] As mentioned above, the focus is generally presented within a framework of information that the readers already know about ("given information") or may even be conscious of at that point ("active information"). In Acts 12:1, the focus "*laid hands on some who belonged to the church*" is set within an active time frame ("*about that time*") and also connects to a given participant ("*Herod the king*"). The time expression provides orientation and the participant is sentence topic; these two expressions, in different ways, connect the focus to things that are already known. When there is an orientation expression, it commonly occurs before the core as a point of departure, as in Acts 12:1 with *"about that time."* The connective translated "now" (Greek δέ) links the entire sentence—actually, here, the larger discourse unit—to the preceding context.

As mentioned above, in the default case information structure contains a topic and a focus (often called a "comment" on the topic), and the core of the clause, consisting of the verb with its arguments, occurs in the the language's basic word order. In Koiné Greek, the basic word order is verb-subject-object

---

[20] Ibid., 132.

[21] Surveys of information structure choices relevant to New Testament Greek are provided by Levinsohn, *Discourse Features*, 2–47 and Steve Runge, *Discourse Grammar of the Greek New Testament: A Practical Introduction for Teaching and Exegesis* (Peabody, Mass.: Hendrickson, 2010), 181–200.

[22] There are rare exceptions. In a conversation such as *How are you today? Fine. And you?,* the utterance *And you?* contains a topic—*you*—without a focus.

(vso), which we can observe in the original of Acts 12:1: "laid (v) Herod the king (s) hands (o)." In the following discussion we will ignore points of departure and connectives in order to concentrate on the clause core.

Special-purpose information structure occurs in different ways. Here we consider two: marked topic (the topic receives heightened attention) and marked focus (the focus receives heightened attention). In New Testament Greek, the most common signal of these constructions is word order: marked topic or marked focus almost always occurs before the verb. In some cases, special particles occur as signals as well.

We have already noted an example of marked topics in Acts 12:5:

> So **Peter** (*μέν* "on one hand") was being kept in the prison,
> but **prayer** (δέ "on the other hand") for him was being made fervently by the church to God.

Both "Peter" and "prayer" are marked topics in Greek; each occurs before its verb and is followed by a special particle: μέν "on the one hand" or δέ "on the other hand." As grammatical subjects, they would likely be taken as sentence topics in any case, but here their order and particles give their topic status heightened prominence. Due to the particles, the motivation for this marked topic construction is transparent: the sentence contrasts Peter's situation and the church's prayer for it.

Marked focus occurs in this same story in relation to the iron gate which lead out into the city in v. 10:

αὐτομάτη	*ἠνοίγη*	*αὐτοῖς*	"[it] opened for them by itself"
by.itself	it.was.opened	to.them	

Here, the expression *αὐτομάτη* "by itself" occurs before the verb as a marked focus; it is the essential piece of new information that the author communicates by means of the clause—how the prison gate was opened. Both with the marked topics in v. 5 and the marked focus in v. 10, special attention is directed to a specific clause constituent. Information structure is attention management on the local level, that is, on the level of the sentence and its immediate context.

Koiné Greek has extreme flexibility of word order, and this is commonly used to signal marked topic or marked focus. Special-purpose information structure is very frequent, much more so than in many of the languages into which the New Testament is translated. The NASB translation of vv. 5 and 10 above is in the basic word order for English (SVO), with no indication that the original has special-purpose information structure. This raises two related translation issues:

- Should a translation always try to signal, in some way, whenever the original has special-purpose information structure?
- Should a translation ever use special-purpose information structure where the original does not have it?

We will not deal with the second question here.[23] But for the first question, I believe that an answer should be given in the negative: translating every instance of special-purpose information structure would be both unnatural and distracting in most languages. It would be unnatural, because even though the target language may have grammatical means to signal a particular marked construction (for example, "it was by itself that the gate opened for them" in v. 10), people would rarely talk that way. Further, in languages with more conservative use of information structure, frequent marked structures would be distracting in the same way that a person like myself finds it distracting to read something that had been marked with a highlighter pen fifteen or twenty times per page. According to a preliminary count, the parable of the prodigal son—to take a narrative passage at random—has about six times as many instances of marked focus than in modern English translations and about three times as many instances of marked topic.[24] So although translating every instance of special-purpose information structure might give valuable information about attention management in the source text, it would make for painful English, increasing the load on the general reader. On this issue, I believe that Pastor James's comment is relevant for translation: "It is my judgment,

[23] For this and related questions, see Robert A. Dooley, "Source-language Versus Target-language Discourse Features in Translating the Word of God," *Journal of Translation* 1/2 (2005): 1–18. Cited 22 September 2005. Online: http://www.sil.org:8090/siljot/2005/2/siljot2005-2-01.html.

[24] Ibid., 11.

therefore, that we should not make it [unnecessarily] difficult for the Gentiles who are turning to God" (Acts 15:19 NIV).

Signals of central participants

Probably all languages use discourse topics—broad-level foci of interest around which authors organize discourses and major discourse units. That is good news for translators, because ways can generally be found so that discourse topics in the original come across as discourse topics in the translation. However, the source and target languages commonly use different kinds of signals to make discourse topics clear. Let us limit our discussion here to narratives in which a discourse topic is a central participant for a paragraph, an episode, or the text as a whole. Translators generally recognize—in the abstract—that languages have their own ways to signal the centrality of a participant. Signals are of two main kinds: formal signals, which use specific linguistic elements to indicate a central participant, and conceptual signals, which seek to convey the same information through knowledge management—that is, by organizing the content as, in some sense, being about the participant. All languages use conceptual signals for discourse topics, but they differ widely in the use of formal signals. In particular, certain languages have linguistic forms and patterns which they use *exclusively* for a central participant and for no others, while other languages use referential forms and patterns indiscriminately for all participants, or perhaps for all that are more or less prominent. A central participant who is indicated by exclusive forms or patterns of reference is known as a VIP (Very Important Participant).[25] Thus while all languages have central participants, not all languages signal them using exclusive linguistic means as VIP s. Further, languages which do have exclusive VIP marking may not choose to use it in every narrative situation.

Koiné Greek is one language which has exclusive signals for VIP s, using these along with conceptual signals in certain situations. "In the Gospels, Jesus is the global VIP,"[26] but certain paragraphs or episodes have their own central

---

[25] See Levinsohn, *Discourse Features*, ch. 8; and Robert A. Dooley and Stephen H. Levinsohn, *Analyzing Discourse: A Manual of Basic Concepts* (Dallas: SIL International, 2001), 58–61.

[26] Levinsohn, *Discourse Features*, 143.

participants, and others have no apparent central participant. The apostle Peter is the central participant for the episode of Acts 12:1–19a, but in the opening paragraph (vv. 1–6) King Herod is the central participant, although Peter is also referred to.

Some ways which Koiné Greek uses to signal central participants and VIPs are the following:

- When the particle ἰδού "lo, behold" is followed by a reference to a participant being introduced, it indicates that participant as being thematic and generally central for a particular discourse unit.[27]
- The definite article can also help identify central participants. It is used differently in Koiné Greek than in many other languages. With proper names, the definite article is not used when the participant is being introduced or is being reintroduced after a time of not being actively referred to, but does commonly occur once the participant is introduced and is active. When Peter is reintroduced in Acts 12:3 after being nonactive in the latter part of chapter 11, his name occurs without the article. But after this, his name has the article in vv. 5, 6, 7, and 11. As was mentioned above, Peter is the central participant for the short episode of Acts 12:1–19a, but at that point there is no central participant in a global sense for the book. In the second part of Acts, however, the apostle Paul is signaled as the central participant, in fact, as VIP. During that section, Paul remains active conceptually even when he is not being referred to. Thus, after a section (Acts 18:14b–17) in which he is not referred to, his reintroduction in v. 18 has the definite article.[28] That is because high-level central participants can remain latently active even over stretches where they are not being referred to. The definite article can thus be used to help determine the status of participants as high-level central participants.
- A related phenomenon occurs at the onset of narrative discourse units. At such places authors commonly update their readers as to

[27] Van Otterloo, "Towards an Understanding," 34; and Levinsohn, *Discourse Features*, 197.

[28] Levinsohn, *Discourse Features*, 153.

> time ("at that time") and place ("there"), and it is common as well for participants to be referred to explicitly, as by name, even those which are currently active. Thus, at the onset of a new discourse unit in Acts 8:30, Philip is referred to by name ("And when *Philip* had run up, he heard him reading Isaiah the prophet"), even though he was active in the preceding context.[29] But when there is a central participant for a larger discourse unit, it is common for him to be exempt from this referential updating. Thus in the Gospels, where Jesus is global VIP, he is normally *not* referred to explicitly at the onset of discourse units.[30] At the onset of a new discourse unit in Matt 4:12, for example, Jesus is referred to in Greek without even a pronoun ("Now when Ø heard that John had been taken into custody, Ø withdrew into Galilee"). That indicates that Jesus is the central participant of a larger unit (actually globally), since other participants undergo referential updating at the onset of lesser units.

Linguistic signals of central participants are part of attention management. The author is saying, "This is who I am primarily interested in talking about; let me direct your attention to him or her." Translators should be aware of attention-directing in the original text and attempt to reproduce it—the overall function, that is, not necessary any particular signal of it—in a natural way in the translation. This may not always be possible, however. When English translations name Jesus at the beginning of discourse units in the Gospels where the Greek has zero, this may amount to a tacit admission that the only evidence is conceptual, rather than linguistic, for Jesus as the global central participant. That may be necessary, if for English readers the difference between "Jesus" and "he" in Matt 4:12 and similar places has to do with clarity and naturalness of reference instead of centrality of participants.[31]

---

[29] Ibid., 142.

[30] Ibid., 143.

[31] The NASB in its 1995 update does this at Matt 4:12: "Now when *Jesus* heard that John had been taken into custody . . ." In this place, the NASB first edition has the pronoun "He."

Conclusion

All texts, in all languages, use both knowledge management and attention management to communicate the message. The distinction between the two is essentially between communicating the facts and organizing the message around one particular salient concept, thus directing the readers' attention to something or someone in which the author has a particular interest at that point. In this paper I have discussed five signals of attention management in the Koiné Greek of the New Testament: the development marker δέ, ἰδού "lo, behold," the historical present, special-purpose information structures, and signals of central participants. Although attention management is distinct in principle from knowledge management, in practice the two dimensions interact in complex ways and operate on different levels.

Attention management is like marking a written text with a highlighter pen. As I have indicated by briefly comparing Koiné Greek and English, languages can signal attention management to different degrees as well as in different ways. What in one language might be appropriate might come across as unnatural to readers of another language. Where one language might want to highlight something in every sentence, readers in another language might find that degree of marking distracting. Where one language might use highlighting sparingly, readers in another might find that kind of practice uninteresting. Reader expectations need to be respected.

This makes for important translation issues. In some cases, not all of the signals in the original text can actually be translated, nor can all of the discourse functions be represented, if the aim is a natural translation. That is, in attention management as in certain other areas of language, patterns of natural expression can be in systematic conflict with the worthy goal of signaling everything explicitly—a property of machine languages but not of human language. One language may be precise and explicit in signaling some area while another is lax, requiring readers to infer information from the context. For example, some languages signal gender in pronouns while others do not; some signal whether the addressee is included in "we" while others do not. What is not signaled must be inferred, at least to the extent that it affects the coherence of the discourse. Since human languages differ in these ways, they will surface in translation. But not all translation is for that reason more vague than the original. In some areas, the target language can require the translation to be more explicit than the original!

How does the goal of faithfulness in translation fare with these issues of (non-)explicitness? The general question is not dealt with here, but it obviously deserves attention. From my own experience, though, it has generally been possible to keep translation within two limits: in regard to knowledge management, it seems to be generally possible for average readers to understand translated facts in a correct way (sometimes with the help of other readers or of helps that are furnished outside of the text); and in regard to attention management, it seems to be generally possible to avoid systematic over-signaling and under-signaling, keeping within the kinds and frequency of signaling that are roughly as natural for readers of the translation as the original text apparently was for its readers, given that inference from context will sometimes need to have a larger or smaller role.

Bibliography

Dooley, Robert A. "Source-language Versus Target-language Discourse Features in Translating the Word of God." *Journal of Translation* 1/2 (2005): 1–18. Cited 22 September, 2005. Online: http://www.sil.org/siljot/2005/2/46692/siljot2005-2-01.pdf.

———. "Explorations in Discourse Topicality." *SIL Electronic Working Papers* 2007-010. Cited 12 October, 2007. Online: http://www.sil.org/silewp/2007/silewp2007-010.pdf.

Dooley, Robert A. and Stephen H. Levinsohn. *Analyzing Discourse: A Manual of Basic Concepts.* Dallas: SIL International, 2001.

Hinds, John. "Organizational patterns in discourse." Pages 115–34 in *Discourse and Syntax.* Edited by Talmy Givón. Syntax and Semantics 12. New York: Academic Press, 1979.

Lambrecht, Knud. *Information Structure and Sentence Form: Topic, Focus, and the Mental Representation of Discourse Referents.* Cambridge Studies in Linguistics. Cambridge: Cambridge University Press, 1994.

Langacker, Ronald W. "Discourse in Cognitive Grammar." *Cognitive Linguistics* 12/2 (2001): 143–88.

Levinsohn, Stephen H. *Discourse Features of New Testament Greek: A Coursebook on the Information Structure of New Testament Greek.* 2nd ed. Dallas: SIL International, 2000.

———. "Towards a Typology of Story Development Marking (Repeatedly Naming the Subject: The Hebrew Equivalent of Greek Δέ)." *Journal of Translation* 2/2 (2006): 31–42. Cited 21 March, 2007. Online: http://www.sil.org/siljot/2006/2/48006/siljot2006-2-04.pdf.

Mann, William C. and Sandra A. Thompson. "Rhetorical Structure Theory: Toward a Functional Theory of Text Organization." *Text* 8/3 (1988): 243–81.

Runge, Steve. *Discourse Grammar of the Greek New Testament: A Practical Introduction for Teaching and Exegesis*. Peabody, Mass.: Hendrickson, 2010.

Schank, Roger C. "The Structure of Episodes in Memory." Pages 237–72 in *Representation and Understanding: Studies in Cognitive Science*. Edited by Daniel G. Bobrow and Allan Collins. New York: Academic Press, 1975.

Tomlin, Russell S., Linda Forrest, Ming Ming Pu, Myung Kim Hee. "Discourse Semantics." Pages 63–111 in *Discourse as Structure and Process*. Edited by Teun A. van Dijk. Discourse Studies: A Multidisciplinary Introduction 1. London: Sage Publications, 1997.

Van Otterloo, Roger. "Towards an Understanding of 'Lo' and 'Behold': Functions of ἰδού and ἴδε in the Greek New Testament." *Occasional Papers in Translation and Textlinguistics* 2/1 (1988): 34–64.

Background

How Orality Affects the Use of Pragmatic Particles, and How It Is Relevant for Translation

Regina Blass

Introduction

Blakemore introduced the term "constraints on relevance." These constraints have a procedural function, mainly consisting of discourse particles like "so," "after all" and "but."[1] Later it was recognized that morphological inflection, pronoun, speech act, prosody, mood indication, tense, and aspect markers, etc., also fall under the same group of phenomena.[2] Procedural information does not contribute to the conceptual representation of an utterance, but it can inferentially enrich utterances. It is an instruction to the cognitive system to manipulate conceptual representations via inferential processes. The inferential process is constrained by the search for optimal relevance. The coding devices which constrain the type of inference which should be performed over the conceptual representation of the utterance provide an effective way to save the hearer processing effort, effectively helping the relevance-driven utterance interpretation process.

---

1 Diane Blakemore, *Semantic Constraints on Relevance* (Oxford: Blackwell, 1987); Diane Blakemore, *Understanding Utterances* (Oxford: Blackwell, 1992); Diane Blakemore, *Relevance and Linguistic Meaning: The Semantics and Pragmatics of Discourse Markers* (Cambridge; New York: Cambridge University Press, 2002).

2 Deirdre Wilson and Dan Sperber, "Linguistic Form and Relevance," *Lingua* 90, no. 1 (1993): 1–25.

Lately, it has been realized that many of the phenomena that were taken as mainly facilitating comprehension are now seen as markers that support argumentation. Humans do not only want to convey information, they want to persuade the audience to accept and believe their messages. Humans, according to Sperber et al., are epistemically vigilant and that vigilance will have to be overcome in order for one's message to be not only understood but believed.[3] One assumes that markers like "so," "after all" and "but" and evidentials fall under that category.

Doing fieldwork amongst the Sissala people I often recorded oral texts and sometimes that was done with an audience and sometimes without one. I realized that what was used orally would not always be transcribed later on and my assistants told me that one cannot write those. Those were particles like attention holders. On the other hand what was told without an audience or written from the start often was realized less frequently. I saw that especially with intensifiers.

Obviously, all prosodic information, accept tone, would fall under that category as well. Intonation is normally not written. There are some markers that are accompanied with intonation and/or stress orally, which again cannot be taken over in written form. Others might be accompanied with gestures. Unless one describes the gestures in written form this is also a problem between orality and written form.

Then there are cases where oral uses are less acceptable in written form. What is different with many procedural markers from conceptual lexical items is that they are optional, except of course for tense, aspect and mood indicators. Also complementisers are often not optional. For those that are optional, it depends on how much context is available to derive the information without the markers inferentially. That might vary in oral from written circumstances.

As far as the phenomena are concerned that are argumentation geared, their use is dependent on who the communicator believes the addressee will accept her message.

[3] Dan Sperber et al., "Epistemic Vigilance," *Mind & Language* 25, no. 4 (2010): 359–393.

Straight testimony will be enough in a case where the assumption is that the addressee will accept one's message, but a lot of strengthening of one's own position is necessary where that cannot be guaranteed. Here too the message might be phrased differently in an oral situation from a written one.

Before I introduce these markers in more detail let me say a bit more about procedures.

Procedural markers

As Sperber and Wilson point out, utterance interpretation consists of (at least) the following tasks:[4]

1. Recognition of the propositional form expressed, disambiguation and enrichment.
2. Recognition of the attitude of the speaker toward what was said (propositional form) and implicated.
3. Recognition of the speech act performed.
4. Recognition of the implicatures conveyed.

In all of these stages special procedural markers may occur that guide the interpretation process. All of these markers convey procedural information concerning inference processes relating to all the above stages.[5]

The most common procedural markers are those that are constraining implicatures and those that are constraining explicatures.

Constraints on implicatures

Implicatures are contextual assumptions and implications giving rise to various cognitive effects which the speaker must have intended to convey if the utterance is to seem relevant to the hearer. As Blakemore has argued, many so-called discourse connectives must be seen as encoding procedural

---

[4] Dan Sperber and Deirdre Wilson, *Relevance: Communication and Cognition* (Oxford: Blackwell, 1986). Deirdre Wilson and Dan Sperber, "Relevance Theory" in *The Handbook of Pragmatics* (ed. L. R. Horn and G. Ward; Oxford: Blackwell, 2004), 607–32.

[5] Wilson and Sperber, "Linguistic Form and Relevance."

information in the sense of constraining the use of context in such a way that the access of particular, intended, contextual assumptions and/or implications (implicatures) are achieved in order to derive particular types of cognitive effects the utterance containing them is to achieve (contextual strengthening, elimination, implication). Consider utterances (1) and (2):[6]

(1) Romeo likes to please Juliet.
(2) He is Juliet's favorite.

These two utterances could be construed as being in a variety of relations to each other: for instance, they could just be a list of two facts or beliefs; or one could be construed as providing evidence for the truth of the other. In that case, one of the two propositions would be a conclusion, and the other evidence to support the conclusion. The problem is that either proposition could be a conclusion, and either could be supporting evidence, depending on the circumstances and the speaker's intention.

Constraints on explicatures

The explicatures of an utterance are constructed by enriching the logical form linguistically encoded in such a way that it expresses a determinate proposition and expresses optionally as a higher level explicature a description of a speech act or a description of a propositional attitude.

Wilson and Sperber claim that procedural phenomena can play a role in this.[7] They mention the question particle *ti* in French, which is used in some dialects and claim is that this particle does not encode a conceptual representation but a constraint on higher level explicature.

Unlike the phenomena introduced by Blakemore, these constraints on higher level explicatures seem to encode a procedure for constructing an explicature on a higher level rather than being conceptual.

---

[6] Blakemore, *Semantic Constraints on Relevance*; Blakemore, *Understanding Utterances*; Blakemore, *Relevance and Linguistic Meaning: The Semantics and Pragmatics of Discourse Markers*.
[7] Wilson and Sperber, "Linguistic Form and Relevance."

Ifantidou shows that evidentials like speech act and attitudinal markers function on higher level explicatures.[8] I introduced the notion "interpretive use marker" with the particle *re* in *Relevance Relations in Discourse*, which indicates metarepresentation (second order communication).[9]

My claim[10] is that *ja* in German has as its only constraint the function of constraining the proposition expressed to be embedded in a higher level explicature expressing the full evidence of mutual manifestness, while unstressed *wohl* constrains less than full evidence of mutual manifestness.

Signals to Do Something or Keep Something in Mind

These, according to Wharton, are also procedural markers but their function is more on the level of the performance of a communicative act.[11] Attention holders and intensifiers belong to these.

Types of procedural markers in oral and written use: signals

Attention indicators

Markers that are not used in written form are often markers that are supposed to keep the attention of the hearers going. They are what Wharton would call "signals." In Sissala, which is a Niger-Congo Gur language, they have a marker *ha* which I noticed to be used in story telling whenever the narrator was trying to keep the attention of the audience. It is also used whenever

---

[8] Elly Ifantidou, *Evidentials and Relevance* (Amsterdam: John Benjamins, 2000); Elly Ifantidou, "Evidentials and Relevance" (Ph.D., London: University of London, 1994).

[9] Regina Blass, *Relevance Relations in Discourse: A Study with Special Reference to Sissala* (Cambridge University Press, 1990).

[10] Regina Blass, "Particles, Propositional Attitude and Mutual Manifestness," in *Pragmatic Markers and Propositional Attitude* (ed. Gisle Andersen and Thorstein Fretheim; Amsterdam: John Benjamins, 2000), 39–52.

[11] Tim Wharton, "Meaning and Showing: Relevance-Theoretic and Gricean Intentions." *Intercultural Pragmatics* 5/2 (2008): 131–152.

someone wants to get someone's attention, e.g., if someone walks behind me and wants me to recognize her and stop, she might say

(3) *Ha* Regina, *ha*.

These markers were refused to be written and were never used in Bible translation. However, I could imagine that the Bible in oral form, especially the Jesus film, those might be employed.

Intensifiers

In Sissala there is an intensifier marker *de* whose function it is to make particular lexical items more salient or mark particular utterances in discourse as of relevance for the outcome of the story.[12]

(4) The chameleon and the spider went and made farms next to each other.
The spider harvested a lot,
The chameleon harvested little.
The chameleon *de* caught flies,
And made a pretty garment.

He asked the spider whether he
wanted the garment in exchange for millet.
The spider said "Yes."
The spider made his wife bring millet to the
Chameleon and filled all his granaries.
One day the spider went to his mother-in-law's funeral.
He greeted all the people. All of a sudden,
the flies *de* of the garment flew away,
and *de* left, and left him *de* sitting naked.
The chameleon walked away.

My solution for use of this marker has been that it minimizes processing effort by guiding the hearer to the most important information (i.e. information which is crucial to the main intended contextual effects).

[12] Blass, *Relevance Relations in Discourse: A Study with Special Reference to Sissala*, 83.

These markers are optional. They do not have to occur. Often in writing they do not occur, since the non-visibility of the audience seems to have an influence on the use of the markers. However, they were used in Bible translation.

Markers that optionally occur

Markers that guide the inferential process in communication

Markers like "so," "after," "all," "but," are basically optional. They are used to facilitate processing and/or to help in argumentation to overcome the vigilance of the addressee.

If the implicatures in communication can be drawn without the help of the particles they do not need to occur. However, that might be different in an oral situation where the physical environment also helps in interpretation from the written kind.

Moreover, they might occur for the reason of argumentation, in order to overcome the vigilance of the addressee and to persuade the audience. In an oral situation the speaker might be more aware of who exactly the addressees are and may use or not use any supporting evidence for his claim. So the use of the particles may vary for argumentation reasons also.

Markers that help establishing explicatures

Procedural indicators on base explicature

1. Pronouns

Procedural indicators that function on the base level are, for instance, pronouns. Their use is dependent on the accessibility of a referent. The marker helps in retrieving this referent. The use of pronouns will vary in written and oral use. In an oral situation the referent might be more easily accessible and so pronouns might be used more easily or on the other hand be replaced by demonstratives or articles.

2. Resemblance markers

Resemblance markers can assist in establishing explicatures but must not be interpretive use markers. The particle "so" in English and German is often used to just indicate a resemblance, which may be a proposition, part of an utterance, an assumption or a non-verbal indication.[13]

(5) Jesus loves you, and *so* do I (resembles part of an utterance, functions on base level).
(6) John is *so* small (resembles an assumption, functions on base level).
(7) John is *so* small (indication by hand, functions on base level).

This particular use has an effect on the concept formation which will be an *ad hoc* concept according to Wilson and Carston.[14]

These uses are different from the one in (8):

(8) The economy is strengthening, *so* Frau Merkel (resembles a proposition, functions on higher level explicature).

All these markers could be left out or explained differently. Surely, there will often be a difference between oral and written use.

Procedural indicators on higher level explicature

1. Evidentials and interpetive use markers

Evidentials and interpretive use markers are dependent on how much the speaker thinks he has to provide evidence for what he says. Here the trust of the communicator in the audience plays a big role.

---

[13] Regina Blass, "Resemblance Markers and Concept Formation," in *Procedural Meaning: Problems and Perspectives* (ed. K. Turner and K. Heusinger; Current Research in Semantics and Pragmatics Series; Amsterdam: Emeralds Publishing, forthcoming).

[14] Deirdre Wilson and Robyn Carston, "A Unitary Approach to Lexical Pragmatics: Relevance, Inference and Ad Hoc Concepts," in *Pragmatics*, ed. Noel Burton-Roberts, Palgrave Advances in Linguistics (Basingstoke: Palgrave Macmillan, 2007), 230–259.

In Sissala the interpretive use particle *re* is only obligatory in certain complementizer positions; otherwise it could be left out. There might be a difference in use between the oral and written form.[15]

(9) This plant is medicine *re* (it is said).

2. Knowledge markers

"Knowledge marker" is a term that I created for markers that indicate that you and I have a common ground.[16] They function on higher level explicature. The second constraint of "after all" indicates mutual manifestness. German *ja* "also" has this function and so does *mana* in Hausa, an Afro-Asiatic, Chadic language. In all three languages—German, English and Hausa—a procedural particle can be used to indicate that both the speaker and hearer have something mutually manifest. Consider (10B: a, b and c):

(10) A: He is wearing shorts (in a Moslem country).
B: a. German: Er ist *ja* zu Hause.
b. English: *After all,* he is at home.
c. Hausa: Kasarsu ce *mana*.

These markers need not to be used and may occur less in writing, since the common ground might not be so obvious.

Markers that are accompanied with intonation or non-verbal acts

With intonation

Obviously in writing intonation is normally not written and so the addressee will have to depend on the context and the marker alone to derive the intended interpretation. That is especially the case with echoic markers which always come with an attitude. That attitude might be indicating agreement, disagreement or puzzlement.

[15] Blass, *Relevance Relations in Discourse: A Study with Special Reference to Sissala.*
[16] Regina Blass, "Particles, Propositional Attitude and Mutual Manifestness," in *Pragmatic Markers and Propositional Attitude*, ed. Gisle Andersen and Thorstein Fretheim (Amsterdam: John Benjamins Publishing Company, 2000), 39–52.

For instance in Kikuyu[17] the marker *ati* may be used to indicate echoic use with agreement, disagreement or indicate puzzlement. Consider (11):

(11) A: It is a nice day today.
B: *Ati* (according to intonation: agreement, disagreement [perhaps irony], or puzzlement)

In writing it would have to be made clear, if it does not become clear by the context, which attitude is meant.

With non-verbal communication

Some markers are especially prone to be used in an oral situation. That is the particle *so* in English as in German. For instance if I say:

(12) He is *so* tall (he holds his hand up to his hip).

Then this depends on some measure that I might indicate to show the exact height.

Many non-European languages also have these kinds of markers, as do Bantu languages.

In written form this would have to be indicated; in oral form it would be seen in the physical environment. Thomas Mann, in *der Zauberberg* uses German *so* a number of times. He usually explains in brackets what the measure is.

Confirmation markers

It seems that every language has confirmation seeking markers. Some can be oral and written and others can only be oral. They are amongst the clearest to show that speakers seek the acceptance of what they are saying to overcome the vigilance of the addressee.

In German there are regional markers like *gel*, *ne*, *woll*, that are often used especially in conversation to seek the acceptance of what has been said by the speaker.

---

[17] J. Gathumbi, *The Metarepresetation Marker* ati *in Kikuyu* (MA Thesis [partial requirement], Nairobi Evangelical Graduate School of Theology, 2000).

(13) This was a good decision *gel/ne/woll* "was it not?"

There is, however, also a form that can be used in written and oral form. That is *nicht wahr*, which would be "is it not?" in English or *ne c`est pas?* in French.

Those oral forms would not be used in written form and if used at all would have to be replaced with the version that is acceptable in writing.

Other markers that are reserved more for oral use and other for written use

German:

(1) John is a good presenter.
Er ist *ja auch* Lehrer (oral preferance). "*After all*, he is a teacher."
Er is (ja) *schließlich* Lehrer (written preference). "*After all*, he is a teacher."

Conclusion

The main aim in this study was to show that in the area of procedural phenomena, oral and written use might be divergent. This has, of course, consequences for translation. Not all oral phenomena is supposed to be written; others—for instance those that are accompanied with intonation or non-verbal communication—cannot be used in written form unless they are described. Others again have to be different in oral use from written. However, all of those oral phenomena may be used in oral translation. It is therefore important to consider not only the written text in something like the Jesus film but all the divergent phenomena I mentioned above.

This has only been a small sample, but further research on the subject, as well as its application to Bible translation, is necessary.

Bibliography

Andersen, Gisle. and Thorstein. Fretheim, eds. *Pragmatic Markers and Propositional Attitude.* Amsterdam: John Benjamins, 2000.

Blakemore, Diane. *Semantic Constraints on Relevance*. Oxford: Blackwell, 1987.

———. *Understanding Utterances*. Oxford: Blackwell, 1992.

———. *Relevance and Linguistic Meaning: The Semantics and Pragmatics of Discourse Markers*. Cambridge: Cambridge University Press, 2002.

Blass, Regina. *Relevance Relations in Discourse: A Study with Special Reference to Sissala*. Cambridge: Cambridge University Press, 1990.

———. "Particles, Propositional Attitude and Mutual Manifestness." Pages 39–52 in *Pragmatic Markers and Propositional Attitude*. Edited by G. Andersen and T. Fretheim. Amsterdam: John Benjamins, 2000.

———. "Resemblance Markers and Concept Formation." In *Procedural Meaning: Problems and Perspectives*. Edited by K. Turner and K. Heusinger. Current Research in Semantics and Pragmatics Series. Emeralds Publishing, forthcoming.

Gathumbi, J. "The Metarepresetation Marker *ati* in Kinkuyu." MA Thesis (partial requirement), Nairobi Evangelical Graduate School of Theology, 2000.

Ifantidu, Elly. *Evidentials and Relevance*. Amsterdam:John Benjamins, 2000.

Sperber, Dan. "The Modularity of Thought and the Epidemiology of Representations." Pages 39–67 in *Mapping the Mind: Domain Specificity in Cognition and Culture*. Edited by L. A. Hirschfeld and S. A. Gelman. New York: Cambridge University Press, 1994.

Sperber, Dan, F. Clement, C. Heintz, O. Mascaro, H. Mercier, G. Orrigi, D. Wilson. "Epistemic Vigilance." *Mind & Language* 25/4 (2010): 359–93.

Sperber, Dan and Deirdre Wilson. *Relevance: Communication and Cognition*. Oxford: Blackwell, 1995.

Wharton, T. "Meaning and Showing: Relevance-Theoretic and Gricean Intentions." *Intercultural Pragmatics* 5/2 (2008): 131–152.

Wilson, Deirdre and Robyn Carston, "A Unitary Approach to Lexical Pragmatics: Relevance, Inference and Ad Hoc Concepts.".

Wilson, Deirdre and Dan Sperber. "Relevance Theory." Pages 607–32 in *The Handbook of Pragmatics*. Edited by Laurence R. Horn and Gregory L. Ward. Oxford: Blackwell, 2004.

———. "Linguistic Form and Relevance." *Lingua* 90/1 (1993): 1–25.

Organization and Allusion in Ezekiel 20

R. J. Sim

Introduction

It is a pleasure to contribute to a festschrift for Stephen Levinsohn. Stephen was already a member of SIL International when I joined, and represents the best of SIL International in combining strong interests in linguistics, Bible translation for minority communities, and biblical interpretation. The "discourse turn" was affecting linguistics from the 1970s, and Stephen pursued this from the outset within Robert Longacre's approach, applying discourse analysis to both source and receptor languages. In recent years, like others among us, he has moved to cognitively based approaches, and this present paper is offered as part of the festschrift. For Stephen, biblical interpretation is driven by its value for translators, and this paper will approach the task with this constantly in mind.

Several recent articles deal with the oracle of Ezek 20, and the contribution of recent monographs on Ezekiel make it opportune to revisit the chapter. The present paper builds on and expands this recent work, and extends it with insights from linguistics and recent work in pragmatics and communication. For this the paper follows a literary approach to discourse, looking at thematic development, by attention to the constraints that discourse particles place upon interpretation, and introducing a recent approach to the re-presentation of material paralleled in the Torahic literature, echo questions, denials, and irony.

There is enough in Ezek 20 about discoursal and rhetorical issues to occupy a monograph. This paper can only be an overview, giving selective attention to parts of the oracle.[1] The chapter is fairly repetitive when read. Thus, I will follow recent work in making this a key to the way in which the evaluation of Israel's (Judah's) past is organized.[2] The present paper gives an overview of Ezek 20:1–44, focusing in detail on vv. 1–5, 11–24.

In the first section we consider briefly the chapter's unity and genre, followed by brief discussion of several pertinent phrases or concepts in the second section. The third section discusses the oracle's internal organization and development, and the final section covers the oracular content of the prelude (vv. 3–5a) and the period in the wilderness (vv. 5b–26) in more detail, looking at rhetorical development through the use of allusions.

Unity and genre

Literary unity

There is no real dissension over treating Ezek 20:1-44 as a literary unit, although small parts of the oracle are often considered to be secondary.[3] The short, dated narrative setting which opens the episode (v. 1) provides a clear initial boundary.

A separate oracle follows, introduced (v. 45 EV; 21:1 HB) by "and the word of Yhwh came to me." This short oracle (20:45–49 EV; 21:1–5 HB) takes up a new topic and is sufficient indication that Yhwh's oracle to the gathered and seated elders ends in Ezek 20:44.

The oracular word of Yhwh runs through vv. 5–44, and as so often in the Hebrew prophets, comes to an abrupt end, with no explicit closure or further

---

[1] The paper is an extract from a larger project on Ezek 20, whose focus is the difficult vv. 25–26, aspects of which have been presented in recent years in SBL International Meetings; see items listed in the references. Although rigorously limited by concerns for space, it is hoped that discussion in this paper demonstrates how recent cognitive work can enhance literary analysis of biblical text.

[2] For example, Leslie C. Allen, "The Structuring of Ezekiel's Revisionist History Lesson (Ezekiel 20:3–31)," *CBQ* 54 (1992): 448–62; Lyle Eslinger, "Ezekiel 20 and the Metaphor of Historical Teleology: Concepts of Biblical History," *JSOT* 81 (1998): 93–125.

[3] Allen, "Structuring." See Walther Zimmerli, *I am Yahweh* (ed. Walter Brueggemann; trans. Douglas W. Stott; Atlanta: John Knox Press, 1982).

reference to the participant audience. We are left to infer that Yhwh's word to the prophet and the prophet's communication of this to the people were both accomplished.

Genre

Although the oracle is generally treated as an historical account of sorts, it is neither narrative nor chronicle, but rather an explanatory (and hence interpretive) criticism of Israel's history. This distinction will assist us later in understanding how it is organized and developed.

First, it is not narrative or "reportage." It is not an account or history of Israel's origins. Events and their participants are not focal; events are not narrated, but mentioned—in the sense of Jacobson—as occasions for criticism. As we shall see, much of the oracle deals with Israel's past by allusion to other material.

Rather, it is an oracle. There are various marks of oracular utterance: see the various formulaic expressions.[4] By definition oracles present a divinity's pronouncements to a human audience, and could potentially be given in any genre. An inspection of the OT is sufficient to show that *ne'um* "oracle" is a kind of communicative event falling within the social institution of prophecy in ancient Israel,[5] which the community recognized. It included warnings and announcements of Yhwh's displeasure among other typical speech acts, but the linguistic form and nature of an oracle could employ any resources of the language, and were not restricted in genre.

Mentions of episodes in Israel's origins and past history lend the oracle a superficial similarity to narrative reportage, but it interprets and evaluates history rather than reporting it. Thus it is expository and explanatory. Yhwh frames his complaint through references to Egypt; the wilderness; the land; the giving of the Law; Israel's idolatry (vv. 13,16 presumably refer to the golden calf episode in Exod 32; compare Ezek 20:15 with Exod 32:10, 14.),

---

[4] Zimmerli, *I am Yahweh*; James E. Robson, *Word and Spirit in Ezekiel* (LHBOTS 447; London: T. & T. Clark, 2006).

[5] T. L. Wilt, " 'Oracle of Yahweh': Translating a Highly Marked Expression," *BT* 50/3 (1999): 301–4.

the Sabbath, and so on. In presenting his point of view, Yhwh recalls his grace to Israel, Israel's rebellion, his anger to the point of retribution, and his relenting in mercy. These expressions of Yhwh's various attitudes toward Israel are hung on a skeleton of mentioned historical episodes.

In the approach adopted here it is not necessary to fit the oracle further into a scheme of genres, nor to think in terms of genre bending or blending. The text itself leads readers through, and its expressions sufficiently orient them, if we grant them access to congruent contextual awareness.

Overview of the oracle and significant motifs

Meier claims that Ezekiel has "the most extensively standardized marking of DD [Direct Discourse] in the entire Bible,"[6] without making the text normative.[7] Building on this, Robson argues that the inclusion of the various formulae which mark prophetic speech "indicate[s] that what the prophet is saying in the rhetorical event is not simply a report of what Yhwh has said, but an instantiation of Yhwh speaking in the present."[8]

In dealing with the oracle, I will pick up on Robson's claim and view the oracle as Yhwh's word communicated by the prophet. This is for simplicity and convenience, is closer to the translator's task, and makes no claims whatever about the prophetic experience, the nature of the revelation, or its transmission history.

Secondly, accepting with Robson both reporting and instantiating aspects of the oracle is precisely what defines oracles as metarepresentations: instantiation makes the communication of the oracle to the people an ostensive re-telling, or re-presentation, of a prior communicative event.[9]

---

[6] Samuel A. Meier, *Speaking of Speaking: Marking Direct Discourse in the Hebrew Bible* (VTSup 46; Leiden: Brill, 1992), 324.

[7] See also Ellen F. Davis, *Swallowing the Scroll: Textuality and the Dynamics of Discourse in Ezekiel's Prophecy* (JSOTSup 78; Sheffield: Almond, 1989), 58–59.

[8] Robson, *Word and Spirit*, 39.

[9] Metarepresentation is a technical term in relevance theory, tersely defined as a representation of a representation, or what we can more simply call re-telling or re-presentation, as the latter term has been recently used in biblical studies. Metarepresentation differs from saying something again by being ostensive about its

Several concepts recur in the oracle, and it is as well that we deal with them right away, in overview, before considering the oracle itself in detail.

The self-presentation and recognition formulas[10]

The simple Self-Presentation Formula (SF) "I am Yhwh" occurs three times (vv. 5, 7, 19) and the Recognition Formula (RF) "(you/they will) know that I am Yhwh" occurs six times in the chapter (vv. 12, 20, 26, 38, 42, 44).

Self-presentation formula

The SF ʾănî yhwh (ʾĕlōhêkem) is frequent in the Priestly Writing and Dt-Isaiah, but rare in the remainder of the Old Testament.[11] The briefer form is often expanded by the substantive attribute "your God" which usually follows asyndetically, only rarely taking an initial kî.[12] The three occurrences in chapter 20 are the only occurrences in the book.[13]

Its terse first person form emphasizes it as the fully personal (and interpersonal) disclosure of Yhwh. Its repetitive occurrence in legal statements

> pushes them into the most central position from which the Old Testament can make any statement. Each of these small groups of legal maxims thereby becomes a legal communication out of the heart of the Old Testament revelation of Yhwh.[14]

It is heard on two different occasions; first in Yhwh's mouth in the actual encounter with the divine, and secondly in subsequent times "growing out of the first revelation, when Yhwh's commissioned spokesperson

---

re-presentation of something said or thought on a prior occasion.

[10] The terms self-presentation formula (Selbstvorstellungsformel) and recognition formula (Erkenntnisformel) are established translations of the German terms stemming from Walther Zimmerli, "Ich bin Yahweh," in *Geschichte und Altes Testament* (ed. William Foxwell Albright; BHT 16; Tübingen: J. C. B. Mohr, 1953), 179–209; and idem., *Erkenntnis Gottes nach dem Buch Ezechiel* (ATANT 27; Zürich: Zwingli-Verlag, 1954).

[11] Zimmerli, "Ich bin Yahweh;" and idem., *I am Yahweh*, 13.

[12] Ibid. 3.

[13] Zimmerli, *I am Yahweh*, 5–6.

[14] Zimmerli, "Ich bin Yahweh;" and idem., *I am Yahweh*, 12.

extends the message to the people."[15] The latter case again is what we mean by metarepresentation.

The three occurrences in the oracle fall within embedded direct speech reports. That is, each is a metarepresentation of a previous speech act, now recounted by Yhwh himself; conversely, none is a new speech act spoken by Yhwh as a new disclosure in the oracle. Yhwh is the one who swore in covenant to Israel in Egypt, committing himself to deliver Israel; it is his directive to Israel in Egypt to separate from idolatry; and it is his directive to the second generation in the wilderness not to walk in their father's statutes, but in his statutes. In this last occurrence it is closely followed by the RF.

Recognition formula

The RF **lādaʿat kî ʾănî yhwh** ("they shall know that I am the LORD") includes within it a metarepresentation of the SF, introduced by **kî**. According to Zimmerli, it occurs seventy-eight times, plus eighteen more if we include expansions. This is the highest concentration in the Old Testament.[16] As with the SF, its first person form emphasizes the inter-personal nature of its deontic illocution.

It is always intimately associated with Yhwh's intervention, strongly implying that "behind Yhwh's acts there stands the intention that precisely these acts will bring about knowledge."[17] This "final level of intention of the divine acts" is to create knowledge of God and to elicit this acknowledgement. Yhwh's actions on his people's behalf "live not only in the narrative proclamation . . . but equally in the signs Yhwh has given his people as fixed observances witnessing to his particular actions" on their behalf, with the Sabbath forming a particular sign.[18]

---

[15] Ibid.

[16] John Frederick Evans, "An Inner-Biblical Interpretation and Intertextual Reading of Ezekiel's Recognition Formulae with the Book of Exodus" (DTh diss., University of Stellenbosch, 2006).

[17] Zimmerli, *I am Yahweh*, 37.

[18] Ibid, 70. Note that the Sabbath is referred to in vv. 12, 13, 16, 20, 21, 24, and that the RF occurs in vv. 12, 20, 26. The interplay of Sabbaths, RF, and idolatry in the chapter await further research.

In Ezek 20 the RF occurs six times, three in the developing criticism of Israel's history in the Wilderness (vv. 12, 20, 26),[19] each of which embeds a metarepresentation of earlier historical disclosure, and three new declarations developing the theme of the New Exodus (vv. 38, 42, 44). This chapter has the highest concentration in the book.[20]

Oaths

Yhwh swears an oath three times in the oracle (vv. 3, 31, 33). Furthermore, five times he refers to an oath he swore earlier in Israel's favor (vv. 5 [2x], 6, 28, 42), and twice more he refers to two additional, earlier oaths he swore against his people (vv. 15, 23).

Oaths as speech acts

Oaths are performative speech acts; to utter an oath is to perform the speech act. Oaths are also commissive and conditional statements.

As a commissive, an oath strengthens beyond doubt the assurance that the swearer will keep his word. The commitment is strengthened or enforced by an accompanying curse which appeals to human or divine authority in case of failure to fulfill it.[21]

The full form is typically "May the LORD do so to me if I do (not) thus" or "As the LORD lives." See for example Ruth 1:17; 1 Sam 3:17; 14:44; 2 Sam 3:35; 1 Kgs 2:23. It is thus syntactically conditional in form, but it is the syntactically conditional protasis that is being asseverated, and the apodosis that is conditional (upon failure to fulfill the protasis of the oath).

---

[19] I have shown in a separate paper (R. J. Sim, "Revisiting Ezek 20.25–26: Echo Question, Denial, or Echo of a Third Kind" [paper presented at the SBL International Meeting in Tartu, July 25–29, 2010]) that the occurrence in v. 26 is aberrant in several ways, giving clue to the need to read this occurrence differently, although Zimmerli marked it as secondary, considering it to be an "awkward deviation from the normal formulation" (*I am Yahweh,* 36).

[20] Evans, "Inner-Biblical Representation," 139–40.

[21] Oaths bind those who swear them under necessary obligations, and in general they cannot be set aside. A father or new husband can set aside a daughter's or wife's oath respectively; see Num 30:6, 9, 13.

The imprecations of the apodosis are frequently omitted, leaving the oath as a protasis standing alone. Thus, "If I do X (may I be accursed)" is reduced to "If I do X." This abbreviated form continues to convey the negative illocution "I will (surely) not do it." The opposite case also holds, with ellipsis of the apodosis leaving a negative protasis "If I do not do it," which will have affirmative illocution "I will surely do it."

The three oaths made in the oracle

The Lord swears by his own life (Ezek 17:16) or by himself (Gen 22:16) or by his name, holiness or right hand, and there is no accompanying curse in case of failure.

The three oaths performed within the oracle (vv. 3, 31, 33) are speech acts of the form ḥay-ʾānî ʾim ("As I live, if I will . . ."). In all three, the apodoses are omitted, and the protases stand alone. Verses 3, 31 are affirmative protases, both assuring the gathered elders (v. 1) that consultation will never take place (on this occasion); v. 33 is in the negative, assuring Israel that Yhwh will yet be king over them.

The mentions of earlier oaths

An earlier oath can be referred to by metonyms of the accompanying action, nāśāʾ yad, "raising the hand" as here in vv. 5, 6, 15, 23, 28, 42 or lexically šĕbûʿâ. The oath mentioned five times (vv. 5, 6, 28, 42) and the two other oaths sworn against Israel (vv. 15, 23) are referred to metonymically in this way, for example, nāśāʾtî yādiy lāhem ("I raised my hand to them"; v. 6); and wĕgam-ʾănî nāśāʾtî yādî lāhem ("Moreover I raised my hand to them"; v. 15, 23). Each mention metarepresents the content of the original oath.

There is double mention of the oath in v. 5.

> . . . wāʾeśśāʾ yādî lĕzeraʿ bêt yaʿăqōb
> wāʾiwwādaʿ lāhem bĕʾereṣ miṣrāyim wāʾeśśāʾ yādî lāhem lēʾmōr ʾănî yhwh ʾĕlōhêkem
> I swore to the offspring of the house of Jacob—making myself known to them in the land of Egypt—I swore to them, saying, I am the Lord your God (Ezek 20:5 nrsv).

Here Yhwh commits himself to take Israel out of Egypt, referring to his commitment in the syntactically incorporated form of the RF wāʾiwwādaʿ lāhem ("making myself known to them") with the SF "I am Yhwh your God" appended under lēʾmōr ("saying"). "The land" is Yhwh's expressed sworn commitment in vv. 6, 15, 28, 42 and implied in v. 23.

The remaining mentions (vv. 6, 15, 23, 28, 42) express the content of the oath by means of a particle, with a negative marker where appropriate, and the preposition *l*- plus the hiphil infinitive construct of the verb.[22] In each case, the mention metarepresents the original commissive speech act in the form of indirect speech—in fact, in free indirect speech, since there is no speech verb, only the metonym for the oath, e.g., "I raised my hand to . . ."

In Ezek 20, the oaths reveal Yhwh's positive commitment to Israel on the one hand, and on the other his pending retribution on all nations, including Israel, for wrong. This sets up a dilemma in which Yhwh is committed to Israel through his past oaths on their behalf, and yet is also committed by oath to end its nationhood for persistent rebellion and idolatry. The dilemma will be resolved in another exodus, two-edged, to purge, purify, and restore the nation (vv. 30–44).

Internal organization and development

Turning now to consider how the oracle is organized and developed, we will look first at the episode opening in vv.1–5a, then at selected parts of the oracle in vv. 5b–44.

The prelude: verses 3–5a

> In the seventh year, in the fifth month, on the tenth day of the month, certain elders of Israel came to consult the LORD, and sat down before me.
> v. 2 And the word of the LORD came to me:

[22] Thus, lĕhôṣîʾām ("for bringing out") *l*+hiphil infin. constr (vv. 6, 28); lĕbiltî hābîʾ ("for not bringing in") *l*+NEG + hiphil infin. constr. (v. 15); lĕhāpîṣ (for scattering") *l*+hiphil infin. constr. (v. 23); bahăbîʾî ("by bringing in") *b*+hiphil infin. constr. (v. 42).

> v. 3 Mortal, speak to the elders of Israel, and say to them: Thus says the Lord GOD: Why are you coming? To consult me? As I live, says the Lord GOD, I will not be consulted by you. (v. 4) Will you judge them, mortal, will you judge them? Then let them know the abominations of their ancestors, (v. 5) and say to them: (NRSV)

Verse 1 records briefly when and why this encounter and oracle took place: **wayhî baššānâ haššĕbî῾ît baḥămišiy be῾āśôr laḥōdeš bāʾû ʾănāšîm mizziqnê yiśrāʾēl lidrōš ʾt-yhwh wayyēšĕbû lĕpānāy** ("In the seventh year, in the fifth month, on the tenth day of the month, certain elders of Israel came to consult the LORD, and sat down before me") which we can date to August 591 B.C.E. The verse also records the occasion: some elders of deported Israel seek a consultation (daraš) with Yhwh,[23] and come seating themselves in front of the prophet-priest.[24]

In this setting, vv. 2–5a introduce Yhwh's response addressed primarily to the prophet.

---

[23] The further significance of their wish is obscure. Two years have elapsed since (false) prophet Hananiah's prophecy concerning the end of deportation (Jer 28), and perhaps the elders want to know if the end is in sight (Daniel I. Block, *The Book of Ezekiel Chapters 1–24* [NICOT; Grand Rapids: Eerdmans, 1997], 618, citing Abraham Malamat, "The Twilight of Judah in the Egyptian-Babylonian Maelstrom" in *Congress Volume, Edinburgh, 1974* [ed. J. A. Emerton; VTSup 28. Leiden: Brill, 1974]). Secondly, Zedekiah's "reckless act of political disloyalty is in the air" (Clements, Ronald Ernest. *Ezekiel* [Westminster Bible Companion; Louisville: Westminster John Knox Press, 1996] 89), which will precipitate Nebuchadnezzar's retaliation (2 Kgs 24:18–20; 2 Chr 36:11–14). The uncertainty surrounding Zedekiah's actions may likewise be a cause of enquiry. Or, there may be a broader, less occasional reason on the elders' part, upon which we can only speculate. The suggestion that perhaps the elders were seeking divine approval to establish a sacrificial cult in exile (see vv. 32, 39) seems to overdraw the evidence. More generally, it would seem likely that they looked for a word of hope, the end of exile, and a return home. The strongest conclusion we can reach at this point is that Yhwh's word to the elders is pertinent to their desire to ask for a word from him: having refused to respond to a question in their mind, he gives them an appropriate piece of his own. We ought to revisit this tentative conclusion toward the end of the paper.

[24] This is not the first consultation the elders of Israel sought. See 8:1 and 14:1.

Verses 2–3a consist almost entirely of oracular formulae, including Yhwh's familiar address term to Ezekiel:

- the word-event formula[25] wayhî dbr-yhwh ʾēlay lēʾmōr ("the word of Yhwh came to me"; v. 2);
- the address term ben-ʾādām ("son of man"; v. 3).

Following the address term is the single initial instruction to Ezekiel

- dabbēr ʾet-ziqnê yiśrāʾēl wĕʾāmartā ʾălēhem ("speak to the elders of Israel, and say to them");
- kō ʾāmar yhwh ("Thus says the LORD"; v. 3a);

and an initial declaration (v. 3b) closed immediately by

- kō ʾāmar yhwh ("Oracle of Yhwh / declares Yhwh"; v. 3c).

A second instruction to the prophet (v. 4) is followed by the transitional instruction

- wĕʾāmartā ʾălêhem ("and say to them . . ."; v. 5a) before the oracular formula
- kō-ʾāmar yhwh ("Thus says Yhwh . . ."; v. 5b) which begins the oracle proper.

This provides a fairly heavy formal encapsulation of Yhwh's word (vv. 3–4) and introduction to the oracle itself.

It seems preferable to take vv. 3–4 to be Yhwh's initial word to Ezekiel, the first declaration of which is to be told the elders (note the 2nd plural pronouns [v. 3][26]), and the instruction to Ezekiel (v. 4) is to form the theme of the oracle proper. It therefore summarizes the informative intention of the oracle which follows; more technically, it is a metarepresentation of the oracle's (Yhwh's) informative intention. That is, the speech content of vv. 3–4 represent to Ezekiel what the oracle itself will represent to the elders; this content will be elaborated below.

[25] Robson, *Word and Spirit*, 27ff.

[26] Whether the elders were told this initial part of Yhwh's response at this point, or only during the following oracle (see v. 31) is not entirely clear, but I take it to be part of Yhwh's initial word to Ezekiel, especially in the light of v. 4.

Yhwh's oracle, verses 5b–44

As so often in Old Testament discourses, the oracle captures in a remarkable way both the spontaneity of oral response and the deliberate planning of written discourse. [Perhaps we tend to overlook the interplay of planning and spontaneity in oral societies.]

The addressees

The oracle (vv.5–44) consists in Yhwh's word *to* Ezekiel *for* the elders who came to consult him. At the same time, it is linguistically Yhwh's word *to* Israel *through* Ezekiel. Bear in mind the claim that "what the prophet is saying in the rhetorical event is not simply a report of what Yhwh has said, but an instantiation of Yhwh speaking in the present."[27] In other words, it is addressed to the elders in 2nd person plural; see "you" (plural in v. 3); "your (plural) fathers" in vv. 27; and consistently in vv. 30–44.

The initial part (vv. 5–29) is largely in 3rd person plural because it refers to past generations of Israel while tacitly addressing the elders; see v. 27, which interpolates a 2nd person address to the elders. Verses 30–44 address contemporary Israel directly, through its elders gathered before Ezekiel, in 2nd person plural. This shift in pronominal reference is an indicator of the flow of the discourse, deserving full weight, although not always emphasized.

The asides[28] to Ezekiel in vv. 27, 30, and Israel in v. 39 constitute slight interruptions in the second half of the oracle by addressing the prophet or the nation, and create turns in the development and rhetoric of the oracle. Space forbids discussion in this paper, but while we don't want to make too much of them, neither should we ignore them.

---

[27] Robson, *Word and Spirit*, 39.

[28] The asides to Ezekiel consist of the following oracular formulas: "Therefore, son of man, speak to the people of Israel say to them . . ." (v. 27) and "Therefore say to the house of Israel . . ." (v. 30). The address to Israel states, "As for you, O house of Israel, this is what the Lord God says . . ." (v. 39).

Overview: episodes and motifs

There have now been a number of discussions of the discourse organization of Ezek 20, and a measure of consensus has emerged about the first half. There is less consensus about the organization of the oracle in vv. 27–44.[29] The focus here will be on the flow of meaning through the text, on turns in its organization rather than on distinguishing strict section boundaries, that is, on continuity and change rather than discontinuity.

1. Episodes

The oracle first picks up on several episodes from Israel's past history (vv. 5–29) before speaking about the deported community's present exile and future (vv. 30–44), marked by a switch in pronominal reference (from 3rd to 2nd plural) at v. 30.

Mention of three locations in the first half allows us to distinguish three major episodes: vv. 5–10a "in Egypt"; vv. 10b–14 (17) "in the wilderness"; and vv. 18–22 (24) "in the wilderness."[30] Broadly, these earlier episodes are:

- bĕʾereṣ miṣrāyim ("in Egypt"; v. 5, and vv. 6, 8, 9, 10a);
- ʾel-hammidbār ("in the wilderness"; vv. 10b, 13, 15),
- ʾel-bĕnêhem bammidbār ("to their children in the wilderness"; vv. 18, 21, 23);
- ʾel-hāʾāreṣ ("in the land"; vv. 27–29; and in exile, vv. 30–44).

[29] The differences are sometimes more matters of preference than real, depending on matters of sub-sectioning; there is a fairly strong consensus over major boundaries. Some disagreement appears to arise over attempts to view the "discourse structure" hierarchically, whereas it may be simpler (both theoretically and practically) to view it as linear, with the text itself signalling its development as it unfolds.

[30] Allen, "Structuring," and Eslinger, "Ezekiel 20," set out the details of the text that lead them to section it 5–9, 10–14, 15–17, 18–22, 23–26. We follow their evidence without reviewing it here. Allen is a good review of previous proposals. He provides a detailed justification from the text, distinguishing sections 5–9, 10–14, 15–17, 18–22, 23–26, 27–29, 30–31. He sees a chiastic structure in these, of which vv. 18–22 forms the centre. Eslinger proposes "nine iterations of a five-segment pattern" of recurrent motifs up to v. 44.

As we shall see, the wilderness and exilic episodes are themselves complex. There is a consensus for recognizing a major turn at vv. 18, identified as second generation by the phrase ʾel-bĕnêhem bammidbār ("to their children in the wilderness"). Consensus thus identifies major "boundaries" or turns at vv. 5, 10b, and 18, with minor differences over the transitional nature of v. 10. Further turns following vv. 15, 23, and 25 are discussed below. Thus different scholars posit three, four, five, or more sections in vv. 5–26.

2. Motifs

These episodes from Israel's past are each developed via four recurrent motifs[31] in vv. 5–24 which might be described as

- Yhwh's gracious acts towards Israel (vv. 5–7, 10–12, 18–20);
- Yhwh's contention about Israel's rebellious spirit (vv. 8a, 13a, 21a);
- Yhwh's rising anger and pending retribution at their rebelliousness (vv. 8b, 13b, 21b);
- Yhwh's mercy, for his honor's sake (vv. 9, 14, 22).

The first of the four is implicational, but the remaining three express the motif in the text. Thus

Yhwh's contention about Israel's rebellious spirit
But they rebelled against me and would not listen to me (v. 8a)
But the house of Israel rebelled against me in the wilderness (v. 13a)
But the children rebelled against me (v. 21a)

Yhwh's rising anger and pending retribution at their rebelliousness
Then I thought I would pour out my wrath upon them and spend my anger against them in the midst of the land of Egypt (v. 8b).
Then I thought I would pour out my wrath upon them in the wilderness, to make an end of them (v. 13b).
Then I thought I would pour out my wrath upon them and spend my anger against them in the wilderness (v. 21b).

[31] See Allen, "Structuring," and Eslinger, "Ezekiel 20." Eslinger's recurrent motifs are Acts of Yhwh: covenant arrangements; rebellion and its purification; divine wrath; exile and return; godly face saving.

Yhwh's mercy, for his honor's sake

But I acted for the sake of my name, that it should not be profaned in the sight of the nations among whom they lived, in whose sight I made myself known to them in bringing them out of the land of Egypt (v. 9).

But I acted for the sake of my name, so that it should not be profaned in the sight of the nations, in whose sight I had brought them out (v. 14).

But I withheld my hand, and acted for the sake of my name, so that it should not be profaned in the sight of the nations, in whose sight I had brought them out (v. 22).

The recurrence of these expressions is a major source of the repetition evident in vv. 5–24. Discussion below will focus upon the remaining content of vv. 12–24.

As noted above, both SF and RF occur a surprising number of times in the chapter, in addition to three oaths performed, and seven mentions of earlier oaths Yhwh has previously sworn. It is not always obvious, however, that the SF and RF in vv. 5–26 are precisely placed for particular local rhetorical effect (except for v. 26).

In order to further elucidate the organization of the oracle, we will deal in more detail with a discourse connector, gam ("moreover"),[32] which previous work seems to have largely overlooked.

[32] In the lexicons it is glossed "again, in addition, moreover, indeed." For example, See Francis Brown, S. R. Driver, and C. A. Briggs, *Hebrew and English Lexicon of the Old Testament* (Oxford: Clarendon, 1907; repr., Peabody, Mass.: Hendrickson, 1979), 768, where it is named an additive; R. Laird Harris, Gleason L. Archer, and Bruce K. Waltke, eds., *Theological Wordbook of the Old Testament* (Chicago: Moody Press, 1980), 361a; Christo H. J. Van der Merwe, "An Overview of Recent Developments in the Description of Biblical Hebrew Relevant for Bible Translation," in *Contemporary Translation Studies and Bible Translation: A South African Perspective*, ed. Christo H. J. Van der Merwe and J. A. Naudé (Acta Theologica Supplement 2: Bloemfontein, 2002) 238, 314–17.

3. The role of gam

Measured support for turns at vv. 15, 23, and 25 can be adduced from attention to the particle gam, which introduces the text at each of these three points.

(w) gam occurs four times in these verses, and helps stage its organization. Once we find wĕgam ʾet-šabbĕtôtay ("moreover, my Sabbaths"; v. 12); twice we have wĕgam-ʾănî . . . "moreover, I . . ." (vv. 15, 25) and once gam-ʾănî . . . (v. 23).

12–14	wĕgam ʾet-šabbĕtôtay ("Moreover [I gave them] my Sabbaths")
15–17	gam-ʾănî ("Moreover, I [raised my hand]")
23–24	gam-ʾănî ("Moreover, I [raised my hand]")
25–26	wĕgam-ʾănî ("Moreover, I [gave them no good decrees]")

Leaving the first of these for later, it can be argued that the latter three occurrences indicate new turns in the development of the oracle.

In two unpublished papers, I have discussed the contribution of gam in Hebrew discourse, arguing that gam is an additive particle introducing a further comment which should be read together with a preceding parallel comment, and which is of equal rather than incidental relevance in this context.[33] I have set out the following hypothesis[34] for the contribution of gam to the meaning communicated.

---

[33] See R. J. Sim, "The Hebrew particle gam as procedural marker," paper presented at the SBL International meeting in Auckland, 6–11 July 2008; R. J. Sim, "Hebrew particle gam: a procedural approach to non-declarative usage," paper presented at the SBL International Meeting in Rome, 30 June–4 July 2009. Also see Stephen H. Levinsohn, "Also, Too and Moreover in a Novel by Dorothy Sayers," *Work Papers of the Summer Institute of Linguistics, University of North Dakota Session* 45 (2001). Online: http://www.und.edu/dept/linguistics/wp/2001Levinsohn.pdf, for a discussion of different additives exhibited in a variety of languages.

[34] This proposal is based on a consideration of the (rather vaguer) information in lexicons and wordbooks, as well as in Diane Blakemore, *Semantic Constraints on Relevance* (Oxford: Blackwell, 1987), 91–97. It is in line with the information given in these resources, but makes more specific and testable claims about the role gam

gam introduces a new premise (assumption) into an argument or explanation,
which *either* strengthens a contextual implication already accessible in the context of the argument
or makes a new contextual implication accessible, which is required for understanding the argument.

For present purposes a contextual implication is one which is (i) not expressed in words in a text; (ii) derived by inference in context; and (iii) intended to be a communicated conclusion.[35] We will apply this proposal to the occurrences of gam in Ezek 20.

a. gam in vv.15–17

Now "in the wilderness" (v.10b), adds further to Israel's rebellion after receiving Yhwh's decrees, rulings and Sabbaths, under the scope of gam, vv. 15-17 add that **wĕgam-ʾănî nāśāʾtî yādî lāhem bammidbār.**

- Yhwh swore an oath not to bring Israel into the land (v. 15)
- for the reason that they rejected his decrees and rulings, profaned (ḥll, Piel) his Sabbaths, gave their heart to idols (v. 16)
- and yet Yhwh was again merciful (v. 17).

Two of the recurrent motifs are covered here: Israel's rebellion (v. 16) and Yhwh's mercy (v. 17). A third motif is Yhwh's anger and pending retribution, which are contextual implications of the oath sworn not to bring them into the land (v. 15).

---

plays in guiding the interpretation of texts, which need further confirmation by analysis of the corpus of biblical Hebrew. It is based on work that has developed around the concept of procedural encoding; see for example, Diane Blakemore, *Understanding Utterances: An Introduction to Pragmatics* (Oxford: Blackwell, 1992); idem., *Relevance and Linguistic Meaning: The Semantics and Pragmatics of Discourse Markers* (Cambridge: Cambridge University Press, 2002); Robyn Carston, and Seiji Uchida, eds., *Relevance Theory: Applications and Implications* (Pragmatics and Beyond, New Series 37; Amsterdam: John Benjamins, 1998); Carston, *Thoughts and Utterances*. See the online bibliography at http: //www.ua.es/personal/francisco.yus/rt.html.

[35] For a technical definition, see Robyn Carston, *Thoughts and Utterances: The Pragmatics of Explicit Communication* (Oxford: Blackwell, 2002), 377.

After bringing them into the wilderness from Egypt, Yhwh gave them his decrees, rulings and Sabbaths with the promise of life for obedience but came close to destroying them (vv.10b–14). Now vv. 15–17 is a further, parallel comment of equal relevance, concerning what Yhwh did for Israel, and vv. 15–17 form a partial but congruent repetition of the pattern set out in vv. 10–14.

In the context of Yhwh's oath to bring Israel into "a land that I had searched out for them, a land flowing with milk and honey, the most glorious of all lands" (v. 6), here **wĕgam-ʾănî** now introduces the new premise that

> [Moreover] Yhwh swore not to bring Israel into the land he had given them

This is a negation, by oath, of his earlier commitment to give Israel the land, stated in v. 6 and implied up to v. 13, and nuances his near-decision to finish them in the wilderness (v. 13), for the reasons given in v. 16. Israel's continued rebellion that leads to this oath sworn against them.

b. **gam** in verses 23–24

In vv. 18–22 Yhwh is dealing with the second generation, which renews the cycle of grace-rebellion-anger-mercy seen in vv. 10–14 and 18–22. Still "in the wilderness," we now read in the same words as v. 15, that

- Yhwh swore an oath to scatter and disperse Israel among the nations (v. 23)
- for the reason that they failed to keep his decrees and rulings and profaned his Sabbaths. (v. 24)

This is parallel to vv.15–17, except that now there is no merciful relenting—but an ominous silence!

Verses 23–24 are then a further comment on vv. 18–22, parallel and of equal relevance to them, introducing the new premise

> [Moreover] Yhwh swore to scatter Israel into the lands of other nations

This goes further than the reversal of his earlier commitment to give Israel the land (v. 15) now not only withholding the land, but swearing to scatter Israel, again in response to Israel's continued failure to respond to him.

Taking the role of **wĕgam-ʾănî** into account in this way allows us to set off vv. 15–17 and 23–24 as sections appended to their preceding verses in each case, incidentally confirming previous attempts both to recognize a break in flow and to recognize continuity with their preceding text.

c. **gam** in verses 25–26

The final occurrence of **wĕgam-ʾănî** (vv. 25–26) introduces a further partial play on the pattern set out in vv. 12–24.[36]

4. Schema

So far we have the schema shown below. Viewed in this way, the historical progression is quasi-generational, quasi-locational, and supported by (**wĕ**) **gam-ʾănî**, which perhaps explains some of the differences in locating internal "boundaries." It is attention to **gam** together with the internal organization of the content of each comment that leads us to differ from Allen, Eslinger, Wright, among others, in their respective handling of the discourse, questioning the nature of the relationship between vv. 23–24 and 25–26 to the section vv. 15–26.

verses	episodes	motifs
5–9	Election through sojourn in Egypt	5–7, 8a, 8b, 9
10–14	Exodus from Egypt into the wilderness	10–12, 13a, 13b, 14
15–17	**wĕgam** in the wilderness (possibly alluding to Num 13–14)	
18–22	The wilderness (possibly referring to Num 22:1—36:13)	18–20, 21a, 21b, 22
23–24	**wĕgam** in the wilderness (possibly alluding to Deut 28:64)	
25–26	< **wĕgam** *no-good, non life-affording laws; defiling sacrifices* >	
27–29	In the land	
30–32	In exile, the present generation	
33–44	the future	

36 See R. J. Sim, "The Hebrew particle gam as procedural marker," 2008; R. J. Sim, "Hebrew particle gam: a procedural approach to non-declarative usage," 2009.

5. *Contextual implications*

In each episode there are some obvious (unstated) contextual implications to be derived from these generally recognized motifs, which may be stated roughly as listed below.

> Yhwh intended and acted for Israel's good
> Israel failed in its proper response to his good intentions and actions
> Yhwh felt legitimate anger when Israel spurned his goodness
> Yhwh came to the point of acting in retribution when Israel spurned his goodness
> Yhwh did not act in retribution when Israel spurned his goodness
> Yhwh showed mercy rather than judgment
> Israel failed to respond to Yhwh's grace and mercy by a change in behavior

These contextual implications are being strengthened throughout first half of the oracle. The sub-episodes or addenda with (wĕ)gam-ʾănî strengthen similar contextual conclusions.

6. *The oaths in the two sub-episodes*

There is significant parallelism between the two addenda introduced by gam in both the oaths and the reasons given for making them.

Oaths

> v. 15 I would not bring them into the land that I had given them, a land flowing with milk and honey, the most glorious of all lands,
> v. 23 I would scatter them among the nations and disperse them through the countries,

Reasons

> v. 16 because they rejected my rulings and did not observe my decrees, and profaned my Sabbaths; for their heart went after their idols.

v. 24 because they had not executed my rulings, but had rejected my decrees and profaned my Sabbaths, and their eyes were set on their ancestors' idols.

Both oaths express the nature of Yhwh's pending retribution, and deny the Exodus oath (vv. 5–6). The oaths themselves are opposites (one negative, one affirmative): (i) not to bring the people into the land and (ii) to scatter them through other lands. The reasons given, however, are closely parallel. Note the corresponding pairs of expression "rejected" vs. "not executed"; "not observed" vs. "rejected"; "heart went after" vs. "set their eyes upon." The expression "profaned the Sabbaths" occurs in both.

The content of these two comments therefore partially breaks with the pattern of recurrent motifs as they occur in the three episodes in vv. 5–9; 10–14; 18–22. There is no initial mention of Yhwh's grace. The oaths assume Israel's failure, the oaths are retributive, and the reasons for the oaths follow. Both comments are additional indictments of Israel's failure, of which only the first carries a final expression of mercy.

Each adds a new premise of equal relevance to the charges already made in the episode which precedes it, and each strengthens the contextual implications of each episode. And yet these two oaths against Israel, sworn to the generations in the wilderness, were not fulfilled in their generation. Israel was not scattered in the wilderness, nor was it excluded from entering the land. Two further contextual conclusions may therefore be manifest here:

Yhwh failed to fulfill his oaths against Israel
Yhwh once again, withheld his oaths, out of further grace towards his rebellious people

There can be no doubt that it is the second that is here being made manifest in the oracle and carries Ezekiel's endorsement. Israel may have concluded that prophetic utterances are always delayed (see Ezek 12:22, 24, 27) but the truth involves Yhwh's honor and his grace and mercy toward Israel, not tardiness. At the same time, these two oaths to exclude and to scatter have set the stage as an explanation of the deportation following upon the fall of Jerusalem in

587 B.C.E. The oaths have stood; the delay has ended; Judah has fallen heir to the oaths taken against their ancestors, and they have been scattered.

Further discussion of selected parts of the oracle

This section can deal only with the content of vv. 3–4 of the prelude and with the episodes of Israel's past covered in vv. 10b–24.

Prelude

Nestling among the cluster of oracular formulae, Yhwh's word to Ezekiel for the elders (vv. 3–4) takes the form of (i) a rebuttal of their request for consultation by means of a rhetorical question (with the initial interrogative particle *he*)—"Is it to consult me that you have come?"—which leaves them to derive Yhwh's response, and (ii) an oath which categorically refuses to engage in consultation at their request "By my life, I will not be consulted by you!"

> hălidrōš ʾōtî ʾattem bāʾîm ḥay-ʾāniy ʾim-ʾiddārēš lākem nĕʾum ʾădōnāy yhwh
> "Is it to consult me that you have come? As I live, I will not be consulted by you [lit. "if I will be consulted by you"]. Oracle of Yhwh." (Ezek 20:3b)

The interrogative particle *he* introduces rhetorical as well as real questions, and may have an exclamatory illocution.

The ensuing evaluation of Israel's story (vv. 5b–44) eventually returns to this context (vv. 30–31) with a series of questions culminating in the repetition "How can I let you consult me, men of Israel? As I live, says Yhwh, I will not be consulted by you" (v. 31), before continuing the oracle to its end (vv. 32–44).

Verse 4 is addressed solely to Ezekiel, consisting in (i) a rhetorical question (repeated, both times introduced by the particle *he*) whose intent is to convey an instruction to the prophet, and (ii) an instruction to indict the elders (and ultimately the house of Israel) with the charge ʾet tôʿăbōt ʾăbôtām hôdîʿēm ("Let them know their fathers' detestable practices"). In context this implies that idolatry is Yhwh's reason for refusing to be consulted. Also, although at this point no further communication is entailed, we are led to expect idolatry to be thematic in what an oracle might have to say.

> hătišpōṭ ʾōtām hătišpôṭ ben-ʾādām ʾet-tôʿăbōt ʾăbôtām hôdîʿēm
> "Will you indict them, son of man, will you indict them? Let them know the abominations of their ancestors." (Ezek 20:4 NRSV [altered])

The repetition is presumably intended to urge the task on Ezekiel. So, there are three interrogative sentences in the prelude (vv. 3–4), and two more in mid-oracle (vv. 30–31), the last occurrence of which (v. 31) lacks the interrogative particle *he*.

The range of meaning of špṭ (v. 4) covers the whole judicial process to discern the rights and wrongs of a legal controversy. Ezekiel's word to the elders from Yhwh is itself to consist in showing or telling them (hôdîʿēm, hiphil imperative) their ancestors' detestable practices ʾet-tôʿăbōt ʾăbôtām. The nature of the špṭ required here—the content of "the ancestors' detestable practices" suggests the sense of arraign, indict, or charge, in the sense of announcing the charge against them.

This preliminary (private) communication to the prophet has the effect of keeping the initiative with Yhwh. He responds to the sought-for consultation by this preliminary aside to his prophet, whom he instructs to convey a refusal of their approach as well as something he does wish to tell them.

The oracle: verses 10b–24 in the wilderness

Verses 5–29 explicates the indictment in a critical review of Israel's past. Verses 30–32 bring that indictment up to the present, and vv. 33–44 address the future. Space limits us here to a partial consideration of the oracle, focusing only on vv. 10b–24.

Allusions and echoically used metarepresentations

Throughout this section there are various allusions to events which occur in the Pentateuch; see election, Jacob and Egypt (v. 5); Sinai (v. 11); refusal to enter the land (Num 13–14 in v. 15), which others have noted.

"Might Ezekiel's prophecy be something of an echo-chamber?" asks Evans,[37] under the influence of Hays and Schultz.[38] In this section we will seek to demonstrate a strong affirmation, at least as far as Ezek 20 is concerned, although perhaps in a stricter sense than Evans contemplated. To do that we must first introduce some necessary concepts and definitions.

Philosophers of language have long been aware of the distinction between use and mention, or *de dicto* versus *de re*. More recently, from Sperber and Wilson,[39] the distinction has received increasing attention within the approach of relevance theory to understanding communication. After finding that the more general phenomenon is the use of one representation to represent another representation, terminology has shifted, to the term metarepresentation.[40] A quotation is perhaps the most immediately obvious example of a metarepresentation of another representation. A metarepresentation does not describe a state of affairs, but is an interpretation of an original descriptive representation, and is an interpretive use of language. The resemblance of a metarepresentation to its original as a matter of interpretive resemblance. And, finally, interpretive resemblance can be defined precisely in terms of the meaning properties of the two representations, both the explicatures (the full expression of "what

[37] Evans, "Inner-Biblical Representation," 9.

[38] Richard B. Hays, *Echoes of Scripture in the Letters of Paul* (New Haven: Yale University Press, 1989); and Richard L. Schultz, "The Ties That Bind: Intertextuality, the Identification of Verbal Parallels, and Reading Strategies in the Book of the Twelve"

[39] Dan Sperber and Deirdre Wilson, "Irony and the Use-Mention Distinction," in *Radical Pragmatics* (ed. Peter Cole; New York: Academic Press, 1981), 295–318.

[40] Dan Sperber and Deirdre Wilson, *Relevance: Communication & Cognition (2nd ed.;* Oxford: Blackwell, 1995), 289 n. 25.

is said") and the implicatures, or what is not expressed but part of the meaning conveyed.[41]

> Two utterances, or even more generally, two ostensive stimuli, interpretively resemble one another to the extent that they share their explicatures and/or implicatures.[42]

We can usefully carry this one stage further. When a metarepresentation is used to attribute some aspect of its content or its form to someone else, and also expresses the current speaker's attitude toward what is attributed, it is echoic, or more strictly, an echoically-used expression.

> A representation is used echoically when it attributes some aspect of its form or content to someone other than the speaker herself at that moment and expresses an attitude to that aspect. The attribution may be overt (encoded) or tacit (to be inferred), and, similarly, the expression of attitude may be overt or tacit.[43]

It may be attributed to a known speaker or document, a stereotypical opinion, or a cultural norm or aspiration. Echoically-used expressions intentionally resemble other utterances or thoughts. It is this ostensive resemblance which distinguishes all incidental re-use of words and expressions from echoically used utterances, and characterizes echoic language as *interpretively used representations*. Allusions are metarepresentations which are echoically used.[44]

---

[41] See Ernst-August Gutt, *Translation and Relevance: Cognition and Context* (Oxford: Blackwell, 1990; repr., Manchester: St Jerome Press, 2001), 35–46: and Sperber and Wilson, *Relevance*, 138, 226–31, 237–39.

[42] Gutt, *Translation and Relevance*, 46.

[43] Carston, *Thoughts and Utterances*, 298.

[44] This differs from Hays's definition (*Echoes of Scripture*), in which echoes are the weak extreme, for which it is no longer possible to decide that re-use was not incidental.

Allusions in Ezekiel 20

Fishbane, Livett Kohn, and Evans[45] draw together numerous allusions to Exod 6:2–9 in Ezek 20:5–26, 33–44.[46],[47]

Other scholars have seen Deuteronomic language in Ezek 20. Pons, as well as Hahn and Bergsma,[48] have sought to show how Ezekiel distances himself from

---

[45] Michael Fishbane, "Torah and Tradition," in *Tradition and Theology in the Old Testament* (ed. Douglas A. Knight; Philadelphia: Fortress Press, 1977), 276–77; Risa Livett Kohn, *A New Heart and a New Soul: Ezekiel, the Exile and the Torah* (JSOTSup 358; London: Continuum Sheffield Academic Press, 2002); idem., " 'With a Mighty Hand and an Outstretched Arm': The Prophet and the Torah in Ezekiel 20," in *Ezekiel's Hierarchical World: Wrestling with a Tiered Reality* (ed. Stephen L. Cook and Corrine Patton; Atlanta: Society of Biblical Literature, 2004); and Evans, "Inter-Biblical Interpretation," 178–79, 183. See also Sheldon H.Blank, "Studies in Deutero-Isaiah." *Hebrew Union College Annual* 15 (1940): 1–46; and Herbert Haag, *Was Lehrt die Literarische Untersuchung des Ezechiel-Textes?* (Freiburg: Paulusdruckerei, 1943).

[46] My focus is on a synchronic approach to the text, approaching it as canonical or "inner biblical exegesis," as far as possible without prejudice to questions of the origins and transmission of the text. I assume a firm (fixed) tradition or hard text. This is supported by the detailed verbal allusions. The cumulative nature of these allusions may allow a discussion of their interpretive resemblance in meaning properties to the corresponding Torahic texts—shared meaning properties, both explicatures and implicatures.

[47] Fishbane notes that "the specific verbal tension [in Ezek 20.4–11, 33–36] . . . withstands a point by point comparison with the language of Exod. 6.2–9." See also the discussion of intertextuality in Fishbane, "Types of Biblical Intertextuality," in *International Organisation for the Study of the Old Testament: Congress Volume 1998 Oslo* (ed. A. Lemaire and M. Sæbø; VTSup 80; Leiden: Brill, 2000). Evans goes so far as to conclude that Ezek 20 is "nothing less than a phrase-by-phrase exposition of Exodus 6," even doubting whether "the number and range of parallels" can be satisfactorily based on tradition rather than on a "hard text." We can consider Evans's first comment to be an overstatement, since it is abundantly clear that Ezek 20 also reflects Lev 18:4–5 and Deuteronomy (or at least Deuteronomic theology). Ezekiel does not consider the exodus in such dark colors that he cannot draw upon it (with Kutsko and contra Tuell). In vv. 5–10a allusions form a chiaroscuro between Yhwh's good plans and Israel's idolatrous failure, while in vv. 33–44 he paints a new exodus in two panels: into the wilderness of the nations for judgement and purification (v. 35), then into the land to serve Yhwh as he intended (v. 40).

[48] Scott Walker Hahn and John Sietze Bergsma, "What Laws Were 'Not Good': A

aspects of deuteronomic theology,[49] while Livett Kohn's (2002) recent work has attempted to reveal a fusion in Ezekiel's thinking between P and D.

My own reading is that a detailed resemblance of allusions to Lev 18:4–5 overshadows the part played by Deuteronomic language for our purposes. This will emerge in the following sub-section.

Allusions in Ezekiel 20:11–24

Sprinkle[50] and others have noted the detailed allusions to Lev 18:2–5 in Ezek 20. In Lev 18:2 the SF is uncharacteristically found in the introduction to a

---

Canonical Approach to the Theological Problem of Ezekiel 20:25–26," *JBL* 123/2 (2004): 201–18.

49 For example, Hahn and Bergsma, "What Laws Were 'Not Good,' " 207, suggest that the masculine gender of ḥuqqîm here is intended to indicate an allusion to Deuteronomy. But to maintain this simply because the masculine form predominates there (Hahn and Bergsma count eighteen occurrences of masculine; eight occurrences of feminine form) apparently ignores the rhetorical effect of repeated allusion to Lev 18:5 from v. 11–25. If the change in gender is significant for interpretation, and I also believe it is, it would be better to find its significance elsewhere. Their presentation of evidence is quite limited, and the crucial role claimed for lexemes used for "scatter" is ambivalent. Words from both P (*zrh*) and D (*pwś*) are used. However, a quick look at the sources makes Hahn and Bergsma's conclusion seem unlikely. *zrh* occurs only once in Lev 26:33, and *pwś* three times in Deuteronomy; this is too few to make any significant contrast. In Ezekiel, *zrh* and *pwś* co-occur six times (12:14–15; 20:23; 22:15; 29:12–13; 30:23, 26; 36:19), while *zrh* alone occurs four times (5:2, 10, 12; 6:8), and *pwś* occurs alone five times literally (11:16–17; 20:34, 41; 28:25;) and twice more in a metaphorical passage (34:6, 12). This pattern of usage does not support the conclusion that Ezekiel intends to contrast the language of P and D in this way. Indeed Ezekiel had to use words which others had already used (Bakhtin), but we cannot make much of this. Drawing conclusions from the words used depends crucially upon (i) the choice available, and (ii) the new speaker's intention. For use of another's words to be significant for interpretation, a speaker must intend the other's words to be recognized as part of the interpretation. Hahn and Bergsma intuitively assume this, but their evidence as noted here does not bear them out. After presenting evidence, their argument shifts, and leans much more on possibilities (using words like "may," "might," "perhaps").

50 Preston M. Sprinkle, *Law and Life: The Interpretation of Leviticus 18:5 in Early Judaism and in Paul* (Tübingen: Mohr Siebeck, 2008), 35-40.

discourse, although even here we should note that it forms an inclusio for the declarations in vv. 2–5. As far as I am aware, no one has traced out the allusions in detail, following the chain through vv. 11–26.[51]

1. Leviticus 18:4–5

The verses in Leviticus read

> v. 4 ʾet-mišpāṭay taʿăśû wĕʾet-ḥuqqōtay tišmĕrû lāleket bāhem ʾănî yhwh ʾĕlōhêkem
> v. 5 ûšĕmartem ʾet-ḥuqqōtay wĕʾet-mišpāṭay ʾăšer yaʿăśe ʾōtām hāʾādām wāḥay bāhem ʾănî yhwh
> v. 4 My rulings you shall observe and my decrees you shall keep, following them: I am the Lord your God. (v. 5) You shall keep my decrees and my rulings; by doing so one shall live: I am the Lord. (NRSV [altered])

Leviticus 18:4 uses the verbs ʿśh ("do"), šmr ("keep")—both Qal Impf 2 masc.plu.—and hlk "walk" (Qal infinitive construction) in exhortation to Israel. Lev 18:5 exhorts Israel to "keep" (šmr; Qal vav-consecutive Perfect, 2nd masculine plural) the decrees and rulings.

The same verse conjoins ʾet-ḥuqqōtay ʾet-mišpāṭay,[52] which also occurs in the reverse order in two conjoined clauses in v. 4.

The passage breaks into the following versets

> a you shall observe my rulings,
> b you shall keep following my decrees
> c I am Yhwh your God
> d you shall keep my decrees and my rulings
> e by doing which a man will live
> c' I am Yhwh

(a), (b), and (d) express the same proposition, and so are synonymous for our purposes. The SF is repeated in (c) and (c'), and can be inferred to be the

[51] See also R. J. Sim, "Allusions in Ezk 20.11-26," 2008.

[52] I will consistently translate ḥuqqîm as "decrees" and mišpāṭîm as "rulings" for simplicity, without implying anything further by the choice. ḥuqqōt is feminine plural and mišpāṭ is masculine. Both carry the 1st person singular possessive suffix.

ground of obedience, which is Yhwh's person(al authority). (e) makes the offer of life the outcome of (d). The two main assertions here are

1. Israel shall obey Yhwh's decrees and rulings
2. Yhwh's decrees and rulings afford life to those who obey them

In context, the obvious contextual assumptions (c.a.) underlying the text, assumed rather than expressed, are

c.a. 1 Yhwh gave Israel his decrees and his rulings
c.a. 2 Yhwh's decrees and rulings are good

That is, the passage assumes that Yhwh has previously given decrees and rulings to Israel, and exhorts Israel to keep what it has been given. The second assumption noted here is pervasive, but not always recognized.

Assertions		**Assumptions**	
1	Israel shall obey Yhwh's decrees and rulings	c.a. 1	Yhwh gave Israel his decrees and his rulings
2	Yhwh's decrees and rulings afford life to those who obey them	c.a. 2	Yhwh's decrees and rulings are good

2. Ezekiel 20:11

Leviticus 18:4–5 is first mentioned in Ezek 20:11 in reference to the giving of the law at Sinai.

> wāʾettēn lāhem ʾet-ḥuqqôtay wĕʾet-mišpāṭay hôdaʿtî ʾôtām ʾăšer yaʿăśe ʾôtām hāʾādām wāḥay bāhem
> "I gave them my decrees and showed them my rulings
> By whose observance everyone shall live." (NRSV [altered])

Apart from being shorter and changing pronominal reference from 2nd to 3rd person, this is a clear mention of the Levitical passage in the following respects.

- We find the verbatim conjoined expression ʾet-ḥuqqôtay wĕʾet-mišpāṭay ("my decrees and my rulings") as in Lev 18:5, with the same gender and carrying the 1st singular possessive pronoun suffix.
- Ezekiel 20:11 includes a verbatim quotation of the second verse, ʾăšer yaʿăśe ʾôtām hāʾādām wāḥay bāhem ("in doing which a person lives"). This is the only chapter outside Leviticus where these words are quoted, and I suggest that its verbal identity serves convincingly to make manifest allusion to Lev 18.
- The verbs used refer behind the exhortation in Lev 18:5 to law-giving at Sinai; Ezek 20:11 uses wāʾettēn lāhem ʾet-ḥuqqôtay wĕʾet-mišpāṭay hôdaʿtî ʾôtām, (Lit: "I gave to them my decrees and my rulings I showed them," with ntn and the hiphil of ydʿ "make known.") The two clauses have word order Verb-IO-OBJ and OBJ-Verb-IO, so that the two verbs form a chiasm around the conjoined nouns. The form linguistically resembles Lev 18:4, with a slight change in word order, which is OBJ-Verb in both clauses.

Ezekiel 20:11 expresses the first contextual assumption (c.a. 1), in its allusion to the Levitical passage (giving the decrees and rulings, the contextual implication or c.i.).

c.a. 2 Yhwh's statutes and rules are good
c.i. Israel should keep Yhwh's statutes and rules

Here, the assertions are

1 Yhwh gave Israel his decrees and rulings
2 Yhwh's decrees and rulings afford life to those who obey them

What was assumed (c.a. 1) in the Levitical passage is here expressed as assertion 1; while assertion 1 in the Levitical passage is here assumed (c.a. 1). The second assertion and c.a. 2 are the same in both passages.

Assertions		**Assumptions**	
1	Yhwh gave Israel his decrees and his rulings	c.a. 1	Israel shall obey Yhwh's decrees and rulings
2	Yhwh's decrees and rulings afford life to those who obey them	c.a. 2	Yhwh's decrees and rulings are good

The obvious contextual assumptions (c.a.) underlying the text, assumed rather than expressed, are

c.a. 1 Yhwh gave Israel his decrees and his rulings
c.a. 2 Yhwh's decrees and rulings are good

Observing the decrees and rulings is now referred to only in connection with the life-affording clause, which is cited verbatim. Otherwise, keeping Yhwh's decrees is a contextual implication (c.i.). The second contextual assumption still underlies the allusion.

With these rather minimal differences, the meaning properties of the allusion of the Levitical passage in this verse are unchanged. There can be no reasonable doubt that Ezek 20:11 is a deliberate allusion to Lev 18:4–5, and follows the same logic, advocating the same obedience to the same laws Yhwh gave them.[53]

3. Exodus 31:13–14

Turning now to compare the Exodus and Ezekiel passages in a similar way, we find the following.

> v. 13 . . . ʾak ʾet-šabbĕtōtay tišmōrû kiy ʾôt hiwʾ bênî ûbênêkem lĕdōrōtêkem lādaʿat kî ʾănî yhwh mĕqaddiškem. (v. 14) ûšĕmartem ʾet-haššabbāt kî qōdeš hiwʾ lākem mĕḥallêhā môt yûmāt kî kol-hāʿōśe bāh mĕlāʾkâ wĕnikrĕtâ hannepeš hahiwʾ miqqereb ʿammêhā
> v. 13 You shall keep my Sabbaths, for this is a sign between me and you throughout your generations, given in order that you may know that I, the Lord, sanctify you. (v. 14) You shall keep the Sabbath, because it is holy for you; everyone who profanes it shall be put to death (NRSV)

[53] The direction of literary dependence is notoriously difficult to ascertain, but it seems to be much more plausible that the Priestly Writing is available to Ezekiel in some form in which Lev 18:4–5 is virtually identical to its present form, than the reverse, namely that Lev 18:4–5 is dependent upon Ezek 20:11.

This breaks into two sets of three versets, as follows.

1)	You shall keep (Imperfect) my Sabbaths,	a
2)	for this is a sign between me and you throughout your generations,	b
3)	The sign is so that you may know that I, the LORD, sanctify you.	c
4)	You shall keep (Imperfect) the Sabbath,	a'
5)	because it is holy for you;	b'
6)	everyone who profanes it shall be put to death	c'

(1) and (4) are synonymous, expressing the same proposition in the form of strong directives, with initial ʾak ("surely") strengthening the directive in (1).

Sabbath (2) and holy for Israel (5). It is a mutual relational sign between Yhwh and his people. Keeping the Sabbath is an idiomatic expression for fulfilling all the requirements relevant to the Sabbath institution. Keeping it is Israel's indication of faithfully meeting Yhwh's requirements in expectation of receiving Yhwh's blessings, and simultaneously Yhwh's commitment to bless Israel for their adherence to his requirements.

Secondly, it is a sign by means of which Israel may recognize "I am Yhwh" who sanctifies his people. Yhwh's actions on his people's behalf "live not only in the narrative proclamation . . . but equally in the signs Yhwh has given his people as fixed observances witnessing to his particular actions" on behalf of his people, and again, "This sabbath is also the sacramental sign and warranty of a particular history from whose perspective Israel can recognize both its status as the elected people and Yhwh as the God who both elects and sanctifies his people."[54]

(3) expresses the goal (intention) of the Sabbath sign, which is the knowledge of God as expressed in the Recognition Formula. (3) is reflected in (6), where sanctions against breaking the Sabbath are set out in warning. People who profane the Sabbath will be excluded. There is a sanction against profaning the Sabbath. Profaning ḥll means take it into a state of profanity, by non-observance of its significant nature.

[54] Zimmerli, *I am Yahweh*, 45, 70.

The main assertions are:

3 Israel shall observe Yhwh's sabbaths
4 Sabbaths are a sign between Israel and Yhwh
5 through observing his Sabbath sign, Israel shall come to know Yhwh

In context, the obvious underlying contextual assumptions are

c.a. 3 Yhwh gave Israel his Sabbaths
c.a. 4 Yhwh's intends his Sabbaths for Israel's good

4. Ezekiel 20:12

When dealing with gam above, we set aside the first occurrence, wĕgam ʾet-šabbĕtôtay in v. 12.

Ezekiel 20:11–12 (BHS/WHM 4.2)

> v. 11 wāʾettēn lāhem ʾet-ḥuqqôtay wĕʾet-mišpāṭay hôdaʿtî ʾôtām ʾăšer yaʿăśe ʾôtām hāʾādām wāḥay bāhem. (v. 12) wĕgam ʾet-šabbĕtôtay nātattî lāhem lihyôt lĕʾôt bênî ûbênêhem lādaʿat kî ʾănî yhwh mĕqaddĕšām
>
> v. 11 I gave them my statutes and showed them my ordinances, by whose observance everyone shall live. (v. 12) Moreover I gave them my Sabbaths, as a sign between me and them, so that they might know that I the LORD sanctify them.

The hypothesis introduced above stills holds, but this time, wĕgam ʾet-šabbĕtôtay nātattî lāhem finds its precedent parallel in v. 11, and instructs the hearer-reader to process the following expression in parallel to an antecedent statement of equal relevance to it; here, the giving of decrees and statutes (v. 11). The parallel is reinforced by fronting the object expression to precede the verb in v. 12.

This resembles the Exodus passage in several respects.

- ʾet-šabbĕtôtay ("my Sabbaths") with the personal suffix only occurs in these two passages.
- Yhwh's Sabbath is a sign between Yhwh and Israel, although lacking lĕdōrōtêkem ("for your generations") in Ezekiel.

- The RF is included verbatim as in Exod 31:13, lāda^cat kî ʾănî yhwh mĕqaddĕšām with the infinitive and with a change in pronominal reference in the participial extension.

The main assertions are:

1 Yhwh gave the Sabbath institution to Israel
2 the Sabbaths are a sign between Yhwh and Israel
3 Sabbath-sign is for knowing kî I am Yhwh who sanctifies you

The contextual assumptions are

c.a. 3 Israel shall observe Yhwh's Sabbaths
c.a. 4 Yhwh's intends his Sabbaths for Israel's good

What was asserted in Exodus (ass 1) is an assumption in Ezekiel (c.a. 1); and what was assumed in Exodus (c.a. 1) is asserted in Ezekiel. Assertions 2 and 3 occur in both passages, and c.a. 2 underlies both. Apart from a minor ellipsis (lĕdōrōtêkem ["for all generations"]) and with the loss of kî from Exodus making the second assertion a descriptively used representation, the two passages are extremely close in "meaning properties," expressing or implying the same propositions. Ezek 20:13 picks up the note of profanation of the Sabbath, which in Exod 31:14 was a prohibitive warning, though here it is a denunciation.

The chain of allusions in verses 11–24

The above discussion has traced out the resemblance in detail, firstly to show how close a resemblance is actually established, and secondly to provide a foundation for tracing the chain through v. 24.

Ezekiel 20:11 is the first of a clear seven-fold chain of allusions to Lev 18:4–5 and Exod 31:13–14 in vv. 11–12, 13, 16, 18, 19–20, 21, and 24. We have argued above that the additive wĕgam introduced Sabbaths to the decrees and rulings, and that they should be processed together with equal significance, which is manifested throughout the passage in vv. 11–24.

- The same indictments for failure in vv. 13, 16, 21, 24 all combine reference to decrees, rulings and Sabbaths. Verse 18 is exceptional in replacing Sabbaths by an indictment of Israel's idolatry.

- Reference to **mišpāṭay**, **ḥuqqôtay** and **šabbětôtay** occur together (except in v. 18).
- In each case the form is constant for gender and possessive suffix (except in the prohibitions in v. 18 and vv. 25–26[55]).
- The affirmation of vv. 11–12 to the second generation in the wilderness **běḥuqqôtay lēkû wěʾet-mišpāṭay šimrû waʿăśû ʾôtām** ("walk in my decrees and carefully obey my rulings" (Ezek 20:19) makes more changes in syntactic form, but still resembles Lev 18:4 both linguistically and conceptually. Thus **ʾet-mišpāṭay taʿăśû wěʾet-ḥuqqōtay tišměrû lāleket bāhem** ("keep my rulings and keep walking in my decrees"; Lev 18:4), noting the reversal of "decrees" and "rulings." The effect of this is that **ḥuqqōt** consistently precedes **mišpāṭ** in the string of allusions in Ezek 20, which strengthens consciousness of its source in Lev 18.
- The indictments in Ezek 20:13, 16, 18, 21, 24, ring the changes on the verbs used in Lev 18:4, now in negative: "they didn't walk/keep" (**lōʾ**or **ʿal** with **šmr** ["keep"] or **hlk** ["walk"]), as well as the lexically negative verb **mʾs** ("reject").
- Throughout the passage, failure to observe the Sabbath is simply **wěʾet-šabbětōtay ḥillělû** ("they profaned my Sabbaths"; **ḥll**), in vv. 13, 16, 21, 24, reflecting the prohibitive sanction **lākem měḥallêhā môt yûmāt** ("everyone who profanes it shall be put to death"; Exod 31:14).
- The indictments in the two **wěgam** sections (vv. 15–17, 23–24), in addition to reiterating Israel's failure to observe the decrees, rulings, and Sabbaths, both record a condemnation of Israel's propensity toward idolatry (hearts and eyes).
- Ezek 20:18 enjoins "the children in the wilderness" not to follow their fathers. Here, without warning, we find **běḥûqqê ʾăbôtêkem ʾal-tēlēkû wěʾet-mišpěṭêhem ʾal-tišmōrû** ("Do not walk in your fathers' decrees nor keep their rulings") with the masculine plural

[55] For vv. 25–26, see R. J. Sim, "Revisiting Ezek 20.25–26: Echo Question, Denial, or Echo of a Third Kind" (paper presented at the SBL International Meeting in Tartu, July 25–29, 2010).

construction ḥûqqê. The choice of masculine gender for "the decrees" at this point cannot be accidental in the light of the repeated close resemblances throughout this chapter, and is probably intended to make the contrast between Yhwh's decrees and the ancestors' decrees.[56] The prohibitions to the second generation in v. 18 forbid walking after and keeping their fathers' decrees and rulings, and condemn idolatry, but make no mention of the Sabbath.

Additionally,

- The affirmation of vv. 11–12 to the second generation in the wilderness in vv. 19-20, using the same verbs "walk, obey, keep," lie within an inclusio formed by SF and RF.
- There are three verbatim quotations of the offer of life, ʾăšer yaʿăśe ʾôtām hāʾādām wāḥay bāhem ("in doing which a person lives"; Ezek 20:11, 13, 21).[57]
- Less striking because the RF occurs elsewhere, we might add that the RF occurs in vv. 12, 20, lādaʿat kî ʾănî yhwh mĕqaddĕšām following Exod 31:13–14 verbatim apart from change in person.

In short, both linguistically and propositionally, the resemblances to both Lev 18:4–5 and Exod 31:13–14 in Ezek 20:11–24 are striking and unmistakable.

Israel's failure in vv. 13, 16, 18, 21, and 24 are negative indictments based on (a), (b), and (d). Israel violated the obedience required in the contextual implication noted above, which was an explicature in the Levitical passage.

The two contextual assumptions, c.a. 1 and 2 still underlie or are expressed in each allusive mention.

The offer of life (e) is cited verbatim in vv. 11, 13, 21. The SF (c) is not cited in connection to the allusions to Lev 18:5 (but occurs in the chapter in 20:7, 19). The RF is cited in v. 12 (as well as in vv. 20, 38, 42, 44).

---

[56] Targum Jonathan and later Jewish interpretation distinguish the good and the no-good decrees of v. 25 in this way. But see Sim, "Revisiting Ezek 20.25–26."

[57] See Preston M. Sprinkle, "Law and Life: The Use of Leviticus 18.5 in the Literary Framework of Ezekiel," *Journal for the Study of the Old Testament* 31 (2007): 55-73.

The same propositions and logic run through the chain of seven mentions. Negations, both sentential and verbal antonyms, are antonymous sentences to the Levitical exhortations. Taking into account the negations to warn or indict Israel, each of these allusions has the same meaning properties as in the Levitical passage.

Verse 19 cites (a), (b), and (c), relies on the same two contextual assumptions, and therefore has the same meaning properties (and logic) as the Levitical passage.

Contextual implications

There are some obvious (unstated) contextual implications which can now be derived. First in importance are two which may be stated roughly as listed below.

> The oracle (Yhwh/Ezekiel) is alluding to Lev 18 and Exod 31
> The oracle is endorsing Lev 18 and Exod 31

Allusions are echoic representations, and as such, convey the speaker's attitude to what is metarepresented. Throughout the passage, every indication is that Ezekiel endorses the allusions from Leviticus; conversely, nothing gives any indication of distance between what Leviticus advocates and what Ezekiel advocates in alluding to it.

Within the context created by these, other contextual implications, including those listed above will also be manifest. These contextual implications are being strengthened throughout first half of the oracle. The sub-episodes or addenda with wĕgam-ʾănî strengthen similar contextual conclusions.

Conclusion

Recent scholarship has found echoes of the language of Exodus, Leviticus and Deuteronomy reflected in Ezek 20. The oracle is heavily allusive: vv. 5b–10a draw upon Exod 6:2–9; vv. 10b–26 draw upon Lev 18:4–5 and Exod 31:13–14; vv. 27–29, 32 use language of idolatry familiar from Kingdoms and Chronicles; and vv. 33–44 again allude strongly to Exod 6:2–9. This is surely significant for the rhetoric of the chapter. The Exodus and Levitical allusions are perhaps the least discussed and the most significant, and have formed the focus of attention in the paper.

The rhetoric of Ezek 20:11–26 builds around eight cycles of allusion (vv. 11, 13, 16, 18, 19, 21, 24, 25) which have a close resemblance to Lev 18:4–5 and Exod 31:13–14, and which endorse the Torahic passages without qualification. Together they affirm Yhwh's decrees, rulings and Sabbath laws as good and a means to life. This is how Yhwh expresses his grace toward Israel. By rejecting them, Israel rejects what Yhwh gives, and refuses what is good. So serious is their rebellion! Yhwh's anger is aroused, but instead of judgment he acts in mercy

We have brought out the most remarkable feature of Ezek 20:11–12, namely that it is entirely composed of expressions/propositions used in Exod 31:13–14 and Lev 18:4–5. The major difference is that Ezek 20 is a record in assertive propositions of the giving of the law at Sinai, whereas both torahic passages are directive, expressing Yhwh's desire that Israel obey his given laws. In Ezek 20 we do not meet an allusion that is directive until vv. 19–20.

These allusions provide a highly salient, and accessible background against which the last ones in vv. 25–26 surely must be read, where apparently it is now Yhwh's decrees that are no-good and his rulings that fail to be a means of life. Rather than sanctifying Israel, their sacrifices bring Yhwh's defilement upon the nation.

The high level of repetitiveness in vv. 10b–24 arises from two sources, both noted above: the reiteration of motifs, and the reiteration of allusions to Lev 18:4–5 and Exod 31:13–14. While a superficial reading might consider the passage tediously lacking in creativeness, a close reading uncovers careful crafting in support of the contextual implications noted.

For translation of these little-read passages, the major challenge is surely ensuring that the oracle is read in the light of the Torahic passages. This need is seldom taken account of. It may require a version to take meticulous care in maintaining the verbal, syntactic and interpretive resemblance; but that by itself is less than sufficient. Readers of the oracle need some means of sending them back to Exod 31 and Lev 18 for context.

Bibliography

Allen, Leslie C. *Ezekiel 20–48*. Word Biblical Commentary 29. Dallas: Word, 1990.

———. "The Structuring of Ezekiel's Revisionist History Lesson (Ezekiel 20:3–31)." *Catholic Biblical Quarterly* 54 (1992): 448–62.

Blakemore, Diane. *Relevance and Linguistic Meaning: The Semantics and Pragmatics of Discourse Markers*. Cambridge: Cambridge University Press, 2002.

———. *Semantic Constraints on Relevance*. Oxford: Blackwell, 1987.

———. *Understanding Utterances: An Introduction to Pragmatics*. Oxford: Blackwell, 1992.

Blank, Sheldon H. "Studies in Deutero-Isaiah." *Hebrew Union College Annual* 15 (1940): 1–46.

Block, Daniel I. *The Book of Ezekiel Chapters 1-24*. New International Commentary of the Old Testament. Grand Rapids: Eerdmans, 1997.

Brown, Francis, S. R. Driver, and C. A. Briggs. *Hebrew and English Lexicon of the Old Testament*. Oxford: Clarendon, 1907. Repr., Peabody, Mass.: Hendrickson, 1979.

Carston, Robyn. *Thoughts and Utterances: The Pragmatics of Explicit Communication*. Oxford: Blackwell, 2002.

Carston, Robyn, and Seiji Uchida, eds. *Relevance Theory: Applications and Implications*. Pragmatics and Beyond, New Series 37. Amsterdam: John Benjamins, 1998.

Davis, Ellen F. *Swallowing the Scroll: Textuality and the Dynamics of Discourse in Ezekiel's Prophecy*. Journal for the Study of the Old Testament: Supplemental Series 78. Sheffield: Almond, 1989.

Eichrodt, Walther. *Ezekiel: A Commentary*. Translated by Cosslett Quin. London: SCM, 1970.

Eslinger, Lyle. "Ezekiel 20 and the Metaphor of Historical Teleology: Concepts of Biblical History." *Journal for the Study of the Old Testament* 81 (1998): 93–125.

Evans, John Frederick. "An Inner-Biblical Interpretation and Intertextual Reading of Ezekiel's Recognition Formulae with the Book of Exodus." DTh diss., University of Stellenbosch, 2006.

Fishbane, Michael. "Torah and Tradition." Pages 275–300 in *Tradition and Theology in the Old Testament*. Edited by Douglas A. Knight. Philadelphia: Fortress Press, 1977.

———. "Types of Biblical Intertextuality." Pages 39–44 in *International Organisation for the Study of the Old Testament: Congress Volume 1998 Oslo*. Edited by A.

Lemaire and M. Sæbø. Supplements to Vestus Testamentum 80. Leiden: Brill, 2000.

Gutt, Ernst-August. *Translation and Relevance: Cognition and Context.* Oxford: Blackwell, 1990. Repr., Manchester: St Jerome Press, 2000.

Hahn, Scott Walker, and John Sietze Bergsma. "What Laws Were 'Not Good': A Canonical Approach to the Theological Problem of Ezekiel 20:25–26." *Journal of Biblical Literature* 123/2 (2004): 201–18.

Harris, R. Laird, Gleason L. Archer, and Bruce K. Waltke, eds. *Theological Wordbook of the Old Testament.* Chicago: Moody Press, 1980.

Hays, Richard, B. *The Conversion of the Imagination: Paul as Interpreter of Israel's Scripture.* Grand Rapids: Eerdmans, 2005.

———. *Echoes of Scripture in the Letters of Paul.* New Haven: Yale University Press, 1989.

Kutsko, John F. *Between Heaven and Earth: Divine Presence and Absence in the Book of Ezekiel.* Biblical and Judaic Studies 7. Winona Lake: Eisenbrauns, 2000.

———. "Ezekiel's Anthropology and Its Ethical Implications." Pages 119–41 in *The Book of Ezekiel: Theological and Anthropological Perspectives.* Edited by Margaret S. Odell and John T. Strong. Atlanta: Society of Biblical Literature, 2000.

Levinsohn, Stephen H. "Also, Too and Moreover in a Novel by Dorothy Sayers." *Work Papers of the Summer Institute of Linguistics, University of North Dakota Session* 45 (2001). Online: http://www.und.edu/dept/linguistics/wp/2001Levinsohn.pdf.

———. "Towards a Typology of Additives" *Afrikanistische Arbeitspapiere* 69 (2002): 171–88.

Livett Kohn, Risa. *A New Heart and a New Soul: Ezekiel, the Exile and the Torah.* Journal for the Study of the Old Testament: Supplemental Series 358. London: Continuum Sheffield Academic Press, 2002.

———. " 'With a Mighty Hand and an Outstretched Arm': The Prophet and the Torah in Ezekiel 20." Pages 159–168 in *Ezekiel's Hierarchical World: Wrestling with a Tiered Reality.* Edited by Stephen L. Cook and Corrine Patton. Atlanta: Society of Biblical Literature, 2004.

Malamat, Abraham. "The Twilight of Judah in the Egyptian-Babylonian Maelstrom" in *Congress Volume, Edinburgh, 1974.* Edited by J. A. Emerton. Supplements to Vetus Testamentum 28. Leiden: Brill, 1974.

Meier, Samuel A. *Speaking of Speaking: Marking Direct Discourse in the Hebrew Bible.* Supplements to Vetus Testamentum 46. Leiden: Brill, 1992.

Patton, Corinne. " 'I Myself Gave Them Laws That Were Not Good': Ezekiel 20 and the Exodus Tradition" *Journal for the Study of the Old Testament* 81 (1998): 93–125.

———. " 'I Myself Gave Them Laws That Were Not Good': Ezekiel 20 and the Exodus Traditions" *Journal for the Study of the Old Testament* 69 (1996): 73–90.

Robson, James E. *Word and Spirit in Ezekiel.* Library of Hebrew Bible/Old Testament Studies 447. London: T. & T. Clark, 2006.

Schultz, Richard L. *The Search for Quotation: Verbal Parallels in the Prophets.* Journal for the Study of the Old Testament: Supplement Series 180. Sheffield: Sheffield Academic Press, 1999.

———. "The Ties That Bind: Intertextuality, the Identification of Verbal Parallels, and Reading Strategies in the Book of the Twelve" *SBL 2001 Seminar Papers,* pp.39-57. Atlanta: Society of Biblical Literature, 2001.

Sim, R. J. "Allusions in Ezek 20.11-26." Paper presented at the SBL International Meeting, Auckland, July 6–11, 2008.

———. "Hebrew Particle gam: A Procedural Approach to Non-Declarative Usage" Paper presented at the SBL International Meeting in Rome, June 30–July 4, 2009.

———. "The Hebrew Particle gam as Procedural Marker" Paper presented at the SBL International meeting in Auckland, July 6–11, 2008.

———. " 'I Gave Them No-Good Laws': Audience Search for Meaning in Ezek 20.25-26" Paper presented at Bible Translation 08, Horsleys Green, UK, February 6–8, 2008.

———. " 'I Gave Them No-Good Laws': Ezek 20.25-26." Paper presented at the SBL International Meeting, Vienna, July 22–25, 2007.

———. "Revisiting Ezek 20.25-26: Echo Question, Denial, or Echo of a Third Kind" Paper presented at the SBL International Meeting in Tartu, July 25–29, 2010.

———. "(Un)shared Meaning Properties: Interpretive Resemblance in Ezek 20.25 with Reference to vv. 11-13" Paper presented at the SBL International Meeting in Rome, June 30–July 4, 2009.

Sperber, Dan, and Deirdre Wilson. "Irony and the Use Mention Distinction." Pages 295–318 in *Radical Pragmatics.* Edited by Peter Cole. New York: Academic Press, 1981.

———. *Relevance: Communication & Cognition. 2nd ed.* Oxford: Blackwell, 1995.

Sprinkle, Preston M. *Law and Life: The Interpretation of Leviticus 18:5 in Early Judaism and in Paul.* Tübingen: Mohr Siebeck, 2008.

———. "Law and Life: The Use of Leviticus 18.5 in the Literary Framework of Ezekiel." *Journal for the Study of the Old Testament* 31 (2007): 55-73.

Tuell, Steven Shawn. "Contemporary Studies in Ezekiel: A New Tide Rising?" Pages 241–254 in *Ezekiel's Hierarchical World: Wrestling with a Tiered Reality.* Edited by Stephen L. Cook and Corrine Patton. Leiden: Brill, 2004.

———. "Divine Presence and Absence in Ezekiel's Prophecy." Pages 97–116 in *Book of Ezekiel: Theological and Anthropological Perspectives*. Edited by Margaret S. Odell and John T. Strong. Atlanta: Society of Biblical Literature, 2000.

Van der Horst, P. W. "I Gave Them Laws That Were Not Good: Ezekiel 20:25 in Ancient Judaism and Early Christianity." Pages 94–118 in *Sacred History and Sacred Texts in Early Judaism: A Symposium in Honour of A. S. van der Woude*. Edited by J. N. Bremmer and F. García Martínez. Contributions to Biblical Exegesis and Theology 5. Kampen: Kok Pharos, 1992.

Van der Merwe, Christo H. J. "An Overview of Recent Developments in the Description of Biblical Hebrew Relevant for Bible Translation." Pages 228-45 in *Contemporary Translation Studies and Bible Translation: A South African Perspective*, edited by Christo H. J. Van der Merwe and J. A. Naudé. Acta Theologica Supplement 2. Bloemfontein, 2002.

Wilson, Deirdre, and Dan Sperber "Representation and relevance." Pages 133–153 in *Mental Representations: The Interface Between Language and Reality*. Edited by Ruth M. Kempson. Cambridge: Cambridge University Press, 1988.

Wilt, T. L. " 'Oracle of Yahweh': Translating a Highly Marked Expression." *The Bible Translator* 50/3 (1999): 301–4.

Wright, Christopher J. H. *The Message of Ezekiel*. The Bible Speaks Today. Leicester: InterVarsity Press, 2001.

Zimmerli, Walther. *Erkenntnis Gottes nach dem Buch Ezechiel*. Abhandlungen zur Theologie des Alten und Neuen Testaments 27. Zürich: Zwingli-Verlag, 1954.

———. *Ezekiel*. Vol. 1. Translated by R. E. Clements. Hermeneia. Philadelphia: Fortress Press, 1983.

———. *I am Yahweh*. Edited by Walter Brueggemann. Translated by Douglas W. Stott. Atlanta: John Knox Press, 1982.

———. "Ich bin Yahweh." Pages 179–209 in *Geschichte und Altes Testament*. Edited by William Foxwell Albright. Beiträge zur historischen Theologie 16. Tübingen: J. C. B. Mohr, 1953.

Verbal System

Breaking Perfect Rules
The Traditional Understanding of the Greek Perfect[1]

Constantine R. Campbell

Introduction

For some time, scholars have queried the veracity of the traditional understanding of the Greek perfect tense-form. Traditionally the perfect has been understood as a combination of the aorist and present, which means that according to an aspectual analysis the perfect encodes both perfective and imperfective aspects at the same time so that "it denotes the *continuance* of *completed action*."[2] In English translation, the standard gloss that is used to represent this continuance of a completed action—or the combination of perfective and imperfective aspects—is *I have x-ed*. This understanding—that the Greek perfect communicates a past action with present consequences—has come under investigation from various quarters and for various reasons. Sicking and Stork comment: "Even after many generations of scholars, agreement about the semantic value of the Greek Perfect has still to be reached."[3] While Greek scholarship has yet to reach a consensus on what the perfect

[1] This essay is based on a paper delivered at the Rome SBL conference in July 2009, at which Dr. Levinsohn was present. His insightful interaction has helped to shape what follows.

[2] BDF, § 340 (emphasis original).

[3] C. M. J. Sicking and P. Stork, "The Synthetic Perfect in Classical Greek," in *Two Studies in the Semantics of the Verb in Classical Greek* (Mnemosyne Supplement 160; Leiden: Brill, 1996), 121.

does communicate, one issue that has almost reached the level of consensus is that the older understanding is full of problematic complexities.[4] My own views regarding the Greek perfect are documented elsewhere, and this is not the occasion to present them in detail.[5] On the contrary, what I aim to do here is to suggest that, as a community of scholars who are engaged with Greek, now is the time to leave the old behind.[6]

Rather than rehearse the various theoretical critiques that have been leveled against the traditional view, most of which are easily accessible, I aim to put forth a novel type of critique. The premise is simple: translators choose to translate the Greek perfect *against* the rules *most* of the time.

Of course it is methodologically problematic to argue for the meaning of Greek forms by citing translations of them. This is hopelessly circular, and does not prove anything. However, I believe that translation-based evidence may be useful as a *corroboration* of the results of rigorous academic investigation that

[4] The traditional description requires a great deal of flexibility in order to account for perfect usage. "Sometimes it is the past action that is emphasized, while the present state that emerges is not regarded as significant (the *extensive* or *consummative perfect*). Other times, it is the present result of the verbal action that is emphasized while the past action is less significant (called the *intensive perfect* by some grammars). Additionally, it is admitted that sometimes the perfect expresses a purely aoristic action, thereby not admitting a present result at all (the *aoristic perfect*), or, conversely, the perfect may express only the present result with no hint of a past action in view (either the *perfect of existing state* or the *intensive perfect*)." Constantine R. Campbell, *Verbal Aspect, the Indicative Mood, and Narrative: Soundings in the Greek of the New Testament* (Studies in Biblical Greek 13; New York: Peter Lang, 2007), 162.

[5] See Campbell, *Verbal Aspect*, 161–211. For a summary of my views, see *Basics of Verbal Aspect in Biblical Greek* (Grand Rapids: Zondervan, 2008), 46–51.

[6] Though beyond the scope of this essay, it is quite possible that the traditional approach to the Greek perfect has arisen from Latin. In his discussion concerning the intrusion of the Latin concept of deponency into Greek, Bernard Taylor writes, "At least by the Renaissance, Latin grammar and terminology had become the norm and were used to describe and delimit other languages, not only within, but even beyond the Indo-European family." Bernard A. Taylor, "Deponency and Greek Lexicography," in *Biblical Greek Language and Lexicography: Essays in Honor of Frederick W. Danker* (ed. Bernard A. Taylor, John A. L. Lee, Peter R. Burton, and Richard E. Whitaker; Grand Rapids: Eerdmans, 2004), 170–71.

is guided by linguistic methodological principles. Such research has already identified difficulties for the traditional view of the perfect, and the following translation-based evidence simply supports such findings.

Lost in translation

There are 835 perfect indicatives in the Greek New Testament. I have examined the translation of each one of these perfects in the English Standard Version, which by most estimations is regarded as a fairly conservative translation. The results reveal that, out of 835 perfect indicatives, 484 of these are *not* translated according to the traditional understanding of the perfect. That means that 58 percent of Greek perfect indicative forms in the New Testament are not translated as a past action with present consequences. A few examples will suffice.

> Matt 4:7 ἔφη αὐτῷ ὁ Ἰησοῦς· πάλιν γέγραπται· οὐκ ἐκπειράσεις κύριον τὸν θεόν σου.
> Jesus said to him, "Again *it is written*, 'You shall not put the Lord your God to the test.' "

> Luke 11:7 κἀκεῖνος ἔσωθεν ἀποκριθεὶς εἴπῃ· μή μοι κόπους πάρεχε· ἤδη ἡ θύρα κέκλεισται καὶ τὰ παιδία μου μετ' ἐμοῦ εἰς τὴν κοίτην εἰσίν· οὐ δύναμαι ἀναστὰς δοῦναί σοι.
> and he will answer from within, "Do not bother me; the door *is* now *shut*, and my children are with me in bed. I cannot get up and give you anything"?

> Romans 8:38 πέπεισμαι γὰρ ὅτι οὔτε θάνατος οὔτε ζωὴ οὔτε ἄγγελοι οὔτε ἀρχαὶ οὔτε ἐνεστῶτα οὔτε μέλλοντα οὔτε δυνάμεις
> For *I am sure* that neither death nor life, nor angels nor rulers, nor things present nor things to come, nor powers

This is not to say that all 484 of these perfects *had* to be translated the way in which the translators of the ESV chose to render them. No doubt some of these could have been rendered as expressing a past action with present consequences, and the statistics would vary from one translation to the next. But that is not the point. The issue at hand, rather, is that the translators chose *not* to render these 484 perfects "according to the rules." Apparently, to their minds, other renderings were preferable, no doubt due to the variety of contextual and lexical factors that inform the translational enterprise.

As such, let us pause to reflect upon the significance of this statistic. On the one hand, it is commonplace to refer to "exceptions" to the rules. For example, if 85 percent of Greek aorists refer to the past, then the other 15 percent are regarded as "exceptions" to the rule that the aorist refers to the past. Such "exceptions" are regarded by different scholars as signifying different things. For some, it is simply part of the cut and thrust of language that the rules are there to be broken, or that we are being pedantic if we expect our rules to be more consistently enforced. For others, such exceptions are evidence that the rules are not quite right, and that a better formulated conception would yield a higher level of consistency.

But on whichever side of that coin one finds oneself, may we honestly describe 58 percent of perfects "exceptions" to the rule? When the number of exceptions outweigh the number of non-exceptions, how meaningful is that rule? If ever there were a time to question the validity of a rule based on statistical exceptions, surely this is it.

Before going further, however, it may be objected that these results have included the lexemes οἶδα (*perfect active indicative*, regularly translated by the English present *to know*) and ἕστηκα (*perfect active indicative*, regularly translated by the English present *to stand*), which are already known to be exceptional. These verbs are always translated as exceptions, and therefore they must skew the data. On that point, two suggestions come to mind. First, the statistics are nonetheless compelling even when these lexemes are disregarded. Of the 835 perfect indicatives, οἶδα and ἕστηκα account for 229. This means that, together, these lexemes constitute 27.5 percent of all perfects. Thus, once they are excluded, the figure of nonconformist perfects drops from 58 percent to 30.5 percent. Obviously this is a less impressive figure, but it is still a serious one. While we may say that only 30 percent of Greek perfects are not translated "according to the rules," this is nevertheless a significant quantity of exceptions. Nearly one third of perfects are not translated according to the rules.

In spite of that, I believe it is illegitimate to discount οἶδα and ἕστηκα on the basis that these lexemes are "exceptional." Their exceptional nature is predicated upon the premise that the traditional understanding of the perfect is correct. Since these lexemes never adhere to that understanding, they are regarded as exceptions, and are never dealt with as "real" perfects. But since that traditional understanding of the perfect is the very thing under review here, such a predication is not valid. These lexemes should not be disregarded as evidence simply because they do not adhere to the very theory that is under question. On the contrary, they constitute potent witnesses to the weakness of that theory.

So then, if 58 percent of perfects are not translated by the rendering of a past action with present consequences, how then are they translated? Of the 835 perfect indicatives in the New Testament, 404 (48 percent) are translated as *presents* by the ESV.[7] These 48 percent of perfects are rendered without a hint

[7] Matt 2:5, 20; 3:2; 4:4, 6, 7, 10, 17; 6:8, 32; 7:11; 8:6; 10:7; 11:10; 15:12; 19:11; 20:6, 22, 25; 21:23, 27; 22:16; 24:36, 42; 25:12, 13; 26:2, 24, 31, 45, 46, 70, 72, 74; 27:43, 65; 28:5; Mark 1:2, 15 (x2), 24; 4:13, 27; 7:6; 9:12, 13; 10:19, 38, 42; 11:17, 33; 12:14; 13:32, 33, 35; 14:21, 27, 42, 68, 71; Luke 2:23; 3:4; 4:4, 8, 10, 12, 34; 5:20, 23; 7:27, 47, 48; 8:20, 49; 10:26; 11:7, 13, 44; 12:7, 30, 56 (x2); 13:12, 25, 27; 18:20; 19:46; 20:21; 21:8; 22:57, 60; 23:34; 24:29, 46; John 1:26 (x2); 3:2 (x2), 8, 11, 18, 29; 4:22, 25, 32, 42; 5:32, 42; 6:42; 7:15, 27, 28 (x3), 29; 8:14 (x2), 17, 19, 37, 52, 55 (x3); 9:12, 20, 21 (x2), 24 (x2), 29 (x2), 30, 31; 10:4, 5; 11:22, 24, 27, 49; 12:27, 35, 50; 13:7, 17, 18; 14:4, 5, 9; 15:15, 21; 16:11, 18, 30 (x2); 17:7, 10; 18:21; 19:10, 30, 35; 20:2, 13, 23 (x2); 20:31; 21:15, 16, 17, 24; Acts 1:11, 20; 2:22; 3:16, 17; 4:10; 7:33, 40, 42; 10:37; 12:11; 13:33; 15:15, 17; 20:25, 29; 22:10, 28; 23:5; 26:2, 4, 22, 27; Rom 1:17; 2:2, 19, 24, 25; 3:4, 10, 19; 4:14 (x2), 17; 5:2; 6:16; 7:2 (x2), 14, 18; 8:22, 26, 27, 28, 36, 38; 9:13, 19, 33; 10:15; 11:2, 8, 20, 26; 12:19; 13:12; 14:11, 14 (x2), 23; 15:3, 9, 14, 21, 29; 1 Cor 1:13, 16, 19, 31; 2:9, 11 (x2); 3:16, 19; 4:4 (x2), 6; 5:6; 6:2, 3, 9, 15, 16, 19; 7:14 (x2), 15, 16 (x2), 27 (x2), 34, 37, 39; 8:1, 3, 4; 9:9, 13, 17, 24; 10:7; 11:2, 15; 12:2; 14:16, 21; 15:1, 27, 45; 16:15; 2 Cor 1:19, 24; 5:1, 11, 16; 6:11; 7:4, 13; 8:15; 9:2, 9; 10:7; 11:11, 31, 2 (x4), 3 (x3); Gal 3:10, 13; 4:13, 22, 27; 5:10, 14; Phil 1:19, 25; 2:24, 3:12; 4:12 (x2), 15, 18; Col 1:17; 3:3; 4:3; 1 Thess 1:5; 2:1, 2, 5, 11; 3:3, 4; 4:2; 5:2; 2 Thess 2:6; 3:4, 7; 1 Tim 1:8; 3:5; 5:6; 6:4; 2 Tim 1:5, 12 (x2), 15; 2:9, 19; 3:15; Titus 1:15; 3:11; Heb 2:14; 3:14; 5:12; 6:9; 7:22; 8:6, 13; 10:7, 11, 30; 12:2, 17; Jas 1:6, 23; 4:4; 5:2, 8, 9; 1 Pet 1:16; 4:7; 2 Pet 2:9, 19 (x2); 1 Jn 2:4, 5, 11, 12, 13, 14, 20, 21 (x2); 3:2, 5, 14, 15, 16; 5:15 (x2), 18, 19, 20; 3 Jn 12; Jude 10; Rev 2:2, 9, 13, 17, 19; 3:1, 8, 15, 17, 20; 7:14; 8:2; 19:12, 13.

of past action; they are pure English presents. Again, this does not really prove anything about what the Greek perfect means, but it is nevertheless revealing that the translators of the ESV found it preferable to render nearly half of all perfect indicatives in the New Testament as English presents.

Verbal aspect

The study of verbal aspect has offered a few different possibilities for understanding the Greek perfect—all of which, arguably, are preferable to the traditional conception. I will briefly present three of these, and it will become clear that at least two of the three would have provided the translators of ESV with better grounds for translating half the Greek perfects as English presents.[8]

The first of these is to regard the Greek perfect as perfective in aspect—an option that clearly works with respect to nomenclature. Perfective aspect is used to depict actions externally, as a whole. That is, an action is portrayed in summary form, without regard to its beginning or end. When it comes to perfective aspect, all scholars are agreed that it is encoded by the aorist tense-form,[9] and some (myself included) also regard the future tense-form as perfective.[10]

The key scholars who have argued that the Greek perfect is perfective in aspect are Fanning and Olsen.[11] While both argue for perfective aspect, Fanning and Olsen differ on the other semantic constituents of the perfect indicative. Fanning regards the perfect to be a combination of perfective aspect, past

---

[8] This is not to suggest that the translators of the ESV were unaware of the advances in verbal aspect, and perhaps aspect has informed some of their decisions.

[9] See, for example, Stanley E. Porter, *Verbal Aspect in the Greek of the New Testament with Reference to Tense and Mood* (Studies in Biblical Greek 1; New York: Peter Lang, 1989), 223; Buist M. Fanning, *Verbal Aspect in New Testament Greek* (Oxford Theological Monographs; Oxford: Clarendon, 1990), 97; Rodney J. Decker, *Temporal Deixis of the Greek Verb in the Gospel of Mark with Reference to Verbal Aspect* (SBG 10; New York: Peter Lang, 2001), 95; Mari Broman Olsen, *A Semantic and Pragmatic Model of Lexical and Grammatical Aspect* (Outstanding Dissertations in Linguistics; New York: Garland Publishing, 1997), 202; Campbell, *Verbal Aspect*, 103.

[10] Campbell, *Verbal Aspect*, 139–51.

[11] Fanning, *Verbal Aspect*, 112–20; Olsen, *Aspect*, 202.

tense, and stative *Aktionsart*.[12] Olsen regards the perfect as encoding perfective aspect and *present* tense (rather than past)—and without stativity.[13] The views of both scholars are similar to the traditional view of the perfect—indeed, of all the aspect scholars, their approaches most closely resemble the traditional conception, in which the perfect is understood as depicting a past action with present results. For Fanning, the past action is created by past tense, and the present results are created by the stative *Aktionsart*, all viewed externally via the perfective aspect.[14] Olsen attributes "these temporal qualities to perfective aspect and present tense, respectively."[15]

The challenges that these views encounter are, therefore, quite similar to those encountered by the traditional view. The numerous occurrences of οἶδα and ἕστηκα are described by Fanning as Homerisms that evidently became fossilized.[16] Fanning lists the lexemes that express a "present stative meaning," but with no attempt to describe the way they fit his theory of the perfect (except to say that they are fossilized forms, and therefore exceptional).[17] As for the perfects that appear to behave as aorists (see below for discussion of these), Fanning likewise regards them as exceptions: "On the other hand, there are a few perfects in the NT which display a tendency to become virtual aorists in denoting simply a past action without reference to its present consequence. . . . This tendency is clearly documented in later Greek."[18] He argues that true aoristic perfects are rare, and are nevertheless distinct from aorists "in that they refer not only to a past occurrence but also to some present result of the action."[19] Consequently, Fanning regards purely present

[12] Fanning, *Verbal Aspect*, 112–20.
[13] Olsen, *Aspect*, 232, 251.
[14] See Campbell, *Verbal Aspect*, 189–90.
[15] Olsen, *Aspect*, 232.
[16] Fanning, *Verbal Aspect*, 112 n. 74.
[17] Ibid., 229. Olsen, on the other hand, does not seek to explain such exceptions via the historical development of the language, but simply states that "perfects of verbs unmarked for dynamicity do not entail past events and so may be used to implicate stative situations." Olsen, *Aspect*, 234. This admission, however, that stative lexemes are not accommodated by her view of the perfect, demonstrates its weakness: it is not capable of explaining full usage.
[18] Fanning, *Verbal Aspect*, 112 n. 74.
[19] Ibid., 303. He does not elaborate as to how this present result of the action is

perfects and purely aoristic perfects as exceptions that were produced through the diachronic development of the language: "Exceptions to this pattern lie at either end of the historical spectrum."[20] The difficulty with this analysis is not so much related to the diachronic facts, but to the accommodation of them. To my mind, these "exceptional" uses of the perfect are awkwardly accommodated by Fanning's approach; consequently, an approach that more readily accommodates them is preferable.[21]

While an aspectual approach to the perfect indicative represents an advance over traditional approaches, it appears that the perfective aspect will not advance the matter far, since several of the same challenges remain. At the very least, Fanning's conception of the perfect does not offer much support for the ESV's translational decisions that render nearly half the Greek perfects as English presents. While verbs with perfective aspect may on occasion be translated using an English present (e.g. εὐδόκησα in Mark 1:11), this is quite an unusual manner in which to render perfective aspect, and should only be adopted when there is not a more natural way in which to translate the verb within its context.

The next aspectual approach to the Greek perfect is to regard it as stative in aspect. The key scholars who have argued for this are McKay and Porter.

---

expressed or to be understood, though perhaps a clue can be gleaned from the section regarding the "Perfect of completed action." This use of the perfect places emphasis upon the completion of the action, while "leaving the resulting condition in the background" (p. 297). While the attempt to explain these uses is appreciated, one is left wondering what "leaving the resulting condition in the background" really means. Related to this is Fanning's discussion of transitive lexemes, concerning which he partially adopts McKay's approach (295), which is why I have not interacted with this element of Fanning's approach previously, but addressed McKay directly; Campbell, *Verbal Aspect*, 166–69.

[20] Fanning, *Verbal Aspect*, 112 n. 74.

[21] In Fanning's review of one of my books, he assumes that because I disagree with his views (and those of others, which I am accused of distorting), I have not seriously reflected upon the strengths of such approaches. Rather, my disagreement simply means that, having carefully considered the explanations offered, I found them wanting. See Buist M. Fanning, Review of *Verbal Aspect, the Indicative Mood, and Narrative: Soundings in the Greek of the New Testament*, by Constantine R. Campbell, *JETS* 51/2 (2008): 394–97.

McKay describes the perfect in the following manner: "The perfect [= stative] aspect expresses the state or condition of the subject of the verb, as a result of an action (logically a prior action), but most often with comparatively little reference to the action itself."[22] Porter, on the other hand, takes the emphasis away from the subject of the verb, and attributes stativity to the activity in view: "The Perfect grammaticalizes the speaker's conception of the verbal process as a state or condition."[23]

The stative aspect approach to the Greek perfect represents a significant advance on the traditional approach, and is also preferable to Fanning and Olsen's approaches, which regard the perfect as perfective in aspect. The key strength that stative aspect offers is that there need not be any necessary implication of past action. One significant problem that inflicts the semantic description of the traditional approach to the perfect is that it requires reference to a previous action, even though it is clear in many instances that no such previous action is in view.[24] Porter is no doubt correct, therefore, that any reference to a previous act that results in a state or condition "is a matter of lexis in context."[25] While it will normally be the case that some action has predated (and brought about) the state of affairs in question, that does not mean that the verb itself must give expression to such action. Language must be able to convey the concept of stativity without implicating the action or actions that give rise to that stativity, even when such actions have taken place within the "real world."

Furthermore, stativity may be conveyed by the use of the English present. The concept, *I know*, is clearly stative, and yet is conveyed by an English present. In English, the lexeme *to know* is a naturally stative concept; the English present does not make the lexeme stative, but it is consistent with the lexeme's inherent stativity. As such, stative aspect provides better theoretical grounds for translating nearly half the Greek perfects as English presents: since

22 K. L. McKay, *A New Syntax of the Verb in New Testament Greek: An Aspectual Approach* (Studies in Biblical Greek 5; New York: Peter Lang, 1994), 31.

23 Porter, *Verbal Aspect*, 257.

24 The grammars acknowledge this fact, of course, but the problem remains that the basic "rule" of past action (+perfective aspect) together with present consequences (+imperfective aspect) is compromised.

25 Porter, *Verbal Aspect*, 259.

stativity may be conveyed by the English present, these renderings would thus be "according to the rules" of stative aspect. Not only does stative aspect supply a significant theoretical improvement upon the traditional theory of the Greek perfect, it is one that evidently makes better sense of the practice of translation, as the ESV exemplifies.

A weakness of stative aspect, however, is brought to light by the translation of 9.5 percent of Greek perfects in the New Testament. Eighty of 835 perfects are translated in the ESV with the English past tense, without any hint of ongoing consequences.[26] This is not simply reflective of the difficulties of translating one language into another; in these instances, the context makes it clear that the perfect refers to a simple past action without an ongoing state on view.[27] Some examples follow.

> John 5:33 ὑμεῖς ἀπεστάλκατε πρὸς Ἰωάννην, καὶ μεμαρτύρηκεν τῇ ἀληθείᾳ·
> You *sent* to John, and he has borne witness to the truth.

> 1 Corinthians 13:11 ὅτε ἤμην νήπιος, ἐλάλουν ὡς νήπιος, ἐφρόνουν ὡς νήπιος, ἐλογιζόμην ὡς νήπιος· ὅτε γέγονα ἀνήρ, κατήργηκα τὰ τοῦ νηπίου.

---

[26] Matt 1:22; 13:46; 19:8; 21:4; 25:6; Mark 5:29, 33; 9:42; 14:4; 15:47; 16:4; Luke 1:22; 9:36; 13:2; John 1:3, 15, 32; 3:26; 4:38; 5:33; 6:25, 32, 65; 7:22; 8:41, 42; 14:7; 15:18; 17:4, 8; 18:9, 37; Acts 7:35; 8:14; 10:45; 16:10; Rom 4:21; 9:29; 11:5; 16:7; 1 Cor 2:8; 13:11 (x2); 2 Cor 5:16; 7:3, 5, 14; 11:21; 12:9, 17; 13:2; Gal 2:7; 3:18, 19, 24; 4:23; Phil 3:7; Col 1:16; 2:14; 1 Thess 2:1; 1 Tim 2:14; Heb 4:7; 7:6, 9, 11, 14; 9:18; 10:9; 11:5, 17, 28; Jas 1:24; 1 Jn 4:3; Rev 3:3; 5:7; 7:14; 8:5; 14:8; 19:3.

[27] Incidentally, it is this type of perfect usage that led Wackernagel to develop the category of the "resultative perfect," in which the present result of an action is attributed to the object rather than to the subject of the action. While the so-called resultative perfect was an attempt to salvage the traditional approach to the perfect (by retaining the "ongoing consequences" when there was none with respect to the subject of the verb), the same phenomenon is problematic for the stative aspect approach. See Jakob Wackernagel, "Studien zum griechischen Perfectum," in *Programm zur akademischen Preisverteilung* (n.p., 1904), 3–4; repr. in *Kleine Schriften* (Göttingen: Vandenhoeck und Ruprecht, 1953), 1000–21.

> When I was a child, I spoke like a child, I thought like a child, I reasoned like a child. When *I became* a man, *I gave up* childish ways.

> Hebrews 7:6 ὁ δὲ μὴ γενεαλογούμενος ἐξ αὐτῶν δεδεκάτωκεν Ἀβραὰμ καὶ τὸν ἔχοντα τὰς ἐπαγγελίας εὐλόγηκεν.
> But this man who does not have his descent from them received tithes from Abraham and *blessed* him who had the promises.

This statistic raises difficulties for the stative aspect approach as well as further difficulties for the traditional conception of the perfect. Regarding the latter, not only are half of Greek perfects translated "against the rules" (of past action with present consequences, or +perfective +imperfective) as pure present tenses (+imperfective only), an additional 9.5 percent are translated against the rules—as simple pasts (+perfective only). They are not past actions with present consequences; they are just past actions. The traditional theory now offers a rate of exceptions at approximately 57.5 percent.

However, these perfects that are rendered as simple pasts in English also issue a challenge to the theory of stative aspect. According to McKay, stative aspect (or *perfect* aspect, as he calls it) is able to account for such perfects in the following manner. When there is no clear "state" arising out of the action itself, McKay argues that it is the "state" of the doer of the action that is in view: he or she is *responsible* for the action performed.[28] Consequently, McKay would not regard these "simple-past-perfects" as exceptional; rather, they invoke a different use of stative aspect, which is to underscore the responsibility of the subject of the action. While McKay's approach exhibits certain merits, and is an advance on previous explanations, his solution can result in awkward or forced exegesis and is not ultimately persuasive.[29]

Porter's approach to the perfect requires no extra application for these "simple-past-perfects," since it is concerned with a general state of affairs, rather than the subject of the action per se. Whatever the type of action, a "state" results. Thus, his version of stative aspect appears to account for all occurrences of the

---

[28] McKay, *Syntax*, 32.

[29] For several examples in which McKay's solution proves difficult, see Campbell, *Verbal Aspect*, 166–69.

Greek perfect. Again, however, this solution is not fully persuasive precisely because the subject of the action becomes disassociated from the action itself.[30] In this way, Porter's solution resembles a less-defined version of the resultative perfect (see above). The central problem for the resultative perfect is that the perfect depicts the state of its object rather than its subject. Porter's version of stative aspect behaves similiarly, but instead of attributing stativity to the object of the verb, it attributes stativity to "the situation." If the key meaning of the verb is disassociated from its subject, one wonders why a finite verb is used at all, since a finite verb by definition focuses on the action or state of its subject.[31] Furthermore, the stative aspect approach suffers from the problem that most linguists regard stativity as an *Aktionsart* value rather an aspect.[32]

---

[30] Porter, *Verbal Aspect*, 170–75.

[31] Campbell, *Verbal Aspect*, 169–72.

[32] This is the case among Greek linguists and general linguists alike. See, for example, Albert L. Lloyd, *Anatomy of the Verb* (Studies in Language Companion Series 4; Amsterdam: John Benjamins, 1979), 117–18; Carl Bache, "Aspect and Aktionsart: Towards a Semantic Distinction," *Journal of Linguistics* 18 (1982), 69; Carl Bache, "Verbal Categories, Form-meaning Relationships and the English Perfect," in *Tense, Aspect and Action: Empirical and Theoretical Contributions to Language Typology* (ed. Carl Bache, Hans Basbøll, and Carl-Erik Lindberg; Empirical Approaches to Language Typology 12; Berlin: Mouton de Gruyter, 1994), 52; Buist M. Fanning, "Approaches to Verbal Aspect in New Testament Greek: Issues in Definition and Method," in *Biblical Greek Language and Linguistics: Open Questions in Current Research* (ed. Stanley E. Porter and D. A. Carson; JSNTSup 80; Sheffield: Sheffield Academic Press, 1993), 49–50; Buist M. Fanning, *Verbal Aspect*, 117; T. V. Evans, "Future Directions for Aspect Studies in Ancient Greek," in *Biblical Greek Language and Lexicography: Essays in Honor of Frederick W. Danker* (ed. Bernard A. Taylor, John A. L. Lee, Peter R. Burton, and Richard E. Whitaker; Grand Rapids: Eerdmans, 2004), 206; Zeno Vendler, "Verbs and Times," in *Linguistics in Philosophy* (ed. Zeno Vendler; New York: Cornell University Press, 1967), 147–49; Bernard Comrie, *Aspect: An Introduction to the Study of Verbal Aspect and Related Problems* (Cambridge Textbooks in Linguistics; Cambridge: Cambridge University Press, 1976), 48–51; Martín S. Ruipérez, *Estructura del sistema de aspectos y tiempos del verbo griego antiguo: Análisis funcional sincrónico* (Theses et Studia Philologica Salmanticensia 7; Salamanca: Colegio Trilingüe de la Universidad, 1954), 60; Olsen, *Aspect*, 259–60; Basil Mandilaras, *The Verb in the Greek Non-Literary Papyri* (Athens: Hellenistic Ministry of Culture and Sciences, 1973), 205.

Nevertheless, both McKay and Porter's versions of stative aspect offer a vastly improved approach to the Greek perfect compared to the traditional view.

A third alternative is to regard the Greek perfect as imperfective in aspect, as put forth by Evans and myself.[33] Imperfective aspect is used to depict actions internally, as though unfolding. One of the strengths of the imperfective aspect approach to the perfect is that the 48 percent of perfects in the New Testament that are rendered by the ESV as pure presents are immediately accounted for, since imperfective aspect is frequently translated by the English present (as is the case for the Greek present tense-form, which is also imperfective in aspect). Furthermore, those Greek perfects that really do seem to be stative in context are also accommodated by imperfective aspect: it is generally acknowledged in wider linguistic studies that imperfective aspect is a standard bearer of stative *Aktionsart*.[34] This means that stativity, which is an *Aktionsart* value (or lexical characteristic), is a natural partner to imperfective aspect; imperfective verbs will often be stative in *Aktionsart*, but this stativity is a lexical characteristic not an aspectual one. Thus imperfective aspect is able to accommodate the perfects that are best understood as present-referring, whether they be stative or not.

This leaves the question of those 9.5 percent of perfects that appear to refer to the past, and are translated in the ESV without any suggestion of present consequences. As I have argued elsewhere, such perfects demonstrate a striking similarity to those Greek presents that are labeled "historical presents." The most compelling similarity is the strong overlap of the lexemes that are used for both historical presents and past-referring perfects.[35] If this apparent parallel is taken seriously, it would suggest that what we witness with respect to these past-referring perfects is a kind of parallel to the historical present. Consequently, these perfects should be labeled "historical perfects," as Ruipérez has suggested.[36] Admittedly, it is still debated as to what the significance of the historical present really is, but that is not the point. Whatever the historical

[33] T. V. Evans, *Verbal Syntax in the Greek Pentateuch: Natural Greek Usage and Hebrew Interference* (Oxford: Oxford University Press, 2001), 30–31.

[34] Comrie, *Aspect*, 50–51.

[35] Campbell, *Verbal Aspect*, 187.

[36] Ruipérez, *Aspectos*, 153: "la existencia de un perfecto histórico paralelo al presente histórico."

present means, my point is that those perfects that refer simply to past action are parallel to the historical present. I have also argued that this parallel between present and perfect is—along with other parallels—evidence of their shared aspectual nature,[37] and Ruipérez has claimed that it is evidence that the perfect is *not* stative in aspect.[38] Both tense-forms encode imperfective aspect. If this is correct, it means that the 9.5 percent of Greek perfects that are translated by the ESV as simple pasts are not exceptional: they are historical perfects, which is a function in keeping with what we already know about imperfective aspect.

Conclusion

It should be clear, then, that both stative aspect and imperfective aspect offer explanatory power when it comes to the Greek perfect. The remaining question is which approach has greatest explanatory power and most rigorously accounts for all the trends of usage of the perfect. Obviously, my preference is for the latter approach, but this is not the occasion to further rehash the lines of argumentation in detail. Rather, the point I wish to underline is that either approach—stative aspect or imperfective aspect—both offer stronger solutions to the problem of the Greek perfect than does the traditional understanding.

The translational decisions made by the editors of the ESV reveal that usage of the Greek perfect is more complicated than the traditional approach allows. The "rules" expressed by such an approach must be broken by translators, and frequently so. We have known this to be the case for some time, though perhaps the frequency of this delinquency has not widely been acknowledged. I would suggest, therefore, that it might be time that all who read and study Ancient Greek collectively move beyond the traditional approach to the perfect. Scholars, teachers, and students would do well to put away the old *Aktionsart* analyses and adopt an approach that analyzes the Greek perfect in terms of verbal aspect. Greek grammars and New Testament commentaries could do likewise. I have suggested that perfective aspect will not advance the cause far, but that either stative aspect or imperfective aspect could be adopted

[37] Campbell, *Verbal Aspect*, 185–87.

[38] Ruipérez, *Aspectos*, 153.

with profit. While I regard the latter to be preferable, either approach will see a widespread improvement of our understanding, handling, and translation of the Greek perfect.

Finally, it is worth reflecting a little on what all this means for translation. As a first step, I would suggest that the initial gloss for translating the Greek perfect should *not* be *I have x-ed*. The *have* and the *–ed* is how the *past action with present consequences* understanding of the perfect is reflected in the traditional gloss translation. As we have already seen, for most instances this gloss is not going to work—nevermind its problematic theoretical complexities. Rather, the gloss translation for the perfect should be *I x*, as it is for the present. Whether stative aspect or imperfective aspect is seen as the core meaning of the perfect, either conception may be expressed via this gloss. While it might require nuancing once the context is appreciated, it is nevertheless a better place to begin translating the perfect than is the traditional gloss.

It is also worth noting that *I have x-ed* may well provide the best translation of *some* perfects, depending on the context.[39] My contention, however, is simply that this should not be our starting-point. If the old gloss continues to be our starting-point for translation, the statistics suggest that it will be overturned more often than not.

Bibliography

Bache, Carl. "Aspect and Aktionsart: Towards a Semantic Distinction." *Journal of Linguistics* 18 (1982): 57–72.

———. "Verbal Categories, Form-meaning Relationships and the English Perfect." Pages 43–60 in *Tense, Aspect and Action: Empirical and Theoretical Contributions to Language Typology*. Edited by Carl Bache, Hans Basbøll, and Carl-Erik Lindberg. Empirical Approaches to Language Typology 12. Berlin: Mouton de Gruyter, 1994.

Campbell, Constantine R. *Basics of Verbal Aspect in Biblical Greek*. Grand Rapids: Zondervan, 2008.

[39] The contextual features that will lead to the *I have x-ed* translation will normally involve temporal deictic indicators and lexical factors. If the context suggests that the action on view had begun in the past and was still continuing on into the "present," then the traditional gloss (or some variation of it) will likely provide the most helpful translation.

———. *Verbal Aspect, the Indicative Mood, and Narrative: Soundings in the Greek of the New Testament.* Studies in Biblical Greek 13. New York: Peter Lang, 2007.

Comrie, Bernard. *Aspect: An Introduction to the Study of Verbal Aspect and Related Problems.* Cambridge Textbooks in Linguistics. Cambridge: Cambridge University Press, 1976.

Decker, Rodney J. *Temporal Deixis of the Greek Verb in the Gospel of Mark with Reference to Verbal Aspect.* Studies in Biblical Greek 10. New York: Peter Lang, 2001.

Evans, T. V. "Future Directions for Aspect Studies in Ancient Greek." Pages 199–206 in *Biblical Greek Language and Lexicography: Essays in Honor of Frederick W. Danker.* Edited by Bernard A. Taylor, John A. L. Lee, Peter R. Burton, and Richard E. Whitaker. Grand Rapids: Eerdmans, 2004.

———. *Verbal Syntax in the Greek Pentateuch: Natural Greek Usage and Hebrew Interference.* Oxford: Oxford University Press, 2001.

Fanning, Buist M. Review of Constantine R. Campbell, *Verbal Aspect, the Indicative Mood, and Narrative: Soundings in the Greek of the New Testament.* Journal of the Evangelical Theological Society 51/2 (2008): 394–97.

———. "Approaches to Verbal Aspect in New Testament Greek: Issues in Definition and Method." Pages 46–62 in *Biblical Greek Language and Linguistics: Open Questions in Current Research.* Edited by Stanley E. Porter and D. A. Carson. Journal for the Study of the New Testament: Supplement Series 80. Sheffield: Sheffield Academic Press, 1993.

———. *Verbal Aspect in New Testament Greek.* Oxford Theological Monographs. Oxford: Clarendon, 1990.

Lloyd, Albert L. *Anatomy of the Verb.* Studies in Language Companion Series 4. Amsterdam: John Benjamins, 1979.

McKay, K. L. *A New Syntax of the Verb in New Testament Greek: An Aspectual Approach.* Studies in Biblical Greek 5. New York: Peter Lang, 1994.

Mandilaras, Basil G. *The Verb in the Greek Non-Literary Papyri.* Athens: Hellenistic Ministry of Culture and Sciences, 1973.

Olsen, Mari Broman. *A Semantic and Pragmatic Model of Lexical and Grammatical Aspect.* Outstanding Dissertations in Linguistics. New York: Garland Publishing, 1997.

Porter, Stanley E. *Verbal Aspect in the Greek of the New Testament with Reference to Tense and Mood.* Studies in Biblical Greek 1. New York: Peter Lang, 1989.

Ruipérez, Martín S. *Estructura del sistema de aspectos y tiempos del verbo griego antiguo: Análisis funcional sincrónico.* Theses et Studia Philologica Salmanticensia 7. Salamanca, Spain: Colegio Trilingüe de la Universidad, 1954.

Sicking, C. M. J. and P. Stork. "The Synthetic Perfect in Classical Greek." Pages 119–298 in *Two Studies in the Semantics of the Verb in Classical Greek.* Mnemosyne Supplement 160. Leiden: Brill, 1996.

Taylor, Bernard A. "Deponency and Greek Lexicography." Pages 167–76 in *Biblical Greek Language and Lexicography: Essays in Honor of Frederick W. Danker.* Edited by Bernard A. Taylor, John A. L. Lee, Peter R. Burton, and Richard E. Whitaker. Grand Rapids: Eerdmans, 2004.

Vendler, Zeno. "Verbs and Times." *Philosophical Review* 66 (1957): 43–60. Repr. as pages 97–121 in *Linguistics in Philosophy.* Edited by Zeno Vendler. New York: Cornell University Press, 1967.

Wackernagel, Jakob. "Studien zum griechischen Perfectum." Pages 3–24 in *Programm zur akademischen Preisverteilung.* n.p., 1904. Repr., pages 1000–21 in *Kleine Schriften:* von Jacob Wackernagel. Herausgegeben von der Akademie der Wissenschaften zu Göttingen. Vol. 1. Göttingen: Vandenhoeck und Ruprecht, 1953.

Greek Presents, Imperfects, and Aorists in the Synoptic Gospels
Their Contribution to Narrative Structuring

Buist Fanning

Introduction

I am delighted to contribute to a volume honoring Stephen Levinsohn. His studies of NT discourse have enriched and informed the work of a wide range of researchers from linguists and biblical scholars to Bible translators worldwide.

The first section of this essay will cover general theoretical points about what we should expect Greek presents, imperfects, and aorists to mean based on broad principles. Section two will give observations about usage in particular passages in the Synoptic Gospels with specific focus on how these forms contribute to narrative structure and flow.[1]

Theoretical summary and argumentation: general points in my approach

Verbal aspect

Aspect properly defined is central in the Greek verb but it interacts in predictable ways with closely related features to produce important secondary effects. We

[1] An earlier version of this essay was presented at the Biblical Greek Language and Linguistics Section of the Society of Biblical Literature meeting in New Orleans in November 2009.

should expect aspect to be important in these forms in the Synoptics, but we should read the aspects in connection with these related features to find the full sense that is expressed in these passages.

Verbal aspect should be defined as a "viewpoint" feature. This means that aspect is a matter of the speaker's (or writer's) portrayal or point of view. It is not directly related to the actual character of the situation described. It is governed by what the speaker chooses to focus on, not by features of the objective situation. It particularly means that aspect proper is of a different semantic order than actional characteristics like duration, repetition, boundedness, existing state, and so on—features sometimes labeled *Aktionsarten*.[2]

Some of these closely related features that must be distinguished from aspect itself (i.e., aspect properly understood as viewpoint) are: temporal location, lexical character, adverbials and subject and object phrases, general vs. specific distinctions, discourse effects, remoteness or proximity, and so on. These closely related features, though distinct, interact with aspect in meaningful and somewhat predictable ways. Careful attention to these interactions is an indispensable aid to interpretation. This does not entail confusing aspect itself with these secondary meanings or abandoning the essentially subjective

[2] Buist M. Fanning, "Approaches to Verbal Aspect in New Testament Greek: Issues in Definition and Method," in *Biblical Greek Language and Linguistics: Open Questions in Current Research* (ed. Stanley E. Porter and D. A. Carson; Sheffield: JSOT Press, 1993), 48–49. This raises questions about calling the Greek perfect an aspect with the value of "stativity," as Stanley E. Porter, *Verbal Aspect in the Greek of the New Testament, with Reference to Tense and Mood* (New York: Peter Lang, 1989), 91, 25–59, has done. Stativity is an *Aktionsart* feature, not a viewpoint aspect. In my view the perfect forms represent a quasi-aspect, an aspect feature combined with other features—but not a pure aspect as the Greek present and aorist reflect. See the critique of this in Fanning, "Approaches to Verbal Aspect," 49–50; Trevor V. Evans, *Verbal Syntax in the Greek Pentateuch: Natural Greek Usage and Hebrew Interference* (Oxford: Oxford University Press, 2001), 26–34; Trevor V. Evans, "Future Directions for Aspect Studies in Ancient Greek," in *Biblical Greek Language and Linguistics: Essays in Honor of Frederick W. Danker* (ed. Bernard A. Taylor et al.; Grand Rapids: Eerdmans, 2004), 205–6; and Constantine R. Campbell, *Verbal Aspect, the Indicative Mood, and Narrative: Soundings in the Greek of the New Testament* (New York: Peter Lang, 2007), 169–75

nature of aspectual choice. It is simply a matter of construing the sense of the aspects in the light of their linguistic contexts.

The relation of aspect to three of these other features will now be discussed in broad terms. I will take them up in turn: temporal location, lexical character and adjunct phrases, and discourse effects. The final topic is the main focus of this essay, where I will work more carefully with specific examples of narrative usage in the Synoptics.

Temporal location

Temporal location or "tense" is clearly grammaticalized in the Greek indicative but this must be properly understood. This is an important factor in interpreting the function of these forms in the Synoptics as I plan to show. Let me advance the theoretical argument for grammaticalized tense in three steps.

The first step is to clear up two misperceptions. One is that aspect and temporal location are mutually exclusive. Sometimes the implication is communicated that a grammatical category like Greek tense cannot grammaticalize more than one thing at a time. This implication is especially associated with a general account that runs something like this: people once understood Greek verbs to mean "time" only and then they understood them to mean *Aktionsart* only, but now we know they mean "aspect" only.[3] Actually we know that aspect-tense combinations occur in a number of languages. Smith for example says, "Temporal location and aspect are complementary temporal systems. . . . The expression of temporal location and aspect is intertwined in many languages of the world. It is not uncommon for verbal inflections to encode temporal and aspectual notions simultaneously."[4] A second misperception is that grammaticalized tense is mutually exclusive with the use of temporal adverbs and other deictic elements. It is easy to see that verbs are sometimes modified

---

[3] There is an implied chronological snobbery in this line of thought—what is new must be right; what is old must be wrong—that ought to be resisted.

[4] Carlota S. Smith, *The Parameter of Aspect* (Dordrecht: Kluwer, 1991), 25, 135. See also Bernard Comrie, *Aspect: An Introduction to the Study of Verbal Aspect and Related Problems* (Cambridge: Cambridge University Press, 1976), 94–98, 127, for discussion and examples.

by other temporal indicators, but it is wrong to think that if the adverbs carry a temporal sense then the verbs do not need to or must not. Like many linguistic features there can be multiple levels of reinforcing elements. When we trace the contribution of verbal adjuncts to time reference, this in itself is no argument against grammaticalized tense values in the verb.[5] In both instances of course, we need to argue our case for or against verbal tense and not assume it based on misperceptions.

Secondly, the main argument that has been articulated against temporal values in Greek indicatives is a misconstrual of what grammatical tense represents. I mean by this the assertion that the expected time frame is not true in all cases and therefore the temporal element cannot be valid. This is the point of Porter's contrastive substitution lists: NT examples showing that present, aorist, and perfect can each be used of present, past, future, omnitemporal, and timeless occurrences; consequently, the Greek tenses cannot be said to grammaticalize temporal meaning, "since the same form may be used with a variety of temporal and non-temporal references."[6] McKay refers to this as "a very useful demonstration" of the non-temporal view.[7] Decker provides a similar listing with three or four time-levels for aorist, present, imperfect, and perfect.[8] Regarding the use of present or aorist in Markan parables, Decker says, "The fact that both aorist and present forms are used in similar contexts with identical time reference argues strongly for a non-temporal view of the verb."[9] Along the same line Campbell refers repeatedly to the problem of, as he says, "verbal actions and states that are not always consistent with the supposed temporal values of the present and imperfect tense-forms."[10]

My problem with this line of thought is this: Porter argues in his book that aspect is subjective—it does not correspond to the external facts of the

---

[5] Smith, *Parameter of Aspect*, 136, 139.

[6] Porter, *Verbal Aspect*, 75–79; quotation from p. 78.

[7] K. L. McKay, *A New Syntax of the Verb in New Testament Greek: An Aspectual Approach* (SBG 5; New York: Peter Lang, 1994), 36.

[8] Rodney J. Decker, *Temporal Deixis of the Greek Verb in the Gospel of Mark with Reference to Verbal Aspect* (SBG 10; New York: Peter Lang, 2001), 49–52.

[9] Ibid., 101, 226n55.

[10] Campbell, *Verbal Aspect*, 50. See his comments also on pp. 26–27, 50, 56–57, 98–99, 120–23.

occurrence but is governed by the speaker's choice to conceive things in a certain way.[11] He argues that mood is subjective—it reflects the speaker's conception, not objective notions of truth or falsity.[12] McKay argues that aspect is subjective: it is "not always objectively determined, but depend[s] very largely on the subjective attitude of the speaker or writer."[13] He states that mood is subjective: it gives the "manner of presentation."[14] Decker argues that aspect is subjective: it is "the speaker's view of the situation. . . . The same situation may often be described by two or even three such viewpoints."[15] He states that mood is subjective: it is the speaker's portrayal of certainty of an action.[16] Campbell argues that aspect is subjective: it is how a writer "portrays an action" with no necessary connection to what happens "in reality."[17] He argues that remoteness is subjective: it is "employed according to the author's communicative purposes," not any kind of literal or physical distance.[18] Presumably we could say the same about voice and person and number if we reflect on them a bit. They give us the speaker's subjective contextual choice about how the subject relates to the action or about how the speaker, his addressees, and others are involved in the action, not some objective, real-world distinctions about voice or person and number.

Why is it that of all these features that are potentially clustered together in the Greek verbal morphology (e.g., aspect, mood, voice, person and number, possibly remoteness), location in time is the one element that must pass rigorous tests of objective accuracy or be thrown out? Why does it not follow that tense operates in the same subjective way: it gives the speaker's portrayal of the time of the event or state. In most cases this corresponds more or less to some conception of the actual time of occurrence—hence aorists and imperfects are used overwhelmingly to describe situations prior to the time of speaking, presents overwhelmingly refer to situations contemporaneous with

---

[11] Porter, *Verbal Aspect*, 86, 88, 91.
[12] Ibid., 163–65.
[13] McKay, *New Syntax*, 27–28.
[14] Ibid., 53.
[15] Decker, *Temporal Deixis*, 26, 176 n. 117.
[16] Ibid., 124.
[17] Campbell, *Verbal Aspect*, 11, 52.
[18] Ibid., 15, 52, 97.

the time of speaking, etc.—but in some instances the temporal portrayal is different from the objective time frame in order to serve some rhetorical or descriptive purpose. Wallace, for example, says that tense in Greek "indicates the speaker's *presentation* of the verbal action (or state) with reference to its aspect and, under certain circumstances, its time." He adds that the portrayal "*may* be other than or broader than the *real* time of the event."[19] Comrie also discusses a range of "exceptional" uses of past tenses in English, German, and Norwegian tenses under the umbrella of this more subjective approach to temporal meaning showing that the time reference is a matter of the speaker's portrayal, not objective reality.[20]

To evaluate tense usage against external notions of true or false is inconsistent with how we treat all these closely-related features of verbal semantics. It is also to misunderstand how language works in relation to the world. As Halliday has written in regard to verbal usage, we should not conceive of these things "in terms of true or false." And he adds, "semantics has nothing to do with truth."[21]

When properly understood, it can be seen that Greek indicative verbs grammaticalize tense: they give a subjective portrayal of location in time. The indicative morphology displays a dual significance in combining both aspect and tense in most forms—the future is an exception because it is a pure tense, without aspectual meaning; and the perfects and pluperfects display a quasi-aspect—not a pure aspectual sense, but an "aspect-plus"—along with tense meaning. The status of the future and the perfects within the Greek tense system remains an issue, and this essay will not engage those questions further. But as far as the present, aorist, and imperfect indicatives

---

[19] Daniel B. Wallace, *Greek Grammar Beyond the Basics: An Exegetical Syntax of the New Testament* (Grand Rapids: Zondervan, 1996), 496 (emphasis mine), 498, 527. See this also in Buist Fanning, *Verbal Aspect in New Testament Greek* (Oxford Theological Monographs; Oxford: Clarendon, 1990), 199, 205–6, 221–25, 227–29, 251–52, 265–67, 269–71.

[20] Bernard Comrie, *Tense* (Cambridge: Cambridge University Press, 1985), 19–21.

[21] M. A. K. Halliday, *An Introduction to Functional Grammar* (2nd ed.; London: Arnold, 1994), 76. This is hyperbole of course but it emphasizes the difference between any linguistic description of reality and the reality itself.

are concerned, the evidence is overwhelming that the forms grammaticalize a subjective presentation of location in time.

One further brief point before I leave this issue. I believe there are still no satisfying answers to objections that have been raised against the non-temporal view. See Evans's treatment for example of the augment as a past time indicator.[22] See Wallace on the place of the imperfect in relation to the present.[23] See also my discussion of performative or "instantaneous" presents, which require the present time value of the present indicative. These are uses presenting an action done in the very act of speaking: to say the word is to do the act (e.g., Mark 2:5, 9 "your sins are forgiven"; Acts 9:34 "Aeneas, Jesus heals you"; 25:11 "I appeal to Caesar"). In languages that do not grammaticalize tense, the perfective (i.e., aorist equivalent) is used for these expressions because time does not interfere with the focus on the present moment (see biblical Hebrew usage). But the Greek aorist indicative (since it grammaticalizes past time) is not used for this, and the present indicative (since it grammaticalizes present time) is pressed into service even though the narrow focus on a moment of occurrence is awkward for its imperfective, internal viewpoint.[24] This is characteristic of a mixed tense-aspect system as is found in Greek.

Lexical and compositional features

We must give attention to aspect's combinations with a verb's lexical character and with other phrases that occur with the verb if aspect study is to be valuable for interpreting texts. Aspect by itself is of little interpretive help: the author's subjective choice of action as a whole or in process or stative gives us very little to work with unless we process it in light of broader contextual

[22] Evans, *Verbal Syntax*, 45–50. Decker's observations (*Temporal Deixis*, 39–40 and endnotes) that the augment is very occasionally omitted doesn't impugn its sense when it does occur. It simply reveals the levels of reinforcement that exist with the augment alongside the secondary indicative endings and/or second aorist roots; these morphological features reinforce each other and dropping the augment occasionally does not evacuate the meaning it carries in its overwhelming frequency of occurrence.

[23] Wallace, *Greek Grammar*, 507–9.

[24] Fanning, *Verbal Aspect*, 187–90, 202–5.

features. Even brief suggestions about levels of prominence associated with the aspects provide little help for translators and exegetes needing to probe the meaning further.[25]

So paying attention to how aspect interacts with features of a verb's lexical meaning or with various adjuncts used with the verb (subject and object phrases, adverbs, prepositional phrases, etc.) is essential to finding the larger significance of aspect in a specific context. It is only natural that in seeking to understand one element of a text's meaning we would pay attention to related features and see them in their larger connections with each other. This has always been an important part of good contextual exegesis. This is what Decker for example calls "the verbal complex" that one explores by examining "the total semantic value of the verb and its adjuncts in a particular context, including aspect, lexis, *Aktionsart*, and contextual factors."[26] These interactions have occupied the attention of most of those who study aspect in the wider linguistic field as well as recent treatments of aspect in ancient and NT Greek. In doing so, many have taken as their starting point the verbal taxonomy of Vendler and Kenny that divides verbs and verb phrases into four main groups: states, activities, accomplishments, and achievements. These are based on features of meaning such as change, homogeneity, duration, and boundedness.[27] Though these are hard to nail down precisely, they provide

[25] Porter for example is all too content to mention aspect's differing conceptions of the action and give a brief treatment of levels of prominence without going any further (e.g., *Verbal Aspect*, 324–34, 352–60).

[26] Decker, *Temporal Deixis*, 27. See McKay, *New Syntax*, 28–30, for a similar emphasis on features of the context leading to various "realizations" of meaning. See also Robert E. Picirilli, "The Meaning of the Tenses in New Testament Greek: Where Are We?" *JETS* 48 (2005): 547–53.

[27] Zeno Vendler, "Verbs and Times," *The Philosophical Review* 66 (1957), 43–60; reprinted in Zeno Vendler, *Linguistics in Philosophy* (Ithaca, New York: Cornell University Press, 1967), 97–121; and Anthony Kenny, *Action, Emotion and Will* (London: Routledge and Kegan Paul, 1963), 151–86. See how these features are developed in Comrie, *Aspect*, 41–51; John Lyons, *Semantics* (Cambridge: Cambridge University Press, 1977), 705–18; Carl Bache, "Aspect and Aktionsart: Towards a Semantic Distinction," *Journal of Linguistics* 18 (1982): 57–72; McKay, *New Syntax*, 28–29; Evans, *Verbal Syntax*, 19–21; Evans, "Future Directions," 201–2, 204–5; Campbell, *Verbal Aspect*, 47.

general outlines for careful reflection on contextual features that are valuable for interpretation. More about these shortly.

Working with other features like this to provide insight into the contextual usage of aspect is one of the notable weaknesses of Porter's treatment. He does not pursue aspect's interaction with other elements of the sentence in any detail in his book although he alludes here and there to the potential value of this. He says, for example, at one point, "lexis . . . may provide a point at which Aktionsart can be joined with a theory of verbal aspect."[28] But he never pursues it—and interpreters who rely on him for insight into construing the sense of Greek verbal usage are the poorer for it.

There is one area, however, in which Porter does suggest more specific contextual distinctions of usage for the Greek aspects. In his *Idioms of the Greek NT*, he lays out specific uses of the aspects—what he labels "Verbal Aspect and its Range of Functions." It is a great irony that these turn out to be temporally-based categories: "present for present action," "present for past action," "present for future action," "aorist for past action," "aorist for present action," "aorist for future action," and so forth.[29] He dismisses traditional categories like ingressive, descriptive, customary as "too complicated" and as somehow restricting aspect to an objective description of how the action actually occurred in the real world. But this is a misunderstanding of what is involved.

To explore these interactions is absolutely not to confuse aspect (i.e., viewpoint) with *Aktionsart* (i.e., the nature of the action itself) or to dilute the essentially subjective nature of aspect as the speaker's viewpoint or focus on the action or state. The writers who have been most clear and articulate in distinguishing aspect and *Aktionsart* on semantic grounds have also been at the forefront in affirming and exploring these secondary interactions.[30] The resulting secondary "functions" of aspect phrased in terms of various actional

[28] Porter, *Verbal Aspect*, 87; other places where he mentions this briefly are 35 n. 15, 96–97, 184.

[29] Stanley E. Porter, *Idioms of the Greek New Testament* (2nd ed.; Sheffield: JSOT Press, 1994), 28–42.

[30] Bache, "Aspect and Aktionsart," 57–72; Carlota S. Smith, "A Theory of Aspectual Choice," *Language* 59 (1983): 479–501; McKay, *New Syntax*, 28–29; Evans, *Verbal Syntax*, 19–21.

characteristics (e.g., single vs. repeated, ingressive vs. culminative, specific vs. general) do not deny the primary "definition" of the aspects themselves as subjective viewpoint features.

Porter did not discuss the Vendler-Kenny taxonomy or anything like it in his book and he has been dismissive of it subsequently. For example, his essay in the Danker Festschrift (2004), he cites Verkuyl's 1993 book as having "refuted [the Vendler-Kenny system] in its substance and its application."[31] But this is not what Verkuyl does at all. While he disputes some of the fine points, he accepts the substance of its elements of meaning and their relations to each other and utilizes them extensively in his own work with aspect. Verkuyl's disagreement with Vendler-Kenny has to do with what level it pertains to in syntactical analysis: are these properties of verbs alone or of verb phrases and entire sentences. His argument is that they operate at more than just the lexical level. This is an on-going dispute in the field, but it is a peripheral discussion that does not call into question the relevance of the larger substance of the Vendler-Kenny scheme and its value for aspectual interpretation.[32] I have treated them as operators both at the lexical level and the phrase level (what Verkuyl calls "compositional"), and others in the field have done likewise.[33] But Verkuyl clearly does not argue against features like change, duration, boundedness as relevant for aspectual function.

The other argument Porter musters against my use of Vendler-Kenny is likewise based on a misunderstanding. He amasses word-frequency statistics

---

[31] Stanley E. Porter, "Aspect Theory and Lexicography," in *Biblical Greek Language and Lexicography: Essays in Honor of Frederick W. Danker* (ed. Bernard A. Taylor et al.; Grand Rapids: Eerdmans, 2004), 214. The book in view is Henk J. Verkuyl, *A Theory of Aspectuality: The Interaction between Temporal and Atemporal Structure* (Cambridge: Cambridge University Press, 1993), 33–68.

[32] Ellen Thompson, *Time in Natural Language: Syntactic Interfaces with Semantics and Discourse* (The Hague: Mouton de Gruyter, 2005), 159; and Debra Ziegeler, *Interfaces with English Aspect: Diachronic and Empirical Studies* (Amsterdam: John Benjamins, 2006), 7–8.

[33] See Fanning, *Verbal Aspect*, 127–28; See also Smith, *Parameter of Aspect*, 177–78; Susan Rothstein, *Structuring Events: A Study of the Semantics of Lexical Aspect* (Oxford: Blackwell, 2004), 29–35; and Susan Rothstein, *Theoretical and Crosslinguistic Approaches to the Semantics of Aspect* (Amsterdam: John Benjamins, 2008), 2–3.

to show that "there is no clear correlation between lexical meaning (if it exists as Fanning outlines it) and selection of tense-form."[34] He assumes I am using Vendler-Kenny to argue that "lexical semantic considerations, that is, the semantics of the action depicted itself as expressed by the lexical root, seem to be linked to the frequency of appearance of a particular tense-form."[35] But I make no such claim, explicit or implied, in my discussion of these lexical classes.[36] What I attempt to do, as many others who study aspect have done, is trace the predictable patterns of meaning that emerge when a certain set of lexical features combine with one of the aspects. I have no expectation that lexical meaning drives the selection of a certain aspect; I simply want to explore what larger significance results from whatever combination is used.

One of the contextual features not covered in the Vendler-Kenny taxonomy is the issue of scope, that is, general vs. specific reference. Paying attention to verbal adjuncts like subject and object phrases, adverbs, prepositional phrases, and other features can give us insight into whether an instance of aspect usage has a broad reference or a very specific one in context.[37] This is important for construing the sense appropriately, as will be developed later in this essay.

Discourse functions of Greek tense-aspect in the Synoptics

Many have observed and commented on how verbal aspect operates at the discourse level in some sense.[38] Usually these observations are rather brief

---

[34] Porter, "Aspect Theory and Lexicography," 215.

[35] Ibid., 211.

[36] My only foray into this type of frequency discussion occurs in a different section of my book where I explore a limited number of verbs that, based on actual frequency counts, appear exclusively or almost exclusively in one aspect or the other (Fanning, *Verbal Aspect*, 340–78). Such ideas are not connected to any of my treatments of the Vendler-Kenny lexical classes (Ibid., 42–46, 127–63).

[37] See details discussed in Fanning, *Verbal Aspect*, 170–85, 199, 206, 210–12, 241–49, 286–88, 326–28, 337–39, 383–85.

[38] Herbert Weir Smyth, *Greek Grammar*, rev. by Gordon M. Messing (Harvard: Harvard University Press, 1956), §§ 1898–99, 1909, 1929; A. T. Robertson, *A Grammar of the Greek New Testament in the Light of Historical Research* (Nashville: Broadman, 1914), 837–40; Nigel Turner, *Syntax* (vol. 3 of *A Grammar of New*

and simple, not clearly developed or defined, and this has resulted in some confusion of both terminology and substance. In what follows an attempt will be made to clarify some important definitions and distinctions. Two other introductory points are important: (1) most who have mentioned these discourse functions treat them not as primary or central to the semantics of aspect but as secondary effects of the viewpoint features that are central as laid out earlier;[39] and (2) verbal aspect is only one of many features that ought to be examined in working with discourse analysis. There is broad agreement that this is how the discourse usage should be assessed and I will not pursue these points further here.

Genre distinctions

One of the important tasks in defining aspect usage in discourse is to work with the question of discourse genre. "Discourse" is too broad a term by itself and needs further clarification since there are different types of discourse with important differences in characteristics. Analysis of how one feature like verbal aspect is used in discourse must take into account genre differences even if we discover some common patterns across discourse-types later in the process. So we need to look at different types of discourse. Longacre, for example, begins with a broad categorization of four types (narrative, procedural, behavioral, and expository) based on two features that may or may not be present in the discourse structure ("contingent temporal succession" and "agent orientation").[40] He argues that narrative is marked for both of these

---

Testament Greek; ed. James Hope Moulton; Edinburgh: T. & T. Clark, 1963), 66.

[39] See discussion in Fanning, *Verbal Aspect*, 72–77, and similar stance in Jeffrey T. Reed, *A Discourse Analysis of Philippians* (Sheffield: Sheffield Academic Press, 1997), 112–15. The main figure from general studies of aspect who sees aspect as primarily a discourse feature is Paul J. Hopper. See his essay "Aspect between Discourse and Grammar: An Introductory Essay for the Volume," in *Tense-Aspect: Between Semantics and Pragmatics* (Amsterdam: John Benjamins, 1982), 3–18.

[40] Robert E. Longacre, *The Grammar of Discourse* (2nd ed.; New York: Plenum, 1996), 8–9. Robert A. Dooley and Stephen H. Levinsohn, *Analyzing Discourse: A Manual of Basic Concepts* (Dallas: Summer Institute of Linguistics, 2001), 7–9, follow Longacre in these.

features. Later in his treatment he suggests other features that may provide further genre distinctions, but these will not be taken up here.[41]

Such distinctions need to be observed at the macro level, that is, in regard to the general discourse genre of a NT book for example. Discourse analysis of the Gospels and Acts should be broadly different from analysis of the Epistles since the genres are different.[42] But this also applies at the micro level, the study of individual sections and subsections. Black, for example, begins her study of the historical present in Matthew by laying out four discourse types into which she classified each sentence of Matthew for purposes of evaluating discourse signals: narrative, exposition, speech, and OT quotations. These are described as follows:

> Narrative (events recounted from the evangelist's viewpoint in roughly temporal order, forming the framework for the discourse), exposition (longer discourse sections attributed to Jesus, including parables), speech (conversation; short statements attributed to Jesus, especially as a reply to another's question or statement), or Old Testament quotation (longer citations as indicated in Nestle-Aland, *Novum Testamentum Graece*, 27th edn.).[43]

Her brief description of narrative coheres with the features commonly cited by others who have attempted to characterize its central properties. Temporal progression and agent orientation are the two features emphasized by Longacre as mentioned above. He means by these "a framework of temporal succession in which some (often most) of the events or doings are contingent on previous events and doings" and "orientation towards agents . . . with at least a partial identity of agent reference running through the discourse." Since narrative is

---

[41] Longacre, *Grammar of Discourse*, 9–11; see also Kathleen Callow, *Discourse Considerations in Translating the Word of God* (Grand Rapids: Zondervan, 1974), 12–18.

[42] Stephen H. Levinsohn, *Discourse Features of New Testament Greek: A Coursebook on the Information Structure of New Testament Greek* (2nd ed.; Dallas: SIL International, 2000), 169, 175.

[43] Stephanie L. Black, "The Historic Present In Matthew: Beyond Speech Margins," in *Discourse Analysis and the New Testament: Approaches and Results* (ed. Stanley E. Porter and Jeffrey T. Reed; JSNTSup 170; Sheffield: Sheffield Academic Press, 1999), 122.

in essence telling a story, it is only natural that participants and flow of events would be central. So in working with narrative discourse we should pay attention to the sequencing and relations of events to each other and to the introduction and role of participants in the story. These elements give us the broad framework to which we can add the other sub-genres that are mixed in. We examine the content of longer speeches and of the shorter conversational interchanges, but we see these within the framework of the larger narrative structure of "contingent temporal succession" and "agent-orientation."

These genre differences are why it is important to be sensitive to differences in aspect frequency and usage in speech or exposition as over against narrative proper. Campbell is to be commended for a number of valuable observations along this line, and for incorporating them into his analysis of aspect function.[44] There are clear patterns of aorists, imperfects, and historical presents being predominant in narrative, while speech or exposition has mainly presents, perfects, and futures (see this in Mark 1:1–45). When we study aspect usage in narrative then, we should focus on the narrative segments proper and not the content of longer expositions or shorter conversational exchanges that are mixed in.[45]

This is also why when analyzing narrative we should focus on aspect use in main clauses and pass over most verb forms in subordinate clauses, participles, infinitives, etc. We may discover in a few cases that grammatically subordinate elements fit on the event line—e.g., some adverbial participles or temporal clauses following the main verb or some relative clauses[46]—but for the most part we should concentrate on main clauses.[47]

---

[44] Campbell, *Verbal Aspect, the Indicative Mood, and Narrative*, 3–5 and passim; see also Harald Weinrich, "Tense and Time," *Archivum Linguisticum* 1 (1970): 31–41, and discussion of his work in Fanning, *Verbal Aspect*, 73–74.

[45] Talmy Givón, *Syntax: A Functional-Typological Introduction* (vol. 1; Amsterdam: John Benjamins, 1984), 288; and Levinsohn, *Discourse Features*, 174 n. 5.

[46] Levinsohn, *Discourse Features*, 181–87, 190–96; Dooley and Levinsohn, *Analyzing Discourse*, 83.

[47] Klutz's comments on the discourse use of verbal aspect in exorcism narratives can be faulted for ignoring this proviso. See Todd Klutz, "Naked and Wounded: Foregrounding, Relevance and Situation in Acts 19:13–20," in *Discourse Analysis and the New Testament: Approaches and Results* (ed. Stanley E. Porter and Jeffrey T. Reed; Sheffield: Sheffield Academic Press, 1999), 263–67; and Todd

Because of these genre considerations, I am not persuaded by approaches that claim the same discourse functions for aspect across all genres, narrative, epistolary, expository, and so on. For such overly broad treatment, see for example Porter's early treatments, where Mark 11:1–11, including speeches and narrative sections, and Rom 5:1–5 are analyzed without any distinctions noted.[48] Subsequently Reed suggested modifications from Porter in the interest of accommodating both narrative and non-narrative characteristics but some inaccuracies remained especially regarding how the aspects contribute.[49] These claims will be taken up again in what follows.

Klutz, *The Exorcism Stories in Luke-Acts: A Sociostylistic Reading* (Cambridge: Cambridge University Press, 2004), 49–50, 107–9, 171–73, 222, where prime thematic significance is given to aspectual usage in embedded speech and embedded participles.

[48] Stanley E. Porter and Jeffrey T. Reed, "Greek Grammar since BDF: A Retrospective and Prospective Analysis," *Filologia Neotestamentaria* 4 (1991): 154–56; and Porter, *Idioms*, 302–3. See also *Idioms*, 23, where Acts 16:1–5 and Rom 5:1–2 are treated the same. Likewise Jeffrey T. Reed and Ruth A. Reese, "Verbal Aspect, Discourse Prominence, and the Letter of Jude," *Filologia Neotestamentaria* 9 (1996): 181–99, assume that all genres display the same discourse patterns in regard to aspect usage. See David H. K. Hoe, "Apocalyptic Discourse in Second Peter" (PhD diss., Dallas Theological Seminary, 2008), 328–31, for negative evaluation of the discourse interpretation of aspect given in Reed and Reese. Hoe argues that the discourse effect they describe for aorist vs. present aspect is better attributed to the temporal contrast of aorist (past events and thus background/given information) vs. present (present situation/relevance). A further demonstration of this is the use of imperfects in Jude 9, 18 that function like the aorists in the book (i.e., background/given) rather than being foregrounded as should be expected for their imperfective verbal aspect. The same general critique can be made regarding Martín-Asensio's brief treatment of aspect roles in the discourse analysis of Ephesians. See Gustavo Martín-Asensio, *Transitivity-Based Foregrounding in the Acts of the Apostles: A Functional-Grammatical Approach to the Lukan Perspective* (Sheffield: Sheffield Academic Press, 2000), 44–47.

[49] Reed, *Philippians*, 107–8, 112–15. More recently Porter himself acknowledged certain genre distinctions but did not move away from his earlier claims about how aspect is used to show discourse prominence across the genre types. See Stanley E. Porter, "Prominence: An Overview," in *The Linguist as Pedagogue: Trends in the Teaching and Linguistic Analysis of the Greek New Testament* (ed. Stanley E. Porter and Matthew Brook O'Donnell; Sheffield: Sheffield Phoenix Press, 2009), 57–58.

Foreground and background in narrative

This brings us to the more specific issue of foreground and background in narrative. This area of research has been subject to, as Dry observes, "numerous conflicting claims and assumptions" especially because of "different understandings of the term foregrounding itself."[50] As she notes, this is due in part to its interdisciplinary status as a subject of research in literary criticism, cognitive psychology, and text linguistics and in part to the ambiguous descriptions by scholars who leave key terms ill-defined or expect readers to extrapolate from examples that can illustrate a range of phenomena. She points out that foregrounding should signal greater prominence or salience for the thematic development of the text, but this is not always what is meant by the term.[51]

In linguistic studies that give verbal aspect a role in narrative foregrounding versus backgrounding, the predominant scheme has been to assign the perfective (i.e., external, aorist) aspect to the foregrounding function and the imperfective (i.e., internal, present or imperfect) to the backgrounding function. Scholars who espouse this scheme for language in general or for ancient Greek in particular are numerous.[52] Those of this group who write

---

[50] Helen Aristar Dry, "Foregrounding: An Assessment," in *Language in Context: Essays for Robert E. Longacre* (ed. Shin Ja J. Hwang; Dallas: Summer Institute of Linguistics, 1992), 435.

[51] Ibid., 435, 438, 444, 448.

[52] Smyth, *Greek Grammar* §§ 1899, 1909, 1929; Weinrich, "Tense and Time," 31–41; William. A. Foley and Robert D. Van Valin, *Functional Syntax and Universal Grammar* (Cambridge Studies in Linguistics 38; Cambridge: Cambridge University Press, 1984), 371–73, 397; Joseph E. Grimes, *The Thread of Discourse* (The Hague: Mouton, 1975), 55–70; Callow, *Discourse Considerations*, 12–18; Hopper, "Aspect between Discourse and Grammar," 3–18; Paul J. Hopper and Sandra A. Thompson, "Transitivity in Grammar and Discourse," *Language* 56 (1980): 251–99; Stephen Wallace, "Figure and Ground: The Interrelationships of Linguistic Categories," in *Tense-Aspect: Between Semantics and Pragmatics* (Amsterdam: John Benjamins, 1982), 201–23; Givón, *Syntax*, 287–90; Fanning, *Verbal Aspect*, 74–75, 191; McKay, *New Syntax*, 42–43; C. M. J. Sicking, "Aspect Choice: Time Reference or Discourse Function?" in *Two Studies in the Syntax of the Verb in Classical Greek* (Leiden: Brill, 1996), 85–94; Egbert J. Bakker, "Verbal Aspect and Mimetic Description in Thucydides," in *Grammar as Interpretation: Greek Literature in Its*

about Greek verbs focus on the contrast between aorist and imperfect in narration. They see the aorist as providing the main line, basic narrative framework of sequenced events, the story line or event line, which in narrative can clearly be seen as of primary importance to the narrative task, and thus "foreground." The imperfect in contrast is seen as giving offline, supporting information, setting the scene, explaining circumstances that lie behind the main event line, and thus "background." What is sometimes said is that since the aorist or foreground verbs give the basic framework of the story, the imperfect or background verbs could be left out without losing the main points of the narrative. As Dooley and Levinsohn say, "If only the foreground were available, the resulting representation might be complete in its general outline, but would be sketchy. Background aids in internal and external contextualization."[53]

The strength of this view is that most narrative, especially in the NT, is clearly structured to recount a story and so the main line of more or less sequenced events portrayed by aorists is thematically central and thus should be labeled "foreground."[54] On the other hand, information that is peripheral and supportive should be seen as background.[55] Two weaknesses of the view are that (1) it fails to address the discourse role for the historical present in narrative—the present is imperfective in aspect but it hardly seems to fit the background role that this view might expect it to take; and (2) it fails to account for numerous instances where the imperfect operates like the aorist

Linguistic Contexts (ed. Egbert J. Bakker; Leiden: Brill, 1997), 13–15; Levinsohn, *Discourse Features*, 173–77; Dooley and Levinsohn, *Analyzing Discourse*, 79–83; Campbell, *Verbal Aspect*, 13–14, 91–96, 108–17.

[53] Dooley and Levinsohn, *Analyzing Discourse*, 79.

[54] Dry, "Foregrounding: An Assessment," 442–48, suggests that sequencing of events may not be as thematically important for literary texts with more complex plot structures; for these characterization, setting, symbols, etc. may assume more importance for the theme than an event line. But this does not seem to describe NT narrative, even though the latter features along with the story line have significance nonetheless.

[55] For an early treatment that lines up "carrying the discourse forward" and "contribut[ing] to the progression of the narrative" with foreground prominence and "not in itself contribut[ing] directly to the progression of the theme" with background, see Callow, *Discourse Considerations*, 52–54.

at the level of main line sequenced events.[56] Instances of both of these will be discussed below.

In contrast to the predominant scheme, a few scholars reverse the poles, seeing the perfective (i.e., aorist aspect) as background, the imperfective (i.e., present aspect including present and imperfect indicatives) as foreground; they also add the perfect forms as frontground.[57] In most cases these levels are asserted without much definition and the illustrations that are given do not clarify how the levels are to be understood. One of the more detailed treatments is in Reed's book on Philippians, where he describes three levels of prominence in NT discourse: background, theme, and focus.[58] A few pages later, when he speaks about the contribution of verbal aspect to discourse prominence, he tentatively identifies the same roles that Porter did—aorist for background, present and imperfect for theme, and perfect and pluperfect for focus. But he specifically limits this to non-narrative texts. He also qualifies the scheme by noting that discourse prominence is a secondary feature for aspect, and so not all instances can be expected to fit the pattern.[59]

There are problems with this scheme in regard to narrative.[60] First, it demands the counterintuitive labeling of aorists as background when they carry "the mainline or storyline" of the narrative, as Porter acknowledges in

---

[56] Both of these issues are mentioned by Martín-Asensio, *Transitivity-Based Foregrounding*, 62–63, in his critique of my unqualified affirmation of this scheme in Fanning, *Verbal Aspect*, 74–75, 191. The second is argued also by Shin Ja J. Hwang, "Foreground Information in Narrative," *Southwest Journal of Linguistics* 9 (1990): 78–82.

[57] This approach originates with Porter, *Verbal Aspect*, 92–93; *Idioms*, 23, 302–3, and in this he is followed by others. See Reed, *Philippians*, 112–15 (affirms but with qualification); Thomas R. Hatina, "The Perfect Tense-Form in Colossians: Verbal Aspect, Temporality and the Challenge of Translation," in *Translating the Bible: Problems and Prospects* (ed. Stanley E. Porter and Richard S. Hess; Sheffield: Sheffield Academic Press, 1999), 249–50, 224–52; Klutz, "Naked and Wounded," 263–67; and Klutz, *Exorcism Stories*, 49–50, 107–9, 171–73, 222. These three levels of prominence for the Greek aspects are repeated in Porter's recent essay, "Prominence: An Overview," 54–61.

[58] Reed, *Philippians*, 107–8.

[59] Ibid., 112–15.

[60] See the brief critique in Martín-Asensio, *Transitivity-Based Foregrounding*, 62–63.

his recent work. He does this just after arguing that "the basic framework" of any discourse consists of "mainline" versus "supporting material."[61] To this he adds a quotation from Hopper about narrative: "It is evidently a universal of narrative discourse that in any extended text an overt distinction is made between the language of the actual story line and the language of supportive material which does not itself narrate the main events."[62] Hopper asserts that cross-linguistically the perfective (aorist) aspect is related to the foreground function just described and the imperfective (present/imperfect) to the background function.[63] See also Porter's use of Wallace (1982) earlier in his essay. He quotes Wallace three times and relies on his descriptions of foreground and background in several places.[64] But he fails to cite Wallace's identification of perfective aspect with foregrounding and of imperfective with backgrounding.[65] Nowhere does Porter indicate why he departs from Hopper and Wallace on these significant points.

Second, it distorts aorist usage to say as Reed does that it "support[s] the main plot with secondary participants and events," while the present and imperfect give "major participants and events . . . often occurring along some chronological line." It is also not true that aorists "can often be eliminated without drastically obscuring the main message."[66] These comments about aorist in narrative are easily disproved by examining NT passages like those given at the end of this essay. Aorists are consistently used to recount the main

---

[61] Porter, "Prominence: An Overview," 57.

[62] This quotation is from Paul J. Hopper, "Aspect and Foregrounding in Discourse," in *Syntax and Semantics* (vol. 12 of *Discourse and Syntax*, ed. Talmy Givón; New York: Academic Press, 1979), 213. In spite of this Porter sticks with his disparate view that aorist is background and "present/imperfect . . . are used for the foregrounding . . . of supporting material" (Porter, "Prominence: An Overview," 57). What he does not acknowledge is that this is the opposite of Hopper's view in the essay just quoted.

[63] Hopper, "Aspect and Foregrounding," 215–16.

[64] Porter, "Prominence: An Overview," 51, 54, 59 (quoting Wallace); 51–59 (repeated references).

[65] Wallace, "Figure and Ground," 208–9.

[66] Reed, *Philippians*, 107. See the contrast with the Dooley-Levinsohn quotation cited by note 53.

events involving the central characters which constitute the primary thematic development of the narrative (i.e., foreground).[67]

This view also goes against the common use of imperfects to describe offline occurrences or provide information about setting, characteristics of people and so forth to supplement the main line of the story. Decker, for example, describes the eight imperfects of Mark 6:18–20 as providing "background information" that is "more remote from the main storyline,"[68] and in this he is surely correct. These uses of the imperfect have a particular characteristic that will be detailed below.

Two of the advantages of this view mirror the weaknesses mentioned above for the previous approach: (1) the historic present seems to fit this scheme more naturally since it seems certainly prominent within the narrative context, and (2) the use of imperfects for vivid description of main line, sequenced events also fits better into what narrative foregrounding should include.[69]

Finally a major weakness of the three-fold "planes of discourse" that Porter has proposed and some have followed is the role of perfect and pluperfect forms. While his most prominent, frontground role for these forms has a certain plausibility in its theoretical presentation and it has often been cited as a theoretical construct, it simply does not work in explaining actual usage of the perfect and pluperfect, especially in narrative texts. One preliminary problem noted earlier is that perfects and pluperfects almost never occur as verbs that carry the narrative; they occur predominantly in sections of

---

[67] See Barnard's extensive evaluation of Porter's levels of prominence. He attempts to assess on other grounds what would be the most important elements in various stories in Luke and compares them with what Porter's scheme would suggest. Barnard finds repeatedly that the seemingly most prominent, climactic events are recorded as aorists, contrary to what would be expected. See Jody A. Barnard, "Is Verbal Aspect a Prominence Indicator? An Evaluation of Stanley Porter's Proposal with Special Reference to the Gospel of Luke," *FN* 19 (2006): 9, 12, 14, 18, 28, 29.

[68] Decker, *Temporal Deixis*, 107; see also 142 regarding imperfects in Mark 2:1–12.

[69] Decker (Ibid., 137–38) is mistaken in taking the imperfects of Mark 14:31 as "remote from the storyline." Surely Peter's bold declaration of loyalty (reinforced by the adverb "vehemently") as well as that of the other disciples is vividly descriptive of their repeated responses right on the spot, viewed in an "up close and personal" way.

speech or in embedded uses in relative clauses or as participles or infinitives. From the outset then they are unlikely to have a major discourse role in the narrative sections. Where perfects or pluperfects do occasionally appear in main clauses within narratives, they function typically like imperfects in providing background information to supplement the aorist main line story. See uses of perfect periphrastic participles with imperfect of εἰμί for example in Mark 15:7, 26; Luke 1:7; 5:1; Acts 8:16.[70] Even when we ignore such finer genre distinctions and look at passages across the board (narrative, exposition, speech, epistolary, etc.), examination of actual usage shows that this level of prominence for perfects and pluperfects simply cannot be valid.

Porter's admittedly brief treatment of Mark 11:1–11 asks us to believe that among the most prominent items in the story are the perfect participle descriptions of the colt as "tied up" (vv. 2, 4) and the people who observe the disciples' actions as "standing" there (v. 5).[71] Surely these things are at the other end of the scale of prominence in this story. In his analysis of Acts 16:1–5, he cites as "very significant items" not that Paul chose Timothy and circumcised him and in their travels they passed on the regulations of the Jerusalem council, but the seemingly subsidiary points that people "knew" Timothy's father was Greek and the regulations were "decided" by the council.[72] Hatina in his study of the perfect in Colossians does a classic job of condemning with faint praise. In his summary of results he refers to Porter's

---

[70] Likewise uses of pluperfects in explanatory clauses, as described in Fanning, *Verbal Aspect*, 306–7. See examples in Matt 7:25; Mark 14:44; Luke 8:29; 16:20. So they occupy the opposite end of the scale of prominence: background instead of frontground as Porter proposes.

[71] Porter, *Idioms*, 302–3. He repeats the example of perfects in Mark 11 and defends his view a bit further in "The Greek Language of the New Testament," in *Handbook to Exegesis of the New Testament* (ed. Stanley E. Porter; Leiden: Brill, 1997), 118–19, and in "Prominence: An Overview," 59–61. He cites certain other contextual factors (e.g., OT allusions) that suggest prominence for the description of the colt in vv. 2, 4 (perfect participles). But he does not defend the description of the bystanders as prominent (also perfect participle), and it seems more likely that any prominence arises from other factors, not the use of the perfect. It would be helpful also to see him make the case from other examples instead of repeating the same few instances in multiple publications over two decades.

[72] Porter, *Idioms*, 23; and Porter, *Verbal Aspect*, 93.

view that "the perfect points to those features of the discourse which are very significant," and he states, "I have observed that in Colossians, at least, the hypothesis is plausible in some cases at this preliminary stage," citing as supporting evidence four examples from the total of 19 perfects in the book. Then he says, "What is more, the evidence based on contextual and discourse features certainly does not discredit the hypothesis. It is generally not the case that the perfect is found in a comparatively insignificant position. The verb/participle which Paul chooses to take on the form of the perfect usually plays an important role in the immediate discourse, and sometimes in the broader discourse of the epistle as a whole."[73] Klutz in his several treatments of exorcism stories does a masterful job of trying to show how perfects and pluperfects just might be seen as most prominent, but we are invariably asked to ignore the centrality of powerful actions done to deliver people or the wider effects of such deliverances in favor of highlighting things like participles describing someone's condition or characteristic events that occurred prior to the scene in view.[74] Reed and Reese in their discourse study of verbal aspect in Jude give, I think more wisely, no analysis of the nine occurrences of the perfect in the epistle.[75]

An alternative view

In consideration of these competing descriptions of background and foreground in narrative and their relative strengths and weaknesses, I suggest

---

[73] Hatina, "Perfect Tense-Form in Colossians," 249–50.

[74] Klutz, "Naked and Wounded," 263–67; Klutz, *Exorcism Stories*, 107–9, 171–73. See a similar critique of Klutz' treatment of aspects in Barnard, "Is Verbal Aspect a Prominence Indicator?," 14–16. Earlier in his discussion of miracle stories in Luke's Gospel, Barnard expresses his opinion (pp. 8–9) that the acts of Jesus to deliver should be regarded as the climax and main point of such stories, not descriptions of the serious conditions from which he sets people free. This seems correct, since as he notes it agrees with standard form critical analyses and develops the Lukan thematic emphasis on the expected deeds of the Messiah as drawn from Isaiah (Luke 4:17–21; 7:21–22).

[75] Reed and Reese, "Verbal Aspect, Discourse Prominence, and the Letter of Jude," *FN* 9 (1996): 181–99.

a different three-plus-one-part structure for verbal aspect's contribution to prominence in narrative.

The three-part structure of aorist and imperfect in narrative

The actual usage is better explained, I think, by seeing (1) the aorist as the *foreground* element because of its role in recounting the main line of more or less sequenced events that make up the story and are thus thematically central. (2) The imperfect then should be seen, in part, as adding offline, supporting information, setting the scene, explaining broader circumstances that lie behind the main event line, and so these uses constitute the *background* element in narrative. But (3) other uses of the imperfect clearly fit on the main event line, but do so in providing more vivid, up-close portrayal of the events they recount. They put readers as it were right on the scene as virtual eye-witnesses of the particular details, phases, actions and reactions of the events that are described. This could be called *frontground* or something like it because of the close attention it pays to the narrative events. But rather than see it as a third major "plane of discourse," it is better to regard it as another option alongside the aorist within the foreground or mainline of the narrative. This is thematically as well as literarily more prominent than the aorist foreground events, since the story slows down and forces the reader to take greater account of the events described in this way and their contribution to the larger theme of the narrative. The "plus-one" element will be explained shortly. First, a bit more about the second and third parts just mentioned: the dual role for the imperfect.

Such a division of the NT imperfect into two narrative contrasts with the foreground aorist is consonant with observations Bakker has made about narrative tenses in Thucydides. He notes that sometimes the imperfect provides background to the main line aorist events, but in other places the imperfect recounts main line events themselves.[76] This he attributes to two modes of narration reflecting differing points of view, one more detached and evaluative, the discourse of the knower ("diegetic" is his term for this) and the

[76] Bakker, "Verbal Aspect and Mimetic Description in Thucydides," 13–16. Alexander C. Loney, "Narrative Structure and Verbal Aspect Choice in Luke," *FN* 18 (2005): 5–11, has surveyed and adapted these insights for his study of Luke.

other more immediate, "on the spot" narration, the discourse of the observer (he calls this "mimetic").[77] While the textual characteristics in Thucydides as over against the NT are not exactly the same, the variation in imperfect usage in narration is parallel.

This dual role for the imperfect is rooted in the feature of scope I mentioned earlier. Whether the imperfect fits in as more detached background information, scene setting, and so forth or as main line "on the spot" narration is directly related to whether the context communicates general or specific reference. If an imperfect verb is used in association with broader, characteristic actions or traits, it clearly is offline, subsidiary information (contributing to the narrative in valuable ways but not forming its main story line). On the other hand if an imperfect is used in regard to a specific, narrow situation in context, it slows the story down and gives a more immediate, vivid description of a main line event. See Luke 2:36–38 where the imperfects in vv. 36–37 (relating Anna's course of life and habits of worship) are offline compared to the developing story of Mary and Joseph's temple visit with the infant Jesus that started in 2:22. But the temporal expressions at the beginning of v. 38 clearly bring us back to the specific events of the developing story to describe Anna's effusive and repeated responses to Jesus' presence on that occasion.[78] Then after this episode is wrapped up by the main line aorist of v. 39, we see imperfects returning again in v. 40 to portray background in a somewhat different way: a broad summary of characteristic descriptions of the child Jesus that form the general backdrop and transition to the next main line story, the twelve-year-old Jesus in Jerusalem (vv. 41–51a, with a different item of background provided in v. 41). A similar passage of broad summary background can be

---

[77] Bakker, "Verbal Aspect and Mimetic Description in Thucydides," 28–48.

[78] See also the examples in Mark 5, where the imperfects of vv. 3–5 describing the demonized man's long term deprivations and the failed attempts of others to deal with him are offline compared to the story of Jesus' arrival in vv. 1–2 that is picked up again in v. 6 (aorists throughout). On the other hand the imperfects of vv. 8–10 describe in a lively way the conversational exchange between Jesus and the man/demons at that critical juncture in the story. The imperfect of v. 11 then gives a background detail about the swine nearby to prepare for the main line request and response of vv. 12–13.

seen in vv. 51b–52, as a conclusion to this account and transition to the launching of Jesus's ministry at the time of John the Baptist (chapter three).[79]

Other examples of general, customary imperfects used for background in narrative can be seen in Matt 3:4; 19:22; Mark 5:28; 6:18–20; Luke 5:17; 16:19–21; 22:1–2.[80]

Other uses of specific, descriptive imperfects used for greater foregrounding of mainline events can be seen in Matt 3:14; 4:11; Mark 5:18, 20; 11:5, 9; 12:17, 18; Luke 5:3, 6; 9:34; 24:13–16.[81]

The "plus-one" element of historical present in narrative

The "plus-one" element for verbal aspect in narrative prominence is the historical present (HP). There is certainly a vast quantity of research on the Greek HP that has gone before, and there is no intention to survey its history

[79] Dooley and Levinsohn, *Analyzing Discourse*, 81 n. 52, observe that summary statements are normally backgrounded.

[80] See other uses, especially from Acts, in Fanning, *Verbal Aspect*, 248–49. Campbell, *Verbal Aspect*, 91–96, has some helpful discussion about the use of imperfects to narrate supplementary, simultaneous events, but his examples are not exactly to the point, I think. He cites imperfects in Luke 9:43–45; 19:3a–b, 4b, 7. These imperfects are, however, not simultaneous but sequenced events in the story. A further sign that these are not background features is that they describe specific actions or attitudes existing on that particular occasion, not more general characteristics. Campbell's examples from Luke 19:2, 3c and John 5:16, I think, are truly backgrounded.

[81] See other uses, especially from Acts, in Fanning, *Verbal Aspect*, 243–44, 286–87. Campbell, *Verbal Aspect*, 96–98, briefly notes the possible occurrence of imperfects to narrate main line, not supplementary events. He gives no explanation of this use except to say it "provides an imperfective contrast" to the normal aorists in main line narration. The examples that he cites, however, are clearly specific, descriptive imperfects giving up-close, vivid narration of these events. I think this shows the limited explanatory power of his "remoteness" view of the imperfect. In Campbell's system we would expect the aorist and imperfect, especially at the level of main line narration, to be equally "remote" but instead the imperfect contrasts with the aorists in paying close attention to certain events within the larger past narrative. This is an issue also with the mention of imperfect as "remote" in Decker, *Temporal Deixis*, 107, 137.

here. But it will be evident how what I want to suggest is both dependent on previous research and also tuned a bit differently to the nuances of the HP.

Many have observed that the HP often occurs at transition points in narrative, especially in Mark but to some degree in other books.[82] These transition points or points of discontinuity include things like bringing participants into a new scene, moving participants to a new location in an existing scene, introducing new participants to a scene, and moving between main sections within a scene. These are readily apparent when we examine HP occurrences in the NT, especially in Mark, and I concur that these are important uses, but they ought to be examined further, because they give invaluable insights in regard to the wider significance of the HP. Another common observation in the literature on NT uses of the HP is that it highlights or gives prominence to significant events or speeches. This is the point at which some even greater adjustment is needed, in my opinion, and in this I am departing from what I wrote about the HP in my *Verbal Aspect* book (1990).

For these changes in thinking I am dependent on the work of people like Randall Buth, John Callow, and Stephen Levinsohn.[83] From them I have learned to look for the HP to signal prominence not for the event or speech that the HP itself describes, but for events or speeches that follow it. In other words the HP is prospective or "cataphoric": it anticipates or signals important events or speeches that are about to come in the story. Like other prominence indicators,[84] the HP interjects something unexpected into the narrative not to draw attention to its own action but to prepare the reader for significant

---

[82] See some of the literature cited in Fanning, *Verbal Aspect*, 231–32. This is also the predominant result of the study of John's use of HP by Mavis M. Leung, "The Historical Present in the Fourth Gospel," *JETS* 51 (2008): 703–20; see her summary points (p. 719) revealing transitions in the narrative as central functions.

[83] Randall Buth, "Mark's Use of the Historical Present," *Notes on Translation* 65 (1977): 7–13; Levinsohn, *Discourse Features*, 200–13, 240–55; see also Levinsohn, *Discourse Features*, 202, who cites unpublished seminar notes by John Callow, "The Historic Present in Mark" (1996). This is now developed more extensively by Steven E. Runge, *Discourse Grammar of the Greek New Testament: A Practical Introduction for Teaching and Exegesis* (Bellingham, Wash.: Lexham Press, 2010), 154–75.

[84] For example, "tail-head linkage," Luke's use of ἐγένετο (described by Levinsohn, *Discourse Features*, 177–80, 197–200) and other features described as "forward-pointing devices" by Runge, *Discourse Grammar*, 77–214.

points that are about to be recounted. As Levinsohn says, "what is highlighted by the HP is not so much the speech or act to which it refers but the event(s) that follow."[85]

This is the real point of the transition uses of the HP noted by many. It's not that the actions of "sending, coming, arriving, seeing" that commonly occur in these instances are significant in themselves; instead they prepare the way for the important events about to take place in the new situation that they signal. See this illustrated for example in the HPs in Matt 3:13 (Jesus coming to the Jordan where John was baptizing); 4:5, 8 (the devil taking Jesus to the temple and then to a very high mountain); in Mark 11:1 (Jesus sending disciples for the colt); 11:7 (bringing and preparing the colt for Jesus to ride on); and in Mark 5:15 (the locals coming and seeing the delivered demoniac before they respond with fear and rejection).[86]

Also as Levinsohn and Runge point out, the function of the HP in such cases is not to mark a boundary in the discourse per se. This can be an accompanying effect but is not central to the HP. What it does is to anticipate important events or speeches that are coming and this frequently comes at a point where the scene changes and reinforces the boundary. But in other places the HP comes somewhat after the point of clearest segmentation in order to point forward to significant things still to come in the existing scene (e.g., Mark 2:3; 5:1–11).[87]

This forward-pointing function for the HP when it is used not at the beginning but further into an existing scene is illustrated by examples like Matt 3:15 (it is not John's consent to baptize Jesus that is prominent but the event of the baptism itself, the Spirit descending, and the heavenly voice); 4:11 (not the devil's leaving, but the further supernatural affirmation of Jesus in parallel to the baptism scene); Mark 11:4 (not the untying of the colt itself but the brief interchange of vv. 5–6 that opens the way for the rest of the story). I think these and numerous examples like them show that the common observation mentioned above—that HP signals prominence—is on the right track, but

[85] Levinsohn, *Discourse Features*, 200.

[86] Many other examples can be found in Fanning, *Verbal Aspect*, 232, and in Levinsohn, *Discourse Features*, 200–13.

[87] Levinsohn, *Discourse Features*, 200–2; and Runge, *Discourse Grammar*, 165–69.

needs significant adjustment. When we see an HP in the text, we should look beyond it to how it prepares the way for what follows.

One will perhaps also notice, in connection with looking at these examples, various instances of speech HPs that occur alongside the event HPs I have pointed out. It certainly seems that these are used in the same way, not due to prominence for the specific utterances they record but as referring forward to significant events or speeches that follow them.[88] Note the speech HP in Mark 11:2 that certainly seems parallel to the verb of sending in 11:1. Likewise the speech verbs in Mark 5:7 and 5:9 introduce utterances that are not so important on their own but anticipate the climactic events of deliverance that follow in the story. Similar points can be made in Matt 4:6 (not the devil's temptation but Jesus's response in v. 7; there is an HP as a textual variant for the aorist speech verb in 4:9 which could evidence the same dynamic). Matt 4:10 is a bit harder since Jesus's statement seems significant; but I think it is better to see this as triggering Satan's response in v. 11 which constitutes the end of his enticements—hence the failure of his efforts. This also illustrates that HPs can occur in a shorter or longer series, with one HP pointing forward to a somewhat more prominent one that follows which in turn points forward in a chain of events that build in significance as they go along.

These are important further indicators, I think, that this cataphoric function for the HP is the best explanation even for these most difficult areas of HP usage in the NT: I mean (1) its use to introduce speech (either as a single utterance or in a series of conversational interactions) and (2) its use in a clustered series of actions, especially in John, but also in some places in Mark. In both situations the HPs anticipate what is coming next, and when used repeatedly in a single span of text, they heighten the importance of the series of events overall (e.g., Mark 15:16–27; John 13:3–11; 20:1–29).[89]

The final issue to mention about the HP is how it comes to be used this way. What is it about the present indicative in these situations that produces this forward-pointing function? I think the key to this is the present indicative's

[88] I no longer regard speech HPs to be merely stereotyped uses as I argued in Fanning, *Verbal Aspect*, 233–34, 239.

[89] See Runge, *Discourse Grammar*, 172–73 and Leung, "Historical Present in the Fourth Gospel," *JETS* 51 (2008): 719.

tense-value, not aspect. This is one of the ways in which the writer's portrayal of the event's location in time differs from the expected temporal frame in order to produce a certain rhetorical or discourse effect. It is the unexpected, non-default use of the present temporal location in the sequence of a past referring narrative that causes it to stand out, "a past event portrayed as though just occurring."[90] And as discourse studies have shown, a feature that departs from its default usage slows down the reader's processing and signals a discontinuity. Runge says, "the HP's departure from the expected norm creates a break in the flow of the discourse."[91] So when the HP appears in the sequence of aorists and main line (descriptive) imperfects, it draws our attention and causes us to anticipate significant events or speeches that will follow.

Runge argues that the present indicative is a "mismatch" due to not only to its unexpected temporal meaning but also its unexpected aspectual meaning in a narrative framework carried by aorists.[92] Since he takes the imperfect as predominantly used for background in narrative,[93] the narrative main line would be carried primarily by aorists in his view, and so the insertion of HPs would clearly stand out on both temporal and aspectual grounds. I prefer to focus on the temporal contrast alone because I see a greater role for imperfects in the narrative main line as detailed above. What I see as unexpected then about the HP is the temporal value of the present indicative intruding on the normally past-referring narrative sequence of mostly aorists and some imperfects.

The HP is thus a *tertium quid* in relation to the three levels of prominence I described earlier. It departs from the main line of aorists and descriptive imperfects in a different way than the background imperfects, but still serves as an effective counterpart to signal a different discourse feature: that of anticipation or cataphoric reference to significant events or speeches that are about to come.

---

90 Fanning, *Verbal Aspect*, 229. As Runge, *Discourse Grammar*, 158, says, it is "a mismatch in the grammaticalized time with the discourse time."

91 Runge, *Discourse Grammar*, 161–62. See his detailed explanation of how this works alongside the normal semantic meaning (pp. 158–61, 175).

92 Ibid., 158–61. Runge correctly observes that most HPs recount main line events like aorists do (p. 161).

93 Ibid., 160.

Conclusion

When I finished my dissertation in the summer of 1986, I had become persuaded of two things: that the study of verbal aspect in NT Greek was a complicated endeavor and that the task of sorting things out would not stop with my work! It is complicated mainly because aspect interacts so closely with other features of meaning. Thus understanding aspect and evaluating its contribution to NT interpretation requires two vital steps: seeing aspect for what it really is, in and of itself, apart from these wider features (the "definition" or semantic level) and tracing its significant interactions with these other features in actual usage (the "function" or pragmatic level). It can be seen from this essay that I am still convinced that both of these steps are indispensable. It can be seen further that the task of sorting out these wider interactions has continued to advance. Those of us with the opportunity to work in this area have been able to build on the solid work of others who came before us—I think especially of scholars like E. D. Burton, A. T. Robertson, and Albert Debrunner. I continue to think that their analyses of the NT Greek verb were not so much wrong as too simplistic and, if used without sensitivity to context, potentially misleading. So refining and deepening our understanding of these things was long overdue at that point, a quarter of a century ago—and the task continues!

Bibliography

Bache, Carl. "Aspect and Aktionsart: Towards a Semantic Distinction." *Journal of Linguistics* 18 (1982): 57–72.

Bakker, Egbert J. "Verbal Aspect and Mimetic Description in Thucydides." Pages 7–54 in *Grammar as Interpretation: Greek Literature in Its Linguistic Contexts.* Edited by Egbert J. Bakker. Leiden: Brill, 1997.

Barnard, Jody A. "Is Verbal Aspect a Prominence Indicator? An Evaluation of Stanley Porter's Proposal with Special Reference to the Gospel of Luke," *Filología Neotestamentaria* 19 (2006): 3–29.

Black, Stephanie L. "The Historic Present in Matthew: Beyond Speech Margins." Pages 120–39 in *Discourse Analysis and the New Testament: Approaches and Results.* Edited by Stanley E. Porter and Jeffrey T. Reed. Journal for the Study of the New Testament: Supplement Series 170. Sheffield: Sheffield Academic Press, 1999.

Buth, Randall. "Mark's Use of the Historical Present." *Notes on Translation* 65 (1977): 7–13.

Callow, Kathleen. *Discourse Considerations in Translating the Word of God.* Grand Rapids: Zondervan, 1974.

Campbell, Constantine R. *Verbal Aspect, the Indicative Mood, and Narrative: Soundings in the Greek of the New Testament.* New York: Peter Lang, 2007.

Comrie, Bernard. *Aspect: An Introduction to the Study of Verbal Aspect and Related Problems.* Cambridge: Cambridge University Press, 1976.

———. *Tense.* Cambridge: Cambridge University Press, 1985.

Decker, Rodney J. *Temporal Deixis of the Greek Verb in the Gospel of Mark with Reference to Verbal Aspect.* Studies in Biblical Greek 10. New York: Peter Lang, 2001.

Dooley, Robert A., and Stephen H. Levinsohn. *Analyzing Discourse: A Manual of Basic Concepts.* Dallas: SIL International, 2001.

Dry, Helen Aristar. "Foregrounding: An Assessment." Pages 435–50 in *Language in Context: Essays for Robert E. Longacre.* Edited by Shin Ja J. Hwang. Dallas: Summer Institute of Linguistics, 1992.

Evans, Trevor V. "Future Directions for Aspect Studies in Ancient Greek." Pages 199–206 in *Biblical Greek Language and Linguistics: Essays in Honor of Frederick W. Danker.* Edited by Bernard A. Taylor et al. Grand Rapids: Eerdmans, 2004.

———. *Verbal Syntax in the Greek Pentateuch: Natural Greek Usage and Hebrew Interference.* Oxford: Oxford University Press, 2001.

Fanning, Buist M. "Approaches to Verbal Aspect in New Testament Greek: Issues in Definition and Method." Pages 46–62 in *Biblical Greek Language and Linguistics: Open Questions in Current Research.* Edited by Stanley E. Porter and D. A. Carson. Sheffield: JSOT Press, 1993.

———. *Verbal Aspect in New Testament Greek.* Oxford Theological Monographs. Oxford: Clarendon, 1990.

Foley, W. A., and Robert D. Van Valin. *Functional Syntax and Universal Grammar.* Cambridge Studies in Linguistics 38. Cambridge: Cambridge University Press, 1984.

Givón, Talmy. *Syntax: A Functional-Typological Introduction.* Vol. 1. Amsterdam: John Benjamins, 1984.

Grimes, Joseph E. *The Thread of Discourse.* The Hague: Mouton, 1975.

Halliday, M. A. K. *An Introduction to Functional Grammar.* 2nd ed. London: Arnold, 1994.

Hatina, Thomas R. "The Perfect Tense-Form in Colossians: Verbal Aspect, Temporality and the Challenge of Translation." Pages 224–52 in *Translating the*

Bible: Problems and Prospects. Edited by Stanley E. Porter and Richard S. Hess. Sheffield: Sheffield Academic Press, 1999.

Hoe, David H. K. "Apocalyptic Discourse in Second Peter." Ph.D. diss., Dallas Theological Seminary, 2008.

Hopper, Paul J. "Aspect and Foregrounding in Discourse." Pages 213–41 in *Discourse and Syntax*. Edited by Talmy Givón. *Syntax and Semantics* 12. New York: Academic Press, 1979.

———. "Aspect between Discourse and Grammar: An Introductory Essay for the Volume." Pages 3–18 in *Tense-Aspect: Between Semantics and Pragmatics*. Amsterdam: John Benjamins, 1982.

Hopper, Paul J., and Sandra A. Thompson. "Transitivity in Grammar and Discourse." *Language* 56 (1980): 251–99.

Hwang, Shin Ja J. "Foreground Information in Narrative." *Southwest Journal of Linguistics* 9 (1990): 78–82.

Kenny, Anthony. *Action, Emotion and Will.* London: Routledge and Kegan Paul, 1963.

Klutz, Todd. *The Exorcism Stories in Luke-Acts: A Sociostylistic Reading*. Cambridge: Cambridge University Press, 2004.

———. "Naked and Wounded: Foregrounding, Relevance and Situation in Acts 19:13–20." Pages 263–67 in *Discourse Analysis and the New Testament: Approaches and Results*. Edited by Stanley E. Porter and Jeffrey T. Reed. Sheffield: Sheffield Academic Press, 1999.

Leung, Mavis M. "The Historical Present in the Fourth Gospel." *Journal of the Evangelical Theological Society* 51 (2008): 703–20.

Levinsohn, Stephen H. *Discourse Features of New Testament Greek: A Coursebook on the Information Structure of New Testament Greek*. 2nd ed. Dallas: SIL International, 2000.

Loney, Alexander C. "Narrative Structure and Verbal Aspect Choice in Luke." *Filología Neotestamentaria* 18 (2005): 3–31.

Longacre, Robert E. *The Grammar of Discourse*. 2nd ed. New York: Plenum, 1996.

Lyons, John. *Semantics*. Cambridge: Cambridge University Press, 1977.

Martín-Asensio, Gustavo. *Transitivity-Based Foregrounding in the Acts of the Apostles: A Functional-Grammatical Approach to the Lukan Perspective*. Sheffield: Sheffield Academic Press, 2000.

McKay, K. L. *A New Syntax of the Verb in New Testament Greek: An Aspectual Approach*. Studies in Biblical Greek 5. New York: Peter Lang, 1994.

Picirilli, Robert E. "The Meaning of the Tenses in New Testament Greek: Where Are We?" *Journal of the Evangelical Theological Society* 48 (2005): 533–55.

Porter, Stanley E. "Aspect Theory and Lexicography." Pages 207–22 in *Biblical Greek Language and Lexicography: Essays in Honor of Frederick W. Danker*. Edited by Bernard A. Taylor et al. Grand Rapids: Eerdmans, 2004.

———. "The Greek Language of the New Testament." Pages 99–130 in *Handbook to Exegesis of the New Testament*. Edited by Stanley E. Porter. Leiden: Brill, 1997.

———. *Idioms of the Greek New Testament*. 2nd ed. Sheffield: JSOT Press, 1994.

———. "Prominence: An Overview." Pages 45–74 in *The Linguist as Pedagogue: Trends in the Teaching and Linguistic Analysis of the Greek New Testament*. Edited by Stanley E. Porter and Matthew Brook O'Donnell. Sheffield: Sheffield Phoenix Press, 2009.

———. *Verbal Aspect in the Greek of the New Testament, with Reference to Tense and Mood*. New York: Peter Lang, 1989.

Porter, Stanley E., and Jeffrey T. Reed. "Greek Grammar since BDF: A Retrospective and Prospective Analysis." *Filologia Neotestamentaria* 4 (1991): 154–56.

Reed, Jeffrey T. *A Discourse Analysis of Philippians*. Sheffield: Sheffield Academic Press, 1997.

Reed, Jeffrey T., and Ruth A. Reese. "Verbal Aspect, Discourse Prominence, and the Letter of Jude." *Filologia Neotestamentaria* 9 (1996): 181–99.

Robertson, A. T. *A Grammar of the Greek New Testament in the Light of Historical Research*. Nashville: Broadman, 1914.

Rothstein, Susan. *Structuring Events: A Study of the Semantics of Lexical Aspect*. Oxford: Blackwell, 2004.

———. *Theoretical and Crosslinguistic Approaches to the Semantics of Aspect*. Amsterdam: John Benjamins, 2008.

Runge, Steven E. *Discourse Grammar of the Greek New Testament: A Practical Introduction for Teaching and Exegesis*. Bellingham, Wash.: Lexham Press, 2010.

Sicking, C. M. J. "Aspect Choice: Time Reference or Discourse Function?" Pages 1–118 in *Two Studies in the Syntax of the Verb in Classical Greek*. Leiden: Brill, 1996.

Smith, Carlota S. *The Parameter of Aspect*. Dordrecht: Kluwer, 1991.

———. "A Theory of Aspectual Choice." *Language* 59 (1983): 479–501.

Smyth, Herbert Weir. *Greek Grammar*. Rev. by Gordon M. Messing. Cambridge: Harvard University Press, 1956.

Thompson, Ellen. *Time in Natural Language: Syntactic Interfaces with Semantics and Discourse*. The Hague: Mouton de Gruyter, 2005.

Turner, Nigel. *Syntax. A Grammar of New Testament Greek 3*. Edinburgh: T. & T. Clark, 1963.

Vendler, Zeno. "Verbs and Times." *The Philosophical Review* 66 (1957): 43–60. Reprinted in Zeno Vendler. Pages 97–121 in *Linguistics in Philosophy*. Ithaca, New York: Cornell University Press, 1967.

Verkuyl, Henk J. *A Theory of Aspectuality: The Interaction between Temporal and Atemporal Structure*. Cambridge: Cambridge University Press, 1993.

Wallace, Daniel B. *Greek Grammar Beyond the Basics: An Exegetical Syntax of the New Testament*. Grand Rapids: Zondervan, 1996.

Wallace, Stephen. "Figure and Ground: The Interrelationships of Linguistic Categories." Pages 201–23 in *Tense-Aspect: Between Semantics and Pragmatics*. Amsterdam: John Benjamins, 1982.

Weinrich, Harald. "Tense and Time." *Archivum Linguisticum* 1 (1970): 31–41.

Ziegeler, Debra. *Interfaces with English Aspect: Diachronic and Empirical Studies*. Amsterdam: John Benjamins, 2006.

The Verbal Aspect of the Historical Present Indicative in Narrative

Steven E. Runge

Introduction

The primary purpose of this article is to challenge the view of the historical present (HP) usage held by those claiming that Koine Greek does not grammaticalize tense. The varied use of the present tense-form has supplied some of strongest evidence against the traditional treatment of Greek as a tense-based language. Porter claims that the HP usage generates claims of prominence based upon the inherent prominence value of the tense-form itself, not based upon the pragmatics of the context. It will be demonstrated that the historical usage stands out based upon patterns of usage and how these influence reader's expectations. Koine Greek is best understood as a mixed tense-aspect verbal system, grammaticalizing both in the indicative. Furthermore, those claiming an aspect-only model have not demonstrated the absence of tense, but merely the predominance of aspect. Properly understanding the HP and how it brings about various pragmatic effects will also bring greater clarity to the function of each tense-form in narrative.

The explanation that follows is a functional and typologically-based approach to language. All languages need to accomplish a common set of discourse tasks. Though they all share similar tasks, there is great variety in that they are accomplished from one language to another. Redundancy, interruption and delay are devices commonly used to accomplish pragmatic tasks. The key to differentiating the various tasks lies in assessing the semantic need for the given element in the particular context. Readers and hearers strive to make sense of a discourse. Writers and speakers seek to be clearly understood, and take steps to facilitate this. All rely on an apparently universal expectation that any given element in the discourse is *supposed* to be there[1]. This expectation can generally be summarized in the principle *choice implies meaning*.[2] In other words, if the writer has chosen to do something or include some element, it is assumed that some meaning is associated with it. For example, if I began telling a joke by introducing a one-legged man who owned a three-legged cat, you would be quite confused if this information proved irrelevant to understanding the punch line. People naturally expect that such details are somehow relevant.

I will begin by surveying the various claims made about the HP by traditional grammarians, by linguists, and most recently by those denying the presence of tense in Koine Greek. Most have treated HPs separately, but have failed to reconcile this fact with their overall description of the verbal system. Another element that has been missing is a theoretical framework which can reconcile the divergent claims made about the effects produced by the HP. These claims include marking the beginning or ending of a paragraph, prominence marking, and even that the HP does nothing more than offer a stylistic variation.

Descriptions of the historical present

Despite the view that the HP represents a vulgar usage since it is virtually absent in Luke,[3] Turner provides compelling evidence of its widespread use in "compositional" Greek that could not have been influenced by translation from other languages.[4] The HP debate hinges on how one reconciles this usage with the prototypical present. Four primary explanations describe

---

[1] See Dan Sperber and Deirdre Wilson, *Relevance: Communication & Cognition* (2nd ed.; Oxford, Blackwell, 1986), 50–64.

[2] Stephen H. Levinsohn, *Discourse Features of New Testament Greek: A Coursebook on the Information Structure of New Testament Greek* (2nd ed.; Dallas: SIL International, 2000), viii.

[3] Friedrich Blass, Albert Debrunner and Robert Walter Funk, *A Greek Grammar of the New Testament and Other Early Christian Literature* (Chicago: University of Chicago Press, 1961), 167 (BDF hereafter).

[4] Nigel Turner, *Syntax* (vol. 3 of *A Grammar of New Testament Greek*; ed. James Hope Moulton; Edinburgh: T. & T. Clark, 1963), 61 (MHT3 hereafter).

the grammatical function of the HP, each of which can be reconciled with the discourse processing hierarchy introduced in the third section. Special attention will be given to the implications of each explanation for our understanding of verbal aspect of the HP.

Dramatic use/vividness[5]

The dramatic use of the HP is the most common explanation offered by commentators ostensibly because of modern English usage. Since the present tense-form is believed to grammaticalize present time, the HP usage is believed to essentially transport a past event into the reader's present experience. Wallace states, "The *reason* for the use of the historical present is normally to portray an event *vividly*, as though the reader were in the midst of the scene as it unfolds."[6] In other words, it is the semantics of the verb form that create the effect rather than some other pragmatic means.

Despite the appeal of the vividness explanation in theory, significant problems arise in practice. The semantic classes of HP verbs most frequently found in the HP are verbs of speaking or motion, leading Buth to characterize the former as "haphazard."[7] Why would a writer portray such action as vivid? Campbell raises the problem of distribution, stating, "They are rarely clustered together, but often alternate with aorists."[8] Although isolated chains of HPs may be found, much more frequently they are found in isolation. Reynolds summarizes the situation well: "When in a given passage in the New Testament there are many changes back and forth from aorist to present, it would seem that there is no forgetting of time for vividness."[9] There is good

[5] Cf. MHT3, 61; BDF, 167; Buist Fanning, *Verbal Aspect in New Testament Greek* (Oxford Theological Monographs; Oxford: Clarendon, 1990), 226; Daniel B. Wallace, *Greek Grammar Beyond the Basics: An Exegetical Syntax of the New Testament* (Grand Rapids: Zondervan, 1996), 527.

[6] Wallace, *Greek Grammar*, 526 (emphasis original).

[7] Randall Buth, "Mark's use of the Historic Present," *Notes on Translation* 65 (1977): 7–13.

[8] Constantine R. Campbell, *Verbal Aspect, the Indicative Mood, and Narrative: Soundings in the Greek of the New Testament* (Studies in Biblical Greek 13; New York: Peter Lang, 2007), 58.

[9] S. M. Reynolds, "The Zero Tense in Greek," *Westminster Theological Journal* 32

reason to believe that "temporal transport" is anachronistic to Koine Greek.[10] Brinton claims that the "vividness and excitement are a consequence of the text-organizing function of the historical present, not the primary function of the form."[11] In other words, it is a pragmatic effect of the usage, not a non-cancelable semantic characteristic.

We learn from the vividness explanation that the "historical" use of the present is deemed inappropriate for the discourse context because of the mismatch of temporal or "proximal" semantics of the tense-form to the reference time of the narrative. Vividness adherents reject that the HPs represent prototypical usage, recognizing instead that some other pragmatic function is intended. This leads us into our next point.

Tense reduction/zero aspect

In contrast to the vividness proponents, two divergent proposals attempt to treat the historical usage as within the semantic scope of the present tense. We begin with the tense-reduction and zero-aspect solutions before moving on to the aspect-only proposals in the second section. It is noteworthy that *all three* groups treat the HP separately from their description of "normal" present usage, a fact to which we will return later.

For those claiming that Koine grammaticalizes tense in the indicative mood, a standard proposal is that of *tense reduction*. This view rejects the understanding of HP verbs as true presents, viewing them instead as more of a sequential form like that found in Hebrew. Based on the fact that verbs of perception, motion and speaking are the most frequently occurring HPs, Battle offers the following proposal:

> Matthew and Luke-Acts, especially the former, nearly always connect the historical present to the aorist. Very seldom is it

(1969): 70.

[10] P. Kiparsky, "Tense and Mood in Indo-European Syntax," *Foundations of Language* 4/1 (February 1968): 30.

[11] Laurel J. Brinton, "Historical Discourse Analysis" in *The Handbook of Discourse Analysis* (ed. Deborah Schiffrin, Deborah Tannen and Heidi Ehernberger Hamilton; Malden, Mass.: Blackwell, 2001), 143. This is consistent with the upper levels of the discourse processing hierarchy discussed in the third section.

> tied to an imperfect. This fact can show either that the historical present is substituted for an aorist in what would normally be a chain of aorists, or that the historical present takes the place of the imperfect which would normally be used to break the monotony of continuous aorists. The first explanation seems simpler, and thus better.[12]

Battle understands the HP as a substitute for the aorist motivated by stylistic variation rather than by some definable discourse function. Such a view stands in stark contrast with traditional grammarians.[13] Winer states,

> Strictly and properly speaking, no one of these tenses can ever stand for another, as the commentators have in so many ways maintained: where such an interchange seems to exist, either it exists in appearance only, there being in point of fact some assignable reason (especially of a rhetorical kind) why this tense is used and no other; or else it must be ascribed to a certain inexactness belonging to the popular language.[14].

Although Battle's proposal is to be rejected, his connection of the HP to the aorist indicative is significant. Grammarians have tended to classify HPs as though they were aoristic in nature rather than as a substitute for the imperfect.[15] Wallace presents a similar view:

---

[12] J. A. Battle, "The Present Indicative in New Testament Exegesis" (ThD diss., Grace Theological Seminary, 1975), 128.

[13] See A. T. Robertson, *A Grammar of the Greek New Testament in the Light of Historical Research* (Nashville: Broadman, 1934), 829.

[14] G. B. Winer, *A Treatise on the Grammar of New Testament Greek* (trans. W. F. Moulton; Edinburgh: T. & T. Clark, 1882), 331.

[15] See F. Blass, *Grammar of New Testament Greek* (2nd ed.; trans. Henry St. J. Thackeray; London: MacMillan, 1898), 188. Funk classifies the present as both punctiliar, durative and present time ostensibly based on HP usage. Viewing the HP as temporal transport for vividness explains the classification as "present time," and the preference for the aorist in a narrative context accounts for the aspect being "punctiliar." Robert W. Funk, *Beginning-Intermediate Grammar of Hellenistic Greek* (Missoula, Mont.: Scholar's Press, 1973), §312.2a. Robertson notes that there are exceptions: "The hist. pres. is not always aoristic. It may be durative like the imperfect. This point has to be watched. Blass considers that the historical present 'habitually takes an aoristic meaning,' but room has to be left for the durative

> The *aspectual* value of the historical present is normally, if not always, reduced to zero. The verbs used such as λέγει and ἔρχεται, normally introduce an action in the midst of aorists without the slightest hint that an internal or progressive aspect is intended. The historical present has suppressed its aspect, but not its time. But the time element is rhetorical rather than real.[16]

In claiming this, Wallace is not taking a reductionist view so much as he is reacting to the contextual factors. The context ostensibly expects an aorist form, with no semantic need for present tense or imperfective aspect. His claim about the usage being "rhetorical" rather than semantic evidences an understanding of markedness, even if unstated. His effort to minimize the aspect can reasonably be attributed to the HP's departure from expected norms.

Claims regarding vividness and tense reduction share a fundamental presupposition that the usage represents a marked departure from the expected norms for the present indicative. It differs both in terms of *aspect* and *tense*. Claims of zero-tense or zero-aspect are best understood as attempts to reconcile actual usage with prototypical usage for the particular discourse context.[17] We must not neglect factors that make these solutions appealing in the first place. These scholars are all attempting to account for the apparent substitution of a present form in a context that prototypically expects another tense-form, most typically the aorist.[18]

Aspect-only claims

In the last twenty years a proposal has been popularized that Koine Greek verbs do not grammaticalize tense in any mood, including the indicative.

---

meaning also" (*Grammar*, 867).

[16] Wallace, *Greek Grammar*, 527. See also Kiparsky, "Tense and Mood," 30–57; Reynolds, "Zero Tense," 71–72.

[17] For other problems which make this view untenable, see Campbell, *Verbal Aspect*, 59–61.

[18] McKay makes the keen observation that the HPs that introduce states of affair at the beginning of pericopes are all "presents in place of normal imperfects" (K. L. McKay, *A New Syntax of the Verb in New Testament Greek: An Aspectual Approach* [SBG 5; New York: Peter Lang, 1994], 42).

Porter takes the most aggressive position, claiming that whatever temporal distinction may be present is better explained as spatial rather than temporal in nature.[19] This view has consequences similar to those confronting the traditional grammarians.

Foregrounding prominence

Porter asserts that the HP stands out not because of the mismatch with the "historical" context, but based on the inherent markedness and prominence of the present tense-form compared to the background aorist and less-foregrounded imperfect. In response to Robertson's argument that the HP functions as a substitute for both the aorist and the imperfect Porter states:

> This theory need not be considered at length, since its linguistic imprecision is self-evident. Those who argue for this theory have placed temporal reference as primary, and hence confused the ability of the historic Present to appear in past contexts with aspectual synonymity . . . More importantly, this theory neglects the fundamental formal opposition of the Present/Aorist in Greek and negates the principle that meaning is choice.[20]

Robertson's claim deserves more consideration. First, Robertson is not equating the meaning of the present with these forms; he is simply describing the mismatch of the present tense to a context prototypically filled by an aorist or imperfect. As with Wallace, the critical observation is made that the present is used where an aorist is expected, and a rhetorical meaning is associated with the choice to use the "wrong" form. Far from negating the principle of choice implying meaning, Robertson and Wallace uphold it by treating the "historical" usage as distinct from prototypical use of the present.[21]

---

[19] Stanley E. Porter, *Verbal Aspect in the Greek of the New Testament, with Reference to Tense and Mood* (SBG 1; New York: Peter Lang, 1989), 239.

[20] Porter, *Verbal Aspect*, 194.

[21] Robertson states, "In general one may say that in normal Greek when a certain tense occurs, that tense was used rather than some other because it best expressed the idea of the speaker or writer. Each tense, therefore, has its specific idea. That idea is normal and can be readily understood" (*Grammar*, 829).

In Porter's model, the inherent prominence of the present brings about the pragmatic effects, not the mismatch of the form to the context. Although he holds that "remoteness" is the key distinction between the present and imperfect tense-forms, Porter does not consider the lack of remoteness as contributing to judgments of the HP standing out in narrative contexts; it is the difference in distributional, semantic and morphological markedness compared to the aorist and imperfect forms.[22] He appeals to the foregrounding prominence of the present to explain the effects associated with the HP, not the contextual mismatch of the non-remote form in the remote context. This conclusion leads him to claim that the present tense-form is *always* inherently more marked than either the aorist or imperfect.

If this claim were valid, one should find similar prominence-marking claims made whenever the present is used alongside the aorist. Romans 1:21–27 provides a non-narrative example of such a chain, interrupted in v. 25 by a present indicative in the parenthetical blessing: ὅς ἐστιν εὐλογητὸς εἰς τοὺς αἰῶνας, ἀμήν.[23] Far from prominently marking the most salient information of the pericope, the usage is more likely motivated by the semantic requirements of the context. However claims of such non-historical presents marking prominence are lacking in the literature, except by those applying Porter's model. The traditional grammarians restrict their claims to the historical usage alone.

In terms of function, Porter affirms nearly all of the uses traditionally claimed by grammarians including vividness. In this case the vividness is not based on transporting the past event to present time, but upon Porter's theorized background-foreground-frontground prominence model. While theoretically the present tense-form is always prominent, the HP usage seems to be particularly so. Consider Black's summary regarding the use in Matthew 4, applying Porter's model of verbal aspect:

> In Jesus' temptation in the wilderness, Matthew moves from fewer to more instances of the historic present in subsequent sections of the passage to convey increasing drama as the narrative

[22] Porter, *Verbal Aspect*, 198–207.

[23] Barbara Aland et al., *The Greek New Testament* (4th rev. ed.; Stuttgart: Deutsche Bibelgesellschaft, 1993), 410.

> builds to a climax. In the first exchange between Jesus and the devil, no present tense-forms are used; in the second exchange two appear; in the climactic third exchange, three present tense-forms appear. Intermixed with other tense-forms in a balanced structure, these make his storytelling more vivid.[24]

Porter makes similar assertions regarding the particular pragmatic effects associated with the HP, despite his claim that such effects should *always* be associated with the present tense-form use in contrast to the aorist on the basis of its purported markedness.[25]

The failure to recognize the mismatch in aspect and remoteness/tense leads Porter to describe the effects associated with the historical usage as prototypical. In many respects the pragmatic effects achieved by the historical usage provide the most convincing support for his claim about the inherent prominence of the present tense-form. Decker applies Porter's model to the usage in Mark, affirming the acceptability of the HP usage without consideration as to why it stands out other than to affirm Porter's view: "The reason the speaker chooses it relates primarily to discourse functions, the more heavily marked form (compared to the aorist) drawing attention to key steps in the course of events or argument."[26] Thus, Porter affirms the pragmatic effects associated with the HP, but simply attributes them to other factors.

In contrast, Campbell considers the mismatch of the present tense-form to the narrative context to be a decisive factor, noting that the imperfect indicative would be better suited both in terms of aspect and proximity for narrative proper: "The absence of remoteness is the feature that marks the present tense-form as a distinct choice as opposed to the imperfect."[27] Just as

---

[24] Stephanie L. Black, "The Historic Present in Matthew: Beyond Speech Margins," in *Discourse Analysis and the New Testament: Approaches and Results* (ed. Stanley E. Porter and Jeffrey T. Reed; JSNTSup 170; Sheffield: Sheffield Academic Press, 1999), 135.

[25] See Porter, *Verbal Aspect*, 196–97.

[26] Rodney J. Decker, *Temporal Deixis of the Greek Verb in the Gospel of Mark with Reference to Verbal Aspect* (SBG 10; New York: Peter Lang, 2001), 103.

[27] Campbell, *Verbal Aspect*, 65. Whereas Porter appeals to the inherent markedness of the present, Campbell accurately appeals to the mismatch of the proximity. Porter's discussion of the HP focuses on the inherent markedness of the form, not

the tense-reduction claim views the HP usage as a mismatch on the basis of tense, Campbell arrives at much the same conclusion in terms of proximity, *contra* Porter and Decker. However, though Campbell notes the correlation of the HP to the aorist by "zero-aspect" adherents like Kiparsky, he does not engage the issue of aspectual mismatch that motivates the claim. He only correlates the HP to the imperfect and not the aorist, leading him to propose a new solution to the problem.

"Spill" from reported speech

Campbell offers a new proposal to account for the apparent mismatch of the HP in narrative proper. He notes that current explanations cannot account for claims of prominence or paragraph marking since counter-examples are easily produced (e.g., HPs encoding mundane events or being found within a paragraph). On the basis of so many HPs being used to introduce reported speech, and the fact that the present tense-form is most often found in this context, Campbell proposes that these HPs "are simply the result of *spill* of the imperfective-proximate nature of the discourse that they introduce; they therefore do not indicate any special discourse function."[28] He cites Stephanie Black as another scholar who has reached the same conclusion.[29] While this claim is novel to say the least, it undermines Campbell's overall proposal regarding aspect.

There is no means of independently corroborating the validity of Campbell's *spill.* Questions regarding why it happens in one context and not in another are left unanswered, with no clear way forward. This proposal also seems to contradict his basic premise regarding choice, meaning and aspect. From a functional standpoint, this explanation is not too different from the reductionist solutions in that it essentially dismisses these uses from consideration. Although he explains their presence, Campbell neglects to

---

the mismatch of context versus usage.

[28] Campbell, *Verbal Aspect*, 66 (emphasis original).

[29] Ibid., 66. Black does not characterize the usage as *spill*, rather she follows the earlier claim of Buth that "the use of the historic present in speech margins in Matthew, especially with λέγω, approaches that of a stereotyped idiom" (Black, "The Historic Present in Matthew," 126).

describe their function in a manner that is consistent with his other claims about the role of aspect in discourse. Note that the ostensive spill is not only of *aspect*, but also of *proximity*. Some examples are needed to illustrate the double mismatch of the HP to the discourse context.

The imperfect is used with verbs of speaking prototypically in three discourse contexts. The first is to introduce an ongoing state-of-affair, such as dialoging that occurs concurrently with or preceding the main action. The Pharisees discussion with Jesus's disciples exemplifies this in Example 1, as their speech is part of a series of circumstantial participles introduced by ἐγένετο recounting the meal held at Matthew's house.

Example 1: Matt 9:11

> Καὶ ἐγένετο αὐτοῦ ἀνακειμένου ἐν τῇ οἰκίᾳ, καὶ ἰδοὺ πολλοὶ τελῶναι καὶ ἁμαρτωλοὶ ἐλθόντες συνανέκειντο τῷ Ἰησοῦ καὶ τοῖς μαθηταῖς αὐτοῦ. (v. 11) καὶ ἰδόντες οἱ Φαρισαῖοι ἔλεγον τοῖς μαθηταῖς αὐτοῦ, Διὰ τί μετὰ τῶν τελωνῶν καὶ ἁμαρτωλῶν ἐσθίει ὁ διδάσκαλος ὑμῶν;
> As Jesus was having a meal in Matthew's house, many tax collectors and sinners came and ate with Jesus and his disciples. (v. 11) When the Pharisees saw this *they said* to his disciples, "Why does your teacher eat with tax collectors and sinners?" (NET)

The mainline aorist indicative resumes in v. 12, recounting Jesus's response to the state-of-affairs.[30] These verbs either introduce offline reported speech, or alternatively indirect speech as states-of-affair.

The second context is at the beginning of a long speech, with the imperfect indicative verb being classified as ingressive, inchoative, or inceptive. Consider the introduction of the Sermon on the Mount in Example 2.

[30] Other similar examples are found in Matt 9:21, 34; 12:23; 14:4; 21:11; 27:41, 47, 49; Mark 2:16, 24; 3:21, 22, 30; 4:41; 5:8, 28, 30, 31; Luke 4:22; 9:31.

Example 2: Matt 5:2

> Ἰδὼν δὲ τοὺς ὄχλους ἀνέβη εἰς τὸ ὄρος, καὶ καθίσαντος αὐτοῦ προσῆλθαν αὐτῷ οἱ μαθηταὶ αὐτοῦ· (v. 2) καὶ ἀνοίξας τὸ στόμα αὐτοῦ ἐδίδασκεν αὐτοὺς λέγων,
> When he saw the crowds, he went up the mountain. After he sat down his disciples came to him. (v. 2) Then *he began to teach* them by saying (NET)

In such cases the action is cast more as a state-of-affair than a mainline event, preparing the reader for an extended speech.[31]

The third context is redundant mid-speech quotative frames as in Example 3.

Example 3: Mark 2:27

> καὶ ἔλεγεν αὐτοῖς, Τὸ σάββατον διὰ τὸν ἄνθρωπον ἐγένετο καὶ οὐχ ὁ ἄνθρωπος διὰ τὸ σάββατον· (v. 28) ὥστε κύριός ἐστιν ὁ υἱὸς τοῦ ἀνθρώπου καὶ τοῦ σαββάτου.
> Then *he said* to them, "The Sabbath was made for people, not people for the Sabbath. (v. 28) For this reason the Son of Man is lord even of the Sabbath". (NET)

A verb of speaking is inserted into an ongoing speech, thus reintroducing the same speaker.[32] It is semantically redundant, but has the effect of segmenting a single speech into smaller parts.

In contrast, HP verbs of speaking typically introduce direct discourse in contexts where they are semantically required, such as changes of speaker or at the beginning of shorter speeches. Few are found in the three prototypical discourse contexts of the imperfect verbs of speaking. More broadly speaking, HPs predominately recount mainline action rather than offline action characterizing the imperfect indicatives. Although "spill" explains a minority of the usage, it is preferable to construe all HP verbs as marked

---

[31] Other examples are found in Mark 3:23; 4:2; Luke 3:7; 5:35; 6:20; 10:2; 12:54; 13:6, 18.

[32] Other examples are found in Mark 4:9, 11, 21, 24, 26, 30; 5:9; 6:4, 10; Luke 6:5; 14:12.

usage on the basis of mismatch of tense and aspect intended to accomplish some pragmatic purpose.

Discourse processing hierarchy

Various discourse functions including vividness, paragraph-marking, and prominence-marking have been attributed to the historical use of the present indicative. What is lacking is a theoretical framework that allows the exegete to objectively determine (or as nearly as possible) the discourse function in a given context. The discourse-processing hierarchy that follows provides such a framework. There is a general tendency to claim that a device cannot accomplish more than one discourse task at a time. This tendency runs counter to the actual usage observed in language. Languages are more likely to multi-task than to specialize. Rarely will one idiom only ever accomplish a single thing.

There is a rhyme and reason to how the tasks double up. Instead of creating an "either/or" dichotomy, the processing hierarchy posits that one function is entailed within another. In other words, the hierarchy is simply a prioritized list of assumptions which readers and speakers of a variety of languages appear to utilize in processing discourse. These assumptions have little to do with the specific idiosyncrasies of a given language, and instead seem based upon how human beings cognitively process the world around them. Here is how it works.

Language forms have meanings, including the present indicative. The meaning is shaped by readers forming an understanding of what is prototypical through their use of the language. At some point this understanding shifts from development to judgment, allowing the reader to recognize pragmatically-motivated departures from the expected norms. These norms are not necessarily statistically determinable, but are grounded in the core semantic meaning of the form. When a form like the present indicative is used in a context that fits expected usage, it is understood to be semantically motivated, intended to convey imperfective aspect and proximate temporal deixis. In terms of the processing hierarchy, the determination of an acceptable semantic function ends the quest for an explanation, and the reader moves on.

If a semantic explanation is not found, the quest for relevance moves the reader up the hierarchy to look for an alternative explanation. In the case of the HP, the mismatch of the historical usage with the narrative context leads the reader to judge that some pragmatic function other than conveying the semantics of the present tense-form is intended. The core semantic meaning of the form does not change; it is the reader's understanding of the writer's rationale for its use in the context that changes.

This processing path is evidenced by the attempts of zero-tense and zero-aspect proponents to make the HP more like the expected aorist form.[33] As Campbell notes, the present tense-form is expected in reported speech, not narrative proper. The departure from the expected norm stands out, leading the reader to search about for another explanation. The HP still plays a semantic role, but it is also doing something more.

The first "something more" in the hierarchy is the processing function. This function is accomplished by adding prominence to a discontinuity that was already present in the context. The added prominence moves the reader to segment the text at that juncture, which in turn aids in the organization of the discourse in their mental representation of it.[34] Judgments that HPs signal the beginning or end of a paragraph, or opens a new sequence, etc., are consistent with the quest for relevance described in the hierarchy. If this processing function provides an adequate explanation to the reader, there is no further movement up the hierarchy.

If the device is not needed for processing or represents overkill, then it is accomplishing something else: a discourse-pragmatic function. This function describes the overuse of a device in a series of clauses, like building to a crescendo. It also accounts for the isolated use in a context of relative continuity where the disruption of the discourse is out of place.[35] Using

---

[33] It may be that a minority of HPs are used in place of imperfects, but there is no way to know. The goal here is to reconcile traditional claims made by seasoned grammarians. The explanation offered here would apply just as well to imperfects as to aorists.

[34] Knud Lambrecht, *Information Structure and Sentence Form* (Cambridge Studies in Linguistics; Cambridge: Cambridge University Press, 1994), 43.

[35] Steven E. Runge, *Discourse Grammar of the Greek New Testament: A Practical Introduction for Teaching and Exegesis* (Bellingham, Wash.: Lexham Press,

redundant or unneeded devices effectively disrupts the flow of the discourse, often generating a sense of suspense or build-up which Longacre describes as a "zone of turbulence."[36] Such contexts may be of local interest, such as the introduction of a significant participant using a verb of motion or perception; they may also be used—even clustered with other devices—just before the climax of the discourse.

These components of the processing hierarchy are summarized in Figure 1. Beginning with the semantic function, hearers continue to move up the hierarchy until an acceptable explanation has been reached.

Figure 1 Discourse Processing Hierarchy

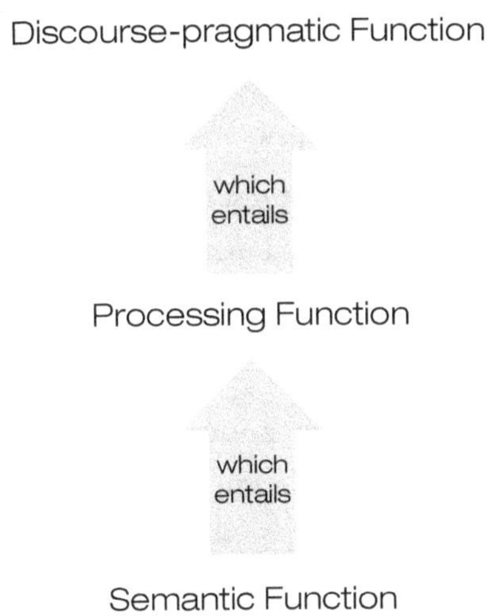

The lower levels are entailed in the higher ones. For example, if a device is deemed to accomplish a discourse-pragmatic function, it still accomplishes semantic and processing functions.

Recall Porter's model which predicts that *every* present tense-form stands out in the "foreground" in comparison to the aorist based on the semantic, morphological and distributional markedness of the present. This explanation works well in describing the HP, but a rigorous application quickly reveals

2010), Section 6.2.

[36] Robert E. Longacre, "Discourse Peak as Zone of Turbulence," in *Beyond the Sentence: Discourse and Sentential Form* (ed. Jessica R. Wirth; Ann Arbor: Karoma, 1985), 81–105.

its problems.[37] Significant actions are often expressed in the aorist, viz. the very mainline of the narrative itself. Within reported speeches, present tense-forms are quite natural, and lack the prominence that Porter claims. The processing hierarchy explains the intermittent success of Porter's model.[38] Prototypical usage fulfills the expected semantic function, eliminating the need to move further up the hierarchy for an explanation. If the usage fits expected norms for reported speech or non-narrative, there are no grounds for claiming special prominence.

The use of the present in narrative proper is quite a different matter. Despite its frequency of usage in Mark and John, it nonetheless is processed as somehow marking something. The usage does not fit the expected semantic function, due to the mismatch of tense/proximity and aspect with the discourse context. The fact that these pragmatic effects are associated with only the historical usage argues for describing this use of the present as marked, not prototypical. To claim that the historical use of the present indicative is prototypical grossly misrepresents its core semantic value. Porter and Decker have demonstrated that the present is used in a variety of contexts, but they have erred in the effort to roll all such uses into the core meaning for the form.

To summarize, if the element is semantically required, nothing more can be claimed about its discourse function. If the element is perceived as redundant or out-of-place, the reader moves on to the processing function. The usage highlights a discontinuity in the discourse to ensure that it is properly processed. Again, if this explanation accounts for the presence of the element in the context, nothing more can be claimed. If the marking of the

---

[37] See Jody A. Bernard, "Is Verbal Aspect a Prominence Indicator? An Evaluation of Stanley Porter's Proposal with Special Reference to the Gospel of Luke," *FN* 19 (2006): 3–29.

[38] Bernard concludes, "With regard to the pronouncement stories it was discovered that many of the prominent points or climactic sayings employ the present tense or sometimes the perfect tense, which is entirely consistent with Porter's proposal. It was also observed, however, that some of these so-called foreground and frontground tenses occur in background contexts. Furthermore, it became evident that Porter's system does not adequately account for certain restrictions upon aspectual choice, which reduces the likelihood that Luke was invariably free to choose verbal aspect" ("Verbal Aspect," 28–29).

discontinuity is more frequent than is needed for simple processing or viewed as excessive based on the relative continuity of the context, the reader moves further up the hierarchy to pragmatic highlighting. This highest function still draws attention to a discontinuity, still plays a semantic role; but in addition to these it draws attention to a significant speech or event which follows.

The discourse processing hierarchy is extrapolated from solid cognitive research from diverse languages regarding the first two levels.[39] The third is based upon consistent anecdotal claims made by linguists, exegetes and anthropologists regarding the perceived pragmatic effects achieved by excessive discontinuity.[40] The consistency of these judgments is further corroborated by the *ad hoc* conclusions reached by NT scholars regarding the HP. This processing hierarchy provides a typologically sound theoretical framework for reconciling the divergent claims associated with the HP. The HP always accomplishes one thing: highlighting a discontinuity in the context that was already present. The claims of paragraph marking, vividness and cataphoric highlighting are better understood as pragmatic effects attributable to how humans process discontinuity.

Reconsidering the aspect of the historical present

Proponents of both tense-based and aspect-based models have consistently acknowledged that the HP seems to be an irregular usage to say the least. There has been a corresponding effort by both groups to somehow normalize the HP. This was seen in the tense-reduction explanation of the traditionalists. The argument by Porter and Decker that the HP does not grammaticalize time is itself a normalization effort. In their view, the highlighting effects achieved by the HP derive from the inherent prominence of the form itself, not by its mismatch with the narrative context.

[39] Readers expect active participants to be minimally encoded. Various empirical and descriptive studies have claimed that such over-encoding is processed in various languages as a marker of discontinuity. See Steven E. Runge, "The Effect of Redundancy on Perceptions of Emphasis and Discontinuity" (Paper presented at the Linguistics and Biblical Hebrew Section of the annual meeting of the Society of Biblical Literature, New Orleans, La., November 22, 2009), 6–7.

[40] Steven E. Runge, "Discourse-Functional Description of Participant Reference in Biblical Hebrew Narrative" (DLitt diss., University of Stellenbosch, 2007), 182–87.

The verbal aspect of the HP is the crux of the tense-aspect debate, in my opinion. The efforts to normalize the usage have only obscured the bigger picture, for both sides have quashed the fact that the HP usage is actually irregular. The claims regarding its discourse functions are a direct result of the marked departure from expected usage. There are significant ramifications for Porter's model if the HP indeed represents marked usage. Before considering the distributional implications, it is important to understand the basic role played by each indicative tense-form in narrative proper.

Asymmetrical description of narrative tense-forms

There is a significant terminological clarification that needs to be made between Porter's use of the terms *foreground* and *background* and the way they are prototypically used in general linguistics.[41] The distinction between *figure/ground, mainline/offline,* and *background/foreground* is typically used to differentiate two aspects of discourse. The foreground is understood to be the main event line of the narrative, one that often forms something of a connected chain of events. These foreground events advance the plot of the narrative. In contrast, background information does not advance the story; instead it fleshes out needed detail. This function has led some to characterize it as offline information. This binary distinction conceives of the action as linear in nature, likely due to the strong correlation of temporal progression with the narrative mainline. Foreground events are the mainline and advance the plot; background information is offline and represents a pause or interruption of the plot.[42]

---

[41] Porter describes his usage as though it were representative stating, "Recent work by linguists in the analysis of discourse differentiates the planes of discourse into three (see Chapter 21): background, foreground and frontground" (*Idioms*, 23). However, he inverts the meaning of foreground and background because of his interest in prominence, thus casting more of a 3-D picture rather than a linear portrayal of the action. My research within linguistic literature revealed no usage of the term *frontground* relating to aspect, action or anything of the type. Instead computer programmers use it as the antonym for background (ostensibly based on the front/back opposition). The only usages I found consistent with Porter's usage were either by Porter himself, or those applying his model in NT studies.

[42] Foley and Van Valin correlate the semantics of certain verb classes with grounding.

Foley and Van Valin note a significant natural correlation between verbal aspect and the foreground/background distinction.[43] The perfective aspect portrays the action "*as a whole*"[44] or as "a complete and undifferentiated process."[45] Since the perfective conceptualizes the action as complete or as a whole, it is not surprising that completed, past-time events are most often portrayed using perfective aspect. This is not to say that perfective action is always past tense, but simply notes the natural correlation. In contrast, imperfective aspect portrays the action as *incomplete*, but without the same kind of natural correlation with time. The imperfective aspect allows the writer or speaker to establish a state of affairs in which perfective action takes place. This could be in a past- or present-tense context.[46]

Campbell provides a useful description of the relationship between background information and the mainline:

The verbs that portray a high degree of transitivity, where agents are acting upon or "doing things" with other things, are most often the mainline/foreground events. In contrast, less-transitive verbs describing states or activity are strongly associated with background/offline information. William. A. Foley and Robert D. Van Valin, *Functional Syntax and Universal Grammar* (Cambridge Studies in Linguistics 38; Cambridge: Cambridge University Press, 1984), 371. See also Levinsohn, *Discourse Features*, 171–72.

43 Foley and Van Valin, *Functional Syntax*, 371. See Levinsohn, *Discourse Features*, 171–72. Hopper makes a similar point in comparing the correlation of perfective aspect to mainline or foregrounded events, whereas imperfective aspect is associated with support, amplification, or comment on the narration. See Paul J. Hopper, "Aspect and Foregrounding in Discourse," in *Syntax and Semantics* (vol. 12 of *Discourse and Syntax*; ed. Talmy Givón; New York: Academic Press, 1979), 215.

44 Hopper, "Aspect and Foregrounding," 215.

45 Porter, *Idioms*, 21.

46 Foley and Van Valin comment on the natural correlation between foreground/background and perfective/imperfective aspect:

> [T]he perfective aspect is the primary aspectual category found in the temporal structure of narrative discourse in a number of languages and imperfective aspect is primary in durational/descriptive structure (Foley and Van Valin, *Functional Syntax*, 373).
>
> This finding [the statement on p. 373] is not surprising, since perfective aspect codes completed actions and events and imperfective incomplete events and actions and the former fit more naturally into the temporal structure of narrative, the latter into durational/descriptive structure (*Functional Syntax*, 397).

> The mainline of the narrative text is concerned with the major events, actions, and developments that project the narrative in the direction it is going. Without the sequence of mainline events and actions, offline information, such as supplemental information, inside information, speech and so forth, will not make sense; these require the mainline to provide context and to enable the reader to understand how the narrative arrived at the location where such offline material is meaningful. Offline material is contingent and dependent upon the mainline events.[47]

In this way, the mainline events represent the foreground of the narrative, whereas the offline information typically represents a pause in the advancement of plot.

In terms of the Greek verbal system, the aorist tense-form is understood to encode perfective aspect, portraying the action as a complete and undifferentiated whole.[48] Most scholars—regardless of their view on tense—associate the aorist with the mainline events of the narrative, as expected from cross-linguistic usage. Robertson states, "The aorist . . . is not the only way of expressing indefinite (undefined) action, but it is the normal method of doing so."[49] Decker states, "The aorist is the tense normally used to carry the storyline of the narrative—it moves the account along by specifying the basic events."[50] Campbell echoes this sentiment, claiming that the aorist grammaticalizes perfective aspect and is used for mainline material.[51] Porter is in basic agreement as well, if one takes into account his resignification of the terminology.

The aorist has traditionally been associated with the past tense, which makes sense based on its depiction of the action as an undifferentiated whole. The nature of the aspect correlates to completed events, but does not demand it.[52]

---

[47] Campbell, *Verbal Aspect*, 116.
[48] Porter, *Idioms*, 21.
[49] Robertson, *Grammar*, 831.
[50] Decker, *Temporal Deixis*, 107.
[51] Campbell, *Verbal Aspect*, 116.
[52] This is an important distinction overlooked by Campbell. Although he rejects the association of tense with aspect, he nonetheless asserts that "the semantic value of remoteness is also encoded within the aorist indicative" (*Verbal Aspect*, 117).

Since there is no other proximate perfective tense-form in Greek, the aorist must play double duty. This explains the use of the aorist in varied temporal or atemporal contexts. In terms of an asymmetrical model of markedness, the aorist is taken as the default tense-form against which the others are described. As Robertson states, "the aorist is the tense used as a matter of course, unless there was special reason for using some other tense."[53] The frequency of aorist forms is thus understood here as a natural consequence of being the most basic form. By virtue of the discourse task perfective verbs perform in narrative, they prototypically occur in high frequency across languages. So while there is apparent agreement with Porter regarding the aorist form being the default tense, I do not draw the same conclusion regarding its prominence.[54]

The imperfect and present tense-forms are understood to encode imperfective aspect, portraying the action as *incomplete*.[55] The imperfect tense-form is associated with past tense for those accepting the presence of tense,[56] and with remoteness for those using an aspect-only model.[57] The cross-linguistic association of the imperfective aspect with offline or background information is general rather than unequivocal. Campbell aptly notes that although there is a strong correlation between the imperfect tense-form and offline information, "imperfects are also able to function within the mainline of narrative proper alongside the aorist, which is the dominant mainline tense-form."[58] Just as the aorist has been heavily associated with past tense, there seems a similar

---

This connection of perfective action to past-tense or deictic remoteness is better explained as a natural consequence of its nature and usage rather than as a semantic constraint that it encodes.

53 Robertson, *Grammar*, 831.

54 Porter's view presupposes a cause-effect, inversely-proportional relationship between frequency and discourse prominence. In his view, the aorist is the least prominent form due in large part to its high frequency. This leads him to refer to it as the *background* tense, based on its diminished discourse prominence in his model.

55 See Decker, *Temporal Deixis*, 107; Campbell, *Verbal Aspect*, 77; Porter, *Verbal Aspect*, 89.

56 See Robertson, *Grammar*, 882.

57 See Decker, *Temporal Deixis*, 107; Campbell, *Verbal Aspect*, 77; Porter, *Verbal Aspect*, 89.

58 Campbell, *Verbal Aspect*, 96. He cites Luke 2:7; 24:30 and John 4:30 as examples of this usage.

propensity for too strongly correlating the imperfect with offline events. Again, the association is best understood as a natural consequence of the discourse role played by the tense-form rather than as a semantic quality. This is exemplified in the parable of the prodigal son in Example 4.

Example 4: Luke 15:14–16

> v. 14 δαπανήσαντος δὲ αὐτοῦ πάντα *ἐγένετο* λιμὸς ἰσχυρὰ κατὰ τὴν χώραν ἐκείνην, καὶ αὐτὸς *ἤρξατο* ὑστερεῖσθαι. (v. 15) καὶ πορευθεὶς *ἐκολλήθη* ἑνὶ τῶν πολιτῶν τῆς χώρας ἐκείνης, καὶ *ἔπεμψεν* αὐτὸν εἰς τοὺς ἀγροὺς αὐτοῦ βόσκειν χοίρους, (v. 16) καὶ ἐπεθύμει χορτασθῆναι ἐκ τῶν κερατίων ὧν ἤσθιον οἱ χοῖροι, καὶ οὐδεὶς ἐδίδου αὐτῷ.
>
> v. 14 Then after he had spent everything, a severe famine *took place* in that country, and *he be*gan to be in need. (v. 15) So he went and *worked for* one of the citizens of that country, who *sent* him to his fields to feed pigs. (v. 16) He was longing to eat the carob pods the pigs were eating, but no one gave him anything.

Most of the actions of the prodigal are encoded using aorists (indicated by italics), even the two verbs of being in v. 14 describing the famine and his need. The actions are viewed as an undifferentiated whole. The imperfects (indicated by bolding) in v. 16 describe ongoing states of affair rather than whole events. These states of affair set the stage for disclosing his decision to return home in v. 17. His decision was not made in a vacuum, but in response to his ongoing need and neglect.

The present tense-form functions as the proximate imperfective counterpart to the imperfect. Although it shares the same aspect, the present is associated with concurrent action by those using a tense-model,[59] and with deictic proximity by those advocating a tense-less model.[60] Decker describes present tense-forms as "often used for various facets of present time reference. This may be in reference to an activity presently in progress . . . or to a condition presently in existence."[61] Campbell provides a compelling case for the strong

[59] E.g., Robertson, *Grammar*, 864.

[60] Porter, *Verbal Aspect*, 207–8.

[61] Decker, *Temporal Deixis*, 99.

association of the present tense-form with direct discourse, ostensibly due to speech being closely related to the speaker in time and/or space.[62] The strength of this correlation provides the impetus for his proposed explanation of the HP representing "spill" from reported speech.

To summarize, the aorist tense-form is understood to be the default form for narrative proper, prototypically used for mainline events to advance the storyline. In contrast, the use of the imperfect marks the action as imperfective in nature, often providing offline description or states-of-affair, but not advancing the narrative. The imperfect has an almost exclusive association with past time reference, whereas the usage of the aorist is less consistent.[63] The present tense-form is differentiated from the aorist by virtue of its aspect, and from the imperfect tense-form by virtue of its tense/proximity.

Mismatch of historical present in narrative proper

The characteristic use of the aorist indicative for mainline events affects the reader's expectations. Using something other than the aorist implies that a meaning is associated with this choice. If a writer wants to portray a narrative action as imperfective, the preferred tense-form is the imperfect. It matches the context in terms of tense/proximity, but contrasts in terms of aspect. If this is the case, what is the relationship of the HP to this system of narrative tense-forms.

We have already noted that the HP is primarily associated with perfective actions rather than with imperfective ones. The present tense-form contrasts with both the aorist and imperfect. It is understood to mark some discourse feature that the aorist or imperfect forms would *not* mark. If the HP was simply intended to mark imperfectivity, there would be no distinction between it and the imperfect form.

There are no claims of prominence, tense-reduction, etc., associated with the use of the imperfect. Hence the HP represents a mismatch of aspect compared to the perfective aorist. The HP also stands out in narrative proper because of its tense/proximity. Mainline narrative events are prototypically past time or

---

62 Campbell, *Verbal Aspect*, 37–48, 50–52.

63 Decker, *Temporal Deixis*, 104–6.

remote. The use of a present or proximate form thus represents a mismatch of both tense and aspect in the discourse context. If the HP somehow lost its imperfectivity or proximity, the mismatch would be diminished.

I contend that the use of the present tense-form in narrative proper is *always* intended to mark the presence of a pragmatic feature of discourse, namely highlighting the presence of a natural discontinuity. Regardless of whether the verb is one of propulsion or speech, the usage is construed as intentionally marking this feature. Use of the present tense-form in narrative proper is a non-default usage of the form. In contrast, those advocating a tense-less description of the verb system have described this widespread use of the present as conclusive evidence for the *absence* of tense. Such a claim both misrepresents the usage and the temporal distribution of the forms.

Impact of HP usage as marked on temporal distribution of tense-forms

The aspect-only model of the verbal system claims that what has typically been expressed as a temporal distinction between the tense-forms is better understood as deictic in nature. Furthermore, this deictic distinction is primarily spatial in nature rather than temporal. Nevertheless, Porter acknowledges regarding the distinction between present and imperfect that "it is as this juncture alone that tense forms in Greek—the Imperfect and Pluperfect—approach time-based tense forms."[64] Decker too recognizes the fine distinction between deictics and tense: "Despite the nearly exclusive use of the imperfect form to express past time in Mark, this does not require that the semantic value of the imperfect be defined as that of past time."[65] After referring to the deictic explanations of Porter, Millhouse and Decker, Campbell states "the temporal reference of the imperfect indicative is difficult to disprove, since it is quite consistently past-referring."[66]

If a stronger case could be made for distributional consistency of the tense-forms, then the need to appeal to spatial rather than a temporal

---

[64] Ibid., 207

[65] Ibid., 106.

[66] Campbell, *Verbal Aspect*, 86.

deixis would diminish as well. Porter and Decker rely upon distributional information for support. They also rely heavily upon their portrayal of the HP as prototypical usage.

Statistics can be a double-edged sword, as their interpretation is heavily affected by presuppositions. As presuppositions change, so do the conclusions yielded by the data. I illustrate this by reconsidering Decker's data regarding the temporal distribution of the three primary indicative tense-forms found in narrative proper.[67] Table 1 contains Decker's figures from Mark that treat the HP as though it were representative use of the present.[68]

Table 1	**Aorist**	**Present**	**Imperfect**
Past	88.6 %	38.8%	97.5%
Present	1.6%	34.2%	Ø
Undefined	9%	6.6%	2.5%
Future	0.8%	20.4%	Ø

At first blush, only the imperfect appears to show a high degree of consistency, exceeding 95%.

Porter and Decker have compellingly shown that Greek is not primarily tense-based. If, however, Greek is a mixed tense/aspect system as the traditional grammarians and typologists have claimed, we should expect to find a strong temporal consistency in the distribution, with the possible exception of the aorist. As noted earlier, the aorist lacks a proximate perfective counterpart, and could thus be expected to manifest more variation. If the language is mixed tense/aspect, one could also expect aspectual considerations to trump temporal ones in certain contexts, leading to something less than 100% consistency.

Since the HP is marked both on the basis of its tense/proximity and aspect, the data cannot legitimately be included in the prototypical description; it must be treated separately. To do otherwise is to misrepresent the core meaning of the present tense-form. It would ignore the fact that the pragmatic effects associated with the HP are only claimed for the historical usage in narrative

67 The usage of the perfect indicative in Mark is too limited to be considered here.

68 Decker, *Temporal Deixis*, 95, 99, 104–6.

proper, not those found in non-narrative contexts like reported speech. In order to truly understand the core semantic meaning of the forms, pragmatically marked usage must be excluded from the overall count.

Another factor is the treatment of temporally undefined data. Due to its atemporal reference, the usage is likely motivated by the core aspectual meaning of the form, as suggested by Smythe[69] rather than by its temporal reference. If this use is part of the core meaning of the form, it should either be included with the core use of the form, or excluded altogether. With respect to the temporal discussion, undefined usage does not prove anything one way or the other.

Table 2 excludes the HP data from the present on the basis that they are not prototypical. In the first column under each tense-form, the "undefined" data is added to the prototypical on the basis that these tokens represent aspectual considerations overriding temporal ones. The second column removes the undefined altogether from consideration. Viewed in this way, they neither prove nor disprove temporal distribution since there is no temporal basis on which to judge.

Table 2	**Aorist**		**Present**		**Imperfect**
	With undefined	Without undefined	With undefined	Without undefined	With/ without undefined
Past	97.4%	97.6%	Ø	Ø	100%
Present	1.7%	1.6%	83.75%	89.2%	Ø
Future	0.08%	0.8%	16.25%	10.8%	Ø

This exercise illustrates that statistical conclusions greatly depend upon one's presuppositions. Changing the presuppositions impacts the conclusions drawn. Understanding the HP usage as non-prototypical significantly impacts the data. For a language which does not grammaticalize temporal information, distributional data approaching or exceeding the 90% seems implausible. The undefined data in each category is reasonably understood as

[69] H. W. Smythe, *A Greek Grammar for Colleges* (New York: American Book Company, 1920), 412.

aspectually-driven, where the aspectual considerations override the temporal ones. Reclassifying the HP and undefined references clarifies the distributional picture. Although one would hardly expect 100% consistency in the usage, Decker's modified data is approaching that in all but the present. We are now in a position to describe the verbal aspect of the present tense.

Aspect and tense of the present indicative

The only distributional anomaly remaining is the use of the present tense-form for both present and future reference. Gerhard Mussies offered a proposal in 1971 which is suggestive. Rather than classifying the present as communicating present time, he classified it instead as grammaticalizing *non-past* reference. Porter and Decker acknowledge this usage, but see it as further evidence for the disassociation between Greek tense and time. Comrie also describes the Ancient Greek verbal system as using a past/non-past distinction.[70] It is important to understand exactly what is meant by "non-past."

The present tense-form often functions as an unmarked form for non-past reference. Comrie states, "Past versus non-past is . . . the basic tense split in many European languages, with sub-divisions within non-past (especially future as opposed to present) being at best secondary."[71] In English this is exemplified in the ambiguity of the present progressive form. Consider the following example.

Example 1:

Unmarked reference	Explicit future reference
I am going to the store.	I will go to the store. I am going to the store on Friday.

The future reference of the present tense-form is also found in Finnish, German, English, Old English, Old French, Latin, and Ancient Greek. So in classifying the present as "non-past," Mussies and Comrie are describing the potentially ambiguous non-past reference of the present. If the writer wants

[70] Bernard Comrie, *Aspect: An Introduction to the Study of Verbal Aspect and Related Problems* (Cambridge: Cambridge University Press, 1976), 53, 97.

[71] Bernard Comrie, *Tense* (Cambridge: Cambridge University Press, 1985), 49.

to explicitly mark something as future, the future tense-form or a temporal deictic marker can be used to make the temporal reference explicit.

Lyons also maintains that the present is best construed as non-past, not on the basis of the progressive, but based on the timeless or gnomic usage. "Whereas the past tense does typically refer to 'before-now,' the non-past is not restricted to what is contemporaneous with the time of utterance: it is used for 'timeless' or 'eternal' statements (The sun rises in the east, etc.) and in many statements that refer to the future ('after-now')."[72] More recent studies could be produced discussing this phenomenon, but the work of Comrie and Lyons is cited because their ideas are part of the foundation Porter assembled to support his prominence-based theory of aspect.[73]

To deny the presence of tense in a language based on its ability to refer to more than one temporal sphere ignores the more widespread function and description of tense. It is not only the present tense-form that functions as non-past, but also the perfect. Mussies and Comrie both treat the perfect as non-past. Understood in this way, they form a very elegant system. In the same way that the past-referring imperfect functions in opposition to the present, the past-referring pluperfect functions in opposition to the perfect in the stative.

Table 3	**Imperfective**	**Stative**
Past	Imperfect	Pluperfect
Non-past	Present	Perfect
Future	Future	Future Perfect

The usage of the perfect in Mark is too limited for Decker's data to be useful, other than to note that it primarily has present reference, with a few future

[72] John Lyons, *Introduction to Theoretical Linguistics* (Cambridge: Cambridge University Press, 1968), 306.

[73] See T. Parsons, "The Progressive in English: Events, States and Processes," *Linguistics and Philosophy* 12/2 (1989): 213–41; M. Fludernik, "The Historical Present Tense in English Literature: an Oral Pattern and its Literary Adaptation," *Language and Literature* 17 (1992): 77–107; Nesselhauf, N., and U. Römer, "Lexical-Grammatical patterns in Spoken English," *International Journal of Corpus Linguistics* 12/3 (2007): 297–333.

references. The discussion of the perfect is intended to illustrate the heuristic value of such typological-tested concepts like "non-past." Far from disproving the presence of tense in Greek, the use of the present and perfect conform to expected usage for a mixed tense-aspect system. These factors leave the claim that Greek does not grammaticalize tense difficult to accept.

Conclusion

Porter has done a great service in advancing our understanding of the role of aspect in the Greek verbal system. His threefold classification of the tenses into perfective, imperfective and stative is consistent with the descriptions provided by Robertson and Winer regarding the relationship between the tenses and "kind of action" they express. The aspectual description is also consistent with the cross-linguistic discourse functions of aspect, notwithstanding Porter's resignification of background and foreground. Alongside these advances, however, setbacks were introduced by presupposing that Koine Greek does not grammaticalize tense. At the heart of this was the analysis of the historical present.

I have demonstrated that the HP is best construed as non-typical usage. The pragmatic effects associated with its use in narrative proper[74] are conspicuously missing in regard to reported speeches and epistolary literature, since the latter usage is construed as prototypical. Only those applying Porter's model make such claims, they are not found in earlier grammars or commentaries. The prominence that Porter assigns to the present by virtue of its inherent markedness is likely derivative of the marked rather than default usage. The pragmatic effects derived from the historical use of the present tense-form in Greek are also consistent with HP usage in older Indo-European languages, making Porter's claims of the present's global prominence all the more implausible.[75] Including the historical usage in the prototypical description of the present has confused the description of the verbal system rather than clarified it.

---

[74] To narrative proper I would add apocalyptic material, as it is often conveyed as first-person narrative, utilizing historical usage for pragmatic purposes just as in narrative. John's use of the HP in Revelation provides manifest examples of this.

[75] One must also ask whether Porter's proposal is typologically consistent with a tense-less language. See Comrie, *Tense*, 50–53.

Reclassifying the historical usage of the present has a dramatic effect on the distributional picture of the verbal system, bringing about the kind of distributional consistency one would expect from a mixed tense-aspect system. The only other missing element was the recognition that future reference of the present and perfect tenses represents not only acceptable, but possibly expected usage for an Indo-European language. The notion that these are non-past tenses predates the work of McKay or Porter, but was not given due consideration. In terms of the distributional data, my proposal explains more than 95% of the usage for the major tenses, based on the data available from Decker's work in Mark.

It is impossible to draw any definitive conclusions from this study on the basis of Mark's usage alone. As stated earlier, one would not expect 100% consistency in the temporal reference in a mixed tense/aspect language. The impact of tense and aspect on Greek usage is indeed complex, but it is not unknowable. The remarkable consistency exemplified by the distributional data calls for a wider analysis of the usage not only in the NT, but more broadly in Koine. Decker states, "an approach which attempts to minimize semantic exceptions and which simplifies grammatical explanation (without sacrificing precision) is to be preferred."[76] The outline of the verbal system sketched above provides an elegant description that reconciles traditional claims with typological expectations from modern linguistics. The idea that the core semantic meaning of the tense-forms are non-cancelable is also upheld. The marked usage of the HP cancels neither tense nor aspect. It is these very things that make it stand out as marked in the first place. Efforts to cancel either the tense or aspect resulted from failing to treat the marked usage as non-prototypical.

Porter suggests three criteria for evaluating a theory. It must be:[77]

1. Inclusive: able to explain the largest amount of the data,
2. Rational: able to analyze and evaluate the data,
3. Productive: able to provide a foundation for further work.

---

[76] Decker, *Temporal Deixis*, 39.

[77] Porter, *Verbal Aspect*, 5.

While the conclusions drawn here are necessarily limited due to the application to Mark, the simplicity with which 95% of the data can be explained suggests that it will indeed provide a productive base for further research. The limited goal of this paper was to demonstrate the potential payoff of a typologically grounded model in addressing the conundrum of the Greek verbal system. There is indeed a way forward in the debate, but it necessitates reformulating current explanations of the historical present.

Bibliography

Aland, Barbara et al. *The Greek New Testament*. 4th rev. ed. Stuttgart: Deutsche Bibelgesellschaft, 1993.

Battle, J. A. "The Present Indicative in New Testament Exegesis." ThD diss., Grace Theological Seminary, 1975.

Barnard, Jody A. "Is Verbal Aspect a Prominence Indicator?" *Filología Neotestamentaria* 19 (2006): 3–29.

Black, Stephanie L. "The Historic Present in Matthew: Beyond Speech Margins." Pages 120–39 in *Discourse Analysis and the New Testament: Approaches and Results*. Edited by Stanley E. Porter and Jeffrey T. Reed. Journal for the Study of the New Testament: Supplement Series 170. Sheffield: Sheffield Academic Press, 1999.

Blass, Friedrich. *Grammar of New Testament Greek*. Translated by Henry St. J. Thackeray. 2nd ed. New York: MacMillan, 1905.

Blass, Friedrich and Albert Debrunner. *A Greek Grammar of the New Testament and Other Early Christian Literature*. Translated and edited by Robert W. Funk. Chicago: University of Chicago Press, 1961.

Brinton, Laurel J. "Historical Discourse Analysis." Pages 138–60 in *The Handbook of Discourse Analysis*. Edited by Deborah Schiffrin, Deborah Tannen and Heidi Ehernberger Hamilton. Malden, Mass.: Blackwell, 2001.

Buth, Randall. "Mark's Use of the Historical Present." *Notes on Translation* 65 (1977): 7–13.

Campbell, Constantine R. *Verbal Aspect, the Indicative Mood, and Narrative: Soundings in the Greek of the New Testament*. New York: Peter Lang, 2007.

Comrie, Bernard. *Aspect: An Introduction to the Study of Verbal Aspect and Related Problems*. Cambridge: Cambridge University Press, 1976.

———. *Tense*. Cambridge: Cambridge University Press, 1985.

Decker, Rodney J. *Temporal Deixis of the Greek Verb in the Gospel of Mark with Reference to Verbal Aspect*. Studies in Biblical Greek 10. New York: Peter Lang, 2001.

Fanning, Buist M. *Verbal Aspect in New Testament Greek.* Oxford Theological Monographs. Oxford: Clarendon, 1990.

Fludernik, M. "The Historical Present Tense in English Literature: An Oral Pattern and its Literary Adaptation." *Language and Literature* 17 (1992): 77–107.

Foley, William A., and Robert D. Van Valin. *Functional Syntax and Universal Grammar.* Cambridge Studies in Linguistics 38. Cambridge: Cambridge University Press, 1984.

Funk, Robert Walter. *A Beginning-Intermediate Grammar of Hellenistic Greek.* Missoula, Mont.: Society of Biblical Literature, 1973.

Hopper, Paul J. "Aspect and Foregrounding in Discourse." Pages 213–41 in *Syntax and Semantics. Vol. 12 of Discourse and Syntax.* Edited by Talmy Givón. New York: Academic Press, 1979.

Kiparsky, P. "Tense and Mood in Indo-European Syntax." *Foundations of Language* 4/1 (February 1968): 30–57.

Lambrecht, Knud. *Information Structure and Sentence Form: Topic, Focus, and the Mental Representation of Discourse Referents.* Cambridge Studies in Linguistics. Cambridge: Cambridge University Press, 1994.

Levinsohn, Stephen H. *Discourse Features of New Testament Greek.* Dallas: Summer Institute of Linguistics, 2000.

Longacre, Robert E. "Discourse Peak as Zone of Turbulence." Pages 81–105 in *Beyond the Sentence: Discourse and Sentential Form.* Edited by Jessica R. Wirth. Ann Arbor: Karoma, 1985.

Lyons, John. *Introduction to Theoretical Linguistics.* Cambridge: Cambridge University Press, 1968.

McKay, K. L. *A New Syntax of the Verb in New Testament Greek.* Studies in Biblical Greek 5. New York: Peter Lang, 1994.

Nesselhauf, N., and U. Römer. "Lexical-Grammatical patterns in Spoken English." *International Journal of Corpus Linguistics* 12/3 (2007): 297–333.

Parsons, T. "The Progressive in English: Events, States and Processes." *Linguistics and Philosophy* 12/2 (1989): 213–41.

Porter, Stanley E. *Verbal Aspect in the Greek of the New Testament, with Reference to Tense and Mood.* Studies in Biblical Greek 1. New York: Peter Lang, 1989.

Reynolds, S. M. "The Zero Tense in Greek." *Westminster Theological Journal* 32 (1965): 68–72.

Robertson, A. T. *A Grammar of the Greek New Testament in the Light of Historical Research.* Nashville: Broadman, 1914.

Runge, Steven E. "Discourse-Functional Description of Participant Reference in Biblical Hebrew Narrative." DLitt diss., University of Stellenbosch 2007.

———. *Discourse Grammar of the Greek New Testament: A Practical Introduction for Teaching and Exegesis*. Bellingham, Wash.: Lexham Press, 2010.

———. "The Effect of Redundancy on Perceptions of Emphasis and Discontinuity." Paper presented at the Linguistics and Biblical Hebrew Section of the annual meeting of the Society of Biblical Literature, New Orleans, La., November 22, 2009.

Smythe, H. W. *A Greek Grammar for Colleges*. New York: American Book Company, 1920.

Sperber, Dan and Deirdre Wilson. *Relevance: Communication & Cognition. 2nd ed.* Oxford: Blackwell, 1995.

Turner, Nigel. *Syntax*. Vol. 3 of *A Grammar of New Testament Greek*. Edited by James Hope Moulton. Edinburgh: T. & T. Clark, 1963.

Wallace, Daniel B. *Greek Grammar Beyond the Basics: An Exegetical Syntax of the New Testament*. Grand Rapids: Zondervan, 1996.

Winer, Georg Benedikt. *A Treatise on the Grammar of New Testament Greek Regarded as a Sure Basis for New Testament Exegesis*. 3rd ed. Translated by W. F. Moulton. Edinburgh: T. & T. Clark, 1882.

Particles and Participles

A Helpful Partnership

Margaret G. Sim

Circumstantial participles[1]

In Koine Greek as in the earlier periods of the language circumstantial participles are famously underdetermined.[2] Although they have a "circumstantial" relationship to the rest of the sentence in which they occur there is no morphological marking on the participle itself to indicate this, in spite of the fact that many grammar books confidently identify temporal, causal, concessive, conditional or "final" participles. Of course such logical relations between participles and the main clause must be identified but this identification is possible only by inference from the context, there being no temporal or logical markings in the participle itself.[3] It is the case, however, that there are some particles which function in a way which guides a reader to a particular interpretation and it is with two of these particles that this paper is concerned. Although participles have almost disappeared in the modern language and signs of this were apparent from shortly after the time of the New Testament writing, in the New Testament itself participles are alive and

[1] Margaret G. Sim, "Underdeterminacy in Greek Participles," *Bible Translator* 55 (2004): 348–59, discusses the general approach to underdeterminacy in participles.

[2] See below for a discussion of underdeterminacy.

[3] One exception to this would be the future participle which was much more common in earlier Greek as well as in secular Koine and which carried the notion of "purpose."

well. Since this is the case any guide to identification of logical relationships is well worth considering.

In certain passages of the New Testament there are two particles—καίπερ and ὡς—which when accompanying a circumstantial participle are used to constrain the options available to the reader either by making the concessive relationship salient and in some cases exclusive or by prompting the reader to view the information following as being a thought or belief of the subject of the sentence. We shall see that the use of the former particle becomes necessary when another logical relationship—perhaps a causal one—between a participle and the main clause might be a more relevant reading but which the author wishes to block. This was also a feature of literary Greek and examples from Xenophon will be adduced as being parallel to several occurrences of καίπερ which are found in Hebrews.

The particle ὡς was widely used *inter alia* to introduce a comparison between nouns, phrases or clauses but when introducing a clause which contains a circumstantial participle it invites the reader to view the clause as expressing the thought or belief of the subject of the sentence. Again we have examples from both the New Testament and Xenophon to support this claim. It is also the case that the same particle almost always points to a conditional reading of the participle, but that is a weaker claim than the former and will be discussed below.

Relevance Theory as an aid to exegesis

A modern theory of cognition—Relevance Theory[4]—which considers the role of particles such as καίπερ and ὡς as constraints on relevance giving instructions to the reader may be more useful for examining the function of such particles than attempting to identify a discrete lexical meaning for each. It also encourages the exegete to ask what other relationship might be relevant to the reader but which the author has chosen to block in order to focus on the concessive or conditional force. Further the concept of *underdeterminacy*

[4] Dan Sperber and Deirdre Wilson were the authors of this cognitive approach which was outlined first in their *Relevance: Communication & Cognition* in 1986 and the second edition in 1995.

is crucial in understanding both the way in which circumstantial participles operated and the reason for their demise in the later language.

This paper does not attempt to discuss Relevance Theory in detail or examine its analytical base but attempts to use its principles and approach as a more solid basis for exegesis than the intuitive guessing which occasionally seems to be the rationale upon which particles are translated and participles classified. Relevance Theory is based upon the premise that humans communicate with one another in the belief what is said is "relevant" to the hearer. Both speaker and hearer (or writer and reader) engage with one another assuming that what is said has relevance. Of course they may be mistaken in this but it is manifestly obvious that we do not merely throw random words at one another. These words relate to situations, contexts in which both speaker and hearer share a common body of knowledge. Humans do not make remarks or even signs without an assumption that the hearer will increase her[5] knowledge by listening or will be able to reassess some information previously held. This does not necessarily or even usually involve a conscious process, but even a superficial consideration of why we communicate with one another involves the belief that the listener will have some interest in what we have to say. This might not necessarily be of benefit to the hearer, but it will be relevant to her.

In the physical world humans begin to infer as soon as they see another human, attributing intent and predicting actions, before verbal communication has begun.[6] Even in the text of the New Testament there are several examples of inferencing which began from viewing actions or even potential actions with no word spoken.[7] The example from the Gospel of John noted below is very clear. The onlookers were wrong, but the inferencing began from their viewing the actions of Mary.

This inferencing is necessary because we do not say all that we "mean." Language is *underdetermined.* This may operate at different levels—ambiguous words,

---

[5] The speaker or writer is referred to by the masculine personal pronoun and the hearer or reader by the feminine pronoun.

[6] Note Robyn Carston, *Thoughts and Utterances* (Oxford: Blackwell, 2002), for further elaboration of this point.

[7] Mark 3:1–2; John 11:31; Acts 21:27–29.

pronominal reference or missing constituents—but a hearer disambiguates, assigns identity to a referent or supplies a constituent by making the necessary inferences. The common polite exchange "Coffee?" regularly elicits the response "Yes, please" although neither speaker "says" all that is "meant." Participles in Greek are underdetermined in terms of logical relationship, but the principle of relevance is what guides the hearer to identify such a relationship. We infer a relationship of time, cause, condition or concession from the context of the whole utterance.

The burden of this study is the exploring of the use of the particular particles καίπερ and ὡς to constrain the interpretation of the participle which they accompany. It may seem from what has been said that relevance alone will provide the correct relationship, but if more than one relationship is possible, or if the speaker wishes to emphasize the content of the participial phrase as being contrary to expectation, or indicate conditionality or even pretense, then he will constrain it by adding καίπερ or ὡς. To demonstrate what has been stated I will consider the three verses in Hebrews in which a participle occurs with the particle καίπερ: 5:8, 7:12 and 12:17 but also we will examine other circumstantial participles which may most relevantly be interpreted as concessive but which occur without the addition of this particle, namely Heb 3:16; 5:12; 7:28; 11:4, 39. Examples from Xenophon's *Hellenica* will be examined also.

With reference to the particle ὡς when used with a circumstantial participle we will consider Acts 3:12; 28:19; 1 Cor 7:29; and 2 Cor 5:20. Examples from Xenophon's *Anabasis* will also be presented.

Examples of καίπερ *as a constraint on relevance*

This particle was more common in earlier Greek, occurring in Homer as two separate morphemes: καί περ.[8] It gives a clear idea of concession when used with a participle but is found only five times in the New Testament, three of these being in Hebrews. After Homer it seems to co-occur with participles

[8] John D. Denniston, *The Greek Particles* (Indianapolis, IN: Hackett Publishing, 1996), 486-87.

while the particle καίτοι occurs with indicative verbs.[9] Now we have stated already that there are many participles in the New Testament which have concession as the most relevant relationship, but the point at issue is whether or not the addition of this particle guides the reader to a concessive relationship when its omission might allow another relationship to be more relevant. That is why the following examples from Hebrews have been chosen.

Hebrews 5:8

> καίπερ ὢν υἱός, ἔμαθεν ἀφ' ὧν ἔπαθεν τὴν ὑπακοήν
> Although being a son, he learned obedience from the things which he suffered

Now the issue here is that a concessive relationship indicates a fact which is contrary to expectation, but human experience would see the relationship as causal: "because he was a son he learned obedience."[10] This expectation has led many of the older commentators to look more carefully at the concept of "son" and consider that this meant "Son," that is "Son of God" rather than a comment on father/son relationships in human terms. "It is the most natural thing in the world for a son to learn obedience by suffering; indeed our author makes this very point in 12:5ff."[11]

Westcott comments: "In one sense it is true that the idea of Sonship suggests that of obedience; but the nature of Christ's Sonship at first sight seems to exclude the thought that He should learn obedience through suffering."[12] Ellingworth points out that in this epistle the Sonship of Christ is not related to earth but to an eternal or heavenly state, which probably means that this verse "implies a contrast between this eternal status on the one hand, and the learning process of Christ's earthly life on the other."[13]

---

[9] It does occur with a participle in Hebrews 4:3.
[10] In modern British society this assumption would be questioned!
[11] F. F. Bruce, *The Epistle to the Hebrews* (NICNT; Grand Rapids: Eerdmens, 1990), 103.
[12] B. F. Westcott, *Epistle to the Hebrews* (Grand Rapids: Eerdmans, 1980 reprint), 128.
[13] Paul Ellingworth, *The Epistle to the Hebrews* (NIGTC; Grand Rapids: Eerdmans, 1993), 293.

In pagan literature also the play on the verbs ἔμαθεν and ἔπαθεν was used to indicate the connection between learning and suffering in general.[14] Moffatt points out, apropos of quotations from Aeschylus, Pindar and Philo which refer to a play on such verbs, that in these authors the subjects referred to were people who were required to suffer in order to learn, in other words they were obdurate offenders.[15] This would have been part of the cognitive environment or encyclopedic knowledge of the hearers/readers of these works at that time.

These comments all relate to the fact of the participle's being marked by καίπερ as concessive, contrary to expectation. It may be deduced from this that had the particle καίπερ not been present another logical relationship would have been more relevant, namely that of cause "because he was a son." Although this could be seen as possible, the writer's focus on the particular nature of "sonship" in question would have been weakened, and the addition of the particle constrains the concessive force of the participle.

Hebrews 7:5

> καὶ οἱ μὲν ἐκ τῶν υἱῶν Λευὶ τὴν ἱερατείαν λαμβάνοντες ἐντολὴν ἔχουσιν ἀποδεκατοῦν τὸν λαὸν κατὰ τὸν νόμον, τοῦτ᾽ ἔστιν τοὺς ἀδελφοὺς αὐτῶν, καίπερ ἐξεληλυθότας ἐκ τῆς ὀσφύος Ἀβραάμ·
>
> Those from the sons of Levi who received the priesthood have a command to receive the people's tithes according to the law, that is their brothers' (tithe) although they are descended (having come from the loins of) Abraham.

Moffatt sees this phrase as emphasizing the status of the Levites: even their "brothers" paid tithes to them;[16] but Ellingworth relates this more generally to the status of the sons of Abraham as a group: "The cumulative effect of the last part of the verse is to emphasize the dignity of the Israelites as descendants

---

[14] Bruce, *Hebrews*, 103.

[15] James Moffatt, *Epistle to the Hebrews* (Edinburgh: T. & T. Clark, 1963 reprint), 67.

[16] Ibid., 94–95.

of Abraham and members of God's chosen people . . . and the authority of the Levitical priests over them."[17]

The effect of the concessive clause is to highlight the common ancestry of those receiving the tithe and those paying it, while acknowledging that this is contrary to expectation: the greater receives tithes from the lesser. "We might have expected naturally that the right of tithing (like the privilege of blessing) would have been exercised only by one superior by birth."[18] The phrase "although they had come from Abraham" also denies the latter expectation, and sets the scene for the exegesis which follows.

Some of this argument is derived from the encyclopedic knowledge which would be accessed by the first readers, namely that in the ancient world it was assumed that a proportion of the spoils of war would be dedicated to a deity or rather the priest who operated on his behalf.[19] If Abraham gave a tenth of the spoil to Melchizedek then he was acknowledging a higher authority. It would follow then that even Abraham's descendants would have to acknowledge such authority.

Hebrews 12:17

> μετανοίας γὰρ τόπον οὐχ εὗρεν καίπερ μετὰ δακρύων ἐκζητήσας αὐτήν.
> For he found no place of repentance, although he sought it with tears.

The context in Genesis focuses on the blessing which Esau bitterly regretted losing, but the context here in this epistle is more concerned with the impossibility of repentance for those who have committed apostasy. Bruce and Westcott take αὐτήν to refer to the blessing (as in Genesis) but Ellingworth and Moffatt see it as related to repentance since that is the point the author is making. "Repentance," however, is being used not so much as acknowledgement of wrong and turning from it as regret for past behavior and a futile desire to revisit that scene with the possibility of changing it.

[17] Ellingworth, *Hebrews*, 364.

[18] Westcott, *Hebrews*, 176–77.

[19] Bruce, *Hebrews*, 140.

The logic of this sentence seems to preclude any interpretation other than a concessive one which may lead to the question as to why the particle καίπερ was necessary. I suggest, however, that the particle here strengthens the point being made by the author that his hearers should avoid apostasy and bad behavior since Esau, acting on impulse, found no way of retracing his steps or changing his past behavior when the result of his action became clear. It is only Esau's selling of his birthright which is the focus; no mention is made of Jacob's role in deceiving Isaac into giving him the blessing of the firstborn. Indeed there is an inference that if Esau had not given away his birthright he would not have "missed" the blessing.[20] The message is clear in v. 25: See that you do not refuse him who is speaking. Tears later will not change anything. Montefiore comments: "Esau stands as a frightening example of the irreversible results of immoral or irreligious conduct on the part of the elect."[21] This was exactly the point which the writer wanted to make.

Other participles in Hebrews with concessive force

We have considered those examples of the use of the particle καίπερ to constrain the logical relationship which the participle brings to the sentence, but there are many examples in the NT of participles which are concessive and yet which lack such a constraining particle. Since καίπερ only occurs five times in the NT with three of these examples being in Hebrews and the others in 1 Peter and Philippians, it will be obvious that this is so.[22] I have noted several of these in the same book to illustrate the optional nature of the role of καίπερ. These are now delineated below.

Hebrews 3:16

> τίνες γὰρ ἀκούσαντες παρεπίκραναν;
> For who, although they heard, rebelled?

---

[20] In terms of Relevance Theory this would be called a "weak implicature."

[21] Hugh Montefiore, *Epistle to the Hebrews* (Peabody, Mass.: Hendrickson, 1987), 226.

[22] Matt 7:11; Luke 11:13; John 12: 37 are clear examples.

Ellingworth supports a concessive reading as do many English translations (NLT as well as RSV, ESV which put "yet" with the main verb). The logic of the sentence requires this, making a particle such as καίπερ unnecessary. The whole burden of the preceding and following sections is the plea to the readers not to be obdurate as were the Israelites of an earlier generation. The contrast between "hearing" and "hardening the heart" is very prominent. The expectation was that those who heard would obey, but the fact was contrary to expectation: although they heard, they disobeyed.

Hebrews 5:12

> καὶ γὰρ ὀφείλοντες εἶναι διδάσκαλοι διὰ τὸν χρόνον, πάλιν χρείαν ἔχετε τοῦ διδάσκειν ὑμᾶς
> For although you ought to be teachers by this time (because of the time), you need again someone to teach you

The contrast between what was expected and what was the actual situation is the reason for the concessive relationship being the most relevant in this context. (RSV, ESV, GNB add "yet" in the main clause and NLT adds "instead.") There is no need for a constraining particle. The use of ὀφείλοντες may also cause the reader to anticipate a situation that should be realized but ultimately is not.

Hebrews 7:28

> ὁ νόμος γὰρ ἀνθρώπους καθίστησιν ἀρχιερεῖς ἔχοντας ἀσθένειαν, ὁ λόγος δὲ τῆς ὁρκωμοσίας τῆς μετὰ τὸν νόμον υἱὸν εἰς τὸν αἰῶνα τετελειωμένον.
> For the law appoints men as priests although they have weaknesses/having weaknesses, but the word of the oath (coming) after the law appoints a son who has been made perfect for ever.

This is potentially a concessive participle! I do not insist on it, but to me it seems a very relevant interpretation! I cannot adduce any evidence from English translations but it does seem that by ignoring the contrast here the focus on the perfect nature of Christ's priesthood may be lost and that is a crucial part of the argument.

Hebrews 11:4

> καὶ δι᾽ αὐτῆς ἀποθανὼν ἔτι λαλεῖ.
> and through it (his faith) although he is dead he still speaks

In this case it may be said that although καίπερ is not present, ἔτι in the main clause acts as a constraint also. I maintain, however, that the function of ἔτι is to make prominent the contrast between the past and the present: someone who died long ago is still "speaking" metaphorically to the readers of this letter. The translations are united in giving the participle ἀποθανὼν concessive force here.

Hebrews 11:39

> Καὶ οὗτοι πάντες μαρτυρηθέντες διὰ τῆς πίστεως οὐκ ἐκομίσαντο τὴν ἐπαγγελίαν,
> And all these although well attested through (their) faith did not receive the promise

The only commentator to concede concession here is Zuntz,[23] but the translations either add "though" to the participial clause or "yet" to the main clause. The expectation following from the fact of someone being attested through faith is that that person will receive what was promised to those who had faith. There is no other logical relationship possible and so there is no need for the constraining particle καίπερ.

Examples from Xenophon

Hellenica 5.1.13

> ἐκ δὲ τούτου οἱ μὲν Ἀθηναῖοι, ὥσπερ ἐν εἰρήνῃ, ἔπλεον τὴν θάλατταν.
> οὐδὲ γὰρ τῷ Ἐτεονίκῳ ἤθελον οἱ ναῦται καίπερ ἀναγκάζοντι ἐμβάλλειν,
> ἐπεὶ μισθὸν οὐκ ἐδίδου.

[23] Bruce, *Hebrews*, 343.

> From this point the Athenians used to sail the sea as in peacetime. For the (Lacedaemonian) sailors were not willing to sail out for Eteonicus, although he was compelling/trying to compel them since he did not give them pay.

Here it seems that καίπερ constrains the participle to a concessive relationship, it being just possible that Eteonicus by trying to force the issue was then the cause of the sailors' refusal. The subsequent paragraph reinforces this since the same sailors later were willing to sail out with another general with no prospect of reward. The use of καίπερ gives the information which was counter to expectation: in spite of an attempt at compulsion Eteonicus was not successful, while the clause introduced by ἐπεί marks a reason for the sailors' refusal rather than the compulsion.

Hellenica 5.4.24

> οἱ δ' ἔφοροι ἀνεκάλεσάν τε τὸν Σφοδρίαν καὶ ὑπῆγον θανάτου. ἐκεῖνος μέντοι φοβούμενος οὐχ ὑπήκουσεν· ὅμως δὲ καίπερ οὐχ ὑπακούων εἰς τὴν κρίσιν ἀπέφυγε.
>
> But the Ephors called Sphodrias back and impeached him on a capital charge. He, however, since he was afraid did not obey. But nevertheless although he did not obey the charge he was acquitted.

In this example the combination of ὅμως as well as καίπερ makes the concessive force very clear. His acquittal was completely contrary to expectation. This sets the scene for the subsequent narrative which explains why this perversion of justice took place. It is just possible that a reader might infer that he was acquitted because he didn't show up (that is if there were no particle to constrain the meaning) but the wider context makes the concessive force clear and the particle guides her in the right direction.

Examples of ὡς as a constraining particle

As older grammarians have shown, care has to be exercised in the interpretation of this particle. Its use with indicative verbs is straightforward but when occurring with a participle it may give the impression of introducing pretense. Of course in many cases it will be seen to do just this thing, but this is derivable only from the context and it is safer to read it as giving procedural instructions to the reader to expect a "thought or assertion of the subject of the main verb."[24] Its use does seem to distance the writer from the thought but not always to disown it. It may be comparable in some ways to the English "apparently" or "it seems" which is similarly neutral and does not commit the writer to belief or disbelief. An example from Luke's account of the parable of the shrewd manager illustrates this well:

Luke 16:1

> καὶ οὗτος διεβλήθη αὐτῷ ὡς διασκορπίζων τὰ ὑπάρχοντα αὐτοῦ.
>
> and he was charged with (as) wasting his (the rich man's) assets.

In this example the charge is introduced by ὡς thus leaving open the question as to whether or not the charge was true.[25] The use of the same particle below presents the positive and negative, false and true accusations of the Corinthians:[26]

Second Corinthians 6:8–10

> ὡς πλάνοι καὶ ἀληθεῖς, ὡς ἀγνοούμενοι καὶ ἐπιγινωσκόμενοι, ὡς ἀποθνῄσκοντες καὶ ἰδοὺ ζῶμεν, ὡς παιδευόμενοι καὶ μὴ θανατούμενοι, ὡς λυπούμενοι ἀεὶ δὲ χαίροντες, ὡς πτωχοὶ πολλοὺς δὲ πλουτίζοντες, ὡς μηδὲν ἔχοντες καὶ πάντα κατέχοντες.
>
> (We are presented as) deceivers and truthful, unknown and well recognized, dying/about to die and look still living, as

---

[24] W. W. Goodwin *Syntax of the Moods and Tenses of the Greek Verb* (London: MacMillan, 1889, reissued 1965), 342.

[25] Luke's presentation of Pilate as introducing the leaders' charge against Jesus as ὡς ἀποστρέφοντα τὸν λαόν (23:14) leaves open the question of whether or not Pilate accepted that, while the following clause indicates that in fact he had found no basis for that charge.

[26] I appreciate that there are different interpretations of these highly condensed clauses, but the particle does seem to introduce the thoughts or accusations of some of the recipients of the letter.

> being disciplined and not being killed, as grieving and always rejoicing, as poor but enriching many, as having nothing and possessing everything.

The presentation of two contrasting opinions following the particle is an excellent illustration of the flexibility of the participle in Greek. Translations and commentators treat these contrasts in two main ways: as contrasting views held among the Corinthians or as actual aspects of Paul's life as an apostle. The difficulty with the latter view of course is the initial phrase. We might identify Paul as being unrecognized, poor, disciplined and having nothing, but we would balk at considering him deceitful! Thrall who supports the view of these participles as actually descriptive sees this first phrase as "transitional" noting that these are adjectives and not participles.[27] The omission of a main verb to guide the interpretation is of course the issue, but if we read the particle as introducing opinions then it seems to lead us to seeing these participles as indicating the opinions of the recipients of the letter without denying that the second participle may present the reality of the varied circumstances of Paul's life.

The majority of examples of ὡς when occurring with participles indicate that a conditional relationship is the most relevant one. The writer of Luke-Acts is by far the most prolific user of this particle as a temporal conjunction with an indicative verb.[28] In conjunction with a participle, the Pauline correspondence and Luke-Acts have many examples: sixteen times[29] in the former, eight times in the latter. The context as always is the deciding factor, but this particle does seem to nudge the reader in this direction.[30] We shall consider the examples from Acts 3:12; 28:19; 1 Cor 7:29; and 2 Cor 5:20.

---

27 M. E. Thrall, *2 Corinthians 1–7* (2nd ed.; London: T. & T. Clark, 2004), 464.

28 This of course is the most common use of this particle.

29 This count takes multiple occurrences together such as in 1 Cor 7:29–31 as one.

30 In speaking of the earlier language Goodwin, *Moods and Tenses*, 343, aptly comments: "The question whether the clause with ὡς gives the real or the pretended opinion of the leading subject is also determined (if at all) by the context."

Acts 3:12

> ἰδὼν δὲ ὁ Πέτρος ἀπεκρίνατο πρὸς τὸν λαόν· ἄνδρες Ἰσραηλῖται, τί θαυμάζετε ἐπὶ τούτῳ ἢ ἡμῖν τί ἀτενίζετε ὡς ἰδίᾳ δυνάμει ἢ εὐσεβείᾳ πεποιηκόσιν τοῦ περιπατεῖν αὐτόν;
> Seeing (this) Peter responded to the people, "Men of Israel, why are you amazed at this or why do you stare at us *as if by (our) power or piety we had made this man walk*?"

Here the inclusion of the particle suggests a conditional interpretation of the participle πεποιηκόσιν which is reinforced several verses later by the assertion that it was faith in the "author of life" which healed the man, that is: it was not Peter and John. Although this particle may also introduce causal or temporal relationships it is hard to find an unequivocal interpretation of such in NT texts.[31]

Acts 28:19

> ἀντιλεγόντων δὲ τῶν Ἰουδαίων ἠναγκάσθην ἐπικαλέσασθαι Καίσαρα οὐχ ὡς τοῦ ἔθνους μου ἔχων τι κατηγορεῖν.
> But when the Jews spoke against (this) I was compelled to appeal to Caesar, not as if I had anything of which to accuse my nation.

This is a more complicated use of ὡς. There seems to be a clause missing: "not as if . . . but in order that" and in fact the Western text includes just such a clause.[32] The clause is distancing Paul from the (perhaps voiced) belief that his appeal to Caesar was a direct complaint against the Jews. ὡς introduces the representation of the belief but the preceding negative denies that this was Paul's motive in his appeal. In speaking to the Jews in Rome he had to make clear that from his perspective his relationship with his own people was still strong.

---

[31] A. T. Robertson, *A Grammar of the Greek New Testament in the Light of Historical Research* (4th ed.; Nashville: Broadman, 1934), 1128, suggests 1 Cor 7:25 but I do not find this the most relevant reading.

[32] C. P. Barrett, *Acts* (2nd ed.; London: T. & T. Clark, 2002), 1239, also sees this text as "sharpening the narrative." The Western text reads: αλλ ινα λυτρωσωμαι την ψυχαν μου εκ θανατου.

The verses below include five examples of clauses introduced by ὡς which bear a conditional relationship to the sentence as a whole, and the clause which precedes each one in particular.

First Corinthians 7:29–31

> τὸ λοιπόν, ἵνα καὶ οἱ ἔχοντες γυναῖκας ὡς μὴ ἔχοντες ὦσιν, καὶ οἱ κλαίοντες ὡς μὴ κλαίοντες καὶ οἱ χαίροντες ὡς μὴ χαίροντες καὶ οἱ ἀγοράζοντες ὡς μὴ κατέχοντες, καὶ οἱ χρώμενοι τὸν κόσμον ὡς μὴ καταχρώμενοι·
> For the rest/in summary those who have wives should be as those who do not have wives, those who weep (should be) as those who don't weep, those who rejoice as those who do not rejoice and those who trade as those who hold back and those who have dealings with the world as those who do not make use (of it).

Again the conditional force is identified through the context and not because of the particle per se but the presence of the particle does give the reader a clue to the relationship of the clause it accompanies to the one preceding. Since it is also widely used in the NT as introducing a comparison (when occurring with a main verb, a phrase or even a noun alone) it fulfils two functions here.

Second Corinthians 5:20

> ὑπὲρ Χριστοῦ οὖν πρεσβεύομεν ὡς τοῦ θεοῦ παρακαλοῦντος δι᾽ ἡμῶν·
> So we are ambassadors on behalf of Christ *as if* God is urging through us.

The clause is a genitive absolute with the following sentence expanding what was being urged: "be reconciled to God." Thrall[33] translates the particle here as "with the conviction that" taking the clause as a representation of Paul's belief. While agreeing that the ὡς clause is a representation of Paul's belief, my own opinion is that the conditional force is still relevant here since it reinforces

[33] Thrall, *2 Corinthians*, 437, and F. Blass and A. Debrunner, *A Greek Grammar of the New Testament* (trans. and ed. Robert W. Funk; Chicago: University of Chicago Press, 1961) §425 (p. 3).

the metaphor. Consider also the prominent position of ὑπὲρ Χριστοῦ in both sentences, which enhances the metaphor.

Xenophon's Anabasis

Of course, in addition to the New Testament usage, the classical authors regularly used ὡς with participles. I have selected a few of many from Xenophon's *Anabasis*. These show the particle as introducing a clause which contains a pretext, that is, a reason presented which both the reader and the author know to be untrue.

Anabasis 1.1.6

> ὡς ἐπιβουλεύοντος Τισσαφέρνους ταῖς πόλεσι.
> as if Tissaphernes was plotting against the cities

The whole context here (not given!) was that Cyrus had decided to raise an army against his brother but was doing this in secret or rather giving a false reason for raising troops in the Peloponnese.

Anabasis 1.1.11

> Πρόξενον δὲ τὸν Βοιώτιον ξένον ὄντα ἐκέλευσε λαβόντα ἄνδρας ὅτι πλείστους παραγενέσθαι, ὡς ἐς Πισίδας βουλόμενος στρατεύεσθαι, ὡς πράγματα παρεχόντων τῶν Πισιδῶν τῇ ἑαυτοῦ χώρᾳ.
> He (Cyrus) ordered Proxenos the Boetian, his friend by treaty, to come to him taking as many men as possible, *as if* he wished to fight against the Pisidians, *as if* they were undertaking enterprises/causing trouble in his country.

In this example Cyrus gives two pretexts for the raising of troops, the context being the same as the previous example in which the real reason for the amassing of an army could not be stated openly. Brownson in the Loeb translation has "saying that" and "as he said" for the two occurrences of ὡς.[34]

---

[34] Xenophon, *Anabasis, Books 1–3* (trans. Carleton Brownson; LCL; London: Heinemann, 1932).

This translation brings out the implicit statements which must have been articulated: I want to fight the Pisidians; the Pisidians are causing trouble in my country. Neither of these of course was true and the use of ὡς guides the reader to this interpretation.

In all these examples the particle ὡς occurs with a participle and guides the reader to interpret the following clause as giving the thought or assertion of the subject but with the idea that this may not be true. The context then confirms this reading of the participle as conditional.

Development and demise of circumstantial participles

Participles in Greek were very much a literary construction and, even by the fourth century C.E., were disappearing in the written language in favor of subordinate clauses. Jannaris[35] ascribes the demise to "vagueness" and "morphological inconvenience," referring to the need to use the context to identify the relationship and the complicated morphological form which identified gender, number and tense. We do however see considerable use of participles in the New Testament exhibiting a range of implicit (or underdetermined) logical relationships. But in addition to the use of participles with concessive force we can also note the use of subordinate clauses introduced by ἐι καί (x10) and the two uses of καίτοι as well as ὅμως and μέντοι. The latter can be seen in Heb 6:9, an interesting occurrence given that this writer uses καίπερ three times with a participle even though there are only two other occurrences in the New Testament corpus. Even καίπερ (after Homer) seems to be used only with participles and as one unit in contrast to the Homeric καί . . . περ.[36]

Summary

This paper has been concerned with two particular "constraining" particles: καίπερ and ὡς. I have claimed that καίπερ gives the reader instructions to read the following participle as having a concessive relationship to the

[35] A. N. Jannaris, *An Historical Greek Grammar* (London: MacMillan, 1897), 504–5.

[36] Denniston, *Particles*, 486–87.

rest of the sentence. If it is omitted then any concessive relationship will be deduced from the context alone. It also strengthens a concessive reading even in those cases in which there is no serious alternative, as in the examples from Xenophon. The particle ὡς is much more widely used both as introducing a temporal clause when it occurs with an indicative verb and as an indicator of comparison when used with nouns, adjectives or phrases. The particular use of ὡς, which is the focus of this paper, is as a constraint on the interpretation of the participle which it introduces. Apart from references by earlier grammarians such as Robertson and Blass, its use with participles has not been in focus. I have claimed that it presents the thought or assertion of the subject but frequently it indicates a potential situation which may or may not be true. Thus, the common translation is "as if." The context is the deciding factor but the particle acts as a constraint, giving the reader what Relevance Theory calls "procedural instructions" for interpretation. These particles have been chosen to highlight the usefulness of Relevance Theory as an aid to exegesis and the recovery of the cognitive environment of those to whom the text was first addressed.

Bibliography

Barrett, C. P. *Acts, 2nd ed.* London: T. & T. Clark, 2002.

Blass, F. and A. Debrunner. *A Greek Grammar of the New Testament. Translated and edited by Robert W. Funk.* Chicago: University of Chicago Press, 1961.

Bruce, F. F. *The Epistle to the Hebrews.* New International Commentary on the New Testament. Grand Rapids: Eerdmans, 1990.

Carston, Robyn. *Thoughts and Utterances.* Oxford: Blackwell, 2002.

Denniston, J. D. *The Greek Particles.* 2nd ed. Oxford: Oxford University Press, 1950.

Ellingworth, Paul. *The Epistle to the Hebrews: A Commentary on the Greek Text.* New International Greek Testament Commentary. Grand Rapids: Eerdmans, 1993.

Goodwin, W. W. *Syntax of the Moods and Tenses of the Greek Verb.* 7th ed. London: MacMillan, 1879.

Jannaris, A. N. *An Historical Greek Grammar.* London: MacMillan, 1897.

Moffatt, James. *A Critical and Exegetical Commentary on the Epistle to the Hebrews.* Edinburgh: T. & T. Clark, 1963 reprint.

Montefiore, Hugh. *Epistle to the Hebrews.* Peabody, Mass.: Hendrickson, 1987.

Robertson, A. T. *A Grammar of the Greek New Testament in the Light of Historical Research 4th ed.* Nashville: Broadman, 1934.

Sim, M. G. "Underdeterminacy in Greek Participles." *Bible Translator* 55 (2004): 348–59.

Sperber, Dan and Deirdre Wilson. *Relevance: Communication & Cognition. 2nd ed.* Oxford: Blackwell, 1995.

Thrall, M. E. *2 Corinthians 1–7: A Critical and Exegetical Commentary on the Second Epistle to the Corinthians.* International Critical Commentary Series. 2nd ed. London: T. & T. Clark, 2004.

Westcott, Brooke Foss. *The Epistle to the Hebrews: The Greek Text with Notes and Essays.* Grand Rapids: Eerdmans, 1980 reprint.

Xenophon. *Anabasis, Books 1–3.* Translated by Carleton Brownson. Loeb Classical Library. London: Heinemann, 1932.

Xenophon. *Hellenica.* Translated by Carleton Brownson. Loeb Classical Library. London: Heinemann, 1918.

Pragmatics

The Semantic Effect of Floating Quantifiers in New Testament Greek

Lindsay J. Whaley

All varieties of ancient Greek are characterized by flexibility in the ordering of words. There are clear limits to this flexibility (e.g., definite articles always precede the noun that they modify), and certain arrangements of constituents are far more common than others (e.g., subjects are far more likely to precede direct objects than the reverse order). Even so, the range of permutations is impressive, and it includes the possibility of discontinuous constituents:

(1) ὅταν πειρασμοῖς περιπέσητε ποικίλοις
"whenever you face trials of many kinds" (Jas 1:2 NIV)

The clause in (1), where the verb intervenes between the noun πειρασμοῖς "trials" and its modifier ποικίλοις "many kinds," exemplifies discontinuity, or hyperbaton as it has been called traditionally. Given the frequency of hyperbaton in ancient Greek texts, it is surprising that relatively little work has appeared that explores the motivations for the use of discontinuous constituents by Greek authors.[1] In this paper, I examine one type of hyperbaton, the discontinuity between a quantifier and the noun it quantifies,

[1] For the most comprehensive treatment, see A. M. Devine and Laurence D. Stephens, *Discontinuous Syntax: Hyperbaton in Greek* (Oxford: Oxford University Press, 2000). More limited discussions can be found in J. de Vries, "Untersuchungen über die Sperrung von Substantiv und Attribut in der Sprache der attischen Redner" (PhD diss., Göttingen, 1938); K. J. Dover, *Greek Word Order* (Cambridge: Cambridge University Press, 1960); Stephen H. Levinsohn, *Discourse Features of New Testament Greek* (Dallas: Summer Institute of Linguistics, 1992); Stéphanie J. Bakker, *The Noun Phrase in Ancient Greek* (Leiden: Brill, 2009).

in an effort to describe the syntactic properties of the construction and the pragmatic effect that the discontinuity produces.

(2) πρῶτον μὲν τοῖς ἱππεῦσιν ἅπαν κυκλοῦται τὸ χωρίον
"First off, he surrounded the whole place with his calvary."
(*J.W.* 7.211)

As can be seen from the example in (2), the quantifier ἅπαν "all," which modifies the object noun phrase τὸ χωρίον "the region," does not appear contiguous to that phrase. Rather, the verb of the clause intervenes between the quantifier and the quantified noun phrase. Very similar constructions arise in a number of languages (e.g., English, Hebrew, Samoan, and Mohawk, to name just a few), where they are commonly referred to as "Quantifier Float." For convenience I will adopt this terminology for Hellenistic Greek as well, though by doing so I am not making a claim that the constructional is necessarily homologous across languages.

In this paper, I propose that Quantifier Float serves to highlight the information that the quantifier conveys in particular ways. In the first section, I provide a general overview of quantifiers in Hellenistic Greek. I then discuss the properties of Quantifier Float in Greek, making some observations about similarities and differences that the construction has with analogues in other languages. Finally, I will comment on the likely programmatic motivations for its use.

Though the analysis offered in this paper might very well extend to ancient Greek more broadly, I restrict attention to Koiné Greek texts written in the first two centuries C.E. A change in word order tendencies from Homeric Greek to Hellenistic Greek has been well documented.[2] To my knowledge, no one has yet examined how such changes may have impacted information packaging in clause structure, but it would not be surprising if there were concomitant changes in how word order was employed for emphasis and focus. Therefore, a more restrictive timeframe is warranted pending further research into these issues. It should be noted, however, that the conclusions

[2] For example, see Ann Taylor, "The Change from SOV to SVO in Ancient Greek," *Language Variation and Change* 6 (1994): 1–37.

that I reach about the semantics of quantifier float are compatible with claims made for earlier varieties of Greek.

Quantifiers in Hellenistic Greek

In the most general of terms, quantifiers are nominal modifiers that indicate quantity, contrasts in quantity, or scope.[3] A roster of such elements in Hellenistic Greek is furnished in Table 1.

INTERNAL QUANTIFIERS		EXTERNAL QUANTIFIERS	
ἄλλος	other	ἀμφότεροι	both
ἕκαστος	each	ἅπας	all, every
ἕτερος	other, the other	μόνος	only
ὀλίγος	few, little	ὅλος	whole
οὐδείς	none, no one	πᾶς	all, every
πολύς	many		
τις	a, certain		
εἷς, δύο	one, two, . . .		

Table 1. Hellenistic Greek Quantifiers[4]

[3] Much work on quantification in natural language employs a broader notion of quantifier which also includes certain verb modifiers (such as auxiliary verbs and adverbs), as well as some affixes. The justification for a more inclusive category rests on the fact that the logico-semantic properties of all of these grammatical elements bear some resemblance. Even so, a distinction is typically made between D-quantifiers (or, determiner quantifiers), which quantify entities, and A-quantifiers, which quantify events. My use of the term "quantifier" in this chapter is equivalent to the notion "D-quantifier."

[4] Other words such as ἄμφω "both," ἄττα "certain ones," δεῖνα "such a one," and σύμπας "altogether" are also properly listed as quantifiers in Classical Greek. However, due to their infrequency in Hellenistic Greek texts, I do not include them in the discussion here. The intensive pronoun αὐτός, which can be used in attributive position meaning "same," shares many properties with external quantifiers. I have not included it in the discussion of this chapter because it does not obviously carry quantificational semantics.

This particular group of words is not treated as a unified category in standard Greek reference works because the words do not obviously share any single morphological or syntactic property. Instead, individual members of the list above have been variously classified as indefinite pronouns, interrogative pronouns, indefinite adjectives, adjectives, or numerals. This tack has been utilized with great effectiveness in the Greek philological tradition in that the quirky distributional or inflectional patterns specific to one or to a small set of these quantifiers are underscored. There are, however, also disadvantages in treating these sundry elements as distinct. Most significantly, it misses the fact that there are certain syntactic patterns which are characteristic of this set of lexemes and that there are intriguing syntactic regularities which are associated with the two subgroups in Table 1: internal quantifiers and external quantifiers. The remainder of this section examines such patterns.

The distribution of internal quantifiers is akin to adjectives. Thus, when these words modify an articular noun, they are placed in the so-called attributive position, either in between the article and the noun (3a) or after the noun with a repeated article (3b).[5]

(3) a. τὴν πολλὴν ἀγάπην αὐτοῦ
"his great love" (Eph 2:4 KJV)

b. αἵ ἁμαρτίαι αὐτῆς αἵ πολλαί
"her many sins" (Luke 7:47 NIV)

Internal quantifiers, though sharing this distributional trait with adjectives, differ in other ways. For example, internal quantifiers commonly appear in clauses without any accompanying head noun or article. In these instances, they have a substantive use; i.e., they take on a role normally associated with a noun, such as the object of a verb (4a) or the object of a preposition (4b).

(4) a. πολλά τε παρὰ τῶν Χαναναίων λαβόντες
"and taking many things from the Canaanites"
(*Ant.* 5.134)

[5] The internal quantifiers τις and οὐδείς do not appear with articular nouns because they are inherently non-definite and therefore incompatible with the use of an article.

b. καὶ διέτριβεν μεθ̓ ὀλίγων
"He stayed with a few friends." (*Mart. Pol.* 5.2)

While this use of internal quantifiers is common, it is utilized more sparingly with adjectives,[6] and even then only with a relatively small number of adjectives, such as κακός "evil" and τυφλός "blind".

Another difference between internal quantifiers and adjectives is that only the former are used in partitive constructions (5).

(5) a. οὐκ ὀλίγα πρὸς τῆς φιλοσοφίας ὠφέληνται οἱ πολλοὶ αὐτῶν
"Most of them have been helped not a little by philosophy." (Lucian, *Bis. acc.* 8)

b. ἀποστέλλει δύο τῶν μαθητῶν αὐτοῦ
"He sent out two of his disciples." (Mark 11:1 NIV)

In the partitive construction, the quantificational word is not properly considered a nominal modifier because it does not agree in case with the noun that appears in conjunction with it. Rather, the quantifier receives its case-marking based on the grammatical role it plays in the sentence; the noun, pronoun, or noun phrase with which it appears is placed in the genitive.

In contrast to internal quantifiers, members of the set of external quantifiers are unlike adjectives in their distribution. They are usually placed in the predicative position when modifying nouns. That is, they appear before the article (6a), or they are placed after the noun, but without a repeated article (6b).

(6) a. καὶ ἐθαυμάσθη ὅλη ἡ γῆ ὀπίσω τοῦ θηρίου
"And all the world wondered after the beast." (Rev 13:3 KJV)

b. ἡ σελήνη ὅλη ἐγένετο ὡς αἷμα
"The whole moon turned blood red." (Rev 6:12 NIV)

This distribution is the same as the distribution of demonstrative pronouns (7).

(7) a. ἀληθῶς οὗτος ὁ ἄνθρωπος υἱὸς θεοῦ
"Truly this man was the son of God." (Mark 15:39 KJV)

[6] Karl Brugmann, *Griechische Grammatik* (Beck: Munich, 1900).

b. ὄντως ὁ ἄνθρωπος οὗτος δίκαιος ἦν
"Certainly this was a righteous man." (Luke 23:47 KJV)

Although (6) and (7) reveal a shared property in the distribution of demonstrative pronouns and external quantifiers, the two categories are best kept disjointed because their syntactic properties differ in other important ways. One obvious case is the ability of external quantifiers, and the inability of demonstratives, to appear alone with an article (8).

(8) a. ὁ <u>μόνος</u> ἔχων ἀθανασίαν
"[the one] who alone has immortality" (1 Tim 6:16 ESV)

b. ἄρα οἱ <u>πάντες</u> ἀπέθανον
"Therefore, all have died." (2 Cor 5:14 ESV)

c. Φαρισαῖοι δὲ ὁμολογοῦσιν τὰ <u>ἀμφότερα</u>
"but the Pharisees confess both." (Acts 23:8 KJV)

d. ὁ γὰρ δεσπότης καὶ δημιουργὸς τῶν ὅλον θεός
"For God is the ruler and creator of all." (*Diogn.* 8.7)

While external quantifiers can occur before or after the noun that they modify, they canonically appear in the former position (9).

(9) a. προσαγορεύτε <u>πάντας</u> τοὺς ἁγιους.
"Greet all the saints." (*Mart. Pol.* 20:2)

b. καὶ ἐθαυμάσθη <u>ὅλη</u> ἡ γῆ ὀπίσω τοῦ θηρίου.
"And all the world wondered after the beast."
(Rev 13:3 KJV)

c. πέπρακται δ᾽ οὖν αὐτοῖς οὐδὲν ἐν <u>ἅπαντι</u> τῷ βίῳ πέρα τῆς ἐλπίδος.
"Therefore, they have done nothing in all their life except to hope."
(Lucian, *Merc. cond.* 8)

The placement of an external quantifier after a noun typically arises in one of three cases: in conjoined noun phrases (cf. Matt 9:35 πόλεις πάσας καὶ τὰς κώμας "all the towns and villages" NIV); where the placement of the quantifier after the noun also situates the quantifier at the end of a clause where it receives heavy emphasis (cf. John 16:13 ὁδηγήσει ὑμᾶς εἰς τὴν ἀλήθειαν πᾶσαν "he will guide you into all truth," NIV); and where the placement of the quantifier after the noun also situates the quantifier right before a verb phrase. I discuss the third case below where I suggest that this represents an instance of Quantifier Float.

To this point, I have suggested that there are two kinds of quantifiers—internal and external—which can be differentiated respectively from adjectives and demonstratives. The two kinds of quantifiers can also be distinguished from each other on distributional grounds, though there are some qualifications which should be made explicit. First, the placement of internal quantifiers in attributive position and external quantifiers in predicative position is only a strong heuristic for determining category membership because attributive position is not the exclusive domain of internal quantifiers. External quantifiers do arise in attributive position, albeit infrequently (10).[7]

(10) a. ἀπώλεσάς σου τὴν πᾶσαν ἐλπίδα
"having destroyed all your hope." (*Herm. Mand.* 5.1.7)

b. καὶ τὴν δόξαν τὴν παρὰ τοῦ μόνου θεοῦ οὐ ζητεῖτε;
"do [you] not seek the glory which comes from the only God?" (John 5:44 ESV)

c. τὸ ὅλον σῶμα ἀπῃώρηκεν αὐτοῦ
"He supports his whole body." (Philo, *Conf.* 38)

In addition to being uncommon, the attributive use of external quantifiers bears greater syntactic restrictions. Unlike adjectives and internal quantifiers,

[7] The rarity of external quantifiers in attributive position is also true of Classical Greek. See Basil Gildersleeve, *Syntax of Classical Greek from Homer to Demosthenes* (vol. 2; New York: American Book Company, 1911). He notes, for instance, that the attributive use of πᾶς "all, whole" arises only around 125 times in the entire corpus of Platonic writings. If anything, πᾶς occurs attributively less often in Hellenistic texts. It is found in this position only eight times in the New Testament (Acts 19:7; 20:18; 21:21; 27:37; Rom 16:15; Gal 1:2; 5:14; 2 Pet 1:3), and only once each in *Herm. Man.* 5.1.7 and *Mart. Pol.* 17:2.
The attributive use of ὅλος is even less common. There are no instances in the New Testament. It does seem to occur in select Papyri, and I have found it in 2 Macc 8.18 as well as in the writings of Clement of Alexandria (where it is usually in the phrase τὸν ὅλον ἄνθρωπον). I have not found any instances of ἀμφότεροι being used attributively in Hellenistic texts.

which can be placed in between an article and a noun (often called the first attributive position), or after the noun with a repeated article (the second attributive position), external quantifiers only arise in the former. That is, examples like those in (11) are unattested.[8]

(11) a. τὴν ἐλπίδα τὴν πᾶσαν "all hope"
b. τοῦ θεοῦ τοῦ μόνου "the only God"
c. τὸ σῶμα τὸ ὅλον

In a somewhat qualified form, then, we can use the distribution of quantifiers in definite noun phrases as a diagnostic of whether they are internal or external. Of course, for inherently indefinite quantifiers, such as τίς "a certain, one" and οὐδείς "none, no one," the diagnostic will be irrelevant. For these two elements, however, a second difference between the syntax of internal and external quantifiers allows for their classification. As noted above, the partitive construction is employed commonly with internal quantifiers. External quantifiers are not used in this way.

On the basis of distributional evidence within the noun phrase, it has been possible to demonstrate how internal and external quantifiers differ from one another, and how each differs from adjectives and demonstratives respectively. However, little has been said about what properties are shared by the two subgroups of quantifiers other than their quantificational semantics. One such commonality is the capacity for both types of quantifiers to undergo Quantifier Float, where the quantifier appears to float away from the noun phrase that it modifies. Instances with internal quantifiers are provided in (12) and with external quantifiers in (13).

---

[8] To my knowledge, there are no exceptions to this generalization in Hellenistic Greek. There are a handful of putative counter-examples from earlier texts, though these are rare and often arise in instances of discontinuous noun phrases (i.e., the noun with which a quantifier is semantically affiliated is not contiguous to the quantifier). Gildersleeve, *Syntax of Classical Greek,* notes two cases which suggest that the restriction to first attributive position is not fully operative for Classical Greek: Herodotus Book II.112, ὁ χῶρος οὗτος ὁ συνάπας "the whole place" (note the atypical placement of the demonstrative which suggests that the quantifier is in apposition to the noun phrase), and Isocrates (*To Philip* 86) τοῦ λογοῦ τοῦ σύμπαντος "the whole argument."

(12) a. οὗτος ὁ ἄνθρωπος πολλὰ ποιεῖ σημεῖα
"this man performs many signs." (John 11:47 ESV)

b. ἡ μνᾶ σου δέκα προσηργάσατο μνᾶς
"your mina has earned ten minas more." (Luke 19:16 ESV)

c. ἐγὼ οὐδεμίαν εὑρίσκω ἐν αὐτῷ αἰτίαν
"I find in him no fault at all." (John 18:38 KJV)

(13) a. ἡ δὲ Μαρία πάντα συνετήρει τὰ ῥήματα ταῦτα
"And Mary treasured up all these things" (Luke 2:19 NIV)

b. ὅλη συγχύννεται Ἰερουσαλήμ
"All Jerusalem was in confusion." (Acts 21:31 ESV)

c. καὶ μόνος ἠγνόει τὰ κατ' αὐτὸν Ἀντίπατρος
"Antipater was the only person ignorant of the rumors about himself." (*J.W.* 1.614)

As the examples demonstrate, Quantifier Float involves a syntactic disassociation between a quantifier and a quantified noun phrase. In the next section, I outline some features of this construction in Hellenistic Greek.

Quantifier Float in Hellenistic Greek

As can be seen in (2), (12) and (13), a characteristic feature of the Quantifier Float construction is that the quantifier does not arise in its canonical position but rather appears directly before the verb phrase. The disassociation is relatively easy to see when the quantified noun phrase is post-verbal. However, the quantified noun phrase can also be preverbal (14) in which case it is not obvious whether the quantifier has floated or is simply at the right edge of the noun phrase.

(14) ὅταν οὖν τὰ ἔργα τῆς μητρὸς αὐτῶν πάντα ποιήσῃς
"when, therefore, you perform all the deeds of their mother" (*Herm. Vis.* 3.8.5)

The syntactic independence of the quantifier πάντα in (14) is much less clear than in the previous examples because it is contiguous to the noun phrase it modifies.[9] One could posit that the quantifier is fully contained within

[9] The same sort of indeterminacy arises in other languages with Quantifier Float. In

the noun phrase, and therefore that (14) is not a case of Quantifier Float. However, external quantifiers have a strong predilection for placement before the noun they modify, unlike πάντα in (14), which makes the Quantifier Float analysis plausible. In the case of πᾶς and ὅλος, for example, the ratio of pre-nominal to post-nominal is on the order of 10:1 in the New Testament,[10] and a high percentage of post-nominal uses of these quantifiers has them immediately preceding a verb (hence, they could be analyzed as instances of Quantifier Float).

In each of the examples of Quantifier Float provided so far, the quantifier is situated immediately before a verb. However, the position of a floated quantifier is not determined by a verb per se, but by a verb phrase. In general terms, we can say that the quantifier appears on the left edge of the verb phrase. There are several reasons to formulate the rule for quantifier placement in this way. For present purposes, let it suffice to discuss just one of them. When a clause has a complex predicate consisting of a copula (e.g., εἰμί "be" or γίνομαι "be, become") and an adjective, a noun, or a prepositional phrase, a floated quantifier is placed before the entire predicate and not the copula. A representative example is given in (15).

> (15) καὶ τὰ ἐμὰ <u>πάντα</u> σά ἐστιν
> "All I have is yours." (John 17:10 NIV)

In (15) the quantifier is found directly before the predicate adjective σά "yours" and not the copula itself.

While Quantifier Float is permitted with all quantifiers, there is a significant limitation on the use of internal quantifiers: the quantified noun phrase from which the internal quantifier floats is either a partitive genitive (16) or it is anarthrous, that is, the noun is not accompanied by an article (see the examples in 12).

---

a pattern very similar to Greek, the English quantifier "all" (as in "All the boys have left") clearly floats in sentences such as "The boys have all left." It may also arise in post-nominal position but contiguous to the quantified noun phrase, "The boys all have left."

[10] William J. Johnston, *The Use of πᾶς in the New Testament* (New York: Peter Lang, 2004).

(16) Ἐκ δὲ τῆς πόλεως πολλοὶ ἐπίστευσαν εἰς αὐτὸν τῶν Σαμαριτῶν
"Many of the Samaritans from that town believed in him."
(John 4:39 ESV)

An additional observation relevant to this restriction is that when internal quantifiers float, they are never accompanied by an article. These facts suggest that Quantifier Float is not always possible for internal quantifiers, but that one of these two conditions on the structure of quantified noun phrases must also hold true.

Quantifier Float in Greek varies from the construction in other languages in two important ways. First, in many languages quantifiers can only float when construed with subject noun phrases, or subjects and direct objects, whereas in Greek (as well as a handful of others languages such as Basque and Albanian) it is possible with subject, objects and obliques. More significantly, the set of quantifiers that floats is much more robust in Greek than in other languages with Quantifier Float. The typical pattern is for a single quantifier (usually a universal quantifier meaning "all") to be able to float or a very small set (such as English with "all," "both" and "each"). Finally, the "landing site" for the quantifier varies cross-linguistically. The most common site is post-verbally. Greek, however, like English uses the preverbal position.

The semantic effect of Quantifier Float

The position at the left edge of a verb phrase has been identified as a slot in clause structure dedicated to focused constituents in many languages: Tzotzil and other Mayan languages, Hungarian, Udi, Somali, Russian and Bulgarian to name a few.[11] Notably, compelling evidence has also been provided that

[11] Judith L. Aissen, "Topic and Focus in Mayan," *Language* 68 (1992): 43–80; Casper de Groot, *Predicate Structure in a Functional Grammar of Hungarian* (Dordrecht: Foris, 1989); Katalin É. Kiss, "NP Movement, Operator Movement, and Scrambling in Hungarian," in *Discourse Configurational Languages* (ed. Katalin É. Kiss; Oxford: Oxford University Press, 1995), 207–43; Alice C. Harris, "Focus in Udi" in *NSL 8: Linguistic Studies in the Non-Slavic Languages of the Commonwealth of Independent States of the Baltic Republics* (ed. Howard Aronson; Chicago: Chicago Linguistic Society, 1996), 201–20; Marco Svolacchia, Lunella

this a focus position in the ancient Greek used by Herodotus.[12] Moreover, in their masterful examination of hyperbaton in Classical Greek, Devine and Stephens note the frequency for modifiers (not just quantifiers) to appear preverbally when separated from the nouns that they modify and conclude that this is used as a focus strategy.[13]

In the same vein, I propose that floated quantifiers in Hellenistic Greek are used to indicate focus. By focus, I mean unpredictable, and usually new, information that is being introduced into discourse. This includes information being given in contrast to other details of the text and information that fills in a gap that exists in the readers' presuppositions. Taking some of the examples from above in their broader context will help clarify how Quantifier Float is used for purposes of focus. The context which precedes (13a), for instance, describes the appearance of angels proclaiming the birth of the Messiah to some shepherds. Once the shepherds locate the baby that had been described to them, their reaction was immediately to spread the news to others.

> (17) When they had seen him, they spread the word concerning what had been told them about this child, and all who heard it were amazed at what the shepherds said to them. But Mary treasured up all these things (ἡ δὲ Μαρία <u>πάντα</u> συνετήρει τὰ ῥήματα ταῦτα) and pondered them in her heart (Luke 2:17–19 NIV).

By virtue of using the Quantifier Float construction, the author has placed the quantifier πάντα in focus position underscoring the contrast between the shepherds, who are vocal in sharing their knowledge about the significance of the birth, and Mary, who remains silent despite having a much more robust

---

Mereu and Annarita Pugielli, "Aspects of Discourse Configurationality in Somali," in *Discourse Configurational Languages* (ed. Katalin É. Kiss: Oxford: Oxford University Press, 1995), 65–98; Tracy Holloway King, *Configuring Topic and Focus in Russian* (Dissertations in Linguistics; Stanford: CSLI, 1995); Roumyana Izvorski, "On Wh-movement and Focus-movement in Bulgarian" (paper presented at COSOLE 2, University of Tübingen, 1993).

[12] Helma Dik, *Word Order in Ancient Greek. A Pragmatic Account of Word Order Variation in Herodotus* (Amsterdam Studies in Classical Philology 5; Amsterdam: Gieben, 1995).

[13] Devine and Stephens, *Discontinuous Syntax*, 31–32.

understanding of the event. The hyperbaton provides this sense of contrast; it also supplies a new, and somewhat surprising, bit of information. Mary opted not to speak about the revelation that had been given to her at all. Rather, against expectations, she treasured it in her heart.

Or consider (14) from above, which exemplifies a different sort of contrastive focus. This instance of quantifier float arises in a text in which a number of moral virtues are enumerated and described as the offspring of one another stretching back in a chain to a shared mother "Faith."

> (18) The first of them who is clasping her hands is called Faith. Through her the chosen of God are saved. The second, who is girded and looks like a man, is called Continence; she is the daughter of Faith. Whosoever then shall follow her becomes blessed in his life, because he will abstain from all evil deeds, believing that if he refrains from every evil lust he will inherit eternal life. "But who are the others, Lady? They are daughters one of the other, and their names are Simplicity, Knowledge, Innocence, Reverence, and Love. When therefore you perform all the deeds of their mother (ὅταν οὖν τὰ ἔργα τῆς μητρὸς αὐτῶν πάντα ποιήσῃς), you can live (*Herm. Vis.* 3.8.5).

In the first part of the passage, the pattern of naming a virtue and then indicating its unique powers for life is established. Faith has the special status of saving God's chosen ones. Continence keeps the chosen ones from lust. The lists of the other virtues is then provided with the implication that each possesses its own unique, though related, dispositions necessary for eternal life. Then, contrary to the expectations set up by this pattern, the deeds are all assigned to Faith. The use of Quantifier Float puts πάντα in a focused position, nicely capturing the summation of the deeds and highlighting the fact that each and everyone of them is expected.

Finally, consider (13b) which represents a different type of focus, one which is not contrastive. Instead, it cleverly uses information found in the prior context in a way that provides highly unpredictable information to one of the characters (as opposed to the reader). In this passage, some detractors of the apostle Paul stir up trouble for him by rousing up a crowd, first in the temple in Jerusalem and then more broadly in the city.

> (19) The whole city (ἡ πόλις ὅλη) was aroused, and the people came running from all directions. Seizing Paul, they dragged him from the temple, and immediately the gates were shut. While they were trying to kill him, news reached the commander of the Roman troops that the whole city of Jerusalem was in an uproar (ὅλη συγχύννεται Ἰερουσαλήμ) (Acts 21:30–31 NIV).

As the commotion in the city increases to the point of violence, a report of this fact comes to the man charged with preserving order. The quantifier ὅλη appears in focused position underscoring the unexpected nature of the news to the commander.

Conclusion

In the preceding sections, I have provided a non-traditional classification of quantifiers in an effort, on the one hand, to underscore the shared properties of a set of lexemes that are often treated as distinct word classes and, on the other hand, to describe one type of hyperbaton that is found widely in Hellenistic Greek texts. This construction, which I have labeled Quantifier Float based on analogous constructions in other languages, may very well function in the same way as other types of hyperbaton,[14] but I have treated it uniquely to simplify my proposal that Quantifier Float is used to focus quantifiers.

The discussion of focus effects revealed that they are not uniform and are often subtle. This, of course, places a burden on a translator to determine whether the focus of the quantifier needs to be represented in the translation, and if so, how. In the case of English, focus is typically expressed through prosody or specialized syntax that has very different properties than Quantifier Float in Hellenistic Greek. In situations where part of the motivation for the Quantifier Float is to express the surprising nature of the quantity, it is certainly possible to employ apposition or peculiar idioms to underscore this fact. For example, the Quantifier Float construction exemplified in (19) might be rendered "Jerusalem, all of it, is in confusion" or "the whole of Jerusalem is in confusion." In other instances, such as (17), it is less obvious

[14] As is assumed, for example, by Divine and Stephens.

that the quantification *per se* is what should be highlighted. Here the focus is contrastive between the shepherds being expressive and Mary being silent. Less important, and perhaps not important at all, is a contrast between "all things" and "some things" or "no things." For this case of Quantifier Float, the translation of the focus effect would center around the contrast in subjects, e.g. "Mary, for her part, treasured all these things pondering them in her heart." Finally, some cases of Quantifier Float, such as that in (18), may be best left alone without any effort to capture them in translation. The focus provided by the Quantifier Float in (18) is recoverable from the general flow of the passage, making additional rhetorical devices redundant in a sense.

Bibliography

Aissen, Judith L. "Topic and Focus in Mayan." *Language* 68 (1992): 43–80.

Bakker, Stéphanie J. *The Noun Phrase in Ancient Greek*. Leiden: Brill, 2009.

Brugmann, Karl. *Griechische Grammatik*. Beck: Munich, 1900.

de Groot, Casper. *Predicate Structure in a Functional Grammar of Hungarian*. Dordrecht: Foris, 1989.

de Vries, J. "Untersuchungen über die Sperrung von Substantiv und Attribut in der Sprache der attischen Redner." PhD diss., Göttingen, 1938.

Devine, A. M. and Laurence D. Stephens. *Discontinuous Syntax: Hyperbaton in Greek*. Oxford: Oxford University Press, 2000.

Dik, Helma. *Word Order in Ancient Greek: A Pragmatic Account of Word Order Variation in Herodotus*. Amsterdam Studies in Classical Philology 5. Amsterdam: Gieben, 1995.

Dover, K. J. *Greek Word Order*. Cambridge: Cambridge University Press. 1960

Glidersleeve, Basil. *Syntax of Classical Greek from Homer to Demosthenes*. Vol. 2. New York: American Book Company, 1911.

Harris, Alice C. "Focus in Udi." Pages 201–20 in *NSL 8: Linguistic Studies in the Non-Slavic Languages of the Commonwealth of Independent States of the Baltic Republics*. Edited by H. Aronson. Chicago: Chicago Linguistic Society, 1996.

Izvorski, Roumyana. "On Wh-movement and Focus-movement in Bulgarian." Paper presented at COSOLE 2, University of Tübingen, 1993.

Johnston, J. William. *The Use of πᾶς in the New Testament*. New York: Peter Lang, 2004.

King, Tracy Holloway. *Configuring Topic and Focus in Russian*. Dissertations in Linguistics. Stanford: CSLI, 1995.

Kiss, Katalin É. "NP Movement, Operator Movement, and Scrambling in Hungarian." Pages 207–43 in *Discourse Configurational Languages*. Edited by Katalin É. Kiss. Oxford: Oxford University Press, 1995.

Levinsohn, Stephen H. *Discourse Features of New Testament Greek*. Dallas: Summer Institute of Linguistics, 1992.

Svolacchia, Marco Lunella Mereu and Annarita Pugielli. "Aspects of Discourse Configurationality in Somali." Pages 65–98 in *Discourse Configurational Languages*. Edited by Katalin É. Kiss. Oxford: Oxford University Press, 1995.

Taylor, Ann. "The Change from SOV to SVO in Ancient Greek." *Language Variation and Change* 6 (1994): 1–17.

The Discourse Function of ἀλλά in Non-Negative Contexts

Rick Brannan[1]

Introduction

Robert Funk, in his *Beginning-Intermediate Grammar of Hellenistic Greek*, writes:

> Negatives, conjunctions, sentence connectors, and subordinators may be termed *function words* or *structure signaling words*. The point of these labels is that such words are nearly lexically empty, i.e. they have little or no dictionary meaning of their own. However, they are grammatically significant in indicating the structure of sentences and parts of sentences. Some of them are so common as to require acquaintance at the grossest level of the language. This simply means that one must learn how they function early in the process. One may guess at the meaning of lexically full words, or leave them blank when reading, but one must know the grammatical "meaning" of function words to be able to proceed at all.[2]

[1] While I have never met Stephen Levinsohn, his work has influenced me. From my initial read of Dooley and Levinsohn's *Analyzing Discourse*, to my examination of sections in his *Discourse Features of New Testament Greek*, to my working through portions of his *Textual Connections in Acts*, my understanding of how the Greek of the New Testament works has been strengthened, and I am better for it. I'm honored to contribute to this volume commemorating his work to date, and look forward to learning more from him in the future.

[2] Robert W. Funk, *Beginning-Intermediate Grammar of Hellenistic Greek* (Missoula, Mont.: Scholar's Press, 1973), 475.

The conjunction ἀλλά is one of these "function words." As Funk describes, ἀλλά is "nearly lexically empty." Yet by distilling several senses of ἀλλά, many grammars and lexicons import lexical freight upon ἀλλά. Each instance of ἀλλά is then evaluated by determining which "sense" fits best, often by testing the translation with sense-based English glosses: "but," "indeed," "yet," etc.

The perspective of this article is different. The focus is not on how to translate ἀλλά, or how to determine what "sense" a particular instance may be. Instead, the focus is on how to understand the function of ἀλλά in context with the hopes that this will bear better exegetical fruit.

A working hypothesis regarding ἀλλά

Virtually every grammar, monograph and lexicon article that discusses ἀλλά notes that it is an "adversative" conjunction.[3] Several go so far as to say that it is a "strong adversative."[4] Upon an examination of every instance of ἀλλά in the New Testament and the Apostolic Fathers, one learns that the vast majority of instances of ἀλλά in these corpora (approximately 80%)[5] involve the comparison of two items (phrases, clauses or otherwise), one of which uses a negator. It is this larger context that is "adversative"; ἀλλά itself does not create the adversity or contrast. It is more proper in such instances to

[3] For example, Stanley E. Porter, *Idioms of the Greek New Testament* (Sheffield: JSOT Press, 1999), 205; A. T. Roberston, *A Grammar of the Greek New Testament in the Light of Historical Research* (Bellingham, Wash.: Logos Research Systems, 2006), 1187–88; Friedrich Blass and Albert Debrunner, *A Greek Grammar of the New Testament and Other Early Christian Literature* (trans. and ed. by Robert W. Funk; Chicago: University of Chicago Press, 1961), §448.

[4] For example, Herbert Weir Smyth, *Greek Grammar* (rev. by Gordon M. Messing; Cambridge, Mass.: Harvard University Press, 1956), §2775.

[5] In the 638 NT instances, 510 instances use negators in one or both statements, 84 have no negation present, and 44 are questionable as regards to negation, using terms like οὐκέτι or μηκέτι. If the marginal instances are counted as non-negative, the ratio is 510/638, or approximately 80%. Including the marginal situations as negatives, the ratio is 554/638 or approximately 87%. For the 352 instances in the Apostolic Fathers, 249 use negation, 76 have no negation present, and 27 are questionable for a ratio of 249/352 or approximately 71%. Including the marginal situations as negatives, the ratio is 276/352, or approximately 78%. By far, the most common case is for ἀλλά to be used in conjunction with a negative statement.

speak of ἀλλά as being used in adversative contexts. But ἀλλά is used in other contexts as well, as the standard lexicons and grammars readily display.

This leads to the larger and more appropriate question: What function does ἀλλά play in discourse? Recall Funk's distinction between function words which are "lexically empty" and other words which are "lexically full."[6] One must understand the function of ἀλλά, not simply substitute sense-derived glosses, in order to understand what a particular passage communicates. Proposed guidelines for understanding the role of ἀλλά in a given passage include:

- ἀλλά involves enhancing the contrast between two things. To understand a particular instance, the two contrasting items must be located. The antecedent item[7] usually directly precedes the ἀλλά; but it may be discontiguous[8] and it may even be a general assumption in the current context.[9] Context (e.g., presence of a negator, contrast based on word choice) determines the degree of contrast between the two items.
- ἀλλά involves correction or replacement. The second item either corrects or replaces the first. "Correction" is when the second item sharpens, redirects or clarifies the first item. "Replacement" is when the second item wipes the first item off of the table and replaces it completely. In discourse, the correction or replacement has the effect of making the second item more prominent than the first.

Applying these two guidelines when examining New Testament passages that contain instances of ἀλλά will result in clearer understanding of passage flow; this in turn bears exegetical fruit.

---

[6] Funk, *Beginning-Intermediate Grammar,* 475.

[7] Terminology is somewhat difficult. This paper uses terms like "antecedent item" to refer to the first statement of the two that ἀλλά joins. Additionally, when appropriate, "counterpoint" and "point" are used. In other contexts, words like "protasis" and "apodosis" (language usually used when discussing conditional statements) is used to refer to the former and latter statements or ideas joined by ἀλλά .

[8] J. D. Denniston, *The Greek Particles* (Oxford: Oxford University Press, 1950), l.

[9] Ibid.

The balance of this paper will ground these guidelines in the existing literature and apply them to non-negative instances of ἀλλά within the synoptic gospels.[10] The goal is to demonstrate the reliability and usefulness of the guidelines toward understanding the discourse function of particular instances of ἀλλά in the New Testament and in other early Christian literature.

The literature: grammars and monographs

Grammars

Herbert Weir Smyth, *Greek Grammar*

Smyth is the standard classical Greek grammar, and surveys a larger amount of literature than grammars that focus upon New Testament/Hellenistic Greek. Smyth follows the somewhat standard approach of isolating contexts in which ἀλλά occurs, and then discussing each context to delimit senses. Smyth's overall description is a helpful starting point:

> ἀλλά, a strongly adversative conjunction (stronger than δέ) connects sentences and clauses, and corresponds pretty closely to *but*; at times ἀλλά need not or cannot be translated. . . . ἀλλά marks opposition, contrast, protest, difference, objection, or limitation; and is thus used both where one notion entirely excludes another and where two notions are not mutually exclusive. ἀλλά is often freely repeated in successive clauses.[11]

Smyth makes plain that ἀλλά commonly stands between two things, marking relationship of some sort between those two things. §2781 notes that "ἀλλά is sometimes found after an affirmative statement" though no distinction is made between positive and negative succeeding statements.

---

[10] Specifically, this paper examines all non-negative instances in the synoptic gospels that have a synoptic parallel. For the purposes of this paper, the constitution of a "non-negative instance" of ἀλλά is thus: If the statement previous to or following ἀλλά contains a negator, it is not examined. If the negative/non-negative status is unclear (e.g. terms like οὐκέτι or μηκέτι), it is not examined. There are over 80 NT "non-negative" instances using this arrangement.

[11] Smyth, *Grammar,* §2775.

Friedrich Blass, Albert Debrunner and Robert Walter Funk, *A Grammar of the Greek New Testament and Other Early Christian Literature* (BDF)

BDF provides a longer treatment for ἀλλά in §448. The article's breakdown is based on context of occurrence; paying attention to the patterns of the larger context in which ἀλλά occurs. Eight different contexts are noted; the use of ἀλλά with a negated clause or phrase is prominent, particularly in the first two: "(1) It appears most frequently as the contrary to a preceding οὐ. . . . (2) With an οὐ also used as the contrary to a preceding positive clause ('but not')."[12] These two contexts provide the majority of instances where the order is negative-ἀλλά-positive (first item) and positive-ἀλλά-negative (second item). Items 3–5 are largely variations on items 1–2, though it is noted that ἀλλά can occur at "with a stronger reference to the difference than δε would have provided," listing John 8:26 as an example. Item 6 notes how ἀλλά can be used "to introduce an additional point in an emphatic way," listing 2 Cor 7:11 as an example. BDF's final item notes ἀλλά ἤ as exceptive (equating ἀλλά ἤ with εἰ μή).

Overall, the description in BDF accurately reports the contexts of ἀλλά in the New Testament, yet outside of its first two contextual descriptions it pays little attention to ἀλλά interplay and resulting function with immediately preceding material. So ἀλλά is either indicative of a contrast (when occurring between negative and positive elements), or ἀλλά brings an exceptive or emphatic connotation to the immediate context.

Robert Walter Funk, *Beginning-Intermediate Grammar of Hellenistic Greek*

Funk's *Beginning-Intermediate Grammar of Hellenistic Greek* is perhaps the most brief (outside of supplied examples) and the most helpful, at least for

---

[12] The exclusive mention of οὐ is interesting, particularly because nearly 100 of the 638 instances of ἀλλά in the NT occur in conjunction with μή (approx. 15% [98/638]), not οὐ. A similar ratio of μή instances occurs in the Apostolic Fathers (approx. 20% [74/352]).

considerations of the discourse function of ἀλλά. In §627, Funk writes that ἀλλά

> is commonly preceded by a negative (*not* . . . *but* . . ., cf. §617), although it is also used in other ways (§628). In combination with a negative, ἀλλά is employed to join grammatical elements of the same order, as is the case with other conjunctions. . . .
> . . . §628: ἀλλά not preceded by a negative may mark a transition to something contrasted or different.[13]

Funk's description is helpful because he acknowledges the primary use of ἀλλά with a negative but does not limit it to this context. He also reminds us that ἀλλά joins things—that it is, after all, a conjunction. It does not simply act alone or on following material; it is in some sort of relationship with preceding material as well. Most importantly, in §628 Funk notes the aspect of contrast commonly seen when ἀλλά is used without a preceding negator.

Richard Young, *Intermediate New Testament Greek: A Linguistic and Exegetical Approach*

Young's article notes four primary senses of ἀλλά: contrast, emphasis, exclusion and transition. On contrast, Young notes, "Semantically, propositions introduced with adversative conjunctions (e.g., I came to fulfill the law) are more prominent than the propositions with which they are contrasted (e.g., I did not come to destroy the law)."[14] Young's point is important for understanding the function of ἀλλά at the discourse level. In Matt 5:17, the statement after ἀλλά is more prominent than the negated statement before it. The point of the passage is that Jesus came to fulfill the law. While the antecedent statement is true, the statement following is the one that is highlighted in the overall context. Stating the point like this ("I did not come to destroy the law, *but [ἀλλά] to fulfill it*") highlights it in a way that the simple statement on its own ("I came to fulfill the law") can never achieve.

---

[13] Funk, *Beginning-Intermediate Grammar,* 494–95.

[14] Richard A. Young, *Intermediate New Testament Greek: A Linguistic and Exegetical Approach* (Nashville: Broadman & Holman, 1994), 180.

Lexicons

Henry George Liddell, Robert Scott, Henry Stuart Jones and Roderick McKenzie, *A Greek-English Lexicon* (LSJ)

LSJ's general description of ἀλλά is fairly standard:

> used adversatively to limit or oppose words, sentences, or clauses, stronger than δέ, usu[ally] in first position, but occasionally postponed[15]

Thus LSJ support the notion of ἀλλά functioning between two items (words, sentences or clauses), "limiting" or "opposing" them. The balance of the article is a catalogue of collocational information categorized in three parts: first, "simple oppositions"; second "whole sentences"; third, when ἀλλά is joined with other particles (e.g. ἀλλ' ουν, ἀλλά γαρ). But most of the subentries focus on isolating a collocation and providing a gloss for the context.

Johannes P. Louw and Eugene Albert Nida, *A Greek-English Lexicon based on Semantic Domains* (Louw-Nida)

Louw-Nida provide a rather conventional view of ἀλλά, classing it in domains 89 ("Relations," articles 96 and 125) and 91 ("Discourse Markers," articles 2 and 11). Thus Louw-Nida break ἀλλά into four primary senses, providing glosses of "but" (89.125), "and" (89.96), "yet" (91.2) and "certainly" (91.11). The primary entry is 89.125, which describes ἀλλά as a "marker of emphatic contrast." The article at 89.96 seems to provide a place to describe the unique instance of 2 Cor 7:11. The other senses, categorized as discourse markers, cover the use of ἀλλά in transitions (91.2, somewhat like BDAG's second and third senses, discussed below) and as a "marker of contrastive emphasis" (91.11). How "contrastive emphasis" differs from "more emphatic contrast" is not specified. While some heed is paid to the function of ἀλλά in discourse contexts, this seems more in use of categorization (as "Relations" and "Discourse Markers") and in use of the term "marker" to describe ἀλλά.

---

[15] Henry George Liddell, Robert Scott, Henry Stuart Jones and Roderick McKenzie, *A Greek-English Lexicon* (rev. ed; Oxford: Clarendon, 1996), 67.

Walter Bauer, Frederick W. Danker, William Arndt and Gingrich, *A Greek-English Lexicon of the New Testament and Other Early Christian Literature* (BDAG)

BDAG's general description takes much the same approach as LSJ:

> gener[ally] adversative particle (orig. neut. pl. of ἄλλος, "otherwise") indicating a difference with or contrast to what precedes, in the case of individual clauses as well as whole sentences.[16]

The article itself recognizes the same breakdowns as other articles and grammars. The primary (most common) syntactic context is first, that of ἀλλά after a negative or after μεν with adversative force, providing gloss translations of "but, yet, rather." The second sense is that of "a transition to someth[ing] different or contrasted" when whole clauses are compared. Upon examination this really is not much different than the first sense as connection between two clauses is involved, along with primarily negative examples. A third sense describes ἀλλά before independent clauses noting the function is "to indicate that the preceding is to be regarded as a settled matter, thus forming a transition to someth[ing] new." Apart from specifying the involvement of independent clauses, it is difficult to see how this third sense differs much from the second (or the first). Both are labeled as transitions, though one is to something "different or contrasted," the other is "to something new." This is a relatively thin difference. Also, most of the examples given in this sense involve no negator preceding ἀλλά, however some portion involve a negator in the ἀλλά clause itself. The differences in these entries seem to be based on different syntactic contexts surrounding ἀλλά, not necessarily different aspects of ἀλλά itself. The last two entries provide further difference of syntactic context (in the apodosis of a conditional statement, and used with an imperative) without much difference noted in the overall function of ἀλλά in such contexts.[17]

---

[16] Walter Bauer, Frederick W. Danker and William Arndt, *A Greek-English Lexicon of the New Testament and Other Early Christian Literature* (3rd ed.; Chicago: University of Chicago Press, 2000), 44.

[17] Though note that BDAG describe the special case 2 Cor 7:11 in item 4b (the reference is the only likely example) as "rhetorically ascensive."

Horst Robert Balz and Gerhard Schneider, *Exegetical Dictionary of the New Testament* (EDNT)

After a usage review noting that the Paulines and Johannines are responsible for most instances of ἀλλά, EDNT provide a general definition as follows:

> The adversative particle ἀλλά is etymologically derived from ἄλλος. Therefore it actually means *differently* and refers to that which is different, to contrasts, separations, and new beginnings.[18]

As with most grammars and lexica, the etymological derivation provides a grounding point for the definition. The general sense of otherness, seen here by the term "differently," is common. This does help in providing for the notion of contrast so often seen in the contexts in which ἀλλά occurs. From here, the definition consists of a series of rough descriptions of syntactic context aligned with English glosses and reference lists. So again the reader is left with the impression that ἀλλά has a range of senses that can be translated into English, and even citation listings for many of them.[19]

Monographs and articles

J. D. Denniston, *The Greek Particles*

Denniston's treatment is too voluminous to handle in any completeness here. Generally, Denniston sketches four "methods of connexion": additional, adversative, confirmatory and inferential. He notes that ἀλλά can be generally classed as an adversative. Of adversatives, he further notes:

> (b) Adversatives are of two kinds: eliminative adversatives, used often where one of two contrasted members is negative, the true being substituted for the false (*par excellence* μὲν οὖν and

[18] Horst Robert Balz, and Gerhard Schneider, eds., *Exegetical Dictionary of the New Testament* (6 vols.; Grand Rapids: Eerdmans, 1990–1993), 1:61.

[19] Like BDAG's description of 2 Cor 7:11 as "rhetorically ascensive," EDNT describe 2 Cor 7:11 as "rhetorical intensification" with, in 2 Cor 7:11's case, "terms juxtaposed for intensification".

> normally ἀλλά), and balancing adversatives, where two truths of divergent tendency are presented (δέ, μήν, μέντοι, etc.).[20]

In describing "eliminative adversatives" (other grammars/lexicons typically call them "strong adversatives"), Denniston notes a substitutionary or corrective aspect to the commonly seen instances of ἀλλά with a negator along with the implicit notion that contrast exists between both items.

Further along in his introduction, Denniston notes some peculiarities to the manner in which some conjunctions, including ἀλλά, connect things:

> The connexion established is, normally, of course, between consecutive units of speech: words, phrases, clauses, or sentences. There are, however, certain exceptions. In dialogue, owing to the quickness of thrust and parry, or the self-absorption of one of the participants, a speaker sometimes links the opening of his speech to his own preceding words, not to the intervening words of the other person. . . . *In S.El.1035 (p. 443) ἀλλ' οὖν looks back to 1017-26: or perhaps it would be truer to say that its point d'appui is the general situation, the whole attitude of Chrysothemis, rather than any particular set of words*, an explanation which applies also to E.*Alc*.713 (καὶ μήν, p. 354), and IT 637 (μέντοι, p. 405).[21]

Denniston introduces and supports the idea that ἀλλά can be used to connect discontinuous text, and that it can even be used to contrast or counter "the general situation" instead of "any particular set of words."

Jakob Heckert, *Discourse Conjoiners in the Pastoral Epistles*

Heckert's work examines the discourse function of several conjunctions within the Pastoral Epistles. One of the conjunctions treated is ἀλλά. After a brief survey of "traditional scholars," "traditional scholars of the New Testament" and "discourse linguists," Heckert posits that ἀλλά is a marker of contrast:

> The basic function of the adversative particle ἀλλά in the pastoral epistles is to mark global contrast, although this function may

---

[20] Denniston, *Greek Particles*, xlix.

[21] Ibid., l (emphasis added).

> be modified to a degree, depending on the presence or absence of a negative marker and its position in relation to ἀλλά. Even in the set construction ου μονον . . . ἀλλά καὶ, ἀλλά functions contrastively within the limits set by οὐ μόνον, on the one hand, and καὶ, on the other.[22]

Heckert isolates five contexts that ἀλλά appears in within the Pastoral Epistles: when preceded by a negative marker, when followed by a negative marker, with no negative marker, with the set construction ου μονον . . . ἀλλά καὶ, and when combined with a non-negative particle. Heckert's overall conclusion is:

> Thus, when a negative marker *precedes* ἀλλά, the second conjunct replaces a rejected proposition; when a negative marker *follows* ἀλλά the expectations raised by the preceding conjunct are denied; *and when a negative marker is absent, the second proposition corrects the expectations initiated by the first one.*[23]

Heckert's work shows that discourse function of ἀλλά as a marker of contrast is relatively stable, and that surrounding context (presence or absence of negatives, or use in combination with other non-negative particles such as γε) contributes to the degree of contrast between the conjuncts joined by ἀλλά. Also relevant is Heckert's conclusion that, in addition to being a marker of contrast, use of ἀλλά is associated with correction or replacement.

Stanley E. Porter and Matthew Brook O'Donnell, "Conjunctions and Levels of Discourse"

Porter and O'Donnell presented this paper to the 2006 symposium of the Linguistics Institute of Ancient and Biblical Greek (LIABG). Porter and O'Donnell posit

> that there are three axes along which the conjunctions function. One of these is vertical, and the other two are horizontal. Selection of a given conjunction requires that one of the two

[22] Jacob K. Heckert, *Discourse Function of Conjoiners in the Pastoral Epistles* (Dallas: Summer Institute of Linguistics, 1996), 19.

[23] Ibid., 28 (emphasis added).

> horizontal axes be chosen, and that a level on the vertical axis be chosen. The vertical axis is a cline of discourse levels, while the horizontal axes represent two different clines, one of continuity-discontinuity and the other of logical-semantic relations.[24]

Porter and O'Donnell place ἀλλά on the axis of continuity-discontinuity, noting that ἀλλά indicates a high degree of discontinuity[25] and can function at multiple levels along the vertical axis of discourse level.

> The conjunction ἀλλά only functions at the lower levels (but perhaps not the lowest level of the word). This conjunction joins word groups in Matthew 9:13: "he did not come to call the just but sinners"; clauses in Mark 4:17: "they do not have roots in themselves but they are for a time"; and clause complexes in 1 Thessalonians 5:15: "watch lest someone return evil for evil but always pursue the good both to others and to all."[26]

The levels of discourse on the vertical axis "move from the conjoining of words to word groups to clauses to clause complexes to paragraphs to discourses."[27] In the above statement they note ἀλλά functions at the word group, clause and clause complex levels and potentially at the word level. However, later in the paper, they assert:

> An initial analysis indicates that there are a limited number of conjunctions that function at all of the levels of discourse. These include only καὶ, δέ, ἀλλά and some of the negative conjunctions, such as οὐδέ and μηδέ. All of the rest of the conjunctions are more circumscribed in the linguistic levels at which they may be used.[28]

---

[24] Stanley E. Porter and Matthew Brook O'Donnell, "Conjunctions and Levels of Discourse" (paper presented at the Symposium of the Linguistics Institute of Ancient and Biblical Greek, Hamilton, Ont., August 24–26, 2006), 150–51.

[25] Ibid., 152. Along the continuity-discontinuity cline, the most continuous conjunctions are καὶ and τε; levels of discontinuity increase along the cline, from low levels (τέ and τότε) to mid levels (δέ, μὲν, οὖν and γάρ); to high levels of discontinuity (ἀλλά , πλήν and ὅμως).

[26] Ibid., 151.

[27] Ibid.

[28] Ibid., 151–52.

Thus, according to Porter and O'Donnell, ἀλλά marks a high level of discontinuity and can be used as a conjoiner at various discourse levels; at least including word group, clause and clause complex levels but perhaps including word, paragraph and even discourse levels.

Steven Runge, "Teaching Them What NOT to Do"

In a paper presented to the Evangelical Theological Society in 2007,[29] Runge examined the phenomena of negation from the perspective of discourse grammar. Outside of simple negated clauses, Runge isolated negation patterns, some of which include the use of ἀλλά.[30] Regarding each of the examples featuring the use of ἀλλά, Runge notes, "In each instance, the negated clause functions as a counterpoint, highlighting the 'point' which is introduced by ἀλλά."[31] Earlier in the section concerning negation and ἀλλά, he defines point and counterpoint, noting that they work in concert with each other to set the point in prominence:

> The result of providing a negative answer followed by a positive one is to create a rhetorical "counterpoint-point" set.[32] . . . the negated clause serves to highlight something that functions as a *counterpoint* in order to set the stage for a more important *point* that follows. Use of the counterpoint-point strategy results in effectively giving the positive answer more emphasis than it would have otherwise received using only the positive answer.[33]

---

[29] Steven Runge, "Teaching Them What NOT to Do: The Nuances of Negation in the Greek New Testament" (paper presented at the Annual Meeting of the Evangelical Theological Society, San Diego, Cal., November 13–16, 2007). Cited 23 May, 2008. Online: http://www.logos.com/media/academic/runge/negation_pragmatics.pdf.

[30] Ibid., 7–11. Pattern 3, "Emphasis on corrective or restrictive information introduced by ἀλλά/εἰ μή," particularly example groups 11–13 which focus on instances of ἀλλά .

[31] Ibid., 9n21.

[32] Runge, *Discourse Grammar of the Greek New Testament* (Peabody, Mass.: Hendrickson, 2010). 92–100 (§4.3) uses the term "point-counterpoint set," which is the terminology that this article uses as well.

[33] Runge, "Teaching Them What NOT to Do," 7–8, (emphasis original).

Runge (building on Heckert[34]) further notes a restrictive or corrective aspect to the point-counterpoint sets that feature use of ἀλλά:

> In roughly one quarter of the instances of negation found in the Greek NT, there is a counterpoint-point strategy at work to restrict or correct the negated clause by supplying additional information introduced by either ἀλλά or εἰ μή.[35]

Runge demonstrates that structures that feature ἀλλά and that rely on a rhetorical use of negation, such as "not that, but (ἀλλά) this" use the first half of the structure (the "counterpoint") to bring the second half (the "point") into even more prominence in the current discourse.[36] Importantly, Runge does not limit the point-counterpoint set to use with ἀλλά; he also includes examples that rely on εἰ μή as the hinge. In DGGNT,[37] he demonstrates that point-counterpoint sets are flexible and not bound to particular grammatical or vocabulary requirements.[38]

Building on Runge's insights, one contention of the current paper is that point-counterpoint sets that use ἀλλά as a hinge need not require a negative counterpoint.

---

[34] Heckert, *Discourse Function*, 18.

[35] Runge, "Teaching Them What NOT to Do," 8.

[36] Note that "counterpoint" and "point" have their origin as strict logical terms where the counterpoint is a foil that is relatively useless to the current context and the point is the salient bit that overshadows and knocks out the counterpoint. In Runge's application, the terminology is not intended to be this strict. Instead, counterpoint and point are used to isolate the two items/areas that are working in conjunction with each other, with the prominent/salient bit encoded in the point. But complete or strict replacement is not implied by Runge's usage of this terminology. His usage of counterpoint is more in line with the *Concise OED's* second sense, "a thing forming a pleasing or notable contrast with something else."

[37] Runge, *Discourse Grammar*, 92–100 (§4.3).

[38] For example, the counterpoint-point structure need not involve ἀλλά or εἰ μή at all; it could be denoted by a prospective (anticipatory) μὲν followed (at some point, not even contiguously) by δέ, ἀλλά , καὶ or asyndeton. Denniston also notes such structures, though he describes them using traditional grammatical terminology.

Annemieke Drummen, *Discourse Cohesion in Dialogue Turn-Initial ἀλλά in Greek Drama*

Drummen's comments are very helpful in coming to understand the discourse function of ἀλλά because they are based on a survey of classical Greek comedy and tragedy. She surveyed a range of "turn-initial ἀλλά"[39] in twenty-four different plays.[40] She concludes:

> The general function of the discourse marker ἀλλά is said to be that it substitutes one element for another. . . . In all cases investigated the function of turn-initial ἀλλά can be interpreted as marking a correction of the preceding words or actions. The corrected (substituted) element is either an explicitly stated element, a presupposed element, an implication, or the discourse topic.[41]

Drummen's research on the use of turn-initial ἀλλά in classical Greek confirms the primary function of ἀλλά as one of correction or substitution.

Summary of descriptions of ἀλλά

Smyth's work brings to light ἀλλά's marking of some relationship between two items. Funk's similar recognition that ἀλλά joins things (§627) along with Young and Runge's individual but complementary assertions regarding an antecedent statement being used as a foil to make a succeeding statement more prominent (Runge labels these point-counterpoint sets) contribute much to the picture. Denniston's articles on ἀλλά and μὲν arrive at similar conclusions (recall his "eliminative adversatives") and further demonstrate how the statement antecedent to ἀλλά may be discontinuous or even a general situation instead of particular text.

39 Here "turn-initial" indicates the beginning of a speaker's "turn" in Greek drama.

40 Six plays each from Aristophanes, Aeschylus, Sophocles and Euripides.

41 Annemieke Drummen, "Discourse Cohesion in Dialogue: Turn-Initial ἀλλά in Greek Drama" in *Discourse Cohesion in Ancient Greek* (ed. Stéphanie Bakker and Gerry Wakker; Amsterdam Studies in Classical Philosophy 16; Leiden/Boston: Brill, 2009), 135–54.

Heckert's description is most directly applicable to the current study. His view of ἀλλά as a "marker of global contrast" that, in non-negative contexts, indicates correction or replacement is central to arriving at a brief, unified and consistent view of the discourse function of ἀλλά. Drummen's similar conclusions in her survey of classical Greek comedy and tragedy strengthen this assertion. Porter and O'Donnell complement this with their description of ἀλλά as marking a high level of discontinuity between conjoined items. Runge's further work, with the concept of point-counterpoint sets that can use ἀλλά (among other words and structures) as a hinge provides further framework with which to evaluate non-negative instances of ἀλλά in the New Testament and other contemporary literature.

With all of this in mind, consider again the "working hypothesis":

- ἀλλά involves enhancing the contrast between two things.
- ἀλλά involves correction or replacement.

Thus, when examining items joined by ἀλλά, one should ask two questions:

1. What items (words, phrases, clauses) are being contrasted?
2. What is the correction or replacement that is taking place?

With this in mind, examples from the New Testament will be examined.

New Testament examples

It is impossible to work through each non-negative instance of ἀλλά in the New Testament in the scope of this paper. Instead, each instance in the synoptic gospels will be evaluated. The goal is to evaluate these instances using the working hypothesis to arrive at an understanding of in-context usage. For each instance, citations in BDF and BDAG will be noted. They will play a role in the discussion.

In addition to examining individual non-negative instances of ἀλλά in the synoptic gospels, the synoptic parallels,[42] where available, will also be examined. In most cases, different information structures present the same

[42] Parallels from Kurt Aland, *Synopsis of the Four Gospels: Greek-English Edition of the Synopsis Quattor Evangeliorum* (United Bible Societies: New York, 1982).

information in different ways. This will help shed light on the function(s) that ἀλλά plays within the larger discourse.

Matthew 9:18 (|| Mark 5:23 || Luke 8:41)

Regarding classification, BDF cites this instance in §448(3), noting ἀλλά is used "before commands or requests."[43] BDAG classifies in sense 5 "with an imperative to strengthen the command."[44] These are both correct in identifying the collocation of ἀλλά with a command, but both descriptions focus on the placement of ἀλλά in respect to what follows and pay little attention to the items that ἀλλά conjoins.

In this case, there are two clauses joined by ἀλλά; "My daughter has just died" (where "My" refers to "a ruler" in the previous clause) and "come and lay your hand on her and she will live."

The parallels in Mark and Luke disclose that the "ruler" in this instance is Jairus. His daughter has died (disclosed in the counterpoint); he desires Jesus to restore her to life (disclosed in the point). In this case, there is a degree of contrast involved in Jairus' request. He asks for Jesus to move his daughter from the state of death (τελευτάω) back into the state of life (ζάω). The underlying contrast is both lexical (contrast between death and life) and grammatical (between the aorist and future tenses). In this instance, ἀλλά functions as a hinge between the counterpoint and the point, heightening the contrast and shifting the focus onto the point: Jairus believes that if Jesus comes and touches his daughter, Jesus will restore her to life.

The Markan and Lucan parallels

The differences between the synoptic accounts of this event are notable. In the Markan and Lukan accounts, Jairus initially represents his daughter as being sick unto the point of death but still alive; information of the girl's death comes later from a servant who arrives on the scene (Mark 5:35 || Luke 8:49). In Matthew she is represented as being dead throughout Jesus and Jairus' interaction.

---

[43] BDF, 3.

[44] BDAG, 45.

In Mark, Jairus' request is twofold: "so that she be made well and live." The request in Luke is much more subtle: "he implored [Jesus] to come to his house." But recall that in Matthew, the request is not to make Jairus' daughter well, but for Jesus to place his hands on her so that she may live again.

Matthew, compressing the event of Jesus and Jairus' initial interaction, packs all of the contrast and drama of the event into Jairus' request that Jesus, by touching his daughter, restore her life from death. Jairus by his statement shows that he thinks Jesus is able, with his very touch, to restore the dead to the living. Mark and Luke both spread this aspect of the drama out. First, Jairus requests that Jesus heal his daughter (Mark only refers to Jesus healing through touch; Luke has Jairus requesting that Jesus simply come to his house to heal, with means unspecified). Then the interlude with the healing of the woman with the issue of blood, who is healed through touching Jesus' garment, which shows the power of Jesus to heal by touch. Only after this do Mark and Luke update the reader with the further information that Jairus' daughter has died. They both do this by focusing on the hopelessness of the situation; now that the daughter has died there is no reason to further bother Jesus. But Jesus overhears this report (Mark 5:36 || Luke 8:50) and goes to Jairus' house anyway, where his touch—in all accounts he takes the daughter by the hand—restores her to life.

In Matthew, Jairus' request is larger and more hopeless. Instead of asking Jesus to heal his daughter from a grave illness, he asks that his dead daughter be restored to life. Each synoptic account uses different grammatical means to make this request: Mark focuses on means, requesting Jesus' touch to reverse the slide from death back toward life. Luke focuses on Jairus' method of request, passionately imploring that Jesus come to his house to heal his dying daughter. Matthew's version, with ἀλλά in a non-negative context, relies on the contrast between death and restoration to life to quickly establish the impossibility of the situation.

All three instances end the same, with Jesus' touch restoring Jairus' daughter to life. Matthew's use of ἀλλά in a non-negative context is the only instance that places all of the contrast at the head of the story, previous to the healing of the woman with the issue of blood.

Mark 9:12–13[45] (|| *Matthew 17:11–12)*

Many commentators translate μὲν in v. 12 as an intensifier (e.g., "indeed"[46]), but it instead provides a clue that a point-counterpoint set is in the text. Often the point-counterpoint set involves a μὲν . . . δέ comparison,[47] but in this case the structure is more complex. There are two such sets in the text; with one building on the other. The first set is indicated by μὲν . . . καὶ; the second involves that entire μὲν . . . καὶ structure as the counterpoint and the ἀλλά clauses (through the end of v. 13) as the point.

The "son of man" content seems strange because it appears to be an interlude of sorts between the statements concerning Elijah. This difficulty is noted by many commentators and several different approaches are taken.[48] France treats it best by noting the μὲν . . . καὶ relationship:

But the μέν in the first clause alerts us that Jesus will not simply repeat what the scribes are saying, but will add his own distinctive angle to the teaching about Elijah. Instead of a further statement with δέ, however, the following clause takes the form of a rhetorical question, challenging the disciples to expand their mental horizon beyond what the scribes have taught.[49]

France also catches the further connection between vv. 12 (μὲν . . . καὶ) and 13 (ἀλλά):

> Verse 13 resolves this puzzle by establishing two important connections: first, that the prophecy of Elijah's return has already been fulfilled, so that the experiences of Jesus as Son of Man are part of the same sequence of events as the return of Elijah;

---

[45] This specific instance is not cited in either BDF or BDAG.

[46] H. B. Swete, *The Gospel According to St. Mark: The Greek Text with Introduction* (New York: MacMillan Company, 1898), 193. Here Swete offers "it is true."

[47] Cf. Runge, *Discourse Grammar*, 72–100 (§4, "Point-Counterpoint Sets").

[48] One approach is to posit Aramaic influence, see Craig Evans' discussion of Maurice Casey's approach to this problem in Craig A. Evans, *Mark 8:27–16:20* (WBC 34b; Nashville: Thomas Nelson, 2001), 43. Another is to redact the text by moving the clause concerning "son of man" previous to the reference to Elijah; H. B. Swete discusses (and dimisses) this approach (*Mark*, 193).

[49] R. T. France, *The Gospel of Mark: A Commentary on the Greek Text* (NIGTC; Grand Rapids: Eerdmans, 2002), 358.

> second that (in contrast with the language of Mal. 4:5–6) the experience of "Elijah" has been of rejection and ill-treatment (ἐποίησαν αὐτῷ ὅσα ἤθελον), which thus foreshadows what is to happen to the Son of Man.[50]

So what is the function of ἀλλά in v. 13? As has been mentioned before, ἀλλά is a marker of contrast and it also indicates correction or replacement of concepts. These are both evident in the state of Elijah's arrival. Verse 13 stipulates that Elijah has come (correcting the question in v. 12 about Elijah's arrival) and further indicates that Elijah has suffered much, as the Messiah will suffer much.[51]

The Matthean parallel

The parallel in Matthew arranges the same content somewhat differently. The "son of man" clause (v. 12b) is moved after the overall comparison. Additionally, the overall comparison uses μὲν . . . δέ instead of the μὲν . . . ἀλλά of Mark. The comparison in Matthew is cleaner[52] than in Mark, but it is different due to using δέ as the primary point-counterpoint hinge instead of ἀλλά. As δέ is a marker of development,[53] Matthew's version uses Elijah's state of being already come as a step on the developmental path to his conclusion, that because Elijah has already come, the Messiah must be on Earth and will suffer. The same ones that did not recognize John the Baptist as Elijah and therefore persecuted him will also not recognize Jesus as Messiah, and will therefore persecute Jesus as well. What happened to John (persecution and death) will also happen to "the Son of Man."

Mark 11:31–32[54] *(|| Matthew 21:25–26 || Luke 20:5–7)*

In this instance, ἀλλά stands between two conditional clauses, the second of which is incomplete; a point-counterpoint set is not present. Jesus has just

---

[50] Ibid.

[51] Ibid., 360.

[52] Ibid., 358, notes that in Mark "the sequence of clauses is clumsy," but Matthew's is a " 'tidied-up' parallel."

[53] Heckert, *Discourse Features*, 37–57.

[54] This specific instance is not cited in either BDF or BDAG.

responded to a question posed by the scribes and chief priests (v. 28) with a counter-question (vv. 29–30). Verses 31 and 32 portray the debate behind the response to Jesus in v. 33.

Based on Jesus' question in v. 30, "Was the baptism of John from heaven or from man?," only two answers are possible: "from heaven" or "from man." The structure of vv. 31–32 presents these alternatives, showing that neither alternative is viable for the present context which includes a large crowd. Jesus relies on the disparity of opinion on this very question between the crowd and the scribes and chief priests as France indicates: "The effectiveness of Jesus' ploy depends on his being aware of popular feeling on the subject, which it would be unwise of [the scribes and chief priests] to flout in this public place."[55]

In this instance, ἀλλά is the hinge between two non-viable options. Recall the contention that ἀλλά is a marker of contrast; here the contrast is implicit between the possible answers "from heaven" or "from man." Also recall that the use of ἀλλά involves correction or replacement of concepts between juxtaposed items. Here the first answer "from heaven" is presented and dismissed using a conditional statement. Then, after ἀλλά, a second answer is presented, replacing the first. This answer is equally untenable, so much so that the apodosis of the conditional statement is not even filled. On this incomplete conditional statement, France notes:

> The four words that remain, ἀλλὰ εἴπωμεν ἐξ ἀνθρώπων, can be construed either as the beginning of a second conditional clause matching ἐὰν εἴπωμεν ἐξ οὐρανοῦ in v. 31, but with the ἐάν left unexpressed, or as a further deliberative question, "But shall we say 'From men'?," or even as a tentative decision on their part, "But let us say 'From men,' " which is then aborted by their recognition of the diplomatic gaffe that would involve. While the general sense is clear, the syntax is awkward, and the decision on how to punctuate the aposiopesis after ἀνθρώπων is a matter of taste.[56]

[55] France, *Mark*, 455. See also Evans, *Mark*, 207.

[56] France, *Mark*, 455.

Neither "from heaven" nor "from men" is an appropriate answer in the current context with a large and disagreeable crowd present. The use of ἀλλά between the conditional statements heightens the contrast between the available options and also, in conjunction with the conditional statements, shows that the scribes and chief priests have no available recourse and therefore must answer, "We do not know" (v. 33).

The Matthean and Lukan parallels

Matthew and Luke each record this event as well, though they use δέ between the conditional statements, and they provide an answer to the second conditional statement. What difference does the use of δέ in Matthew and Luke make?

The difference is subtle but appreciable. In Matthew and Luke, the use of δέ marks development of argument; the scribes and chief priests are working through the alternatives to see which is most feasible to use in response to Jesus' counter-question. Contrast is present by virtue of the options, but it is not heightened. In Mark, however, the "from man" alternative is out of the question as a response before the dialogue even begins due to the role of the crowd; thus the conditional need not even be completed. In other words, the contrast between the options is heightened in Mark's version of the story; ἀλλά marks and reinforces this heightened contrast in comparison to the accounts in Matthew and Luke.

Mark 14:27–28[57] *(|| Matthew 26:31–32)*

This episode takes place just after the meal in the upper room. Jesus has predicted his betrayal and alluded to his death. Verse 27 shifts the scene to the Mount of Olives and Jesus instructs his disciples that they will all "fall away," citing Zech 13:7. After the citation, ἀλλά is used to transition a statement about where Jesus will be after he is raised from the dead.

On its surface, the two statements—a point-counterpoint set with "you will fall away" as counterpoint and "after I am raised up" as the point—seem

[57] This specific instance is not cited in either BDF or BDAG.

unrelated. However, the use of ἀλλά shows that Jesus is really instructing his disciples what to do after he has been raised from the dead. They will fall away and scatter during the trial and crucifixion, but Jesus gives them the information they need to reassemble after the resurrection. The use of ἀλλά as the hinge between counterpoint and point marks and heightens the contrast between being scattered at the crucifixion and being regathered in Galilee after the resurrection. It also offers a correction to the scattering by giving the disciples the means to regather in Galilee after the resurrection.

The Matthean parallel

Matthew has a few differences. First, τότε is used to introduce the words of Jesus, not καὶ.[58] Second, Matthew specifies the time of the falling away: "this night." Third, the quotation formula in v. 31 uses γάρ; Mark uses ὅτι to introduce the whole thing as a subordinate clause. Fourth, Matthew adds "the flock" to qualify "sheep." Fifth and most notably, Matthew uses δέ where Mark uses ἀλλά.

According to Heckert,[59] γάρ is best described as a marker of strengthening or confirmation. In Matthew, the quotation is used to strengthen Jesus' assertion that the disciples will fall away that night. The following statement with Jesus going before them into Galilee, conjoined using δέ in Matthew, is a further development of Jesus' point. By the use of τοτε as a conjunction, the addition of "this night," the use of γάρ to strengthen and confirm Jesus' assertion regarding falling away, and the developmental use of δέ, one can see a more temporal flow in Matthew's presentation of the episode. While the disciples will fall away at the trail and through the crucifixion, they also know that Jesus will be awaiting them in Galilee to gather them together again.

Mark, by his use of point-counterpoint set with ἀλλά as its hinge, presents the scattering and instructions concerning regathering as less of a progression and more of a change of state.

---

[58] On the use of τότε as a sentence conjunction, see Stephanie Black, *Sentence Conjunctions in the Gospel of Matthew: Narrative Discourse* (Sheffield: JSOT Press, 2002), 218–53.

[59] Heckert, *Discourse Features*, 36.

Conclusion

This paper has proposed and applied two guidelines regarding ἀλλά to instances occurring in non-negative contexts with the goal of providing a basic method for examining instances of ἀλλά in the New Testament and other early Christian literature. These two guidelines are:

- ἀλλά involves enhancing the contrast between two things.
- ἀλλά involves correction or replacement.

The association of these elements with the presence of ἀλλά was confirmed through the examination of several grammars, lexicons, monographs and articles. Several instances, including all non-negative instances in the synoptic Gospels, were examined to determine which items are conjoined, how contrast between the items is made evident, and if correction or replacement is present. In each examined instance, ἀλλά indicated the presence of varying degrees of contrast. An element of correction or replacement was also identified in each instance.

Further, the importance of the contrast and correction/replacement in each passage (as opposed to deriving senses to assist in translation to English) was discussed and shown to be relevant for understanding the discourse function of ἀλλά and, therefore, helpful in the process of exegesis. These guidelines, then, appear to be reliable and helpful for the examination of passages that use ἀλλά.

Bibliography

Aland, Kurt. *Synopsis of the Four Gospels: Greek-English Edition of the Synopsis Quattor Evangeliorum*. New York: United Bible Societies, 1982.

Drummen, Annemieke. "Discourse Cohesion in Dialogue Turn-Initial ἀλλά in Greek Drama." In *Discourse Cohesion in Ancient Greek. Amsterdam Studies in Classical Philosophy 16*. Edited by Stéphanie Bakker and Gerry Wakker. Leiden/ Boston: Brill, 2009.

Balz, Horst Robert, and Gerhard Schneider, eds. *Exegetical Dictionary of the New Testament*. 3 vols. Grand Rapids: Eerdmans, 1990–1993.

Bauer, Walter, Frederick W. Danker, and William Arndt. *A Greek-English Lexicon of the New Testament and Other Early Christian Literature*. 3rd ed. Chicago: University of Chicago Press, 2000.

Black, Stephanie. *Sentence Conjunctions in the Gospel of Matthew: Narrative Discourse.* Sheffield: JSOT Press, 2002.

Blass, Friedrich. *Grammar of New Testament Greek.* Translated by Henry St. J. Thackeray. 2nd ed. New York: MacMillan, 1905.

Blass, Friedrich and Albert Debrunner. *A Greek Grammar of the New Testament and Other Early Christian Literature.* Translated and edited by Robert W. Funk. Chicago: University of Chicago Press, 1961.

Denniston, J. D. *The Greek Particles.* 2nd ed. Revised by K. J. Dover. Oxford: Oxford University Press, 1950. Reprint, Indianapolis: Hackett Publishing Company, 1996.

Dooley, Robert A. and Stephen H. Levinsohn. *Analyzing Discourse: A Manual of Basic Concepts.* Dallas: SIL International, 2001.

Evans, Craig A. *Mark 8:27–16:20.* Word Biblical Commentary 34B. Nashville: Thomas Nelson, 2001.

France, R. T. *The Gospel of Mark: A Commentary on the Greek Text.* New International Greek Testament Commentary. Grand Rapids: Eerdmans, 2002.

Funk, Robert Walter. *A Beginning-Intermediate Grammar of Hellenistic Greek.* Missoula, Mont.: Scholars Press, 1973.

Hagner, Donald A. *Matthew 1–13.* Word Biblical Commentary 33A. Dallas: Word, 1993.

Heckert, Jacob K. *Discourse Function of Conjoiners in the Pastoral Epistles.* Dallas: Summer Institute of Linguistics, 1996.

Liddell, Henry George, Robert Scott, Henry Stuart Jones, and Roderick McKenzie. *A Greek-English Lexicon.* Rev. ed. Oxford: Clarendon, 1996.

Louw, Johannes P., and Eugene Albert Nida. *Greek-English Lexicon of the New Testament: Based on Semantic Domains.* 2nd ed. New York: United Bible Societies, 1989.

Luz, Ulrich. *Matthew 8–20: A Commentary on Matthew 8–20.* Hermeneia. Translated by James E. Crouch. Minneapolis: Fortress Press, 2001.

Merriam-Webster's Collegiate Dictionary. 11th Edition. Springfield, Mass.: Merriam-Webster, 2003.

Morris, Leon. *The Gospel According to Matthew.* Pillar New Testament Commentary. Grand Rapids: Eerdmans, 1992.

Nolland, J. *Luke 9:21–18:34.* Word Biblical Commentary 35B. Nashville: Thomas Nelson, 2002.

Plummer, A. *A Critical and Exegetical Commentary on the Gospel According to St. Luke.* International Critical Commentary. London: T. & T. Clark, 1896.

Porter, Stanley E. *Idioms of the Greek New Testament.* 2nd ed. Sheffield: JSOT Press, 1999.

Porter, Stanley E. and Matthew Brook O'Donnell. "Conjunctions and Levels of Discourse." Paper presented at the Symposium of the Linguistics Institute of Ancient and Biblical Greek. Hamilton, Ont., August 24–26 2006. Online: http://www.liabg.org/liabg/symposium2006/Proceedings.pdf.

Robertson, A. T. *A Grammar of the Greek New Testament in the Light of Historical Research.* 1919. Reprint, Bellingham, Wash.: Logos Research Systems, 2006.

———. *Word Pictures in the New Testament.* Oak Harbor, Wash.: Logos Research Systems, 1997.

Runge, Steven. "Teaching Them What NOT to Do: The Nuances of Negation in the Greek New Testament." Paper presented at the annual meeting of the Evangelical Theological Society. San Diego, Cal., November 13–16, 2007. Online: http://www.logos.com/media/academic/runge/negation_pragmatics.pdf.

———. *Discourse Grammar of the Greek New Testament: A Practical Introduction for Teaching and Exegesis.* Peabody, Mass.: Hendrickson Publishers, 2010.

———. *The Lexham Discourse Greek New Testament.* Bellingham, Wash.: Logos Research Systems, 2008.

———. *The Lexham Discourse Greek New Testament: Introduction.* Bellingham, Wash.: Logos Research Systems, 2008.

Smyth, Herbert Weir. *Greek Grammar.* Rev. by Gordon M. Messing. Cambridge, Mass.: Harvard University Press, 1956.

Soanes, Catherine, and Angus Stevenson. *Concise Oxford English Dictionary.* 11th ed. Oxford: Oxford University Press, 2004.

Spence-Jones, H. D. M., ed. *St. Luke Vol. II.* The Pulpit Commentary. Bellingham, Wash.: Logos Research Systems, 2004.

Swete, Henry Barclay. *The Gospel According to St. Mark: The Greek Text with Introduction.* New York: The MacMillan Company, 1898.

Thrall, Margaret E. *Greek Particles in the New Testament: Linguistic and Exegetical Studies.* New Testament Tools and Studies. Volume 3. Grand Rapids: Eerdmans, 1962.

Young, Richard A. *Intermediate New Testament Greek: A Linguistic and Exegetical Approach.* Nashville: Broadman & Holman, 1994.

Information Structure Issues in Copular εἶναι Clauses[1]

Nicholas A. Bailey

What is the information structure of the following εἶναι clauses? Which constituent expresses the "sentence topic" (i.e., what is to be taken as the common ground between the speaker and hearer) and which one expresses the "focus" (i.e., the constituent that is unpredictable, that makes the sentence informative)?[2]

> Mark 8:29 καὶ αὐτὸς ἐπηρώτα αὐτούς, Ὑμεῖς δὲ τίνα με λέγετε εἶναι; ἀποκριθεὶς ὁ Πέτρος λέγει αὐτῷ, Σὺ εἶ ὁ Χριστός.
> [Jesus] asked them, "But who do you say that I am?" Peter answered him, "You are the Messiah."
> John 11:25 εἶπεν αὐτῇ ὁ Ἰησοῦς, Ἐγώ εἰμι ἡ ἀνάστασις καὶ ἡ ζωή·
> v. 24 Martha said to him, "I know that he will rise again in the resurrection on the last day." (v. 25) Jesus said to her, "I am the resurrection and the life."

As an approximation, we can compare the potential information structure of the Greek copular clause in Mark 8:29 with the following English paraphrases, where capital letters indicate primary sentence stress. Which paraphrase

---

[1] I am grateful for comments on an earlier version of this paper from an audience at Horsleys Green, February 14, 2004, as well as for many helpful comments from Tony Pope on the current version. I take full responsibility for any errors.

[2] Unless noted otherwise, translations are from the NRSV. Bold type in the cited translations is my own. And except where noted, the cited New Testament text is from Nestle-Aland 27th Edition.

approximates the intended meaning of the Greek? An oral reading requires a reader to commit to one stress pattern or another, and thus to a certain information structure, since sentence stress placement is a key element in the expression of information structure categories in English.

(1) A: YOU are the Christ.
B: You are the CHRIST.
C: You ARE the Christ.

Does the Greek constituent order require one interpretation and discount the others? Do the subject pronouns (σύ in Mark 8:29 and ἐγώ in John 11:25) automatically render these subject constituents as focal, or "emphatic," to use a term of traditional grammarians? How are sentences like (1.c), which involve "polar-focus," expressed in Greek?

These are questions that I attempt to answer in this article for New Testament copular εἶναι clauses, especially ones with a present tense indicative form. One conclusion that I shall draw is that the order SJ–εἶναι–CMP (SJ=subject, CMP=complement) is ambiguous and that it is compatible with either a focal complement or a focal subject. In fact, I will argue that the above two illustrated clauses have different structures. The correct analysis of John 11:25 is reflected by "I am the light of the world," where the subject ἐγώ is focal, and the correct analysis of Mark 8:29 is (1.b) "You are the CHRIST," where the complement (i.e., predicate) ὁ Χριστός is focal. Thus, in such clauses, a subject need not be topical, and nominal complements and subject pronouns are not necessarily focal. So there is no simple formula for determining the significance of constituent orders in such copular clauses. Nevertheless, some general principles and notable tendencies in constituent order patterns can be identified that will aid exegetes in their analysis.

Such information structure interpretations are often ignored by exegetes, but they can be crucial to understanding a passage. Since the form SJ–εἶναι–CMP is ambiguous, as I will argue, an exegete must consider the broader context when determining a clause's information structure. But sometimes it can be difficult to determine which interpretation is correct, in which case the exegete may be tempted not to commit to a particular interpretation. However, even if the exegete wishes to remain neutral, his (or her) job is not complete until he has cast his vote for the interpretation that seems most likely.

In any case, oral readers do not have the "luxury" of being non-committal, since, unlike written English, the spoken language requires sentence stress and in this way conveys more information structure clues than the written language does. Nor do all Bible translators have this luxury, since the linguistic resources of some languages necessarily require writers to use constructions that are, pragmatically speaking, more restricted (and precise) in meaning than an English clause like "You are the Christ" when stripped of its intonation. Later I will illustrate this dilemma with data from Kurmanji-Kurdish.

In what follows, I treat different sets of copular clauses in Koine Greek. My discussion touches on issues of constituent order, the function of subject pronouns, and the assignment of subject and complement. This discussion will set the stage for the final sections, which treat some theologically weighty copular clauses in John's Gospel; some of these clauses have been featured in the literature, but the discussions have suffered because biblical scholars typically neglect to distinguish between grammatical relations (subject vs. complement) on the one hand, and pragmatic relations (topic vs. focus vs. polarity) on the other.

My discussion focuses on present indicative forms of εἶναι, although I occasionally cite examples with other forms of εἶναι, flagging them accordingly. The reason for my treating primarily present indicative forms is because they *tend* to behave differently than other forms of εἶναι and other verbs. The latter occur clause initially much more frequently than do present indicative forms of εἶναι. This difference in behavior makes sense in so far as the present indicative forms of εἶναι (except for εἶ "2.sg") are considered to be enclitics (i.e., a subtype of "postpositive," in Classical terminology). They are considered enclitics because normally they lack an accent and do not occur clause initially.[3] But the matter is not at all straightforward, since, occasionally, we do find such forms occurring initially, and it is well-known that existential and thetic (presentational) uses of εἶναι, regardless of tense, often occur clause initially.[4] In existential and thetic uses, εἶναι is not copular

[3] For some details on the accentuation and word order of ἔστιν, see A. T. Robertson, *A Grammar of the Greek New Testament in the Light of Historical Research* (1923; repr., Nashville: Broadman, 1934), 233–34.

[4] Given the inconsistent behavior of present tense indicative εἶναι, both Kenneth

because it lacks a true complement.[5] So it is methodologically important to restrict my claims primarily to present indicative forms. Having said that, it is still occasionally helpful to cite clauses with other forms. This is justified by the fact that the distinction between enclitic and non-enclitic (or postpositive and non-postpositive) for copular clauses does not affect the position of the subject and complement *relative to each other*, but only the position of εἶναι, and so copular clauses of all types, in my opinion, still share many characteristics.

Elsewhere I have written about existential and thetic (presentational) uses of εἶναι. So this present article, with its focus on copular clauses, treats a very different use of εἶναι. Both uses of εἶναι are in fact ones that have not featured extensively in Stephen Levinsohn's work. I hope that this present study, as well as my previous work, are appropriate tributes to one who has taught me much about the discourse-pragmatics and information structure of New Testament Greek.

Some basic information structure concepts

Before turning to the Greek data, we must first define some basic concepts of information structure analysis. I will present my discussion in a framework based on Lambrecht's work.[6] This discussion presupposes a distinction

---

James Dover, *Greek Word Order* (Cambridge: Cambridge University Press, 1968), 13, and Helma Dik, *Word Order in Ancient Greek: A Pragmatic Account of Word Order Variation in Herodotus* (Amsterdam Studies in Classical Philology 5; Amsterdam: J. C. Gieben, 1995), 32n32, avoid assuming it is always an enclitic (or "postpositive"). Elsewhere, I have discussed constituent order in thetic (i.e., presentational) clauses with εἶναι and noted that εἶναι precedes its subject about half the time; in such cases εἶναι is, ignoring conjunctions, usually clause initial (Nicholas A. Bailey, "Thetic Constructions in Koine Greek" [Ph.D. diss., Amsterdam: Vrije Universiteit, 2009], 116, 233–37).

[5] Existential and thetic uses of εἶναι are often translated by "there BE" in English, as illustrated by the thetic clause in John 21:25, where ἔστιν is clause initial: Ἔστιν δὲ καὶ ἄλλα πολλὰ ἃ ἐποίησεν ὁ Ἰησοῦς "But there are also many other things that Jesus did." Such clauses are not copular because they lack a predicating element, i.e., an adjective, nominal, or prepositional phrase that functions as a predicate complement to εἶναι. See Bailey, "Thetic Constructions," 127–34.

[6] Knud Lambrecht, *Information Structure and Sentence Form* (Cambridge Studies

between grammatical relations (subject vs. object vs. complement) and information structure relations (alias pragmatic relations). The two most important and foundational information structure relations that will feature in our discussion are "(sentence) topic" and "focus."

The (sentence) topic[7] is that part of a sentence which the speaker assumes the hearer will take as the common ground between the speaker and hearer, i.e., it expresses part of the "pragmatic presupposition." An utterance with a topic serves to say something informative "about" that topic. Most typically, the topic phrase refers to an entity that has already been evoked in the discourse (i.e., it is an idea that is "activated" or "semi-activated" in the mind of the hearer) or it refers to an entity that is in some way "accessible" to the hearer, e.g., because it can be inferred from the context. As is well known, cross-linguistically, the subject constituent prototypically (and most frequently) expresses the topic, although there are many exceptions to this generalization, as will be illustrated in our data. So a subject is not necessarily topical.

In contrast to the topic, the "focus domain"—or "focus" for short—is that part of a sentence which expresses an unpredictable element that *in relation* to the topic, or some presupposed element, makes the sentence informative, i.e., it makes the sentence a "pragmatic assertion." Since the subject prototypically expresses the topic, the predicate prototypically expresses the focus.[8] In English and many other languages, an element of the focus domain is always prosodically stressed (i.e., spoken with intonational prominence), but some topic expressions may also be stressed, especially if contrastive.

The following examples illustrate the same semantic proposition ("the children went to school") expressed in three different contexts.[9] Note that the

in Linguistics; Cambridge: Cambridge University Press, 1994); and idem., "When Subjects Behave like Objects: An Analysis of the Merging of S and O in Sentence-Focus Constructions," *Studies in Language* 24 (2000): 611–82.

[7] Sentence topic is not to be confused with "discourse topic." A sentence topic is necessarily expressed by a linguistic element in a sentence. A discourse topic is what a discourse is about. It need not be referred to explicitly in each sentence of a discourse, and it may not even be expressed explicitly in a discourse.

[8] See Lambrecht, *Information Structure*, 131–33, 141, 296; Bailey, "Thetic Constructions," 11.

[9] These examples and analyses are based on ones by Lambrecht, *Information*

presupposition and assertion, in tandem with the topic and focus domains, vary according to context ([. . .]$_{\text{FOC}}$ = focus domain, [. . .]$_{\text{TOP}}$ = topic domain).[10] In (2), the topical element is of the more typical sort, a single constituent, the subject. But in (3) and in (4), the topical element is of a special type, namely a full proposition minus a variable, and the focal constituent (which makes the sentence informative) supplies the missing variable, thus completing the proposition. Such a topical element is called "a topical open proposition" (= [. . .]$_{\text{TOP'L OP}}$).[11] The proposition is called "open" because it is missing an element. (See also below on examples (6) and (7).)

(2) Context:	A: Tell me about the children. (or What did the children do?)
Info. Structure:	B: [They]$_{\text{TOP}}$ [went to SCHOOL]$_{\text{FOC}}$
Presupposition:	a comment is being made about the discourse relevant topic "the children"
Assertion:	"comment = went to school"
(3) Context:	A: Where did the children go?
Info. Structure:	B: [They went to]$_{\text{TOP'L OP}}$ [SCHOOL]$_{\text{FOC}}$
Presupposition:	the open proposition, "the children went to x," is the topical element
Assertion:	"x = school"
(4) Context:	A: Who went to school?
Info. Structure:	B: [The CHILDREN]$_{\text{FOC}}$ [went to school]$_{\text{TOP'L OP}}$
Presupposition:	the open proposition, "x went to school," is the topical element
Assertion:	"x = the children"

Structure, 121–27, 223–35.

[10] While pragmatic presupposition and assertion have to do with the speech act made by the utterance, information structure, including focus structure and topic structure, are the grammatical reflexes of those pragmatic roles.

[11] Lambrecht, *Information Structure*, 75, 156, applies the term "topic" only to those presuppositional expressions that are sentence arguments (e.g., subject and object constituents, nominalized constituents, etc.), not to open propositions (p. 122). However, since an open proposition is part of the presupposition (i.e., the common ground), it is the most topic-like element of the clause—therefore I call it "topical."

Sentences (2) and (3) have the same surface form, "They went to SCHOOL," where the noun phrase SCHOOL alone is stressed, and thus this form is to a certain degree functionally ambiguous. So the difference in meaning is a reflex of the different information structures (which reflect the different contexts the sentences are used in). In (2) the focus domain includes the entire predicate "went to SCHOOL," but in (3) it includes only the noun phrase SCHOOL.[12] This kind of situation is not unlike other areas of language where one form can have more than one sense or be appropriately used in more than one context.

Now consider example (5), which has not only the same prosodic form as (4) but also the same information structure:

(5) Context:	A: incorrectly believes it was the teachers who went to school.
Info. Structure:	B: [The CHILDREN]$_{\text{FOC}}$ [went to school]$_{\text{TOP'L OP}}$
Presupposition:	the open proposition, "x went to school," is the topical element
Assertion:	"x = the children"
Implicature:	The identity of those *who* went to school is being corrected: it was not the teachers but the children.

According to Lambrecht,[13] the difference in meaning between (4) and (5) is *not* a difference in information structure proper, since the domain of the focus and topical elements are identical and both serve to *identify* the relevant entity in an open proposition.[14] Instead, the meaning difference arises from the fact that (5) conveys the implicature that the speaker is correcting a wrong belief

[12] Thus, a focus domain (or "projection") can be larger than just the word or phrase that is stressed.

[13] See Lambrecht, *Information Structure*, 286–91 on contrastiveness and 122–23, 214–15, 222 and 228 on constituent-focus (alias "argument-focus"). See also Enric Vallduví and Maria Vilkuna, "On Rheme and Kontrast," in *The Limits of Syntax* (ed. Peter Culicover and Louise McNally; vol. 29 of *Syntax and Semantics*; San Diego: Academic Press, 1998), 79–108, esp. 84–85.

[14] It is also true that (5) might carry a stronger stress than (4), but the placement of the stress is the same, and so, according to Lambrecht, the information structure in such English sentences is identical.

held by the hearer.[15] This type of focus structure is often called "contrastive focus," since the identity of "children" contrasts with that of "teachers".[16] As a "rule of thumb" test for contrastive focus, Chafe and later Lambrecht suggested that, if you can insert a phrase like "rather than (instead of, not)" after a focal constituent or its clause without changing the meaning of the original assertion, then it is a case of contrastive focus (i.e., the constituent is a corrective focal constituent). Thus, we could paraphrase (5) as "The CHILDREN went to school, not the teachers."[17]

In the literature, structures like (4) and (5), where a single constituent in a clause is focal, are known by different terms. I shall call this focus type "constituent-focus." Other terms for this include "argument-focus" (Lambrecht's preferred term), "narrow focus," and "focus-presupposition." Constituent-focus, where a single constituent is focal, contrasts with "predicate-focus," where the entire predicate is focal, as in (2), and with structures where the subject and predicate as a unit are focal (as in thetic/presentational constructions).

Content question words, like what, who, where, etc., in questions are also considered to be instances of constituent-focus, as illustrated by (6). The question word expresses the open variable "x" and the rest of the question evokes the open proposition.[18] Reciprocally, the answer to the question is also an instance of constituent-focus, as illustrated by "the CHILDREN" in (7). If

---

[15] That is, it is a conversational implicature—something implied given the context in which the sentence is used—it is not part of the meaning of the construction itself (Lambrecht, *Information Structure*, 291; Vallduví and Vilkuna, "On Rheme and Kontrast," 84–85).

[16] Lambrecht, *Information Structure*, 286–91.

[17] Wallace Chafe, "Givenness, Contrastiveness, Definiteness, Subjects, Topics and Point of View," in *Subject and Topic* (ed. Charles N. Li; New York: Academic Press, 1976, 25–55), 35; Knud Lambrecht, *Topic, Antitopic, and Verb Agreement in Non-Standard French* (Amsterdam: John Benjamins, 1981), 67. There are other subtypes of constituent-focus discussed in the literature; see e.g., Simon C. Dik, *The Theory of Functional Grammar: Part 1: The Structure of the Clause* (Berlin: Mouton de Gruyter, 1997), 330–35.

[18] Knud Lambrecht and Laura A. Michaelis, "Sentence Accent in Information Questions: Default and Projection," *Linguistics and Philosophy* 21 (1998): 477–544; S. Dik, *The Theory of Functional Grammar*, 328–29.

the speaker judges that the open proposition "went to school" is sufficiently activated in the mind of the hearer, it need not be uttered.

(6) [Who]$_{FOC}$ went to school?
(7) [The CHILDREN]$_{FOC}$ (went to school).

English it-clefts, as illustrated by (8), also involve constituent-focus. In this example, "the CHILDREN" again constitutes the focus domain. But it-clefts are more restricted in the kinds of contexts they are used in than are non-clefts.

(8) It was [the CHILDREN]$_{FOC}$ who went to school.

One more focus structure that must be mentioned here is "polar-focus," a category that Lambrecht only discusses in passing, but which others discuss in detail.[19] In polar-focus structures, what is asserted is the truth-value of a presupposed complete proposition. In a context where a complete proposition is topical (it is either fully activated or to some degree accessible), different communicators may hold different beliefs about its truth. If, for example, someone was wondering about the truth of the proposition "the children went to school," another person might assert that it was or was not true, or that it was possibly true.

(9) A: The children WENT to school. / They DID go to school.
B: They DIDN't go. / They did NOT go.
C: They PROBABLY went.

The structural marking of polar-focus in these English examples involves stressing either (i) a verb—i.e., "verb-focus," (ii) a negative particle (not), or (iii) an adverb. Some other languages employ special particles or morphology. As a "rule of thumb" test, a polar assertion functions to answer an explicit or implicit "yes-no" question evoked by the discourse (e.g., "Did they go to school?" or "Didn't they go to school?" or "They didn't go to school, did they?"). Polar assertions also frequently convey corrective implicatures.

[19] Lambrecht, *Information Structure*, 236, 336; S. Dik, *The Theory of Functional Grammar*, 331, 384–86; Tilman N. Höhle, "Über Verum-Fokus im Deutschen" in *Informationsstruktur und Grammatik* (ed. Joachim Jacobs; Opladen: Westdeutscher Verlag, 1992), 112–41.

Finally, I mention the category of "emotive emphasis," which I use as a cover term for the functions of stress and intonation patterns of an emphatic nature, and certain particles that convey a speaker's attitudes or emotions towards a state of affairs (e.g., anger, joy, excitement, surprise, fear, irony, arrogance).[20] Such emotion and attitudes are non-propositional (or "paralinguistic") according to Ladd and for this reason Lambrecht excludes the emotive (or "expressive") component of language from information structure proper.[21] Nevertheless, emotive emphasis interacts with information structure in interesting ways. For example, in English, constituents that are stressed to convey the information structure category of focus can simultaneously be "hosts" for various types of emphatic stress. The reader can no doubt imagine emphatic stress being added to the above illustrated sentences, "They DIDn't go!" and "The CHILDREN went to school!" Moreover, words that evoke a semantic extreme or contrast are especially common hosts for emphatic stress and other special intonation patterns in English. The reader can imagine, for example, "incredible" in (10) and "slaved" in (11) receiving a special stress (in addition to the stress that the nominals "dream" and "homework" would receive). As I understand it, such hosts for emotive emphasis represent salient elements of a broad focus domain.

(10) Last night I [had the most *incredible* dream.]$_{FOC}$
(11) After school, Joe [went fishing at the river]$_{FOC}$ while Jack [*slaved* over his homework.]$_{FOC}$

What is relevant to our discussion is the proposal that certain marked word orders in Greek can serve not only to mark information structure categories like focus, but that an element of a broad focus domain is emotively emphatic. This assumption is implicit in the work of Levinsohn.[22]

[20] I am using the term "(emotive) emphasis" here in a precise way, in contrast to the loose way "emphasis" is used in traditional grammars where it seems to cover any kind of prominence.

[21] D. R. Ladd, *Intonational Phonology* (Cambridge: Cambridge University, 1996), 33–34, 200–2; Lambrecht, *Information Structure*, 239, 254; Bailey, "Thetic Constructions," 40–41, 107–8.

[22] For example, Levinsohn assumes that, in Greek, focus and emphasis are two distinct reasons for preposing a constituent before its verb (Stephen H. Levinsohn, *Discourse Features of New Testament Greek: A Coursebook on the Information Structure*

Some common types of copular clauses

Copular clauses come in many varieties. Some major subtypes include "predicate locatives" (e.g., The children are at school), "predicate adjectives" (e.g., The children are silly), and "predicate nominals" (e.g., He is a teacher). "Predicate nominals," in turn, can be subdivided into at least two major subtypes, ones expressing proper inclusion and ones of the equative sort, according to Payne.[23] Proper inclusion is illustrated by (12), where the predicate nominal "a teacher" indicates a class to which the subject belongs. An equative clause "assert[s] that a particular entity (the subject of the clause) is identical to the entity specified in the predicate nominal," as illustrated by the clauses in (13).[24]

(12) Proper inclusion:	He is a teacher.
(13) Equative:	He is my father. | You are the Christ.

---

of New Testament Greek [Dallas: SIL International, 2000]). He describes emphasis as "express[ing] strong feelings about an item or indicat[ing] that an event is unexpected" (7; see also Bailey, "Thetic Constructions," 106). Focus he defines as "what is relatively the most important . . . information in the given setting" (7; he is following S. Dik). Elsewhere Levinsohn makes clear that such focal constituents may also be "contrastive," and that the contrast may relate to either the preceding context (37, 40) or the following context (55–57).

[23] Thomas E. Payne, *Describing Morphosyntax: A Guide for Field Linguists* (Cambridge: Cambridge University Press, 1997), 114.

[24] Equative clauses go by other names. Kees Hengeveld, *Non-Verbal Predication: Theory, Typology, Diachrony* (Berlin: Mouton de Gruyter, 1992), 80–89, calls them "identification." Hengeveld distinguishes two types of identification: "specification" and "characterization." In the specification type, the predicate complement exhaustively identifies the subject (e.g., The capital of France is Paris), but this is not so in the characterization type (e.g., Paris is [among other things] the capital of France). An even more nuanced discussion is found in Line Mikkelsen, "Copular Clauses," in *Semantics: An International Handbook of Natural Language Meaning* (ed. Klaus von Heusinger, Claudia Maienborn, and Paul Portner; Berlin: Mouton de Gruyter, forthcoming). Mikkelsen distinguishes three types (besides her "predicational" type, which for predicate nominals corresponds to Payne's "proper inclusion"): "specificational" (e.g., *The director of* Anatomy of a Murder *is Otto Preminger*), "identification" (e.g., That (woman) is Sylvia, here with a demonstrative), and "equative" (e.g., Sylvia Obernauer is *her*).

To avoid confusion, I will refer to such predicate elements of copular verbs as "complements" (and reserve "predicate" for the entire verb/copula phrase).

In what follows, our discussion of Greek copular clauses will focus on equative clauses. Much of the discussion will concern (i) the position of a nominal focal constituent (i.e., does it precede or follow the copula?) and (ii) whether it expresses the subject or complement, although we will also treat a few clauses that might in fact involve polar-focus.

Constituent-focus in preverbal and postverbal positions, expressing either subject or complement

One goal of this section is to show that constituent-focus in equative clauses can occur in either preverbal or postverbal positions, and that it can express either the subject or complement. Another goal is to illustrate some typical and non-typical orders in such clauses, some of which are pragmatically determined, but others which are not.

In information questions, question words (e.g., τίς "who, what," ποῦ "where," πόθεν "whence") as a rule always precede their verb, including εἶναι (or the non-verbal predicate if there is no verb). They may come immediately before the copula, as in John 1:19 and 5:12, or earlier, as in Matt 18:1, where something intervenes. As stated earlier, such question words and their answers are considered to be (prototypical) instances of constituent-focus.

> John 1:19 Σὺ $[\text{τίς}]_{\text{FOC}}$ εἶ;
> "Who are you?"
> John 5:12 $[\text{Τίς}]_{\text{FOC}}$ ἐστιν ὁ ἄνθρωπος ὁ εἰπών σοι, Ἆρον καὶ περιπάτει;
> "Who is the man who said to you, 'Take it up and walk'?"
> Matt 18:1 $[\text{Τίς}]_{\text{FOC}}$ ἄρα μείζων ἐστὶν ἐν τῇ βασιλείᾳ τῶν οὐρανῶν;
> "Who is the greatest in the kingdom of heaven?"

Identifying which constituent is the subject in copular clauses is not always easy, especially when the subject is third person. McGaughy worked out a useful set of rules for identifying subject in Greek copular clauses.[25] His rules make use of both syntactic and discourse criteria.[26] According to his rules, τίς is the complement in the two John passages: this is because in 1:19, the copula εἶ agrees with the subject pronoun σύ (rule 1); and in 5:12 the subject is arthrous, i.e., takes the article (rule 3c). But for Matt 18:1, μείζων . . . ἐν τῇ βασιλείᾳ would be the complement since it is anarthrous (i.e., lacks the article).

In the handful of cases I have collected, focal constituents that answer a content question usually precede the verb, especially if the question was just evoked in the discourse. Consider the (anarthrous) name Ἰησοῦς in John 5:15 (which answers the question "Who healed you?") and the pronoun ὑμεῖς in 1 Thess 2:20 (which answers Paul's rhetorical question). According

---

[25] Lane C. McGaughy, *Toward a Descriptive Analysis of EINAI as a Linking Verb in New Testament Greek* (Society of Biblical Literature Dissertation Series 6; Atlanta: Society of Biblical Literature, 1972). McGaughy's rules are ranked in the order they are to be applied (so if Rule 1 applies, one should not look beyond it).
"Rule 1. The subject is that word or word cluster which agrees in person and number with the personal ending (bound morphemes) of the equative verb" (p. 36).
"Rule 2. The word or word cluster with head term in the nominative case is the subject" (p. 39).
"Rule 3. The subject is determined by its antecedent" (p. 40). [Rules 3, including 3a–3d, to varying degrees use discourse criteria to identify subject.]
"Rule 3a. Demonstrative and relative pronouns are subjects" (p. 46). [This rule would not work for English (where the grammatical subject in declarative clauses is defined by its position in relation to the verb). A (demonstrative) cataphoric pronoun in English can either be a subject or complement argument. Compare "THIS is what I want to talk about: xyz" versus "What I want to what to talk about is THIS: xyz" (see 1 Cor 9:3).]
"Rule 3b. The subject is indicated by zero anaphora" (p. 48). [This rule uses topic criteria to identify the subject.]
"Rule 3c. The word or word cluster determined by an article is the subject" (p. 49). [So a definite complement would lack the article, as is typical when preverbal, according to Colwell's rule—see note 31.]
"Rule 3d. If both words or word clusters are determined by an article, the first one is the subject" (p. 53).
[26] Daniel B. Wallace, *Greek Grammar Beyond the Basics: An Exegetical Syntax of the New Testament* (Grand Rapids: Zondervan, 1996) offers a set of three rules for identifying subject (pp. 42–43), which are to a large degree based on McGaughy's.

to McGaughy's rules, in the former Ἰησοῦς is the complement (rule 3c), but in the latter ὑμεῖς is the subject (rule 1).[27]

> John 5:15 ἀπῆλθεν ὁ ἄνθρωπος καὶ ἀνήγγειλεν τοῖς Ἰουδαίοις ὅτι [Ἰησοῦς]$_{\text{FOC}}$ ἐστιν ὁ ποιήσας αὐτὸν ὑγιῆ.
> v. 12 They asked him, "Who is the man who said to you, 'Take it up and walk'?" (v. 13) Now the man . . . did not know who it was. . . . (v. 14) Later Jesus found him in the temple. . . . (v. 15) The man went away and told the Jews that it was Jesus who had made him well.
> 1 Thess 2:20 [ὑμεῖς]$_{\text{FOC}}$ γάρ ἐστε ἡ δόξα ἡμῶν καὶ ἡ χαρά.
> (v. 19) For what is our hope or joy or crown of boasting before our Lord Jesus at his coming? Is it not you? (v. 20) Yes, you are our glory and joy!

But even focal constituents answering an explicit question can be postverbal, as illustrated by the complement Ἰησοῦς in Acts 26:15 (rule 1).

> Acts 26:15 ἐγὼ δὲ εἶπα, Τίς εἶ, κύριε;ὑὁ δὲ κύριος εἶπεν, Ἐγώ εἰμι [Ἰησοῦς]$_{\text{FOC}}$ ὃν σὺ διώκεις.
> I asked, "Who are you, Lord?" The Lord answered, "I am Jesus whom you are persecuting."

---

[27] But Wallace, *Greek Grammar*, 44, esp. note 25, argues that, in clauses with both an arthrous noun phrase and a proper name, the subject will be whichever comes first, in which case anarthrous Ἰησοῦς in John 5:15 would be the subject (he cites John 8:39; 1 John 2:22; 4:15; 5:1, 5). However, given the fairly strong correlations between (i) focality and the lack of the article and between (ii) focality and the predicate (Lambrecht, *Information Structure*), I would still follow McGaughy's rules (see Levinsohn, *Discourse Features*, 148–67, and Bailey, "Thetic Constructions," 121, on the correlation of between the lack of the article and focality). In any case, Wallace unfortunately did not distinguish grammatical relations from information structure categories, in which case I am certain we would agree that Ἰησοῦς in John 5:15 is focal.
See also John 6:63 [τὸ πνεῦμά]$_{\text{FOC}}$ ἐστιν τὸ ζῳοποιοῦν, ἡ σὰρξ οὐκ ὠφελεῖ οὐδέν· which is often translated by an it-cleft (NRSV: "It is the spirit that gives life; the flesh is useless"). According to McGaughy's rule 3d (and Wallace's rules), τὸ πνεῦμά is the subject.

In cases of constituent-focus that only answer an implicit question, the focal element is often postverbal. Consider the subject ὁ πατήρ μου (rule 3d) in John 8:54 (it answers an implicit question "Who glorifies Jesus?" and it is also implicitly corrective, assuming his audience believed that Jesus alone was magnifying himself) and consider the (anarthrous) complement Μωϋσῆς in John 5:45 (rule 3c).[28] (Notice that the NRSV uses an it-cleft for John 8:54.)

> John 8:54 Ἐὰν ἐγὼ δοξάσω ἐμαυτόν, ἡ δόξα μου οὐδέν ἐστιν· ἔστιν [ὁ πατήρ μου]$_{\text{FOC}}$ ὁ δοξάζων με, ὃν ὑμεῖς λέγετε ὅτι θεὸς ἡμῶν ἐστιν,
> If I glorify myself, my glory is nothing. It is my Father who glorifies me, he of whom you say, "He is our God,"
> John 5:45 μὴ δοκεῖτε ὅτι [ἐγὼ]$_{\text{FOC}}$ κατηγορήσω ὑμῶν πρὸς τὸν πατέρα· ἔστιν ὁ κατηγορῶν ὑμῶν [Μωϋσῆς,]$_{\text{FOC}}$ εἰς ὃν ὑμεῖς ἠλπίκατε.
> Do not think that I will accuse you before the Father; your accuser is Moses, on whom you have set your hope.

Since present indicative forms of the copula normally behave as enclitics, it is remarkable that ἔστιν in these last two examples is clause initial. This has led some to read these as existentials (i.e., as non-copular), e.g., "there exists my Father" and "there exists your accuser."[29] But such interpretations are awkward with definite subjects, and in any case, there are other less controversial instances of clause initial copulas, even if rare. Consider, e.g., Heb 11:1, where the subject πίστις is defined (see also Luke 8:11; 1 Tim 6:6;

---

[28] More cases of postverbal constituent-focus in equative clauses include (all are complements) John 1:4 ("the light of all people," imperfect), 9 (imperfect); additional cases might also be Matt 5:13 and 14; Luke 1:19; John 5:35 (imperfect); 6:33; 7:41. More preverbal cases include (all but one is the subject) John 6:63 ("the Spirit"); 8:18; 2 Cor 3:2 (similar to 1 Thess 2:20); Phil 3:3; additional cases might also be Matt 11:3 and parallel Luke 7:19 (which are simultaneously polar); John 8:39 (the complement "Abraham"); 1 Cor 12:27; 1 John 5:6 (e.g., "it is the *Spirit* who testifies").

[29] See Brooke Foss Westcott, *The Epistles of St. John: The Greek Text with Notes and Essays* (3rd ed.; London: MacMillan, 1892), 15, 64, and see D. Theodor Zahn, *Das Evangelium des Johannes* (Leipzig: Deichert'sche Verlagsbuchhandlung Nachfolger: Georg Böhme, 1908), 423.

1 John 1:5; and clauses lacking an explicit subject: 2 Tim 4:11; Titus 3:9; Rev 16:14).

> Heb 11:1 Ἔστιν δὲ πίστις [ἐλπιζομένων ὑπόστασις,]$_{\text{FOC}}$ πραγμάτων ἔλεγχος οὐ βλεπομένων.
> Now faith is the assurance of things hoped for, the conviction of things not seen.

Whatever the case, equative clauses with a present indicative and the order εἶναι–SJ–CMP (or other εἶναι-initial clause type) are indeed rare.[30] More typically, when both subject and complement are explicit, the order SJ–εἶναι–CMP occurs. This order is illustrated by all but the last two copular clauses in Matt 13:37–39. In each clause, it is the complement that is focal (see rules 3d and 3c). (Jesus is explaining a parable the disciples failed to understand. He is answering implicit questions, identifying "Who is the sower?," "What is the field?," etc. So each focal nominal complement identifies a missing element in an open proposition.)

> v. 37 Ὁ σπείρων τὸ καλὸν σπέρμα ἐστὶν [ὁ υἱὸς τοῦ ἀνθρώπου,]$_{\text{FOC}}$
> The one who sows the good seed is the Son of Man;
> v. 38a ὁ δὲ ἀγρός ἐστιν [ὁ κόσμος,]FOC
> the field is the world,
> v. 38b τὸ δὲ καλὸν σπέρμα οὗτοί εἰσιν [οἱ υἱοὶ τῆς βασιλείας·]$_{\text{FOC}}$
> and the good seed are the children of the kingdom;

---

[30] Clause initial forms that are not present indicative are common, especially in non-equative clauses. Examples with the imperfect include Matt 7:8; 14:24 (εἶναι–CMP–SJ); John 18:40; with the future: Mark 10:8; 13:19; with non-finite forms: participial: Acts 27:9; Rom 5:6; infinitival: Acts 18:5 (equative); Rom 4:16 (εἶναι–CMP–SJ). John 11:2 is problematic: ἦν δὲ Μαριὰμ ἡ ἀλείψασα τὸν κύριον μύρῳ, NET: "Now it was Mary who anointed the Lord with perfumed oil." According to the NET's use of an it-cleft, Μαριὰμ is focal, and according to McGaughy's rule 3c, it is also the complement (because anarthrous). That Μαριὰμ is focal requires us to assume (as many commentators do) that John believed his readers would have already heard about a woman who anointed the Lord with oil but they did not know she was this particular Mary who was sister to Lazarus of Bethany. But, as pointed out to me by Tony Pope, taking "who anointed the Lord with perfumed oil, etc." as the topical element is somewhat bizarre since the story about Mary anointing Jesus comes later. According to the Wallace's criteria, Μαριὰμ would instead count as the topical subject (see my note 27).

v. 38c τὰ δὲ ζιζάνιά εἰσιν [οἱ υἱοὶ τοῦ πονηροῦ,]$_{\text{FOC}}$
the weeds are the children of the evil one,
v. 39a ὁ δὲ ἐχθρὸς ὁ σπείρας αὐτά ἐστιν [ὁ διάβολος,]$_{\text{FOC}}$
and the enemy who sowed them is the devil;
v. 39b ὁ δὲ θερισμὸς [συντέλεια αἰῶνός]$_{\text{FOC}}$ ἐστιν,
the harvest is the end of the age,
v. 39c οἱ δὲ θερισταὶ [ἄγγελοί]$_{\text{FOC}}$ εἰσιν.
and the reapers are the angels.
v. 40 Just as the weeds are collected and burned up with fire, so will it be at the end of the age. (v. 41) The Son of Man will send his angels, and they will collect out of his kingdom all causes of sin and all evildoers, (v. 42) and they will throw them into the furnace of fire, where there will be weeping and gnashing of teeth. (v. 43) Then the righteous will shine like the sun in the kingdom of their Father.

I have found that, in equative clauses (excluding infinitival and participial versions), the order SJ–εἶναι–CMP is the most common, and in fact it appears to be an unmarked order (i.e., a "neutral" order, so a discourse-pragmatic explanation would be irrelevant). This order is also very common for non-equative copular clauses. Why certain (focal) complements precede the copula, like "(the) end of (the) age" and "(the) angels" in the last two tokens, is not an easy question to answer.[31] Elsewhere, building on work by John Callow, I have concluded that these two noun phrases are likely preverbal because the speaker wishes to "spotlight" them, i.e., give them special prominence.[32]

---

[31] Despite these NPs lacking articles, they are commonly taken as "definite," i.e., as instances of "Colwell's rule" (E. C. Colwell, "A Definite Rule for the Use of the Article in the Greek New Testament," *JBL* 52 [1933]: 12–21.) Colwell noted that when a nominal complement precedes its copula and refers to a definite (i.e., identifiable) entity, it almost always lacks the article.

[32] See Bailey, "Thetic Constructions," 111–12 for a summary and illustration of Callow's findings (John Callow, "Constituent Order in Copula Clauses: A Partial Study," in *Linguistics and New Testament Interpretation: Essays on Discourse Analysis* [ed. David Alan Black, Katharine Barnwell, and Stephen Levinsohn; Nashville: Broadman, 1992], 68–89). Briefly, Callow notes three possible functions of such preverbal copular complements. They may be (i) contrastive, (ii) emphatic, or (iii) serve to "spotlight" something of special interest in the discourse. That a complement is postverbal may be because it is a long coordinated phrase; otherwise,

This prominence is reflected by the fact that they persist in the discourse (both entities are mentioned again later, in 13:40–41 where they feature at the climax of the parable). Still, since "the Son of Man," who was identified in postverbal position in 13:37, also explicitly persists, the correlations between (i) preverbal position and persistence and (ii) postverbal position and lack of persistence are not perfect.

There are other (syntactic or quasi-syntactic) environments where the position of the copula's complement is probably pragmatically unmarked (i.e., it is determined automatically). The following observations apply to most types of copular clauses, not just ones of the equative sort. Postverbal complements are most typical when the (explicit) subject is a personal pronoun (e.g., ἐγώ) or deictic pronoun (οὗτος, αὕτη, τοῦτο)[33] or a relative pronoun. And preverbal complements are strongly preferred when the clause lacks an explicit lexical subject (or when the subject is left-dislocated and so not in the clause core) and the clause is neither negated, relativized, a question, imperatival, nor infinitival. I have tested this last syntactic environment for εἶναι clauses in much of the New Testament, finding few exceptions.[34] Examples of this constellation with proper inclusion and adjectival complements are common, as illustrated by Matt 14:26 and John 7:12. But there are also occasional examples of the equative sort, as illustrated by Matt 27:42 (I am assuming that βασιλεὺς Ἰσραήλ is definite).

---

statements with postverbal complements appear to be "off the theme-line" (79; in which case the idea usually does not persist) or "downplayed" (78) or in a οὐ/μὴ . . . ἀλλά "not X but Y" construction.

[33] On the preference for postverbal complements when the subject is a pronoun, see McGaughy, *EINAI*, 57 and Levinsohn, *Discourse Features*, 39.
Cataphoric demonstrative pronouns (i.e., deictic pronouns) in copular clauses comprise a special subtype. They are necessarily instances of subject constituent-focus, where what is identified is yet to be revealed in the subsequent discourse. According to my unsystematic counts, they prefer preverbal position (e.g., John 1:19; 3:19; 6:29, 39, 40; 15:12; 17:3; James 1:27; 1 John 2:25; 3:11; 5:6, 9) but also occur postverbally (e.g., Matt 10:2; Acts 8:32, imperfect; 1 Cor 9:3; 1 John 1:5).

[34] Kahn has observed much the same for Homer (Charles H. Kahn, *The Verb "Be" in Ancient Greek* [Indianapolis: Hackett Publishing, 2003]). Kahn (pp. 429–30) treats εἰμί in indicative clauses, whether main or subordinate (but it is not clear to me if he excludes negated clauses or questions).

Matt 14:26 λέγοντες ὅτι [Φάντασμά ἐστιν]$_{FOC}$
But when the disciples saw him walking on the sea, they were terrified, saying, "It is a ghost!"
John 7:12 οἱ μὲν ἔλεγον ὅτι [Ἀγαθός ἐστιν,]$_{FOC}$
some were saying, "He is a good man,"
Matt 27:42 Ἄλλους ἔσωσεν, ἑαυτὸν οὐ δύναται σῶσαι· [βασιλεὺς Ἰσραήλ]$_{FOC}$ ἐστιν,
He saved others; he cannot save himself. He is the King of Israel;

The strong preference for this order where the copula "hangs" on the complement, at least in the above-stated syntactic environments, is of course evidence that εἶναι is behaving like an enclitic (i.e., like a postpositive).

Constituent-focus may also involve a split phrase (i.e., a discontinuous constituent), in which part of the phrase precedes and part follows the copula. To be sure, split phrases are analytically difficult. Presently, I am considering three possible interpretations for such equative copular complements: It may be that (i) the preverbal part alone should be considered the sole focused element, identifying the variable of the open proposition; or (ii) the preverbal element may be the most salient part of the larger focused constituent (because it will feature in the ensuing discourse, or is contrastive or emotive); or (iii), especially when there is no explicit subject, it may simply be a reflex of a default rule of copular clauses in Greek, that some portion of a complex complement (typically the head noun) must precede the verb.

Matt 5:34–35 involves three split phrases, where Jesus gives three reasons why one should not swear and each reason evokes an open proposition ("What is significant about heaven?," "about earth?," and "about Jerusalem?"). In principle, all three could be instances of type (iii), i.e., obeying the default rule. However, in the first two, it could also be that the most salient elements are set off in the preverbal position, and postverbal elements about "God" are topical (part of the open proposition), in which case these would illustrate type (i) and the preverbal elements alone are in the focus domain. But such an argument for the preverbal element πόλις in the third case seems less likely because there no mention of "the Great King" elsewhere in this context. So I assume that the entire constituent, πόλις . . . τοῦ μεγάλου βασιλέως is in the focus domain. If so, this could be an instance of either type (ii) (where πόλις was set off because it is salient) or of type (iii).

> Matt 5:34–35 (v. 34) ἐγὼ δὲ λέγω ὑμῖν μὴ ὀμόσαι ὅλως· μήτε ἐν τῷ οὐρανῷ, ὅτι θρόνος ἐστὶν τοῦ θεοῦ, (v. 35) μήτε ἐν τῇ γῇ, ὅτι ὑποπόδιόν ἐστιν τῶν ποδῶν αὐτοῦ, μήτε εἰς Ἱεροσόλυμα, ὅτι πόλις ἐστὶν τοῦ μεγάλου βασιλέως,
> v. 34 But I say to you, Do not swear at all, either by heaven, for it is the throne of God, (v. 35) or by the earth, for it is his footstool, or by Jerusalem, for it is the city of the great King.

In Matt 23:31, where Jesus tells his hearers "who they are", "sons" may well be intended as a salient element, in which case this would be an instance of type (i) or (ii). However, in John 19:21, it does not make sense to argue that "the king" is more salient or contrastive. Rather this would have to be a case of type (iii).[35]

> Matt 23:31 ὥστε μαρτυρεῖτε ἑαυτοῖς ὅτι υἱοί ἐστε τῶν φονευσάντων τοὺς προφήτας.
> v. 30 and you say, "If we had lived in the days of our ancestors, we would not have taken part with them in shedding the blood of the prophets." (v. 31) Thus you testify against yourselves that you are descendants of those who murdered the prophets.
> John 19:21 Μὴ γράφε· Ὁ βασιλεὺς τῶν Ἰουδαίων, ἀλλ᾽ ὅτι ἐκεῖνος εἶπεν, Βασιλεύς εἰμι τῶν Ἰουδαίων.
> "Do not write, 'The King of the Jews,' but, 'This man said, I am King of the Jews.'"

There are many aspects of split phrases that are not clear to me. Nevertheless, what does seem clear is that an entire split phrase can be a case of constituent-focus.[36]

In summary, this section has shown that constituent-focus in copular εἶναι clauses, especially of the equative type, occurs in a variety of structures. The

[35] Contrast Mark 2:28 (probably not equative) where, given the use of non-conjunctive (and thus focal) καί, it is the postverbal element that is more salient: ὥστε κύριός ἐστιν ὁ υἱὸς τοῦ ἀνθρώπου καὶ τοῦ σαββάτου "the Son of Man is lord even of the Sabbath."

[36] More equative clauses with split complements include Matt 27:40 (υἱὸς . . . τοῦ θεοῦ) and 27:43 (with the inverse order, θεοῦ . . . υἱός); Luke 4:9; 22 (with a polar element); John 1:49 (could be polar-focus; some manuscripts have ἀληθῶς and several lack the split); 9:5; 2 Cor 6:16 (if sanctuary is definite).

focal constituent can be either preverbal or postverbal, and it can express either the subject or complement (the latter being more common in the illustrated examples).[37] Complex focal complements can also be split. Question words like τίς invariably occur initially, but focal constituents answering explicit and implicit questions often do not. When both subject and complement are explicit, the order SJ–εἶναι–CMP is most common (even with complex complements) and it appears to be a default order (this order is also very compatible with relativization, negation, and questions). When there is no explicit subject in the clause core (in which case the subject cannot be focal), and the clause is neither negated, relativized, a question, imperatival, nor infinitival, then there is a strong tendency for the complement (or part of it when complex) to precede the copula, thus CMP–εἶναι, what is again a default order, I believe. These last two observations apply not just to the equative type.

Paired cases of positive-negative constituent-focus

Callow observes that preverbal copular complements are often contrastive (or emphatic or "spotlighting," as I mentioned in footnote 32). But he also notes that postverbal complements may be contrastive if they occur in a οὐ/μὴ . . . ἀλλά "not X but Y" construction.[38] Many instances of this construction in fact involve pairs of contrastive foci (i.e., corrective constituent-focus) where the first focal constituent is usually negated and the second is positive. 1 Corinthians 12:14 and Rom 6:14 are fairly typical instances with postverbal focal complements in non-equative clauses.

> 1 Corinthians 12:14 καὶ γὰρ τὸ σῶμα οὐκ ἔστιν [ἓν μέλος]$_{\text{FOC}}$ ἀλλὰ [πολλά.]$_{\text{FOC}}$
> Indeed, the body does not consist of one member but of many.
> Rom 6:14 οὐ γάρ ἐστε [ὑπὸ νόμον]$_{\text{FOC}}$ ἀλλὰ [ὑπὸ χάριν.]$_{\text{FOC}}$

37 That constituent-focus may occur in both preverbal and postverbal positions is also true for non-copular clauses. See the discussion in Bailey, "Thetic Constructions," 103–9.

38 Callow, "Constituent Order in Copula Clauses," 77–78. See H. Dik, *Word Order*, 38–45 on similar constructions in Classical Greek.

> For sin will have no dominion over you, since you are not under law but under grace.

Equative instances are rare. Mark 13:11 and Matt 10:20 are two instances from parallel passages. Interestingly, in these clauses, the focal constituents are subjects rather than complements, and in Matthew's version, it is noteworthy that the initial subject (ὑμεῖς) is preverbal.

> Mark 13:11 οὐ γάρ ἐστε [ὑμεῖς]$_{FOC}$ οἱ λαλοῦντες ἀλλὰ [τὸ πνεῦμα τὸ ἅγιον.]$_{FOC}$
> When they bring you to trial and hand you over, do not worry beforehand about what you are to say; but say whatever is given you at that time, for it is not you who speak, but the Holy Spirit.
> Matt 10:20 οὐ γὰρ [ὑμεῖς]$_{FOC}$ ἐστε οἱ λαλοῦντες ἀλλὰ [τὸ πνεῦμα τοῦ πατρὸς ὑμῶν]$_{FOC}$ τὸ λαλοῦν ἐν ὑμῖν.
> for it is not you who speak, but the Spirit of your Father speaking through you.

Consider also John 1:8 (with imperfect). Although a marginal example (the second element is not entirely parallel to the first), it may be that the postverbal subject ἐκεῖνος is also focal, given the mention of "the light" in 1:7 (the NRSV's use of "he himself" supports this reading):[39]

> John 1:8 οὐκ ἦν [ἐκεῖνος]$_{FOC}$ τὸ φῶς, ἀλλ᾽ ἵνα μαρτυρήσῃ περὶ τοῦ φωτός.
> v. 7 [John] came as a witness to testify to the light, so that all might believe through him. (v. 8) He himself was not the light, but he came to testify to the light.

But a focal complement can even be preverbal in this construction, as illustrated by the prepositional phrases in (non-equative) John 7:22 and in John 12:30 (with γίνομαι).

> John 7:22 οὐχ ὅτι [ἐκ τοῦ Μωϋσέως]$_{FOC}$ ἐστὶν ἀλλ᾽ [ἐκ τῶν πατέρων]$_{FOC}$

[39] Or John 1:8 could be primarily polar, indicating a strong denial (e.g., He was *not* the light). The only other instance of this construction with an equative clause occurs in 3:28, which may also be primarily polar.

RSV: Moses gave you circumcision (not that it is from Moses, but from the fathers), and you circumcise a man upon the sabbath.
John 12:30 Οὐ [δι' ἐμὲ]$_{FOC}$ ἡ φωνὴ αὕτη γέγονεν ἀλλὰ [δι' ὑμᾶς.]$_{FOC}$
Jesus answered, "This voice has come for your sake, not for mine."

To sum up, the above sample of the οὐ/μὴ . . . ἀλλά construction also presents a mixed picture. The focal constituent may be either the subject or complement and it may come either before or after the copula. Three, if not all four, instances of the equative type that I have found have focal subjects.

Information structure functions of subject pronouns

Traditionally, grammarians and commentators have assumed that certain pronouns, especially nominative ones like ἐγώ and σύ, are "emphatic." From our perspective, "emphatic" is an imprecise designation for a variety of phenomena.[40] Since such subject pronouns occur in many equative copular clauses, it is helpful to outline here some of their major pragmatic uses. I will argue that such pronouns can be either focal or topical; that some are contrastive and others indicate (what I earlier defined narrowly) as "emotive emphasis"; but that still others have the indirect effect of marking a discourse boundary (i.e., a new beginning) or even a discourse peak. (Since the copula always agrees with first and second person pronouns, they express the subject—see McGaughy's rule 1.)

So far we have cited two passages where a subject pronoun was focal according to Lambrecht's definitions: in the copular clause in 1 Thess 2:20 ([ὑμεῖς]$_{FOC}$ γάρ ἐστε ἡ δόξα ἡμῶν καὶ ἡ χαρά "You are our glory and joy") and in the non-copular clause in John 5:45 (μὴ δοκεῖτε ὅτι [ἐγὼ]$_{FOC}$ κατηγορήσω ὑμῶν πρὸς τὸν πατέρα "Do not think that it is I who will accuse you before the Father"). To these can be added more examples, such as ἐγώ in Matt 14:27

[40] On Classical Greek, see Herbert Weir Smyth, *Greek Grammar* (rev. by Gordon M. Messing; Harvard: Harvard University Press, 1956), §1190–1192. On Koine, see Friedrich Blass, Albert Debrunner and Robert Walter Funk, *A Greek Grammar of the New Testament and Other Early Christian Literature* (Chicago: University of Chicago Press, 1961), who state that first and second person nominative pronouns are employed "for contrast or other emphasis" (§277). See also Wallace, *Greek Grammar*, 320–23.

and σύ in 14:28 (in both of which the copula immediately follows, behaving as a postpositive, i.e., in its enclitic-like position; see also John 6:20 and 2 Sam 2:20). These clauses involve ellipsis in that the complement (something like "that which you see") is unexpressed and so the order is SJ–εἶναι.[41] The example in 14:28 is certainly contrastive.

> Matt 14:26–28 (v. 26) λέγοντες ὅτι Φάντασμά ἐστιν, . . . (v. 27) εὐθὺς δὲ ἐλάλησεν ὁ Ἰησοῦς αὐτοῖς λέγων, Θαρσεῖτε, [ἐγώ]$_{FOC}$ εἰμι· μὴ φοβεῖσθε. (v. 28) ἀποκριθεὶς δὲ αὐτῷ ὁ Πέτρος εἶπεν, Κύριε, εἰ [σὺ]$_{FOC}$ εἶ, κέλευσόν με
> v. 26 But when the disciples saw him walking on the sea, they were terrified, saying, "It is a ghost!" And they cried out in fear. (v. 27) But immediately Jesus spoke to them and said, "Take heart, it is I; do not be afraid." (v. 28) Peter answered him, "Lord, if it is you, command me to come to you on the water."

According to Lambrecht's definitions,[42] every case of constituent-focus must be expressed either pronominally or lexically. In other words, there must be a constituent (a phrasal category) which is the host for the focus relation (and in languages like English it would also be the host for the prosodic stress). So in a sentence like υἱὸς ἀνθρώπου ἐστίν in John 5:27, which lacks an explicit subject constituent, the subject could never be an instance of constituent-focus.

> John 5:27 καὶ ἐξουσίαν ἔδωκεν αὐτῷ κρίσιν ποιεῖν, ὅτι [υἱὸς ἀνθρώπου]$_{FOC}$ ἐστίν.
> and [the Father] has given him authority to execute judgment, because he is the Son of Man.

In contrast to the foregoing examples with focal pronominal subjects, we have also noted in passing a subject pronoun that is clearly not focal, σύ in

[41] On analogy to clauses like ἐγώ εἰμι, where ἐγώ is clearly the subject and the complement is unexpressed, I count as the subjects the proper names and nouns in Mark 6:15 (Elijah); 10:47 (Jesus the Nazarene); John 20:14 and 21:4 (Jesus); and 21:12 (the Lord). Colloquial English follows a different pattern than Greek; the focal constituent in a functionally equivalent construction is the complement (e.g., "It's me!" or "It's Jesus").

[42] Lambrecht, *Information Structure*, 214–15.

John 1:19, Σὺ [τίς]$_{FOC}$ εἶ; "Who are you?" (So, it is clear that not all subject pronouns are focal.)[43] In fact, in this particular clause, the pronoun σύ expresses a kind of topic (something that would be covered by Levinsohn's notion of "point of departure," given its initial position and topical function). Moreover, from Lambrecht's perspective, σύ works with εἶ where together they express the (topical) open proposition.

Now, assuming that σύ in John 1:19 expresses a kind of topic, we must underscore that it is not of the contrastive sort, what is known in the literature as a "contrastive topic." The clause it occurs in is portrayed as the first utterance the priests and Levites say to John the Baptist, and there is nothing in particular that its referent could be contrasting with. In fact, it seems to be the norm to use first and second person pronouns, especially in copular clauses, at the beginning of a speech and probably also at the beginning of a new paragraph.[44] We will encounter more examples of such pronouns below.

The use of pronouns as contrastive topics is illustrated several times in John 8:14–15, 23, where the speaker Jesus contrasts himself with his audience. The tokens in 8:14–15 occur in non-copular clauses, and those in 8:23 occur in (non-equative) copular clauses. I assume that the predicates express the focus in each of these clauses. In each case, the contrastive pronominal topic is clause initial.[45]

---

[43] Levinsohn, *Discourse Features*, 39, also assumes that some preverbal pronouns can express topics. But see below on why I do not agree with his analysis of John 8:12.

[44] See the authors cited on 157–58 in Huang (Yan Huang, "Discourse Anaphora: Four Theoretical Models," *Journal of Pragmatics* 3 [2000]: 151–76) who have reported similar phenomena in other languages, and see also Levinsohn (*Discourse Features*, 136, 197) for similar observations on elements other than pronouns. Although more research is needed, clauses like Εἰ υἱὸς εἶ τοῦ θεοῦ "If you are the Son of God" in Matt 4:3 and Luke 4:3, which is the devil's first utterance to Jesus and lacks the subject pronoun, seem less typical.

[45] That 8:23 begins with a topical pronoun ([Ὑμεῖς]$_{TOP}$ ἐκ τῶν κάτω ἐστέ) might simply reflect the previously mentioned tendency at the beginning of speeches and new paragraphs. Or it might be case of a (cataphoric) contrastive topic that anticipates the switch to "I" in the clause.

> John 8:14–15, 23. (v. 14) ὅτι οἶδα πόθεν ἦλθον καὶ ποῦ ὑπάγω· [ὑμεῖς]$_{TOP}$ δὲ οὐκ οἴδατε πόθεν ἔρχομαι ἢ ποῦ ὑπάγω. (v. 15) [ὑμεῖς]$_{TOP}$ κατὰ τὴν σάρκα κρίνετε, [ἐγὼ]$_{TOP}$ οὐ κρίνω οὐδένα. . . . (v. 23) καὶ ἔλεγεν αὐτοῖς, [Ὑμεῖς]$_{TOP}$ ἐκ τῶν κάτω ἐστέ, [ἐγὼ]$_{TOP}$ ἐκ τῶν ἄνω εἰμί· [ὑμεῖς]$_{TOP}$ ἐκ τούτου τοῦ κόσμου ἐστέ, [ἐγὼ]$_{TOP}$ οὐκ εἰμὶ ἐκ τοῦ κόσμου τούτου.
>
> v. 13 Then the Pharisees said to him, "You are testifying on your own behalf; your testimony is not valid." (v. 14) Jesus answered, "Even if I testify on my own behalf, my testimony is valid because I know where I have come from and where I am going, but you do not know where I come from or where I am going. (v. 15) You judge by human standards; I judge no one. . . ." (v. 23) He said to them, "You are from below, I am from above; you are of this world, I am not of this world."

(Levinsohn describes clause initial topical phrases with a similar function as "points of departure" that indicate a "(contrastive) switch.")[46]

Topical subject pronouns (and noun phrases) also occur postverbally, but these are usually not of the contrastive sort.[47] To be sure, it is hard to say what the function of such pronouns is. Still, there seems to be some sort of a continuum: the more a dialogue progresses and the referent continues to be referred to, the more likely the referent will be expressed by a postverbal subject or only indexed on the verb. Consider the polar questions in John 1:19–21, where in the first (1:19) and second (1:21) the subject σύ is preverbal, in the

[46] See e.g., in *Discourse Features*, Levinsohn's discussion of ἡμεῖς in Act 20:6 (pp. 10–11) and of Titus 1:15b (p. 25).

[47] Assuming ὑμεῖς in Matt 5:48 (with future tense, Ἔσεσθε οὖν [ὑμεῖς]$_{TOP}$ τέλειοι ὡς [ὁ πατὴρ ὑμῶν ὁ οὐράνιος]$_{TOP}$ τέλειός ἐστιν, GNT: "You must be perfect—just as your Father in heaven is perfect") is a contrastive topic, it is an exception to this generalization.

third (1:21) it is postverbal,[48] and then finally, in the content question, τίς εἶ in 1:22 lacks σύ.[49]

> John 1:19–22 (v. 19) Σὺ τίς εἶ; (v. 20) καὶ ὡμολόγησεν καὶ οὐκ ἠρνήσατο, καὶ ὡμολόγησεν ὅτι Ἐγὼ οὐκ εἰμὶ ὁ Χριστός. (v. 21) καὶ ἠρώτησαν αὐτόν, Τί οὖν; Σὺ Ἠλίας εἶ; καὶ λέγει, Οὐκ εἰμί. Ὁ προφήτης εἶ σύ; καὶ ἀπεκρίθη, Οὔ. (v. 22) εἶπαν οὖν αὐτῷ, Τίς εἶ; ἵνα ἀπόκρισιν δῶμεν τοῖς πέμψασιν ἡμᾶς· τί λέγεις περὶ σεαυτοῦ;
> v. 19 [. . . the priests and Levites ask John], "Who are you?" (v. 20) He confessed and did not deny it, but confessed, "I am not the Messiah." (v. 21) And they asked him, "What then? Are you Elijah?" He said, "I am not." "Are you the prophet?" He answered, "No." (v. 22) Then they said to him, "Who are you? Let us have an answer for those who sent us. What do you say about yourself?"

Occasionally a clause initial (non-contrastive) topical subject pronoun coming mid-discourse appears to have the effect of highlighting a peak in the discourse (Levinsohn, *Discourse Features*, 197–98, says that "a full noun phrase or other marked encoding of participant reference" can have such a function). Consider Mark 8:29, mentioned in my introduction, where Peter declares who he thinks Jesus is. Given the question-answer formula, the topical pronoun σύ is redundant. In Matthew's version of the passage, σύ also occurs, but in Luke's (Luke 9:20), the focal constituent alone is expressed (Τὸν Χριστὸν τοῦ θεοῦ).[50]

---

48 Although only a hunch that requires further research, it seems that postverbal σύ in Ὁ προφήτης εἶ σύ; in 1:21 and in Κύριε, θεωρῶ ὅτι προφήτης εἶ σύ in John 4:19 is behaving as a postpositive, given its position (even though such accented pronouns usually do not count as enclitics), in which case σύ could hardly be focal or emphatic. For an interesting discussion of cases of σύ and ἐγώ behaving as (enclitic) postpositives, see Helma Dik, "On Unemphatic 'Emphatic' Pronouns in Greek: Nominative Pronouns in Plato and Sophocles," *Mnemosyne* 56.5 (2003): 535–50.

49 There are variations in the manuscripts in both 1:21 and 1:22. But if a rival text were followed in 1:21 (Τί οὖν; Ἠλίας εἶ σύ;), it would not affect my argument, and the variant in 1:22 (Σὺ τίς εἶ;) is not well supported.

50 For more one-phrase answers to content questions, see John 18:5 (Ἰησοῦν τὸν

> Mark 8:29 καὶ αὐτὸς ἐπηρώτα αὐτούς, Ὑμεῖς δὲ τίνα με λέγετε εἶναι; ἀποκριθεὶς ὁ Πέτρος λέγει αὐτῷ, [Σὺ]$_{TOP}$ εἶ [ὁ Χριστός.]$_{FOC}$
> v. 27 [Jesus] asked his disciples, "Who do people say that I am?" (v. 28) And they answered him, "John the Baptist; and others, Elijah; and still others, one of the prophets." (v. 29) He asked them, "But who do you say that I am?" Peter answered him, "You are the Messiah."
> Luke 9:20 εἶπεν δὲ αὐτοῖς, Ὑμεῖς δὲ τίνα με λέγετε εἶναι; Πέτρος δὲ ἀποκριθεὶς εἶπεν, [Τὸν Χριστὸν τοῦ θεοῦ.]$_{FOC}$

Given the climactic nature of such contexts, it is possible that such redundant pronouns (or other grammatically redundant phrases) simultaneously serve as hosts for emotively emphatic intonation, assuming emotive emphasis was expressed in Koine Greek in a similar way as in English.

The pronoun ἐγώ in John 8:58 might be another case, although its occurrence could also be accounted for as a (mildly) contrastive topic (indicating a switch from Abraham). Commentators also see in the formula ἐγώ εἰμι an echo of utterances made by God about himself (Isaiah 40–50 and possibly Exodus 3).[51] In any case, εἰμί alone constitutes the focus domain (εἰμί here, meaning "exist, be (there)" is not copular).

> John 8:58 Ἀμὴν ἀμὴν λέγω ὑμῖν, πρὶν Ἀβραὰμ γενέσθαι [ἐγὼ]$_{TOP}$ [εἰμί.]$_{FOC}$
> v. 57 Then the Jews said to him, "You are not yet fifty years old, and have you seen Abraham?" (v. 58) Jesus said to them, "Very truly, I tell you, before Abraham was, I am."

Ναζωραῖον) and (copular) Luke 8:30 (Λεγιών).

[51] See e.g., D. A. Carson, *The Gospel According to John* (Grand Rapids: Eerdmans, 1991) on John 8:24, 28, 58, and 13:19. Except for 8:58, where εἰμί is clearly not copular, the other passages may have an implied complement. Given different understandings of these verses, translators differ considerably in their renderings, as illustrated by 8:24. NRSV: "for you will die in your sins unless you believe that I am he"; *Die Gute Nachricht:* "*Ich* bin der, an dem sich alles entscheidet" ("*I* am the one on which everything depends"); TEV: "And you will die in your sins if you do not believe that 'I Am Who I Am'"; CEV: "If you don't have faith in me for who I am, you will die . . ."

More examples of redundant pronouns that probably have a highlighting function while perhaps also functioning as hosts for emphatic intonation include Matt 16:18 (σύ, non-equative); Act 9:5; Col 1:17–18 (αὐτός twice and other pronouns in this passage); Rev 22:16 (the second ἐγώ).[52]

To sum up, whatever grammarians might mean by describing certain pronouns, especially nominative ἐγώ and σύ, as "emphatic," it is clear that the functions of these pronouns cannot be reduced to a single parameter. Some are focal, some are topical, and some may be emotively emphatic. Of the topical ones, some are contrastive and others are not. And of the non-contrastive topical ones, some can be explained by their occurrence at the start of a discourse section, while others appear to have the effect of highlighting a discourse peak.[53]

Polar-focus and verb-focus

So far we have not mentioned any Greek examples of polar-focus with the exception of a couple of polar questions (John 1:21) and a few footnoted examples. Levinsohn (*Discourse Features*, 40–41) notes that the clause final position can be for verb-focus. Since his discussion only involves non-copular verbs, I assume he does not have εἶναι in mind. As far as I can tell, neither

[52] We should also mention the Messianic declarations "This is my beloved/chosen son" (Matt 3:17; 17:5; 9:7; Luke 9:35) and "You are my beloved son" (Mark 1:11; Luke 3:22). Since each declaration begins a discourse (as a quote), all the subject pronouns could, in theory at least, be topical. The topical reading makes sense for the σύ versions, assuming that Jesus, the addressee, already knew who he was and that the statements were uttered primarily for the bystanders' benefit. But a focal subject reading makes better sense to me for the οὗτος versions since God would be pointing out to the bystanders *who* the son was.

[53] The different pragmatic effects achieved by the two non-contrastive uses of topical pronouns, which I characterized as "redundant" uses, are not necessarily unrelated. Some types of redundancy lend themselves towards being used in systematic ways in language, especially to achieve certain special effects. Steven E. Runge, *Discourse Grammar of the Greek New Testament: A Practical Introduction for Teaching and Exegesis* (Peabody, Mass.: Hendrickson, 2010), explores some "redundant" uses of certain Greek constructions (e.g., the historical present [p. 32ff], left-dislocation [p. 292ff], besides other constructions). His perspective and area of research is a promising one and may well apply to such redundant uses of pronouns.

polar-focus nor verb-focus in copular clauses influences constituent order in any particular way. Having said that, I admit that it is not easy to identify clear cases of either polar-focus or verb-focus in copular clauses. What I have found in potential tokens reflects the same general constituent order principles found for other copular clauses.

That polar-focus and verb-focus do not normally affect constituent order in copular clauses is clear for clauses with only a copula and subject. Jesus' affirmative answer in Mark 14:62 (and in the parallel Luke 22:70) comes as a response to a polar question and therefore it cannot be a case of subject-focus; instead it functions to affirm the truth of the presupposed complete proposition (the complement is unexpressed).[54] In John 8:58 (repeated from above), non-copular εἰμί is alone focal (meaning "exist"). But in Matt 14:27 (also treated above), the subject alone is focal (see also 2 Sam 2:20).

> Mark 14:62 ὁ δὲ Ἰησοῦς εἶπεν, Ἐγώ [εἰμι,]$_{FOC}$ | Luke 22:70 Ὑμεῖς λέγετε ὅτι ἐγώ [εἰμι.]$_{FOC}$
> v. 61 Again the high priest asked him, "Are you the Messiah, the Son of the Blessed One?" (v. 62) Jesus said, "I am" (Luke: "You say that I am.")
> John 8:58 πρὶν Ἀβραὰμ γενέσθαι ἐγὼ [εἰμί.]$_{FOC}$
> "before Abraham was, I am."
> Matt 14:27 Θαρσεῖτε, [ἐγώ]$_{FOC}$ εἰμι· μὴ φοβεῖσθε.
> "Take heart, it is I; do not be afraid."

Thus, if the subject or verb alone is focal, or if the utterance affirms the truth of a presupposed proposition, the order remains the same (and so εἶναι takes its default postpositive position). Assuming Koine Greek was like other European languages, it too would have used prosodic stress to distinguish subject-focus from verb-focus in the above sentences. In John 9:9, ἐγώ εἰμι and perhaps

[54] I am also assuming with France and others that this is not a divine name formula but a normal idiomatic response with topical subject (R. T. France, *The Gospel of Mark: A Commentary on the Greek Text* [Grand Rapids: Eerdmans, 2002]). But see the discussion of this and similar verses in Catrin H. Williams, *I Am He: The Interpretation of "Anî Hû" in Jewish and Early Christian Literature* (WUNT 2:113; Tübingen: J. C. B. Mohr, 2000).

οὗτός ἐστιν might be two more cases of polar-focus. (Other possible tokens in equative statements include John 1:49; 6:69; 9:20; 11:27.)

> John 9:9 ἄλλοι ἔλεγον ὅτι Οὗτός ἐστιν, ἄλλοι ἔλεγον, Οὐχί, ἀλλὰ ὅμοιος αὐτῷ ἐστιν. ἐκεῖνος ἔλεγεν ὅτι Ἐγώ [εἰμι.]$_{\text{FOC}}$
> v. 8 The neighbors and those who had seen him before as a beggar began to ask, "Is this not the man who used to sit and beg?" (v. 9) Some were saying, "It is he." Others were saying, "No, but it is someone like him." He kept saying, "I am the man."

When both the subject and complement are explicit, the order SJ–εἶναι–CMP is common, as we found with other focus constellations. Consider two likely instances of polar-focus in John 4:29 and 42. In 4:29, the Samaritan woman puts a polar question to the people in her village (μήτι normally expects a negative answer, but she seems to be veiling considerable belief in the proposition). Later, in 4:42, the people confirm their belief in what is essentially the same proposition.

> John 4:29 and 42. (v. 29) μήτι οὗτός ἐστιν ὁ Χριστός; . . . (v. 42) αὐτοὶ γὰρ ἀκηκόαμεν καὶ οἴδαμεν ὅτι οὗτός ἐστιν ἀληθῶς ὁ σωτὴρ τοῦ κόσμου.
> TEV: (v. 28) [The woman at the well] went back to the town, and said to the people there, (v. 29) "Come and see the man who told me everything I have ever done. Could he be the Messiah?" (v. 42) [The people] told the woman, "We believe now, not because of what you said, but because we ourselves have heard him, and we know that he really is the Savior of the world."

The addition of ἀληθῶς "truly" in the last clause is further evidence that the main function of the clause is to confirm the truth of the (topical) complete proposition. However, without native speakers, there is no way to know if ἀληθῶς would have taken the main sentence stress or if another constituent would have. The same order, SJ–εἶναι–ἀληθῶς–CMP, also occurs in John 6:14 and 7:40. But elsewhere ἀληθῶς comes initially (in what would be the prototypical marked focus position in Greek: Matt 14:33; Matt 27:54, imperfect; Mark 15:39, imperfect), or even in the preceding matrix clause (John 7:26 "they truly know that"). Matt 14:33 (paraphrasable as "Truly you

ARE the Son of God") lacks the explicit subject σύ and so the complement precedes the copula as we have seen elsewhere.

> Matt 14:33 οἱ δὲ ἐν τῷ πλοίῳ προσεκύνησαν αὐτῷ λέγοντες, Ἀληθῶς θεοῦ υἱὸς εἶ.
> And those in the boat worshiped him, saying, "Truly you are the Son of God."

Finally, it should be noted that some grammarians have considered clause initial εἶναι to be somehow emphasized. For Westcott, this applies not only to existential uses, but also to occasional copular ones (see above on John 5:45 and 8:54, and see footnote 29).[55] Although this might be an attractive theory, I have found little evidence that substantiates it, especially for copular uses, and what I consider to be good examples of potential verb-focus and polar-focus (illustrated above) do not involve clause initial εἶναι.[56]

To summarize, polar-focus and verb-focus, at least in copular clauses, do not seem to affect constituent order. In such sentences, I suspect that the verb or another element (e.g., ἀληθῶς) would have been the prosodic host for the main sentence stress. Despite these problems, polar-focus and verb-focus are still relevant categories for exegetes and translators.

Some Pivotal ἐγώ εἰμι Clauses in John's Gospel

In this section, I treat from John's Gospel four famous equative ἐγώ εἰμι clauses, in which a correct analysis of the information structure is crucial to understanding John's message about who Jesus is. I shall argue that ἐγώ is very likely a case of subject constituent-focus in each, and that each involves important corrective implicatures. Since the foregoing sections have shown

---

[55] On 1 John 1:5, see e.g., Westcott, *Epistles of St. John,* 15, and on Heb 11:1, see Brooke Foss Westcott, *The Epistle to the Hebrews: The Greek Text with Notes and Essays* (2nd ed.; London: MacMillan, 1892), 349–50.

[56] The best example that I have found that suggests that initial copular εἶναι can involve verb-focus is 1 Tim 6:6: νομιζόντων πορισμὸν εἶναι τὴν εὐσέβειαν. (v. 6) ἔστιν δὲ πορισμὸς μέγας ἡ εὐσέβεια μετὰ αὐταρκείας· TEV: "They think that religion is a way to become rich. (v. 6) Well, religion does make us very rich, if we are satisfied with what we have."

that a preverbal subject pronoun can be either focal or topical, it is necessary to study carefully the context in order to determine which analysis is correct.

Consider first John 11:25:

> 11:25 ['Εγώ]$_{\text{FOC}}$ εἰμι ἡ ἀνάστασις καὶ ἡ ζωή· ὁ πιστεύων εἰς ἐμὲ κἂν ἀποθάνῃ ζήσεται,
> v. 21 Martha said to Jesus, "Lord, if you had been here, my brother would not have died. (v. 22) But even now I know that God will give you whatever you ask of him." (v. 23) Jesus said to her, "Your brother will rise again." (v. 24) Martha said to him, "I know that he will rise again in the resurrection on the last day." (v. 25) Jesus said to her, "I am the resurrection and the life. Those who believe in me, even though they die, will live.

The context suggests that Martha believes the resurrection will happen on a day off in the future, and that Jesus is limited in his power. Since Martha has not fully grasped Jesus' earlier claims that he will raise the dead,[57] Jesus is implicitly correcting her beliefs about what the resurrection is, who he is, and what he can do. So, I take the subject to be a case of constituent-focus. The topical presupposition is "x is the resurrection and the life,"[58] and the assertion is "x = Jesus" (paraphrasable as "It is I who am the resurrection and the life").

Consider now 6:35:

> 6:35 ['Εγώ]$_{\text{FOC}}$ εἰμι ὁ ἄρτος τῆς ζωῆς·
> NIV: (v. 31) "Our forefathers ate the manna in the desert; as it is written: 'He gave them bread from heaven to eat.'" (v. 32) Jesus

---

[57] John 5:21 reads "For as the Father raises the dead and gives them life, so also the Son gives life to whom he will" (RSV). See also 5:25–29 and 6:39–40 and the discussion in Carson (*John*, 412) and F. F. Bruce, *The Gospel of John* (Grand Rapids: Eerdmans, 1983), 244.

[58] The topical presupposition (paraphrasable as "What is the resurrection and the life?") has until this point in the discourse not been activated, and the idea that a person could be equated with an abstract event might have struck Martha as odd. So it is the very act of Jesus' making this statement that instantly made this open proposition a relevant topic for conversation. See Lambrecht, *Information Structure*, 65–73 on "accommodation."

> said to them, "I tell you the truth, it is not Moses who has given you the bread from heaven (τὸν ἄρτον ἐκ τοῦ οὐρανοῦ), but it is my Father[59] who gives you the true bread from heaven (τὸν ἄρτον ἐκ τοῦ οὐρανοῦ τὸν ἀληθινόν). (v. 33) For the bread of God is he who comes down from heaven and gives life to the world." (v. 34) "Sir," they said, "from now on give us this bread." (v. 35) Then Jesus declared, "I am the bread of life. He who comes to me will never go hungry, and he who believes in me will never be thirsty."

The idea of "divine bread" is thematic in the context, and 6:34 suggests the audience assumed that this divine bread is something a person could be given by Jesus or God, like manna. Against the presupposition "x is the bread of life", Jesus makes the exclusive assertion that he himself is that bread ("x = Jesus," paraphrasable as "It is I who am the bread of life"), thereby correcting their understanding (see also the similar clause in 6:41).

The token in 10:7 is another case of subject constituent-focus.

> 10:7 Ἀμὴν ἀμὴν λέγω ὑμῖν ὅτι [ἐγώ]$_{FOC}$ εἰμι ἡ θύρα τῶν προβάτων.
> v. 1 "Very truly, I tell you, anyone who does not enter the sheepfold by the gate but climbs in by another way is a thief and a bandit. (v. 2) The one who enters by the gate is the shepherd of the sheep. (v. 3)The gatekeeper opens the gate for him, and the sheep hear his voice . . ." (v. 6) Jesus used this figure of speech with them, but they did not understand what he was saying to them. (v. 7) So again Jesus said to them, "Very truly, I tell you, I am the gate for the sheep."

The disciples have missed the point of Jesus' analogy and consequently what the gate refers to in 10:1–3, and so Jesus identifies himself with that concept. By implication, he is making another exclusive claim, that he alone is the means to safety and salvation.

---

[59] The NIV takes οὐ Μωϋσῆς . . . ἀλλ' ὁ πατήρ μου in 6:32 as a pair of contrastive foci. While the TEV footnotes this interpretation, its translation reads: "What Moses gave you was not the bread from heaven; it is my Father who gives you the real bread from heaven."

John 8:12 contains another important ἐγώ εἰμι statement. The relevant context is rich.

> 8:12 Πάλιν οὖν αὐτοῖς ἐλάλησεν ὁ Ἰησοῦς λέγων, [Ἐγώ]$_{FOC}$ εἰμι τὸ φῶς τοῦ κόσμου·
> Again Jesus spoke to them, saying, "I am the light of the world. Whoever follows me will never walk in darkness but will have the light of life."

In a brief comment, Levinsohn makes it clear he assumes that it is the complement and not ἐγώ that is focal.[60] This might make sense if we take the clause in isolation, and the fact that Jesus' statement comes at the beginning of a new section might suggest that it is an isolated statement and that the subject takes its default topic function. But a closer look at the passage and John's Gospel suggests that this too is an instance of subject constituent-focus.

"Light" is a recurrent concept in John, coming up several times early in the book (1:4–9; 3:19–21; 5:35) as well as later (11:9–10; 12:35–36, 46), although nothing about light has been stated since 5:35. However, looking back to 7:37, commentators infer that Jesus made the statement in 8:12 during the Feast of Tabernacles, which happens to be a festival where light and light imagery is very prominent. Among other activities associated with this festival, every night four huge lamps were lit in the Court of Women in the Temple, and pious Jews would stay awake all night celebrating. The celebration would end each night with a procession where priests blew trumpets, then turned toward the Temple and declared, "Our fathers who were in this place turned their backs to the temple of God and their faces eastward and threw themselves down eastward before the sun; but we direct our eyes to Yahweh" (see Ezek 8:16, Mishnah, Sukkah 5).[61] Commentators also assume that this festival was to recall the Israelites wandering in the wilderness where God's glory was shown in the fiery pillar by night which guided and protected the people (Exod 13:21–22). In Isaiah (42:6; 49:6 and 51:4), the Servant of the Lord as well as the Lord's law and justice are equated with the light of the nations.

---

[60] Levinsohn, *Discourse Features*, 39.

[61] George R. Beasley-Murray, *John* (WBC 36; Nashville: Thomas Nelson, 1999), 106, 127–28.

Elsewhere, the Lord himself is equated with the light. As Beasley-Murray notes,[62] the image of God as light is associated with his acts of saving power (Ps 27:1 "The LORD is my light and my salvation. Whom shall I fear?"; Pss 44:3; 118:25–27),[63] as well as his appearance and revelation (Ezek 1:4, 13, 26–28, Hab 3:3–4). Besides that, "contemporary Judaism spoke not only of God as the Light of the world but also of the Torah and the Temple" as being light (on God's word and law being light, see Pss 119:105, 19:8, Prov 4:18–19, 6:23, Eccl 2:13).

So, assuming this background was known to the original audience, it would be natural to take Jesus' statement as a claim about "what the light of the world is" ("x is the light of the world"). Thus he would be identifying himself as that light ("x = Jesus") while simultaneously correcting his audience's understanding of what the light was. Further implicatures that his audience could have inferred include that Jesus is equivalent to the Torah, God's word, God's salvation, God's presence and even God himself.

By translating the Greek with "I am the light of the world," as virtually all translations do, a reader who is unaware of this background will likely read the complement as focal (since predicate-focus is the default reading in English). But by using a marked construction, such as a subject-stressed clause (indicated typographically by bolding or italics) or an it-cleft ("It is I who am the light of the world"), the reader is encouraged to search for relevant implications (the details of which can be spelled out in a footnote). To be sure, a predicate-focus construction (e.g., $[\text{I}]_{\text{TOP}}$ $[\text{am the LIGHT}]_{\text{FOC}}$) does not prevent the audience from searching for further significance, but the subject-focus construction is a surer means to get the audience thinking.

Some languages are unlike English where a structure like "I am the light of the world," stripped of its intonation, is compatible with both subject-focus and predicate-focus readings. For example, there is no corresponding

[62] Beasley-Murray, *John*, 128.

[63] The Hallel (Pss 113–118) was recited at the Feast of Tabernacles (and other holidays). Mishnah, Sukkah 3:9–10 refers to Ps 118:25 in particular. Verse 27, at the very end of the Hallel, refers to the "branches" used in the Feast of Tabernacles and to God giving light to the people: (NRSV) "The Lord is God, and he has given us light. Bind the festal procession with branches, up to the horns of the altar."

structure in Kurmanji-Kurdish that is ambiguous in the same way. Instead, one has to choose between a construction like (14), which would necessarily be interpreted as a case of predicate-focus, and a construction like (15), which necessarily involves subject-focus (the copula immediately follows the subject pronoun and the complement can come either before or after this phrase).

(14)	ez	ronaya	dinyayê	me
	1SG	light-of	world	cop.1SG
(15)	. . .	ez	im	. . .
	. . .	1S	cop.1SG	. . .

In such situations, Kurdish translators must commit themselves to the interpretation that seems more likely—they cannot straddle the fence. The translation team for Kurmanji-Kurdish of the former Soviet Union (Moscow 2000), in which I was involved, decided to use subject-focus in John 6:35, 41; 8:12; 10:7, 9, 11; 11:25, besides other ἐγώ εἰμι clauses.

The *Die Gute Nachricht* (1997) is also exemplary in this respect. Although the constituent order SJ–copula–CMP in German is just as ambiguous as it is in English, the translators made the decision to aid the reader by disambiguating the possible readings. They indicated subject-focus by putting *ich* "I" in italics in most of the same passages as the Kurdish translators did (6:35; 8:12; 10:7, 9, 11; 11:25, besides other passages—see also footnote 65 on Bultmann's "recognition formula"). But naturally, in clauses where there is no explicit subject pronoun, like in 9:5 (ὅταν ἐν τῷ κόσμῳ ὦ, φῶς εἰμι τοῦ κόσμου "as long as (I) am in the world, (I) am the light of the world") and 10:36 (ὅτι εἶπον, Υἱὸς τοῦ θεοῦ εἰμι "because (I) said '(I) am the Son of God'"), neither *Die Gute Nachricht* nor the Kurdish translation have subject-focus constructions.

John 20:31 and Acts 18:5

The famous summary statement in John's Gospel, 20:30–31, involves a pivotal copular clause that has aroused considerable debate.

> 20:30–31 (v. 30) Πολλὰ μὲν οὖν καὶ ἄλλα σημεῖα ἐποίησεν ὁ Ἰησοῦς ἐνώπιον τῶν μαθητῶν [αὐτοῦ], ἃ οὐκ ἔστιν γεγραμμένα ἐν τῷ βιβλίῳ τούτῳ· (v. 31) ταῦτα δὲ γέγραπται ἵνα

> πιστεύ[σ]ητε ὅτι Ἰησοῦς ἐστιν ὁ Χριστὸς ὁ υἱὸς τοῦ θεοῦ, καὶ ἵνα πιστεύοντες ζωὴν ἔχητε ἐν τῷ ὀνόματι αὐτοῦ.
> v. 30 Now Jesus did many other signs in the presence of his disciples, which are not written in this book. (v. 31) But these are written so that you may come to believe that Jesus is the Messiah, the Son of God, and that through believing you may have life in his name.

McGaughy, for example, caught the attention of others when he concluded that Ἰησοῦς must be the subject even though, according to his own rule 3c, it would be the complement (since a preverbal complement with definite reference normally lacks the article). He compared this clause to Peter's declaration in Matt 16:16, Σὺ εἶ ὁ Χριστὸς ὁ υἱὸς τοῦ θεοῦ τοῦ ζῶντος "You are the Messiah, the Son of the living God," reasoning that σύ in Matt 16:16 and Ἰησοῦς in John 21:31 "point to what is known; the articular titles function to identify this man and, therefore, are the complements, despite rule 3c." Goetchius and later Carson objected to his interpretation of John 20:31; Carson has argued in multiple publications that it makes more sense to take the clause as answering the question "who is the Christ, the Son of God?"[64] Assuming John's purpose in writing his Gospel was primarily for unbelievers (as Carson argues), or at least partially so, his audience would include people who knew of the promised Messiah and who would want to learn of his identity. But others argue that Ἰησοῦς is the "subject" because (i) it is preverbal and it is a proper name (Wallace), or (ii) it comes in a ὅτι clause (Fee), or (iii) because it is assumed that John was writing primarily to edify believers (Fee).[65] However, none of these reasons are conclusive: (i) or (ii) only reflect tendencies and (iii) is based on (albeit reasoned) speculation.

---

[64] E. V. N. Goetchius, review of Lane C. McGaughy, *Toward a Descriptive Analysis of EINAI as a Linking Verb in New Testament Greek*, *JBL* 95 (1976): 147–49; D. A. Carson, "The Purpose of the Fourth Gospel," *JBL* 106 (1987): 639–51; Carson, *John*.

[65] Wallace's suggestion (*Greek Grammar*, 46) that Ἰησοῦς is the subject because it is preverbal, is still not conclusive, since, as we have seen, subjects in equative clauses can occasionally be postverbal. Gordon D. Fee *To What End Exegesis? Essays Textual, Exegetical, and Theological* (Grand Rapids: Eerdmans, 2001), 29–42, argues that the present subjective (πιστεύητε) reading was original (not the aorist subjunctive πιστεύσητε), and that this reading would be more meaningful for believers. He also argues (41–42n29) that it is normal for a proper name in John to be anarthrous in a

As the reader might now infer, the discussions by McGaughy, Goetchius, Carson, Fee, and Wallace suffer because these authors do not clearly or consistently distinguish between grammatical relations (subject vs. complement) on the one hand, and pragmatic relations (topic vs. focus) on the other.[66] It is not enough to identify either subject or complement since in many languages, including Greek and English, both subjects and predicates (i.e., complements) can express both topical and focal ideas.

What is ultimately of more importance in the analysis of this clause is not the grammatical relations but the information structure relations. From our perspective, Goetchius and Carson take Ἰησοῦς to be focal (and apparently the order is CMP–εἶναι–SJ) in contrast to McGaughy, Wallace, and Fee who take it to be topical (and the order to be SJ–εἶναι–CMP). Although I am not in the position to offer a definitive conclusion, if McGaughy's rules are reliable, then Ἰησοῦς is the complement and somewhat more likely to be focal since the default reading of a complement is a focal one. While this reading makes good sense if John was really writing primarily for non-believers (something that is debated), there is of course at least one other possible reading, that the clause has polar-focus. There is no doubt that, at this point in John's Gospel, the complete proposition "Jesus is the Messiah" is sufficiently established in the discourse,[67] and we might infer that the validity of this proposition represented an important issue to his audience, assuming there were groups

ὅτι clause, in which case Ἰησοῦς need not necessarily be the predicate.

[66] The same applies to Rudolf Bultmann, *The Gospel of John* (Oxford: Blackwell, 1971), 225–26, who for his part offers an interesting discussion of ἐγώ εἰμι clauses, describing four different uses and noting several examples for each from non-biblical sources. In the first three uses, he states that ἐγώ is the "subject," but in the fourth, "the recognition formula," he says ἐγώ is the "predicate." His fourth use is in fact equal to what I am calling subject constituent-focus, and so it is clear that Bultmann was using "predicate" to indicate an information structure category (the informative constituent in the clause), not a grammatical relation. Incidentally, Beasley-Murray, *John,* 89–90, summarizes Bultmann's four categories, but omits Bultmann's non-biblical examples. Bultmann says the following verses make use of the "recognition formula": John 6:35, 41, 48, 51; 8:12; 10:7, 9, 11, 14; 15:1, 5. But "11:25, and perhaps too 14:6" he assigns to the "identification formula," which in my terms would be an equative clause with a focal complement.

[67] This theme is obviously a major one in John, even if the title "Christ" has not been mentioned since 17:3 and "Son of God" since 19:7.

who were opposing this view. Thus, the clause could be functioning to affirm the positive truth-value of this proposition (paraphrasable as "Jesus IS the Messiah, the Son of God"). But having said that, I have not found enough clear cases of polar-focus in Greek copular clauses to make a strong case for this analysis based on constituent order. Moreover, there is no ἀληθῶς "truly" attached to this clause as we found in several similar equative clauses in John (e.g., 4:42; 6:14; 7:26, 40).

If Ἰησοῦς is truly focal, there is nonetheless to my knowledge no standard English translation that clearly conveys this reading (nor the polar reading). The typical English rendering (e.g., NRSV, "Jesus is the Messiah, the Son of God"), where "Jesus" is the subject, biases the reader to take this as the topic (since this is cross-linguistically the default reading of subjects).

In the *Translator's Handbook to John's Gospel,* Newman and Nida do not address these issues for John 20:31. But in their handbook to Acts, they handle a similar problem in Acts 18:5 (see also 18:28).[68] They are convinced that in the context of Acts 18, "the Christ" is a concept that Paul's Jewish audience would believe in, and that what the audience needed convincing of was that it was Jesus, and no one else, who was that Christ. So Ἰησοῦν would be focal, and that makes good sense.

> Acts 18:5 διαμαρτυρόμενος τοῖς Ἰουδαίοις εἶναι τὸν Χριστόν, [Ἰησοῦν.]$_{FOC}$
> When Silas and Timothy arrived from Macedonia, Paul was occupied with proclaiming the word, testifying to the Jews that the Messiah was Jesus.

In light of this, the NRSV rendering here of "the Messiah" as the subject is good, because it encourages the reader to take it as topical. However, it is unfortunate that Newman and Nida conclude that the word order "the Messiah is Jesus"

would seem quite strange to the average reader of the New Testament who would be much more familiar with the person of Jesus than he would with

---

[68] Barclay M. Newman and Eugene A. Nida, *A Translator's Handbook on the Acts of the Apostles* (New York: United Bible Societies, 1972); idem., *A Translator's Handbook on the Gospel of John* (New York: United Bible Societies, 1980).

the designation of Jesus as the Messiah. Therefore, to the reader, it is the Messiahship of Jesus which is presumably the new information, while Jesus, as a historical person, is well accepted as given information.

They recommend repackaging the semantic content of the assertion for the benefit of a modern audience. In essence (as Barrie Evans has pointed out to me), Newman and Nida are setting aside the historical meaning for a meaning that is supposedly more relevant to a modern audience, i.e., a modern "reader meaning." For my part, I think it is better in this case to convey the historical meaning and, if necessary, add a note of explanation. Nor am I convinced that "the Messiah is Jesus" would be especially awkward for readers. If a translator was convinced that it was, he could instead use a cleft ("testifying to the Jews that it was Jesus who is the Christ") or some other construction ("that the [long awaited] Christ was indeed Jesus").

Conclusion

Analyzing the information structure of present indicative copular clauses involves many difficulties, but it is essential to the task of exegesis and translation. I cited evidence that constituent-focus in New Testament Greek is compatible with positions both before and after the copula and with both subjects and complements. Pronouns (including so-called "emphatic" ones) were also shown to be compatible with both topical and focal functions. When considering syntactic environments, we found that, (i) if both subject and complement are explicit, the order SJ–εἶναι–CMP is most common and, I assume, pragmatically unmarked, but (ii) if there is no explicit subject in the clause core, and the clause is neither negated, relativized, a question, imperatival, nor infinitival, then there is a strong tendency for the complement (or part of it when complex) to precede the (present indicative) copula, thus CMP–εἶναι. Although my research has concentrated on equative clauses, these last two observations apply equally to other types of copular clauses. We also found SJ–εἶναι to be the unmarked order in equative clauses where the complement was unexpressed (e.g., ἐγώ εἰμι). It was also argued that polar-focus and verb focus were additional possible information structures, but no constituent orders could be shown to unambiguously instantiate these focus types.

Although many questions remain, motivations were suggested for certain orders, some of which concerned the syntactic environment and others the discourse-pragmatic function. And although linguistic elements like constituent order, paired instances of positive-negative constituent-focus (e.g., with οὐ/μὴ . . . ἀλλά), the presence of a pronoun or of an adverb like ἀληθῶς "truly," etc., can be helpful to the analyst in determining which information structure is correct for a given clause, nevertheless the results of this study suggest that exegetes and translators must still rely heavily on a careful analysis of the context.

At times translators can aid readers in the disambiguation process by using structures that are relatively specific in meaning (e.g., the it-cleft) or whose order favors a reading (e.g., subjects more typically express the clause topic and complements the focus). They can also make use of typographical means (e.g., *italics* or **bold**, CAPS) in order to indicate prosodic stress for focus (or other categories), as was illustrated by the use of italics in *Die Gute Nachricht.* It is unfortunate that typographical means are often frowned upon as being "non-literary" or ridiculed as a "comic book" technique, in English and German writing at least.

Bibliography

Bailey, Nicholas A. "Thetic Constructions in Koine Greek: With Special Attention to Clauses with εἰμί 'be', γίνομαι 'occur', ἔρχομαι 'come', ἰδού/ἴδε 'behold', and Complement Clauses of ὁράω 'see'." PhD diss., Vrije Universiteit Amsterdam, 2009.

Beasley-Murray, George R. *John.* Word Bible Commentary 36. Nashville: Thomas Nelson, 1999.

Blass, Friedrich, Albert Debrunner and Robert Walter Funk. *A Greek Grammar of the New Testament and Other Early Christian Literature.* Chicago: University of Chicago Press, 1961.

Bruce, F. F. *The Gospel of John.* Grand Rapids: Eerdmans, 1983.

Bultmann, Rudolf. *The Gospel of John.* Oxford: Blackwell, 1971.

Callow, John C. "Constituent Order in Copula Clauses: A Partial Study." Pages 68–89 in *Linguistics and New Testament Interpretation.* Edited by David Alan Black. Nashville: Broadman, 1992.

Carson, D. A. *The Gospel According to John.* Grand Rapids: Eerdmans. 1991.

———. "The Purpose of the Fourth Gospel." *Journal of Biblical Literature* 106 (1987): 639–51.Chafe, Wallace. "Givenness, Contrastiveness, Definiteness, Subjects, Topics and Point of View." Pages 25–55 in *Subject and Topic*. Edited by Charles N. Li. New York: Academic Press, 1976.

Colwell, E. C. "A Definite Rule for the Use of the Article in the Greek New Testament." *Journal of Biblical Literature* 52 (1933): 12–21.

Dik, Helma. "On Unemphatic 'Emphatic' Pronouns in Greek: Nominative Pronouns in Plato and Sophocles." *Mnemosyne* 56.5 (2003): 535–550.

———. *Word Order in Ancient Greek: A Pragmatic Account of Word Order Variation in Herodotus*. Amsterdam Studies in Classical Philology 5. Amsterdam: J. C. Gieben, 1995.

Dik, Simon C. *The Theory of Functional Grammar. Part 1: The Structure of the Clause*. Berlin: Mouton de Gruyter, 1997.

Dover, Kenneth James. *Greek Word Order*. Cambridge: Cambridge University Press, 1968.

Fee, Gordon D. *To What End Exegesis? Essays Textual, Exegetical, and Theological*. Grand Rapids: Eerdmans, 2001.

France, R. T. *The Gospel of Mark: A Commentary on the Greek Text*. Grand Rapids: Eerdmans, 2002.

Goetchius, E. V. N. Review of Lane C. McGaughy, *Toward a Descriptive Analysis of EINAI as a Linking Verb in New Testament Greek*. *Journal of Biblical Literature* 95 (1976): 147–49.

Hengeveld, Kees. *Non-Verbal Predication: Theory, Typology, Diachrony*. Berlin: Mouton de Gruyter, 1992.

Höhle, Tilman N. "Über Verum-Fokus im Deutschen." Pages 112–141 in *Informationsstruktur und Grammatik*. Edited by Joachim Jacobs. Opladen: Westdeutscher Verlag, 1992.

Huang, Yan. "Discourse anaphora: Four theoretical models." *Journal of Pragmatics* 3 (2000): 151–76.

Kahn, Charles H. *The Verb "Be" in Ancient Greek*. Indianapolis: Hackett Publishing, 2003.

Ladd, D. Robert. *Intonational Phonology*. Cambridge: Cambridge University Press, 1996.

Lambrecht, Knud. *Information Structure and Sentence Form: Topic, Focus, and the Mental Representation of Discourse Referents*. Cambridge Studies in Linguistics; Cambridge: Cambridge University Press, 1994.

———. *Topic, Antitopic, and Verb Agreement in Non-Standard French*. Amsterdam: John Benjamins, 1981.

———. "When Subjects Behave like Objects: An Analysis of the Merging of S and O in Sentence-Focus Constructions." *Studies in Language* 24 (2000): 611–82.

Lambrecht, Knud and Laura A. Michaelis. "Sentence Accent in Information Questions: Default and Projection." *Linguistics and Philosophy* 21 (1998): 477–544.

Levinsohn, Stephen H. *Discourse Features of New Testament Greek: A Coursebook on the Information Structure of New Testament Greek.* 2nd ed. Dallas: SIL International, 2000.

McGaughy, Lane C. *Toward a Descriptive Analysis of EINAI as a Linking Verb in New Testament Greek.* Society of Biblical Literature Dissertation Series 6. Missoula, Mont.: Society of Biblical Literature, 1972.

Mikkelsen, Line. "Copular Clauses." In *Semantics: An International Handbook of Natural Language Meaning.* Edited by Klaus von Heusinger, Claudia Maienborn, and Paul Portner. Berlin: Mouton de Gruyter, forthcoming.

Newman, Barclay M. and Eugene A. Nida. *A Translator's Handbook on the Acts of the Apostles.* New York: United Bible Societies, 1972.

———. *A Translator's Handbook on the Gospel of John.* New York: United Bible Societies, 1980.

Payne, Thomas E. *Describing Morphosyntax: A Guide for Field Linguists.* Cambridge: Cambridge University Press, 1997.

Robertson, A. T. *A Grammar of the Greek New Testament in the Light of Historical Research.* Nashville: Broadman, (1923, 4th ed.) 1934.

Runge, Steven E. *Discourse Grammar of the Greek New Testament: A Practical Introduction for Teaching and Exegesis.* Peabody, Mass.: Hendrickson Publishers, 2010.

Smyth, Herbert Weir. *Greek Grammar.* Rev. by Gordon M. Messing. Harvard: Harvard University Press, 1956.

Vallduví, Enric and Maria Vilkuna. "On rheme and kontrast." Pages 79–108 in *The Limits of Syntax.* Edited by Peter W. Culicover and Louise McNally. Syntax and Semantics 29. San Diego: Academic Press, 1998.

Wallace, Daniel B. *Greek Grammar Beyond the Basics: An Exegetical Syntax of the New Testament.* Grand Rapids: Zondervan, 1996.

Westcott, Brooke Foss. *The Epistle to the Hebrews: The Greek Text with Notes and Essays.* 2nd ed. London: MacMillan, 1892.

———. *The Epistles of St. John: The Greek Text with Notes and Essays.* 3rd ed). London: MacMillan, 1892.

Williams, Catrin H. *I Am He: The Interpretation of "Anî Hû" in Jewish and Early Christian Literature.* Wissenschaftliche Untersuchungen zum Neuen Testament 2/113. Tübingen: Mohr Siebeck, 2000.

Zahn, D. Theodor. *Das Evangelium des Johannes.* Leipzig: Deichert'sche Verlagsbuchhandlung Nachfolger (Georg Böhme), 1908.

Evaluating Luke's Unnatural Greek
A Look at His Connectives

Randall Buth

Introduction

The discourse parameters of connectors have long been included in textlinguistics.[1] However, sources and outside language interference create turbulence that raise special methodological problems. Luke has provided us with two works: his Gospel and the Acts of the Apostles. These works allow us to observe his diverse patterns in language use. Luke's use of connectives is measurably distinct between his Gospel, the first half of Acts, and the second half of Acts. It is important to bring the concept of "threshold" to a discussion of connectives. Major connectives like καί, δέ, οὖν, τε, μέν, γάρ, τότε, ὥστε, ἀλλά, and πλήν, should be joined to the boundary material of genitive absolutes and the indefinite-subject ἐγένετο clauses in order to present an integrated picture of what Luke is doing. Some of this data is incompatible with the common assumption that Luke is imitating the Septuagint. In this article we discuss the incongruencies within the connective framework, as well as associated structural phenomena, in order to highlight both non-Lukan features and data incompatible with the "imitation" theory. This has implications for the way we read Luke. The surprise for some may be that he is not trying to imitate the Septuagint as much as he is partially smoothing

[1] I would like to thank Stephen Levinsohn for the pioneering, linguistic stimulation that he has provided over the years. I was first privileged to meet him at a Greek Discourse seminar that he organized in Cameroon in 1989. I could only wish that our paths could have crossed more often. Maybe they yet will.

out his sources, some of which go back to Hebrew. The article concludes by comparing relevant sociolinguistic expectations and pointing to the importance of the conclusion of this study for New Testament studies.

In order to understand Luke as a historian we must understand his writing methods. A comparison of Lukan style in Acts and the Gospel is primary data for evaluating him and for understanding his writing methods and use of sources.

The words and structures used for connecting sentences in the Gospel and Acts are primary evidence that Luke was doing something unnatural with his writing style. This article will measure the differences and evaluate their significance. These have been variously explained in the past.[2] Basically, there are five explanations: different author, different time, different genre or literary purpose, imitation of Septuagintal style, and the use of sources.

On positing a different author as an explanation, there is near consensus that one author penned and published both works.[3]

A hundred years ago, John Hawkins in his *Horae Synopticae* recognized this stylistic problem and suggested that considerable time between the Gospel and Acts could account for the difference in style.[4] However, if Luke already knew

---

[2] Due to the amount of required data that lengthens this article, footnotes that document the history of scholarship will be restricted to a minimum of essential or representational citations. The history is immense, as almost every study on the Gospel of Luke needs to take some position on interpreting Luke's Greek style.

[3] Cf. John C. Hawkins, *Horae Synopticae: Contributions to the Study of the Synoptic Problem* (2nd ed.; Oxford: Clarendon Press, 1909; repr., Grand Rapids: Baker Book House, 1968), 183: "Now this last view, which attributes the composition of the third Gospel and of the whole of Acts to the original author of the 'We'-sections, receives very strong support from linguistic considerations." And John Nolland, *Luke 1—9:20* (WBC 35A; Dallas: Word, 1989), xxxiii: "The Acts of the Apostles clearly presents itself as a continuation of the Gospel of Luke (see Acts 1:1–5), and is so accepted by almost all scholars. . . . It is only reasonable to agree with the claim made by the writer of Acts that he is there writing a sequel to a Gospel which he himself had penned." Also Nigel Turner, *Syntax* (vol. 3 of *A Grammar of New Testament Greek*; ed. James Hope Moulton; Edinburgh: T. & T. Clark, 1963), 57: "There is a lingiustic unity throughout his two books, and the final editor has been able to impose his own style upon all his material."

[4] Hawkins, *Horae Synopticae*, 177: "I do not know that much attention has been

a cultured Greek (e.g., Luke 1:1–4 and Acts 1:1–3), and if the connectives show tendencies of translation Greek[5] in the Gospel, and if these features are consistent across many items and show a collective pattern between the Gospel and Acts, then we can be fairly sure that time is not the explanation for the different style.

Some have treated this difference as determined by genre and literary purpose. This is essentially the approach of Stephen Levinsohn in *Textual Connections in Acts*.[6] There are certainly minor refinements that could be argued on the basis of embedded genre, though Acts and Luke are both narratives that essentially share the same linguistic, past-narrative genre.

Another approach is to attribute the differences in style to purposeful imitation by Luke of a Septuagintal style. H. F. D. Sparks has epitomized this approach and he treats the Septuagintal-imitation explanation as almost self-evident, since some of the Lukan unnaturalness lines up with Hebraisms, and because the Hebraisms are not found in Mark.[7] Since the time of Sparks's writing

---

paid to the linguistic differences between the two. These, however, are important in their way; for, while quite insufficient to throw doubt on the common authorship, they seem to suggest that a considerable time must have elapsed between the writing of the two books." Hawkins adds a footnote to this statement: "I do not think that nearly all of them are such as can be caused by differences in the sources used by Luke in the two books; for we know how freely he dealt with Mark, and probably with Q also, in matters of style, and even of vocabulary."

[5] Editor: Translation Greek refers to somewhat unnatural usage that woodenly preserves the forms, preferences or syntax from the source language.

[6] Stephen H. Levinsohn's *Textual Connections in Acts* (Atlanta: Scholar's Press, 1987) is the first comprehensive study applying the developing field of textlinguistics to Acts. Stephen is to be praised and thanked for establishing such a benchmark. Of course, a full respect for his work and conclusions still leaves considerable room to differ on the nature of the textual connections in the Gospel. Cf. p. 173: "The nature of Acts hides an important feature about the distribution of δε and και. DUs ("Development Units," which are primarily associated with δε) must develop *from* some other unit. . . . In contrast with Acts, και often introduces the first sentence(s) of an incident or sub-incident in the Gospel of Luke" (p. 176). "Other differences in the organization structure and purpose of the Gospel of Luke and the book of Acts may also be identified, which influence the use of και" (Ibid.). We will discuss this perspective below after Table 1.

[7] H. F. D. Sparks, "The Semitisms of St. Luke's Gospel," *JTS* 44 (1943): 129–38;

there has been a major change in availability of relevant data. The Dead Sea Scrolls have confirmed what Mishnaic Hebrew specialists already knew: two registers of Hebrew, literary Hebrew and a colloquial Hebrew were in active use during the Second Temple period.[8] With publication of the Dead Sea Scrolls, there was no longer anything problematic about another first-century Jewish messianic community in Jerusalem writing material in Hebrew.

A fifth perspective on Lukan style has been advocated from time to time: the use of Semitized Greek sources.[9]

With this introduction we can proceed to an examination of Luke's connectives in the Gospel and Acts. In order to include the possibility of sources within a linguistic study, we need to deal with something that I call a "threshold." Certain tendencies in translation Greek from a Semitic source lead to predictable choices and frequencies. An editor or compiler who looks at a Greek text with a high frequency of καί needs creative energy to cross a threshold and add δέ, τε, or a host of other possible connectors into a text with ubiquitous καί. This threshold phenomenon tends to preserve καί as the Greek word most closely associated with Hebrew *waw* "and," a word that joins noun phrases as well as verbs and larger sentences. Greek καί also joins nouns and other words below a sentence level. The existence of this threshold

---

and idem., "The Semitisms of Acts," *JTS*, ns 1 (1950): 16–28.

[8] M. H. Segal, "Mishnaic Hebrew and Its Relation to Biblical Hebrew and to Aramaic," *JQR*, O.S. 20 (1908): 647–737; Eliezer Ben-Yehuda, *"Mavo ha-Gadol,"* in *Milon ha-Lashon ha-`Ivrit ha-Yeshanah veha-Hadashah* (Jerusalem: Ben-Yehuda Publications, 1909–1958); J. N. Epstein, *Mavo Lenusah Hamishnah* (Jerusalem, 1948); E. Y. Kutscher, *Leshon Haza"l* (The Language of the Sages)," in Eduard Yechezkel Kutscher, *Hebrew and Aramaic Studies* (Jerusalem: Magnes Press, 1977), 73–107 (Hebrew section).

[9] See Raymond A. Martin, *Studies in the Life and Ministry of the Historical Jesus* (New York: University Press of America, 1995). See especially pp. 3–5: "The more commonly held view, namely Luke's skillful and deliberate imitation of LXX style, is not satisfactory either. The data from Luke-Acts is particularly instructive here. . . . Surely the most probable explanation for this inconsistency is that Semitic sources/traditions are being used." And Randall Buth and Brian Kvasnica, "Temple Authorities and Tithe Evasion: The Linguistic Background and Impact of the Parable of the Vineyard, the Tenants and the Son," in *Jesus' Last Week*, (ed. R. Steven Notley, et al.; Leiden: Brill: 2006), 53–80, esp. the appendix of critical notes on pp. 259–317.

generally results in unnatural Greek frequencies in the second and third generation Greek text. (By third generation, I mean a Greek product that used a Greek text, but that Greek source itself was influenced by a Semitic language. With this brief background we can begin to survey some of the relevant data.

The connector τε certainly needs to cross a threshold to get into a Greek text, as is evidenced by the wide disparity between the 266 examples of τε in the Old Greek Bible[10] (OG) and the 4605 examples in Josephus's writings, which are of a similar magnitude (both collections of writings are approximately 500,000 total words). In order to provide more precise comparisons I have provided a statistic that gives the rate of occurrence per 1000 words of running text.[11]

Table 1. τε ("and" +connection, sameness, +change). τε is more common in natural Greek.

Book	Number	n/1000 (number per 1000 words)
OG(all)	266	0.45 (OG is the Old Greek Bible)
Gen	16	0.43
Exod	21	0.75
Judg—1 Kgs	0 !	0.00
Jdt	0	0.00
Tob	1	0.16
1 Macc	4	0.20
2 Macc	25	1.92
3 Macc	32	5.82
4 Macc	27	3.18
Matt	3	0.14

[10] The statistics for the Old Greek (OG) include the books of 1 Esdras, additions in Greek Esther, Judith, Tobit, 1 Maccabees, 2 Maccabees, 3 Maccabees, 4 Maccabees, Odes of Solomon, Wisdom, Ben Sira, Psalms of Solomon, Baruch, and additions in Greek Daniel. Much of these books were originally written in Greek and a consensus exists on this for 2–4 Maccabees. 1–4 Maccabees will be added to the tables where relevant or available.

[11] Most of the statistics in this paper were generated through the Accordance 8 Bible Software (Oaktree Software). Occasional numbers represent personal manual countings and numbers from other sources are footnoted.

Luke	9	0.38
1 Acts[12]	67	5.72
2 Acts	84	8.58
Josephus	4605	9.03
Ant.	3074	9.76
J. W.	1343	10.40
Life	94	5.78
Ag. Ap.	94	4.41

We see that Genesis has 0.43 τε per 1000 words and the histories of Judges through Kings have zero occurrences. First Maccabees has 0.20 per 1000, while 2 Maccabees, primarily an original Greek composition, has 1.92 per 1000 and 3 Maccabees has 5.82 per 1000. Josephus's writings range from 4.41 per 1000 in *Ag. Ap.*, to 10.40 per 1000 in *J. W.*. With regard to τε, Josephus would appear to be writing a natural Greek,[13] without the restraints of a Semitic source. In the case of *J. W.*, if it was not a complete re-writing, the threshold was so low that it did not constrain the output at all. When we compare the Gospels we find 0.14 for Matthew and 0.38 for Luke. But then we have 5.72 for 1 Acts and 8.58 for 2 Acts. The statistics between the two sub-groups in Acts are regularly different and Martin has shown that 1 Acts has indications of Semitic interference in many subsections.

With τε in 2 Acts we are probably seeing Luke's preferred style. Here he doesn't have a threshold to cross. Even in the Gospel, though, we see that Luke can

[12] Because of previous studies, especially Raymond Martin's statistical approaches, I divide Acts into chapters 1–15:35 ("1 Acts") and 15:36–28:31 ("2 Acts").

[13] Josephus's *J. W.* patterns like normal Greek. Henry St. J. Thackeray (*Josephus* [vol. 2; Loeb Classical Library; Cambridge (Mass.): Harvard University Press, 1978], xiii) says, "The style is an excellent specimen of the Atticistic Greek fashionable in the first century." Even though Josephus claimed to write a first edition in 'the patriarchal language' and then to translate it into Greek, the style and level of Greek do not testify to translation at all and must be considered a thoroughy new edition and re-writing. (In Josephus's own words, he apparently chose Hebrew as the language of writing for posterity, maybe like 1 Macabbees, despite sending the book out to the Jewish diaspora. See *J. W.* 1.3–7 and 5.272, for the Hebrew connection, *Ag. Ap.* 1.50 for a statement of using Greek stylistic assistants.)

cross the threshold, though that threshold or his sources are quite different in 1 Acts. First Acts moves most of the way toward his preferred style.

If we think of the proposed explanations for these statistical differences, it is doubtful that time of writing could explain the dramatic shift from the Gospel to Acts. Imitation of the LXX is possible, though it should be noted that Luke includes τε in his Gospel. Mark never uses τε in his Gospel. A Semitized source for Luke's Gospel is more than possible.[14]

Table 2. μέν (+situation-marking, point of comparison). μέν is common in normal Greek.

Book	Number	n/1000
OG	211	0.36
Gen	7	0.21
Exod	5	0.20
Proverbs	4	0.36
Wisdom	32	4.60
Jdt	1	0.10
Tob	2	0.32
1 Macc	0 !	0.00
2 Macc	62	5.20
3 Macc	20	3.91
4 Macc	36	4.58
Josephus (all)	5495	11.73
Ant.	3160	10.08
J.W.	1952	15.22
Life	136	8.41
Ag. Ap.	247	11.66.

[14] The idea that Luke was expanding his "DU" units in the Gospel with sub-units of καί and τε ("non-developmental conjunctions [within DUs]" [Levinsohn, *Textual Connections in Acts*, 157]) would predict considerably more examples of τε than we find. We have an increase of καί in the Gospel in comparison to Acts (for statistics, see below) but a dramatic 94% *reduction* of τε, the other marker of a "subDU" unit. It would appear that something else was at work in producing the differences between nine occurrences of τε in the Gospel and 151 in Acts. Something is quite different from Acts and an explanation based on a threshold phenomenon would work. I do not consider literary organization to be a plausible explanation of the difference in frequencies.

Matt	20	0.90
Mark	6	0.44
Luke	10	0.43
Acts	48	2.23
1 Acts	23	1.96
2 Acts	25	2.55

μέν shows similar tendencies to τε. OG has 211 examples while Josephus has 5495. The Gospels show a fairly high threshold in Mark and Luke, a slightly lower threshold in Matthew, resulting in more μέν, but definite movement in the direction of normal Greek in Acts with frequencies of 1.96 and 2.55 in 1 Acts and 2 Acts. Luke personally uses μέν less frequently than the contemporary Josephus, but the existence of a threshold in his Gospel and to a much lesser extent in 1 Acts is still visible.

Table 3a. Genitive Absolute (the genitive absolute provides a background comment with a different syntactic subject than the main verb). The genitive absolute is common in normal Greek, and less common in translation Greek.

Book	Number	per 1000	
Gen	13	0.40	
Luke	64	3.28	(*sic*, Luke 3.2827),
1 Acts	33	3.28	(*sic*, 1 Acts 3.2796),
2 Acts	80	9.51	

Table 3b. Genitive participles. For broad comparison, statistics are given below, all of which are "raw," for any and all genitive participles. ("Raw" genitive participle statistics give relative numbers of genitive absolute when reduced):[15]

[15] We do not have a statistical comparison with Josephus limited to the genitive absolute, so we have remained content with an approximation of using the raw genitive participle statistics. The actual number of genitive absolutes will be less than the total number of genitive participles. Compare the raw participle statistics for Luke with the actual absolute statistics.

Book (raw)	hits	hits/1000
OG	1925	3.28
OG (//Heb canon)	1372	3.23
Matt	90	4.07
Mark	54	3.96
Luke	99	4.23 (actual gn.ab.: 3.28)
John	46	2.45
Acts 1:1-15:35	67	5.72 (actual gn.ab.: 3.28)
Acts 15:36-28:31	103	10.52 (actual gn.ab.: 9.51)
Acts (all)	170	7.90 (actual gn.ab.: 6.12)
Gen	50	1.54 (actual gn.ab.: 0.40)
Exod	73	2.94
Lev	63	3.30
Num	81	3.23
Deut	62	2.70
Jdt	19	1.87
Tob	11	1.74
1 Macc	24	1.19
2 Macc	197	15.15
3 Macc	98	16.16
4 Macc	54	6.20
Josephus (all)	7604	16.23
Ant.	5533	17.56
J.W.	1574	12.19
Life	136	8.41
Ag. Ap.	247	11.66

Table 3a lists a connective structure rather than a simple conjunction. The statistics again move similarly to the first examples. Luke writes with the genitive absolute about 3 times per 1000 in both the Gospel and 1 Acts. Second Acts triples that with 9.51 genitive absolutes per 1000 words. Again, we are seeing a threshold effect. For a fast comparison that provides a good overview we have provided Table 3b. It confirms the Greek nature of the structure and its value in separating translational Greek from original Greek, even though it cannot provide exact statistics for genitive absolutes.

Table 4. (clausal) καί/δέ ratio. καί ("and" + addition, +continuity), δέ ("and" + addition, +change). Nigel Turner[16] provides the following statistics.

	clausal καί/δέ
Gen	2.4
Exod	2.1
TestAbr-a	2.0
TestAbr-b	5.0
4 Macc	1.0
"papyri sample"	0.92
Plutarch	0.24
Josephus *Ant.* 1	0.3
Philostratus	0.4
Lucian *Somn.*	0.6
Matt	1.5
Mark	5.0
Luke (parallel Mark)	1.2
Luke "Q"	1.9
1 Acts	1.0
2 Acts	0.6
Acts "we"	0.5

Table 4 concerns the ratio of καί to δέ. This has figured prominently in many stylistic studies of NT Greek, especially Martin. We find a ratio of 0.6 καί for 1 δέ in 2 Acts, with 0.5 in the "we" sections. These are normal Greek styles. A threshold effect begins to be visable in 1 Acts with 1.0. The Gospel has a higher threshold effect with an average of 1.2 καί for δέ in passages that have a parallel in Mark, and even 1.9 in the so-called Lukan "Q." If Luke were using Mark with its 5.0 ratio, then he rather strongly de-Septuagintalizes in order to achieve his 1.2. The same would be said if Luke had a non-Marcan source with a heightened frequency of καί: Luke is de-Septuagintalizing in order to lower the ratio to 1.2.[17]

[16] Nigel Turner, *Style* (vol. 4 of *A Grammar of New Testament Greek*; ed. James Hope Moulton; Edinburgh: T. & T. Clark, 1976), 58.

[17] We prefer to see Luke and Mark as sharing a source, rather than Luke using Mark, but that is outside the scope of this article.

Table 5. οὖν ("so" +significant change, +close connection)

OG	247	0.42
Gen	42	1.14
Gen 1–25	12	0.74
Gen 26–50	30	1.46
Exod	29	1.04
Judg	2	0.11
Jdt	0	0.00
Tob	1	0.16
1 Macc	21	1.04
2 Macc	26	2.00
3 Macc	8	1.45
4 Macc	17	1.95
Matt	56	2.53
Mark	6	0.44
Luke	33	1.41
John	200	10.66
Acts	61	2.84
1 Acts	29	2.47
2 Acts	32	3.27
Josephus (all)	1079	2.30
Ant.	682	2.16
J.W.	263	2.04
Life	70	4.30
Ag. Ap.	64	3.00

Table 5 οὖν brings us to one more threshold item. Luke's Gospel is 1.41 οὖν per 1000 while 1 Acts is 2.84 and 2 Acts is 3.27. Luke's Gospel is similar to 1 Macc 1.15, while his 1 Acts is similar to 2 Macc 2.18. Second Acts moves strongly into a more nuanced Greek usage. The writer of the Gospel of John goes off the chart in Greek with his personal proclivity for οὖν.

All of the above connectives and structures, Tables 1–5, have shown a spread between the Gospel of Luke and Acts. From their large numbers the connectives and structures above must be acknowledged as the main Greek connectors in the language. These connectors are used very frequently by all

Greek writers and they are the connectors and structures that are at the heart of an understanding of Luke's style.

Table 6. μὲν οὖν and μενοῦν (+affirmation, +contrast)

OG	24	0.04
Gen	1	0.03
Exod	2	0.07
Jdt	0	0.00
Tob	0	0.00
1 Macc	0	0.00
2 Macc	7	0.54
3 Macc	7	1.27
4 Macc	4	0.46
Ant.	78	0.78
J.W.	194	1.51
Life	15	0.93
Ag. Ap.	35	1.65
Matt	0	0.00
Mark	1	0.07
Luke	1	0.04
Acts (all)	27	1.25
1 Acts	13	1.11
2 Acts	14	1.43

With Table 6 we move into a less frequently attested collocation, μὲν οὖν. Luke's Gospel has a very low 0.04 frequency per 1000, while 1 Acts and 2 Acts have frequencies significantly higher—1.11 and 1.43, respectively. The same pattern is being attested as in Tables 1–5 where Luke's Gospel differs from Acts and in the direction of Semitic Greek, while the Acts stands with frequencies of original Greek writers, with 2 Acts at the highest end.

This is a fairly good indicator of Greek style and Table 6 documents a semitically induced threshold. However, the frequency of μὲν οὖν will reduce its usefulness for analyzing texts below 5,000 total words. Native Greek writers might be expected to produce only about 1 μὲν οὖν per 1,000 words, and genre could be expected to have an additional effect.

In any case, the pattern for Luke in the Gospel and Acts remains consistent and clear.

Table 7. ὥστε (+result). This appears to be a distinguishing feature of normal Greek.

OG	178	0.3
Gen	8	0.22
Exod	25	0.90
Jdt	0	0.00
Tob	1	0.16
1 Macc	7	0.35
2 Macc	14	1.08
3 Macc	6	1.09
4 Macc	19	2.18
Josephus (all)	334	0.71
Ant.	238	0.76
J.W.	82	0.64
Life	4	0.25
Ag. Ap.	10	0.47
Matt	15	0.68
Mark	13	0.95
Luke	4	0.17
John	1	0.05
Acts (all)	8	0.37
1 Acts	3	0.26
2 Acts	5	0.51

Table 7 shows a low frequency item that might be helpful in creating a grid of items that have a threshold for documents that are translations from, or descendants of, Hebrew sources. The OG and Josephus show a low frequency word, ὥστε, that might be diagnostic for Semiticized Greek. Josephus is roughly twice the frequency of OG. However, ὥστε is somewhat specialized in Greek narrative because it requires a main verb to follow in the infinitive, meaning that the overall clause structure is marginalized within the Greek language. In addition, in Matthew and Mark we have higher frequencies than both 1 Acts and 2 Acts. Supposedly "Semitized" Mark is higher than "clean Greek" 2 Acts. This reflects one of the problems of items that are of low frequency. Nevertheless, 1 Acts at 0.26 and 2 Acts at 0.51 are more frequent than the Gospel of Luke's 0.17. Luke shows his consistent inconsistency.

However, as with οὖν in the Gospel of John, individual writers may use a particular word or structure at a special frequency, thus giving us false positives. This is one of the reasons why we are looking at a whole series of conjunctions and not just one.

Table 8. γε (+stipulation). This word should be more frequent in original Greek, although a translator may idiosyncratically adopt it, as in "OG" 2 Samuel and 2 Kings, where our resulting Greek text has apparently been mixed with the so-called "καί γε recension."[18]

OG	162	0.28	
Gen	3	0.08	
Exod	1	0.04	
Jdt	0	0.00	
Tob	0	0.00	
2 Kgdms (2 Sam)	28	1.39	
4 Kgdms (2 Kgs)	17	0.82	
1 Macc	0	0.00	
2 Macc	0	0.00	
3 Macc	0	0.00	
4 Macc	11	1.26	
Josephus (all)	505	1.08	
Ant.	235	0.75	
J.W.	237	1.84	
Life	3	0.18	
Ag. Ap.	30	1.41	
Matt	4	0.18	
Mark	0	0.00	
Luke	8	0.34	
1 Acts	2 (1 OG)	0.17	(0.09)
2 Acts	2	0.20	

Table 8 γε is a low frequency item that brings us face to face with a word that doesn't meet our expectations. Josephus is higher than the OG and this suggests that γε might be an indicator of Greek style over against translation Greek.

[18] Dominique Barthélemy, *Les Devanciers d'Aquila* (Leiden: Brill, 1963).

However, the 0.20 ratio in 2 Acts is lower than the Gospel of Luke's 0.34 ratio. How does one explain this? First of all, with only two occurrences in 2 Acts, this is an item whose frequency is much too low to rely on, at least in isolation as one item. From the opposite direction, in the Gospel of Luke we find eight examples of γε and this may mean that Luke's sources had more examples of γε than he was used to using himself. There would still be a difference between the Gospel and Acts and reasonable consistency within Acts. However, the low frequency of the item and the possibility of idiosyncratic difference from other Greek writers leave this item with without much value for evaluating Luke's style. It is a kind of static in the data profile.

Table 9. γάρ (+clarification, inference). γάρ may be higher in natural Greek, but the word is influenced strongly by genre.

OG	1522	2.59
Gen	105	2.85
Exod	93	3.34
Prov	102	6.74
Isa	184	5.94
Jdt	36	3.55
Tob	12	1.89
1 Macc	31	1.54
2 Macc	52	4.00
3 Macc	10	1.82
4 Macc	82	9.41
Josephus (all)	3678	7.85
Ant..	2240	7.11
J.W.	1066	8.26
Life	151	9.28
Ag. Ap.	221	10.37
Matt	121	5.61
Mark	66	4.84
Luke	97	4.14
Acts (all)	80	3.72
1 Acts	34	2.70
2 Acts	46	4.70

With Table 9 we have a word that appears to be quite sensitive to genre. In general, the 1,500 examples in OG and 3,700 examples in Josephus would lead to an expectation of a threshold in Semiticized Greek, especially when one considers that the OG statistics include writings that are original Greek compositions.[19] But genre complicates this. γάρ occurs doubly and triply higher in OG Isaiah and Proverbs than in the OG translations of Genesis and Exodus. In our Gospels and Acts the statistics are mixed. Luke is not significantly more "Semitic" than 2 Acts. γάρ needs more careful distinctions within genre and probably a differential control such as ὅτι, similarly to the way in which καί and δέ are compared as a ratio.

Table 10. ἀλλά ("but" +contrast). This is the primary Greek word for marking contrast.

OG	557	0.95
Gen	27	0.73
Exod	11	0.40
Josh	17	1.03
Isa	55	1.78
Job	40	2.25
Jdt	21	2.07
Tob	12	1.89
1 Macc	13	0.64
2 Macc	15	1.15
3 Macc	10	1.82
4 Macc	50	5.74
Josephus (all)	1649	3.52
Ant..	1061	3.37
J.W.	408	3.16
Life	40	2.46
Ag. Ap.	140	6.57
Matt	37	1.67
Mark	45	3.30
Luke	35	1.49

[19] We have not taken the clearly Greek compositions out of the OG total so that the statistical differences, when they occur, would be all the more certain. We consider 2 Maccabees—4 Maccabees to certainly be original Greek compositions.

John	102	5.44
Acts (all)	30	1.39
1 Acts	16	1.37
2 Acts	14	1.43

Table 10 demonstrates that, in the LXX translation of the classical Hebrew narrative of Genesis and Exodus, ἀλλά was not used as frequently as in Greek narratives. Genre is also quite influential as we see in books like Isaiah and Job. However, ἀλλά is a word that was borrowed by colloquial Hebrew, Aramaic, and Syriac. All three languages, Hebrew, Aramaic/Syriac, and Greek were using this word in the first century, so that one might expect that any potential for its use as a diagnostic tool would be diminished.[20] And, in fact, there is virtually no statistical difference between the use of this word in the Gospel of Luke and in Acts, with the Gospel's ratio being just slightly higher.

Table 11. μᾶλλον (+alternative, +addition).

OG	46	0.08
Gen	2	0.05
Exod	0	0.00
Prov	8.	0.53
Jdt	0	0.00
Tob	1	0.16
1 Macc	0	0.00
2 Macc	2	0.15
3 Macc	4	0.73
4 Macc	5	0.57
Josephus	334	0.71
Ant.	243	0.77
J.W.	72	0.56
Life	8	0.49
Ag. Ap.	11	0.52
Matt	9	0.41
Mark	5	0.37

[20] As examples, אלא "but" occurs 981 times in the Mishnah, ܐܠܐ "but" occurs 803 times in the Peshitto NT and 151 times in the Old Syriac Sinaiticus, and ἀλλά "but" occurs 638 times in the NT.

Luke	5	0.21
John	4	0.21
1 Acts	4	0.34
2 Acts	3	0.31

μᾶλλον is a low frequency word that fits our expectations of Luke versus 2 Acts. However, the frequency is so low that it is not a good diagnostic. In addition, it is a word that will be strongly affected by genre, as Proverbs' ratio of 0.53 shows.

Table 12. πλήν "but, except." This is a Greek word that became more common in the Koine dialect.

LXX	230	0.39	
Gen	5	0.14	
Exod	10	0.36	
Judg	12	0.68	
3 Kgdms	14	0.51	(=1 Kings)
4Kgdms	24	1.15	(=2 Kings)
Jdt	1	0.10	
Tob	3	0.47	
1 Macc	7	0.35	
2 Macc	1	0.08	
3 Macc	1	0.18	
4 Macc	1	0.11	
Josephus (all)	75	0.16	
Ant.	33	0.10	
J.W.	34	0.26	
Life	3	0.18	
Ag. Ap.	5	0.23	
Matt	5	0.23	
Mark	1	0.07	
Luke	15	0.64	
John	0	0.00	
1 Acts	2	0.17	
2 Acts	2	0.20	

πλήν is a Koine-ism that might be predicted to have statistics in the opposite direction from those discussed in most of the previous tables above. The OG shows 0.39, quite low by itself while Josephus only has 0.16. Here we have something of interest. It is not distinctive of the OG as a whole, yet we have a translation like Judges where it achieves a frequency five times higher than Genesis.

In the Synoptic Gospels Luke is significantly higher than Matthew or Mark, yet comparisons with Acts, especially 2 Acts, suggest that this may not be coming from Luke. By itself we might attribute this to time between the writing of the Gospel and Acts, but in the light of the above differences consistently patterning between the Gospel and Acts, time is not a first choice as an explanation. Nor is it something truly Septuagintal. It would appear to be a minor indicator of a non-Marcan source, not a creation by Luke.

Table 13 narrative τότε. "Narrative τότε" is a special conjunction that developed within Second Temple-period Aramaic and comes as a calque from translation of late Second Temple-period Aramaic. It is prototypically used in past narrative without adding another conjunction and occurs first in its sentence. It is to be distinguished from "adverbial τότε"/ "adverbial ʾz"/ "adverbial ʾdyn" that can occur in future and proverbial contexts in Hebrew and Aramaic and Greek, and can occur anywhere in a sentence in general prose. (Numbers refer to potential "narrative τότε" as a conjunction and not to all τότε in the work.)

Dan Θ	28	5.21
Dan OG	39	6.96
3 Macc	6	1.17
TJob	26	3.83
1 Esd 3–5	8	4.47
Matt	63	3.43
Mark	0	0.00
Luke	3	0.15
John	0	0.00
1 Acts	11	1.09
2 Acts	9	1.07

A general adverb for "at that time, then" occurs naturally in all three languages, Hebrew (ʾāz), Aramaic (ʾĕdayin), and Greek (τότε). This natural use of "then" in the three languages I will call "adverbial τότε." On the other hand, we frequently find in Matthew something that functions like a conjunction. I will call this τότε "narrative τότε."

narrative τότε	Matt 3:5	τότε ἐξεπορεύετο πρὸς αὐτὸν
conjunction	Mark 1:5	καί ἐξεπορεύετο πρὸς αὐτὸν

Narrative τότε was a development within Aramaic.[21] In all of the Jewish Aramaic narratives from the Second Temple ʾdyn is used as a narrative conjunction. In Greek translations that preserve some of the Semitic flavor of their source, we find narrative τότε. In original Greek documents we sometimes find τότε up to 1.1 times per 1000 in what might appear to be, potentially, a "narrative τότε." But in documents in which there is Aramaic influence, we find frequencies from 3.0 to 9.0.

This grammatical feature will help us considerably in understanding Luke and is an important datum for synoptic studies. In his Gospel, Luke has a potential narrative τότε at a ratio of only 0.15 per 1000, well within typical Greek usage. But in Acts, this percentage jumps to 1.09 in 1 Acts and 1.07 in 2 Acts. The frequencies found in Acts are acceptable as Greek and they show that Luke personally wrote with such a style. It is important to notice the contrast with the ratio in his Gospel. Luke is most probably being influenced in his Gospel by sources that do not have narrative τότε. That tells us two significant things: first, that Luke is probably not using Aramaic-based sources; and second, that Luke is not using Matthew, against the theories of Ferrar-Goulder ("Mark without Q" Mark>Matt>Luke), or Griesbach-Farmer (Matt>Luke>Mark) or Augustine-Butler (Matt>Mark>Luke). Luke has examples of 12 adverbial τότε, many in parallel with either Mark or Matthew. However, not one of Matthew's 60+ examples of narrative τότε penetrate into Luke's Gospel,[22] despite Luke's personal style attested in Acts, which must be called narrative-τότε-friendly.

---

[21] See Randall Buth, "אדין/τότε—Anatomy of a Semitism in Jewish Greek," *Maarav* 5-6 (1990): 33–48.

[22] Matt has 55 to 63 examples: 2:7, 16, 17; 3:5, 13, 15; 4:1, 5, 10, 11, 17 (ἀπὸ τότε); 8:26; 9:6, 14, 29, 37; 11:20; 12:13, 22, 38; 13:36; 15:1, 12, 28; 16:12, 20,

This lack of narrative τότε in the Gospel of Luke should not be attributed to a different time of writing, since Luke is unlikely to have developed a τότε-friendly style if he had not already done so in his travels with Paul or during his two years in Judea.

Likewise, the imitation of the LXX is not a plausible explanation for the difference in narrative τότε between the Gospel and Acts. Luke's style in the Gospel is clearly not a rigorous Septuagintalization, certainly not to the degree that would actively forbid a τότε style. He had no reason to suppress τότε unless he had some secret agenda, such as trying to be purely Hebraic in his Septuagintalization, and anti-Aramaic. That would be a conspiracy theory without basis. Furthermore, if Luke spent time in Judea, he was likely occasionally heard storytelling with narrative τότε like what we find in the Gospel of Matthew, and he would undoubtedly have considered that τότε would give his Greek local Semitic coloring. Actually, Luke appears to be unconcerned about features that were "non-Septuagintal" and we find non-Septuagintal features in abundance in his Gospel, even where Septuagintal idioms were available or were being used. Furthermore, it is improbable that anyone in antiquity would have thought of narrative τότε as being non-Septuagintal and needing repression. In addition to the canonical works of Ezra and Daniel, some pseudepigrapha like the Testament of Job, Adam and Eve, and First Esdras have narrative τότε. And the Gospel of Matthew shows that narrative τότε was an acceptable style in Jewish Greek. Narrative τότε is basically inert toward any imitation theory: it would not need to be avoided either on the basis of the Old Greek or on the basis of Jewish Greek. Therefore, a LXX-imitation theory cannot explain Luke's pattern. Nevertheless, in NT studies the imitation theory is still the primary explanation for Luke's Hebraic elements.

From the other direction, we see that a source hypothesis and a threshold would explain simply and precisely what we have in Luke's Gospel. Luke's Semitized Greek sources did not have narrative τότε. Luke's three examples of

---

21 (ἀπὸ τότε), 24; 17:13, 19; 18:21, 18:32; 19:13, 27; 20:20; 21:1 (καὶ ὅτε . . . τότε); 22:8 (in a parable), 13 (in parable), 15, 21; 23:1; 25:7 (in parable); 26:3, 14, 16 (καὶ ἀπὸ τότε), 31, 36, 38, 45, 50, 52, 56, 65, 67, 74; 27:3, (9), 13, 26, 27, 38, 58; 28:10. This produces a statistic of between 3.00 to 3.43 narrative τότε.

narrative τότε can be viewed as additions that broke through the threshold and allowed some of his natural choice, though at a less than full percentage.

Table 14. "Greek-based" indefinite ἐγένετο + infinitive MAIN verb. (This is typically used for providing setting material. It is Plummer's type "c."[23] It is not a translation from Hebrew and it is never found in the Old Greek Bible.

Matt	0	0.00
Mark	2	0.18
Luke	5	0.26
1 Acts	8	0.43
2 Acts	9	0.49

When we refer to an "indefinite ἐγένετο" structure, we mean an idiomatic use of ἐγένετο that does not have either an explicit subject or a specific subject referent beyond the situation "it" as in, "it happened." The main verb follows any adjunct setting material (like a dative location or time phrase) and is an infinitive. This Greek-based structure mimics a classical idiom συνέβη αὐτὸν ποιῆσαι "and it happened for him to do," which is a verbose way of saying, "he did it." The use of this structure in Luke 3:21 was extended over four infinitive verbs and may be a way that Luke used to demote the baptism scene or to remove it from the main narrative line of events. In Jewish Greek and, marginally, in secular colloquial Greek this infinitive structure was used with ἐγένετο instead of συνέβη. This Greek-based structure was pointed out by Plummer over a century ago as distinct. Furthermore, this Greek-based indefinite ἐγένετο structure never occurs in the Septuagint or Old Greek Bible. The structure occurs five times in Gospel of Luke (3:21; 6:1, 6, 12; 16:22) and seventeen times in Acts (Acts 4:5; 9:3, 32, 37, 43; 10:25 [ὡς ἐγένετο]; 11:26; 14:1; 16:16; 19:1; 21:1 [ὡς δὲ ἐγένετο +infinitive without setting], 5 [ὅτε δὲ ἐγένετο +infinitive without setting]; 22:6, 17; 27:44; 28:8, 17). A Septuagintalizing hypothesis does not explain this situation because it does not occur in the Old Greek and the true Septuagintal structure (Table 15) does not occur in Acts along with all of these indefinite ἐγένετο structures.

[23] Alfred Plummer, *A Critical and Exegetical Commentary on the Gospel According to St. Luke* (ICC; Edinburgh: T. & T. Clark, 1896), 45: "That which takes place is put in the infinitive mood, and this depends upon ἐγένετο."

Furthermore, one may profitably compare the imitation hypothesis with the findings on τότε. The extreme degree of precision and conspiratorial purity in an imitation hypothesis that would be necessary in order to exclude τότε would presumably have excluded these Greek structures as well. But Luke uses them. In fact, we find in Acts that Luke uses them seventeen times. This Greek-based indefinite ἐγένετο may be a piece of Jewish Greek that Luke adopted as his own Greek before ever writing his Gospel.

The structure in Table 14 does not occur in the Old Greek Bible. It should not be considered a Hebraism nor is it a Septuagintalism. Most importantly, it must be distinguished from the Hebraic structure to be mentioned in Table 15 below.

Table 15. "Hebraic" indefinite ἐγένετο (+/- καί) + finite main verb. This structure does not occur in normal Greek but is associated specifically with literary Hebrew, but not with Aramaic, nor with Mishnaic Hebrew. (Plummer type "a" is without καί before the finite main verb and Plummer type "b" is with καί before the finite main verb.)

Plummer type a (. . . –καί +finite verb)		
Matt	5	0.27
Mark	2	0.18
Luke	22	1.13
1 Acts	0	0.00 (zero)
2 Acts	0	0.00 (zero)
Plummer type b (. . . +καί +finite verb)		
Matt	1	0.05
Mark	0	0.00
Luke	12	0.62
1 Acts	0	0.00 (zero)
2 Acts	0	0.00 (zero)

Tables 14 and 15 show both Greek-based and Hebraic "indefinite subject" ἐγένετο structures. These are similar to the genitive absolute in that they provide a mechanism for inserting some background setting material at the beginning of a new unit. The Hebraic ἐγένετο style in Table 15 has a finite main verb. Luke never once uses the Hebraic ἐγένετο structure in Acts. Gustaf Dalman was wrong when he claimed that it occurred in 2 Acts and even in the "we" sections: "Whoever would collect proofs for a Hebrew source gospel should first start with καὶ ἐγένετο . . . the 'We-section' is not free from καὶ ἐγένετο. See Acts 21, etc. Such observations forbid any assumption of a Hebrew source."[24] We all make mistakes, but this one has echoed throughout twentieth-century NT scholarship.[25] The facts are that Luke never used the Hebraic structure in Acts. Not once! The only thing that we know is that Luke used the Greek-based ἐγένετο structure on his own, not the Hebraic one. Of course, it would have been possible for him to create the Hebraic structure by copying it from the Greek Bible. But we have no evidence that he ever did so. Just the opposite: we have evidence that he used the Greek-based structure.

Could time explain this difference between the Greek-based and Hebraic ἐγένετο structures in the Gospel and Acts? Not if we take into account other features. Time could only explain the lack of Hebraic ἐγένετο in Acts as a possibility, though with difficulty, and only in isolation, separated from all other connective phenomena in Luke-Acts. For example, one might hypothesize that Luke used both structures in the 60–70s when writing the Gospel, but then two to three decades later, retreated to the Greek-based structure when writing Acts. That would make him a Septuagintalizer earlier

---

[24] "Wer Beweise für ein hebräisches Urevangelium sammeln wollte, hätte zuerst dies καὶ ἐγένετο nennen müssen. . . . Selbst der 'Wir-Bericht' is nicht davon frei, s. Apg. 21,1.5; 27,44; 28,8.17. . . . Solche Beobachtungen verbieten die Annahme eines hebräischen Originals." Gustaf Dalman, *Die Worte Jesu* (2nd ed.; Leipzig: Hinrichs, 1930), 26.

[25] Cf. Turner, *Style*, 47: "The construction with the infinitive occurs, very rarely in non-Biblical authors, but the preponderance of the strictly Hebraic construction in Luke-Acts indicates that even when Luke sometimes uses the infinitive construction he is still writing Biblical Greek influenced by the LXX (II Acts 19:1; We 16:6, 21:1,5; 27:44; 28:8)." Notice how Turner's comment, "the strictly Hebraic construction in Luke-Acts," ignores the fact that the structure only occurs in the Gospel of Luke. Turner missed a chance to apply his own advice from a later statement (p. 55): "There is no doubt that some of the . . . Semitisms must be attributed to the use of sources." Cf. also, Joseph Fitzmyer, *The Gospel According to Luke I–IX: Introduction, Translation, and Notes* (AB 28; Garden City, New York: Doubleday, 1981), 119, who included Acts 5:7 and Acts 9:19 in his Hebraic list, but Acts 5:7 has διάστημα as subject and is not the Hebraic indefinite construction. Likewise, "Paul" is the subject at Acts 9:19 and is not the Hebraic indefinite construction. These simply follow in Dalman's mistake.

and a non-Septuagintalizer later, despite including other Jewish and Greek Bible items in Acts. And it would be inconsistent if combined with his usage of narrative τότε. One would have to argue that over the same period narrative τότε moved in the opposite direction, from not occurring in his style when it would have been expected, and to appearing more fully when it would not be expected. The time argument also fails to explain the magnitude of the other conjunctives that pattern inconsistently between Luke's Gospel and Acts. Therefore, time cannot be singled out as an explanation for indefinite ἐγένετο structures.

Does imitation of LXX provide an explanation? No, because in his Gospel, Luke uses both the Greek and Hebraic structures, but in Acts he uses the Greek-based structure only. Luke does not use the Hebraic structure on his own.

On the other hand, a source hypothesis for Luke's Gospel should predict this kind of difference. Acts would show Luke's personal style and choices, while his Gospel would reflect a mix of accepting source structures and mixing his own style with these. Again, a threshold exists that lets in a few of Luke's own personal choices, resulting in the mixed phenomena in the Gospel. Presumably, in Acts Luke did not use any source material that contained the Hebraic structure. Therefore, we only find the Greek-based structure. That is a straightforward, simple, and satisfying explanation of the linguistic data. There is further support in this direction from internal consistency.

Table 16 Internal Consistency

Language/Text	Narrative Criteria		Profile
	#13 narrative τότε	#15 Hb ἐγένετο	
Aramaic	+	–	Aramaic
Hebrew	–	+	Hebrew
Greek	–	–	Greek
Matt	+	+	??
Mark	–	+	Hebrew
Luke	–	+	Hebrew
John	–	–	Greek
Acts	–	–	Greek

The co-occurrences for connective structures #13 narrative τότε and #15 Hebraic indefinite ἐγένετο in material from various backgrounds are presented in Table 16. A Greek narrative text with influence from an Aramaic source would test positive for #13 and negative for #15. A Greek narrative text with influence from a Hebrew source would test negative for #13 and probably positive for #15.[26] The OG tests positive for all three sets because it is a collection of documents with all three backgrounds. Luke's Gospel consistently tests as having a literary Hebrew background at some layer.[27]

Complications would arise if a document tested positive for both. Matthew does that. Because of the importance of understanding this phenomenon, I have listed fifteen examples of narrative τότε in Matthew where the wording of the Greek is close to Mark and or Luke.[28] The Greek wording is obviously connected and is either flowing into Matthew or from Matthew. τότε helps us see the direction of the flow. Neither Mark nor Luke ever picks up a narrative

---

[26] The indefinite wyhy structure dropped out of Mishnaic Hebrew and the colloquial language. First Maccabees suggests that it was still in use in literary Hebrew.

[27] Acts tests as Greek.

[28] Matt 3:5 τότε ἐξεπορεύετο πρὸς αὐτὸν Ἱεροσόλυμα καὶ πᾶσα ἡ Ἰουδαία
Mark 1:5 καὶ ἐξεπορεύετο πρὸς αὐτὸν πᾶσα ἡ Ἰουδαία χώρα
καὶ οἱ Ἱεροσολυμῖται
Luke 3:3–7 (parallel pericope, but without this sentence)

Matt 4:11 τότε ἀφίησιν αὐτόν ὁ διάβολος
Mark 1:12–13 (parallel pericope, but without this sentence)
Luke 4:13 καὶ συντελέσας πάντα πειρασμόν ὁ διάβολος ἀπέση ἀπ αὐτοῦ

Matt 9:6 . . . ἐπὶ τῆς γῆς ἀφιέναι ἁμαρτίας – τότε λέγει τῷ παραλυτικῷ
Mark 2:10 . . . ἀφιέναι ἁμαρτίας ἐπὶ τῆς γῆς – λέγει τῷ παραλυτικῷ
Luke 5:24 . . . ἐπὶ τῆς γῆς ἀφιέναι ἁμαρτίας – εἶπεν τῷ παραλελυμένῳ

Matt 8:26 τότε ἐγερθεὶς ἐπετίμησεν τοῖς ἀνέμοις
Mark 4:39 καὶ διεγερθεὶς ἐπετίμησεν τῷ ἀνέμῳ
Luke 8:24 ὁ δὲ διεγερθεὶς ἐπετίμησεν τῷ ἀνέμῳ

Matt 12:13 τότε λέγει τῷ ἀνθρώπῳ, ἔκτεινόν
Mark 3:5 καὶ περιβλεψάμενος . . . λέγει τῷ ἀνθρώπῳ, ἔκτεινόν
Luke 6:10 καὶ περιβλεψάμενος . . . εἶπεν αὐτῷ, ἔκτεινόν

Matt 17:19 τότε προσελθόντες οἱ μαθηταὶ τῷ Ἰησοῦ κατ' ἰδίαν εἶπον
Διὰ τί ἡμεῖς οὐκ ἠδυνήθημεν ἐκβαλεῖν αὐτό;
Mark 9:28 καὶ εἰσελθόντος αὐτοῦ εἰς οἶκον οἱ μαθηταὶ αὐτοῦ κατ' ἰδίαν
ἐπηρώτων
ὅτι ἡμεῖς οὐκ ἠδυνήθημεν ἐκβαλεῖν αὐτό;
Luke 9:37–43 (parallel pericope, but without this sentence)

Matt 19:13 τότε προσηνέχθησαν αὐτῷ παιδία
Mark 10:13 καὶ προσέφερον αὐτῷ παιδία
Luke 18:15 προσέφερον δὲ αὐτῷ παιδία

Matt 21:1 καὶ ὅτε ἤγγισαν εἰς Ἱεροσόλυμα
καὶ ἦλθον εἰς Βηθφαγὴ εἰς τὸ Ὄρος τῶν Ἐλαιῶν
(adv) τότε Ἰησοῦς ἀπέστειλεν δύο μαθητὰς
Mark 11:1 καὶ ὅτε ἠγγίζουσιν εἰς Ἱεροσόλυμα
εἰς Βηθφαγὴ καὶ Βηθανίαν πρὸς τὸ Ὄρος τῶν Ἐλαιῶν
ἀποστέλλει δύο τῶν μαθητῶν αὐτοῦ
Luke 19:29 καὶ ἐγένετο ὡς ἤγγισεν εἰς
Βηθφαγὴ καὶ Βηθανία[ν] πρὸς τὸ ὄρος τὸ καλοῦμενον
Ἐλαιῶν
ἀπέστειλεν δύο μαθητὰς

Matt 22:21	λέγουσιν αὐτῷ	Καίσαρος.	τότε	λέγει	αὐτοῖς
Mark 12:16–17	οἱ δὲ εἶπαν αὐτῷ	Καίσαρος.	ὁ δὲ Ἰησοῦς	εἶπεν	αὐτοῖς
Luke 20:24–25	οἱ δὲ εἶπαν	Καίσαρος.	ὁ δὲ	εἶπεν	πρὸς αὐτοῖς

Matt 26:14 τότε πορευθεὶς εἷς τῶν δώδεκα,
ὁ λεγόμενος Ἰούδας Ἰσκαριώτης, πρὸς τοὺς ἀρχειρεῖς
Mark 14:10 καὶ Ἰούδας Ἰσκαριώθ ὁ εἷς τῶν δώδεκα,
ἀπῆλθεν πρὸς τοὺς ἀρχειρεῖς
Luke 22:3 εἰσῆλθεν δὲ σατανᾶς εἰς Ἰούδαν τὸν καλούμενον Ἰσκαριώτην,
ὄντα ἐκ τοῦ ἀριθμοῦ τῶν δώδεκα,

Matt 26:16	καὶ ἀπὸ τότε	ἐζήτει εὐκαιρίαν	ἵνα αὐτὸν παραδῷ	
Mark 14:11	καὶ	ἐζήτει	πῶς αὐτὸν εὐκαίρως παραδοῖ	
Luke 22:6	καὶ	ἐζήτει εὐκαιρίαν		τοῦ παραδοῦναι αὐτὸν

Matt 26:31 τότε λέγει αὐτοῖς ὁ Ἰησοῦς πάντες ὑμεῖς σκανδαλισθήσεθσε
Mark 14:27 καὶ λέγει αὐτοῖς ὁ Ἰησοῦς ὅτι πάντες σκανδαλισθήσεθσε
Luke 22:31–39 (parallel pericope, but without this sentence)

τότε from Matthew although they do share instances of adverbial τότε.[29]

Matt 26:38 τότε λέγει αὐτοῖς περίλυπός ἐστιν ἡ ψυχή μου ἕως θανάτου μείνατε ὧδε καὶ γρηγορεῖτε μετ᾽ ἐμοῦ
Mark 14:34 καὶ λέγει αὐτοῖς περίλυπός ἐστιν ἡ ψυχή μου ἕως θανάτου μείνατε ὧδε καὶ γρηγορεῖτε
Luke 22:39–41 (parallel pericope, but without this sentence)

Matt 26:74 τότε ἤρξατο καταθεματίζειν καὶ ὀμνύειν ὅτι οὐκ οἶδα τὸν ἄνθρωπον
Mark 14:71 ὁ δὲ ἤρξατο ἀναθεματίζειν καὶ ὀμνύναι ὅτι οὐκ οἶδα τὸν ἄνθρωπον
Luke 22:60 εἶπεν δὲ ὁ Πέτρος· ἄνθρωπε, οὐκ οἶδα ὅ λέγεις

Matt 27:26 τότε ἀπέλυσεν αὐτοῖς τὸν Βαραββᾶν
Mark 15:15 . . . ἀπέλυσεν αὐτοῖς τὸν Βαραββᾶν
Luke 23:25 ἀπέλυσεν δὲ τὸν διὰ στάσιν

[29] The following seven sets of readings are **not** narrative τότε:
Matt 7:5 καὶ τότε διαβλέψεις ἐκβαλεῖν τὸ κάρφος ἐκ τοῦ ὀφθαλμοῦ τοῦ ἀδελφοῦ σου
Mark (no parallel)
Luke 6:42 καὶ τότε διαβλέψεις τὸ κάρφος τὸ ἐν τῷ ὀφθαλμῷ τοῦ ἀδελφοῦ σου ἐκβαλεῖν. (Notice how Luke uses characteristically Greek word order despite a Hebraic idiom. The word order shows Greek sensitivity to presumed sources and argues against an imitation theory.)

Matt 9:15 καὶ τότε νηστεύσουσιν
Mark 2:20 καὶ τότε νηστεύσουσιν
Luke 5:35 τότε νηστεύσουσιν

Matt 12:29 καὶ τότε τὴν οἰκίαν αὐτοῦ διαρπάσει
Mark 3:27 καὶ τότε τὴν οἰκίαν αὐτοῦ διαρπάσει
Luke 11:22 καὶ τὰ σκῦλα αὐτοῦ διαδίδωσιν

Matt 12:43–45 τότε λέγει εἰς τὸν οἶκον μου ἐπιστρεψω . . . τότε πορεύεται καὶ παραλαμβάνει μεθ ἑαυτοῦ ἑπτὰ ἕτερα πνεύματα
Mark (no parallel)
Luke 11:24–26 τότε λέγει εἰς τὸν οἶκον μου ἐπιστρεψω . . . τότε πορεύεται καὶ παραλαμβάνει ἕτερα πνεύματα

Matthew's examples of narrative τότε occur in the middle of material that is identical except for τότε. The Greek is not flowing from Matthew into Mark or Luke, but rather, is flowing into Matthew. It is Matthew's style. Matthew writes Greek with narrative τότε and frequently adds this item in a way that is similar to the way Luke apparently adds δέ to his sources. If we didn't have Mark we might think that Matthew was ultimately derived from an Aramaic narrative. There is an additional clue that confirms our conclusion: Matthew has grouped material into five long discourses and at the end of each discourse's conclusion he has a Hebraic ἐγένετο structure. But that structure does not occur in Aramaic. The fact that both narrative τότε and Hebraic indefinite ἐγένετο occur in the same document means either that two separate sources in two different languages were used by Matthew or that Matthew is writing with his own personal brand of first-century Jewish Greek. Two separate sources are unnecessary and contra-indicated by the highly organized nature of the materials bounded by indefinite ἐγένετο. The five collections of Jesus's teaching are distinctively Matthean and the ἐγένετο structures are tied to those collections. Consequently, one must chose the second hypothesis: Matthew has created the Hebraic ἐγένετο examples.[30] That would lead one to hypothesize that Matthew may be responsible for the Aramaic style, too. As mentioned above, the existence of Mark and a comparison of the wording of Matthew and Mark where they differ only on τότε, allows us to go beyond the linguistic hypothesis and state that Matthew is most probably the one responsible for both his examples of criterion #13 and criterion #15.

Mark and Luke have nothing against τότε per se. They like adverbial τότε, but avoid narrative τότε, even in Mark 2:10 and Luke 5:24 where they

---

Matt 24:16	τότε οἱ ἐν τῇ Ἰουδαίᾳ φευγέτωσαν εἰς τὸ ὄρη
Mark 13:14	τότε οἱ ἐν τῇ Ἰουδαίᾳ φευγέτωσαν εἰς τὸ ὄρη
Luke 21:21	τότε οἱ ἐν τῇ Ἰουδαίᾳ φευγέτωσαν εἰς τὸ ὄρη

Matt 24:23		τότε ἐὰν τις ὑμῖν εἴπῃ	ἰδοὺ ὧδε
Mark 13:21	καὶ	τότε ἐὰν τις ὑμῖν εἴπῃ	ἰδοὺ ὧδε
Luke 17:23	καὶ	ἐροῦσιν ὑμῖν· ἰδοὺ ἐκεῖ, [ἤ]	ἰδοὺ ὧδε

[30] If Matthew and Luke shared a Greek source with a literary Hebrew background, Matthew may have seen quite a few indefinite ἐγένετο examples in the material that he gathered together, perhaps influencing what may be seen in Matthew's Gospel.

are identical in wording, and in including the interruptive "he says." Mark and Luke exhibit this amazing paradox, even though such a distinction has never existed in any grammar book, ancient or modern. In fact, twentieth-century scholarship on Semitisms in the NT has generally missed this lack of narrative τότε in Mark and Luke, not discussing its significance. The evidence above points to Hebrew as the necessary language for any Semitic narrative background.

Sociolinguistics for assuming a Hebrew narrative on Jesus

The conclusions that point to a Hebrew gospel source behind the Greek sources to the Synoptic Gospels fit within a larger picture of what is known about the first century. Because of the tendency in many NT studies to assume that Hebrew was not a realistic option for a narrative about Jesus, we will briefly list some sociolinguistic points. Many of these are seemingly obvious, but often do not receive collective presentation in NT gospel studies where their combined weight may be seen.

1. Qumran Hebrew shows the language choice of a major Jewish sect at the end of the Second Temple period. Qumran Hebrew is multidialectical, including a literary dialect that is an extension of "Late Biblical Hebrew," and a dialect that is close to Mishnaic Hebrew. It must be considered culturally appropriate for a first-century eschatological, messianic group to write in Hebrew.

2. Maccabean Hebrew. The style of 1 Maccabees points to Hebrew as the language of choice for the writing of the history.

3. The sociology of Acts 21:20–26, which includes a Jerusalem messianic movement concerned with following Torah, leads to the natural prediction that they, too, would choose Hebrew as the language for writing a messianic history, and the Torah of their "Second Moses."

4. The most natural reading of Papias's statement in Eusebius (our earliest church history), points to a Hebrew Gospel written by the disciple Matthew, presumably for the Jerusalem church. This statement is direct testimony and not problematic from the perspective of current Mishnaic scholarship. Of course, this tradition refers to a Hebrew source gospel, not

to the canonical Gospel. The canonical Gospel of Matthew was written in Greek, not Hebrew.

5. The Hebrew Bible was in direct use by the first-century Jewish residents of the land of Israel. That is confirmed by the relative lack of Targumim at Qumran, despite the sect's having many Aramaic documents, including two copies of an Aramaic translation of the notoriously difficult[31] Job.[32]

6. The published teachings and decisions of the rabbis recorded in the Mishnah and other rabbinic writings, representing a culture that praised the

---

[31] The Hebrew of the book of Job has been seen as a problematic dialect from pre-Christian times. The Old Greek translation of Job commented on using the help of an Aramaic document for their translation (Job 42:17ff).

[32] The facts on the ground are problematic for the assumptions of many scholars that Aramaic translations were already commonplace. Consider the opening sentence of an article in Willem Smelik, "Language, Locus, and Translation Between the Talmudim," *Journal for the Aramaic Bible* 3 (2001): 199–224: "In a society that had largely lost the ability to speak Hebrew—in both the Diaspora and Palestine—translations of the Torah must have been used quite freely around the beginning of the Common Era." This is true for Job, because Job was written in a unique dialect in the history of the Hebrew language. At least in the land of Israel, we must assume that the Hebrew Bible was commonly accessed directly in the Hebrew language during the Second Temple period. It is only in the second century that Smelik's opening statement starts to find support, as he himself points out: "In Palestine, translations may have found their way into the synagogue much later than in the diaspora, possibly not before the second century CE. While generalizations are quite misleading, this assumption is based on observations that show that the inclusion of translations was not standard to the extent that many scholars assume it was. All the first century sources on Palestine, including Philo, Josephus and the New Testament, refer to all elements within the service, including midrashic expositions, but remain silent about a translation. Only literary sources dating from the second century CE onward relate translations to the synagogue" (p. 206). We can add the archeological evidence of Qumran to that picture of agreement. With over two hundred Hebrew Bible documents, an Aramaic Bible is only represented by 11Q Job (with spelling considerations that point to an outside, eastern origin), 4Q156tg Lev (16:12–15, 18–21; either from a targum or perhaps from a Day of Atonement pilgrimage reading), and 4Q157tgJob. With the two attestations of a Job Targum at Qumran, we should add the testimony of the Old Greek to a Job Targum (Job 42:17ff Greek) so that we see the wide circulation of an Aramaic Job throughout the ancient Middle East.

retention of the original wording of a teacher, show that first-century teachers taught in Hebrew.

7. Story parables are given in Hebrew throughout rabbinic literature, even when found within Aramaic contexts. There are no examples of Aramaic story parables.[33]

8. Linguistic trace elements in the Gospels now join and confirm the above sociolinguistic pictures. If we accept the theory of a Semitic source behind the Synoptic Gospels' Greek source(s), then at least one of those source(s) was Hebrew and not Aramaic. Furthermore, such trace elements would suggest that the synoptic problem cannot be solved without seriously coming to grips with Hebrew.

Conclusion

Luke's connectives are primary evidence that he has used an unnatural style in his Gospel and to a slight degree in the first part of Acts. This is important, primary evidence with far-reaching implications.

Luke's unnatural style in his use of connectives cannot be satisfactorily explained by supposing a long time gap between the writing of his Gospel and the writing of Acts, by supposing a different genre or literary organization, or by hypothesizing a wide-ranging imitation of the Old Greek Bible. The most consistent linguistic explanation is that Luke had access to at least one Hebraized Greek source to his Gospel. He smoothed out the Greek, by and

[33] The lack of Aramaic parables was already noted by Segal over a century ago. Nevertheless, examples abound where this is ignored and not discussed. Cf. Arland Hultgren, *The Parables of Jesus: A Commentary* (Grand Rapids: Eerdmans, 2000), 363, who argues against the originality of the wordplay bn "son" and ʾbn "stone" in the Parable of the Wicked Tenants, on two grounds: (1) it is overly subtle, and (2) it does not work in Aramaic. Apparently, Hultgren was unacquainted with Josephus *J.W.* 5:272, or even Matt 3:9/Luke 3:8 and Luke 19:40 (where the plural doesn't require Hebrew, though there should not be any restriction to Aramaic in the first place). If someone were to argue similarly about Hillel, Gamaliel the Elder, or Yochanan ben Zakkai, they would be considered out of touch with the linguistic, cultural, and sociolinguistic background, on both points.

large, but was limited by a threshold phenomenon that has produced the stylistic inconsistencies noted above.

There is much that could be added to this article in support of a source explanation or against the rather commonly held imitation explanation.[34] Examples of non-Septuagintal Hebraisms would add their confirmation to this thesis. The nature of the uneven style in Luke's Gospel would add to this thesis.

In Luke we have someone who is true enough to his sources to allow unnatural Greek, a Greek somewhat at odds with his own style. Threshold phenomena apparently inhibited the freest use of his connectives. Consistently, his use of major Greek connectives in his Gospel and Acts produces quite different frequencies of use between the Gospel, 1 Acts, and 2 Acts. The data, for both the translation Greek of some of the Old Greek Bible and for Greek documents that are more stylistically natural Greek, can be viewed in Tables 1–8 and 12–15.

What this means for reading and interpretation is that the connectives in the Gospel are slightly stronger than those in the Acts and these connectives

[34] Again, see Martin, *Studies in the Life and Ministry of the Historical Jesus*. See especially pp. 3–5: "The more commonly held view, namely Luke's skillful and deliberate imitation of LXX style, is not satisfactory either. The data from Luke-Acts is particularly instructive here. First of all, consider the book of Acts. The second half (Acts 15:36—28:31) is *consistently* like the original Greek control documents studied. . . . The first half (Acts 1:1—15:35), however, is erratic with respect to occurrence of these 17 criteria—22 of some 58 units having Semitic frequencies. . . . When Luke's Gospel is analyzed by means of these 17 criteria the same erratic distribution occurs. Why is not the entire Gospel written in such deliberately Semitized Greek since the Gospel material is entirely set within a Palestinian environment? And why, as a study of his use of Markan material shows, does Luke tend generally to lessen the Semitic style of Mark (as determined by these 17 criteria), as he does nearly 3/4 of the time? . . . It becomes even more improbable, however, when it is seen that such *erratic Semitic style with respect to these 17 syntactical features appears in both Mark and Matthew!* Is it to be assumed that they, like Luke, are so skilled as to be able consciously to imitate the style of the Greek of the Old Testament so as to give appropriate coloring to their Gospels? And, if so, why do they, like Luke, also do it only in some stories and sayings and not others? . . . Surely the most probable explanation for this inconsistency is that Semitic sources/traditions are being used" (emphasis original).

cannot be assumed to be naturally consistent. The connectives in the Gospel have crossed a threshold and Luke has not reworked all of them into his own style. Some of the blocks of material introduced by καί in his Gospel are more linguistically ambiguous than those in Acts and should not automatically be considered sub-ordinated to a larger δέ unit.

Equally important, the existence of a source(s) that cannot be Mark suggests that the Gospel of Luke may have had more source material than is commonly assumed in commentaries. Apparently, Luke had one or more sources that go back through Greek to a literary Hebrew narrative and he apparently respected his sources to such an extent that he allowed them to measurably influence his own writing style.

Bibliography

Barthélemy, Dominique. *Les Devanciers d'Aquila*. Leiden: Brill, 1963.

Ben-Yehuda, Eliezer. *"Mavo ha-Gadol,"* in *Milon ha-Lashon ha-`Ivrit ha-Yeshanah veha-Hadashah*. Jerusalem: Ben-Yehuda Publications, 1909–1958.

Buth, Randall. "אדין/τότε—Anatomy of a Semitism in Jewish Greek." *Maarav* 5-6 (1990): 33–48.

Buth, Randall and Brian Kvasnica, "Temple Authorities and Tithe Evasion: The Linguistic Background and Impact of the Parable of the Vineyard, the Tenants and the Son." Pages 53–80 in *Jesus' Last Week*. Edited by R. Steven Notley, et al. Leiden: Brill: 2006.

Dalman, Gustaf. *Die Worte Jesu*. 2nd ed. Leipzig: Hinrichs, 1930.

Epstein, J. N. *Mavo Lenusah Hamishnah*. Jerusalem: n.p., 1948.

Fitzmyer, Joseph. *The Gospel According to Luke I-IX: Introduction, Translation, and Notes*. Anchor Bible 28. Garden City, New York: Doubleday, 1981.

Hawkins, John C. *Horae Synopticae: Contributions to the Study of the Synoptic Problem*. 2nd ed. Oxford: Clarendon Press, 1909. Repr., Grand Rapids: Baker Book House, 1968.

Hultgren, Arland. *The Parables of Jesus: A Commentary*. Grand Rapids: Eerdmans, 2000.

Kutscher, E. Y. *Leshon Haza"l* (The Language of the Sages)." Pages 37–107 in *Hebrew and Aramaic Studies*. Edited by Eduard Yechezkel Kutscher. Jerusalem: Magnes Press, 1977.

Levinsohn, Stephen H. *Textual Connections in Acts*. Atlanta: Scholar's Press, 1987.

Martin, Raymond A. *Studies in the Life and Ministry of the Historical Jesus*. New York: University Press of America, 1995.

Nolland, John. *Luke 1—9:20*. Word Bible Commentary 35A. Dallas: Word, 1989.

Plummer, Alfred. *A Critical and Exegetical Commentary on the Gospel According to St. Luke*. International Critical Commentary. Edinburgh: T. & T. Clark, 1896.

Segal, M. H. "Mishnaic Hebrew and Its Relation to Biblical Hebrew and to Aramaic." *Jewish Quarterly Review*, O.S. 20 (1908): 647–737.

Smelik, Willem. "Language, Locus, and Translation Between the Talmudim." *Journal for the Aramaic Bible* 3 (2001): 199–224.

Sparks, H. F. D. "The Semitisms of St. Luke's Gospel." *Journal of Theological Studies* 44 (1943): 129–38.

———. "The Semitisms of Acts." *Journal of Theological Studies*, ns 1 (1950): 16–28.

Josephus. Translated by Henry St. J. Thackeray. Vol. 2. LCL. Cambridge, Mass.: Harvard University Press, 1926–1965.

Turner, Nigel. *Style*. Vol. 4 of *A Grammar of New Testament Greek*. Edited by James Hope Moulton. Edinburgh: T. & T. Clark, 1976.

———. *Syntax*. Vol. 3 of *A Grammar of New Testament Greek*. Edited by James Hope Moulton. Edinburgh: T. & T. Clark, 1963.

The Use of the Article Before Names of Places
Patterns of Use in the Book of Acts

Jenny Read-Heimerdinger

Introduction

My initiation into discourse analysis came about through the study of New Testament manuscripts as it became apparent that many of the features that were of interest to linguists working in the field were also affected by variant readings in the Greek text. The article before proper names was one such feature, and in 1992 I had the pleasure of collaborating with Stephen Levinsohn in producing a study dealing with the special case of names of people in the book of Acts.[1] The overall conclusion was that the article with names of persons is the default way of referring to people by name, reflecting the function of the article to designate entities that are "uniquely identifiable."[2] The discussion set out to demonstrate that when names of persons are anarthrous it is because the participant is prominent at that point in the discourse. In other words, the narrator or person making a speech

[1] Jenny Heimerdinger and Stephen H. Levinsohn, "The Use of the Definite Article before Names of People in the Greek Text of Acts with Particular Reference to Codex Bezae," *FN* 5 (1992): 15–44. The study was adapted in Jenny Read-Heimerdinger, *The Bezan Text of Acts: A Contribution of Discourse Analysis to Textual Criticism* (JSNTSup 236; Sheffield: Sheffield Academic Press, 2002), 116–44; and developed further in Stephen H. Levinsohn, *Discourse Features of New Testament Greek* (2nd ed.; Dallas: Summer Institute of Linguistics, 2000), 150–62.

[2] Levinsohn, *Discourse Features*, 133.

omitted the article in order to bring the named character to the attention of the addressee for one reason or another.[3]

Regarding ordinary nouns, too, salience has been recognized as the overall factor that lies behind the omission of the article before a noun where it would normally be expected. Thus, in a recent study of the use of the article in Plato, David Sansone concludes that the "definite article tends to be more at home with topic than with focus."[4] It is not surprising, then, that the omission of the article should often be observed to be operating in conjunction with other features, notably word order, as combined means to indicate the important information of a sentence, where "important" naturally means "important for the speaker in terms of his or her communication goal" and not in any absolute sense.

Like names of persons, place names also fall into the category of nouns that have a sole, identifiable referent. To use the classification proposed by Stanley Porter, names of places are identifiable as "particular."[5] In fact, they are even more particular than names of persons since there is rarely more than one referent designated by any given geographical name, unlike the many people called Mary, Peter or Jesus, for example, even though in a given context there may well be only one such person. The aim of this present study is to see if the pattern that has been established with respect to the use of the article with names of persons also applies to the names of places. The text selected for examination is the book of Acts, whose subject matter means that of all the New Testament books it has the greatest number of references to place names. Indeed, both the narrative and the speeches abound in references to

---

[3] The conclusion is somewhat different from that reached by the classical grammarian Basil Gildersleeve who concluded that the article was not generally used with proper names in classical Greek: "Proper names being in their nature particular do not require the explicit article, and when the article is used with them, it retains much of its original demonstrative force" (Basil L. Gildersleeve, *Syntax of Classical Greek from Homer to Demosthenes* [2 vols.; New York: American Book Company, 1900–1911], 2:§514. Online: http://www.perseus.tufts.edu).

[4] David Sansone, "Towards a New Doctrine of the Article: Some Observations on the Definite Article in Plato," *CP* 88 (1993): 199.

[5] Stanley E. Porter, *Idioms of New Testament Greek* (Biblical Languages: Greek 2; Sheffield: JSOT Press, 1992), 313.

geographical locations of many kinds, whether associated with the land or the sea: countries, regions, cities, mountains, islands, seas.

In considering the references exhaustively, it becomes apparent that there are, in fact, two distinct patterns in the use of the article before names in these various categories, the principle governing the presence of the article with names of cities being different from that governing its presence with the other geographical entities. In view of the amount of data, especially taking into account the variant readings, thorough treatment of the entire topic would justify two separate studies. In the present essay, therefore, the category of cities is presented with provisional and partial conclusions, following detailed analysis of the other geographical groups.

Briefly stated, the results show that the default pattern is for the article to be present before names of places, unless attention is being drawn to the place. In the case of cities, this includes the first mention of the name in an episode, but other places are not affected by this factor. With respect to everything except cities, the article is omitted only if the narrator is deliberately highlighting the place for its significance to the participant in connection with whom it is mentioned. It is the role of the active participant, rather than the development of the narrative, that tends to be the relevant factor affecting the choice of the article.

Research context

Handbooks of grammar

Consideration of the article with geographical names in the standard grammars suggests that, as with names of persons, there are no real rules. Blass–Debrunner, for example, present a list of observations, noting the "frequent," "many" or "occasional" occurrences of the presence or the absence of the article with certain names or categories but without explanation; Robertson speaks of "obscurity and uncertainty."[6] Other works make no distinction between

---

[6] Friedrich W. Blass, Albert Debrunner and Friedrich Rehkopf, *Grammatik des neutestamentlichen Griechisch* (15th ed.; Göttingen: Vandenhoeck & Ruprecht, 1979), §261 (hereafter BDR); A. T. Robertson, *A Grammar of the Greek New Testament in the Light of Historical Research* (4th ed.; Nashville: Broadman, 1934), 1397.

proper names of people and proper names of places, any "clear and consistent principles" being in any case rated as undetectable.[7] Two authors stand out as offering rather more detailed analysis: Basil Gildersleeve with his monumental work on classical Greek, and G. B. Winer with his focus on New Testament Greek, so often ahead of his time in his clear-sighted acknowledgement of factors operating beyond the sentence level.[8] Gildersleeve identifies the general "rule" that the article is present with geographical names, while noting that exceptions occur chiefly in enumerations, conjoined nouns functioning as a unity and the predicate.[9] On particular categories, he observes among other things that Asia is always arthrous though other names of countries vary; postpositive partitive and chorographic genitives are generally articular; towns/cities are generally anarthrous though the more notable regularly take the article. He suggests that names that are substantivized adjectives (frequently ending in -ια) are more likely to be arthrous.[10] It is telling that, commenting on Gildersleeve's analysis of the spectrum of classical works, Robertson notes that usage of article with names of places "greatly varies among Greek writers."[11]

Winer, for his part, notes that in the New Testament countries and rivers are more often arthrous than cities and that the first mention of a place often causes the article to be omitted, as does a preposition before the name of a city. Overall, he gives the impression that apart from a regular tendency for the first mention of a name to be anarthrous, the presence or absence of the article depends on the nature of the place (e.g., country vs. cities) or

---

[7] E.g., Daniel B. Wallace, *Greek Grammar Beyond the Basics* (Grand Rapids: Zondervan, 1996), 245–47.

[8] Gildersleeve, *Syntax*, esp. 2:§547–§561, as well as specific articles: idem., "On the Article with Proper Names," *AJP* 11 (1890): 483–87; idem., "Problems in Greek Syntax: II. The Article," *AJP* 23 (1902); and G. B. Winer, *A Treatise on the Grammar of New Testament Greek* (trans. W. F. Moulton; Edinburgh: T. & T. Clark, 1882), 139–40.

[9] Gildersleeve, *Syntax*, 2:§568, 603 and 666 respectively.

[10] This claim is also made by BDR but is dismissed by Hemer as "misconceived" (Colin J. Hemer, *The Book of Acts in the Setting of Hellenistic History* (ed. Conrad H. Gempf; Tübingen: J. C. B. Mohr, 1989), 243.

[11] Robertson, *Grammar*, 759.

on the grammatical context (e.g., after prepositions, or in oblique cases) or on the author.

The situation in the grammar books is thus not a little confused, despite some extensive and detailed analysis and a genuine search for general principles. It lends itself to the conclusion that the choice to use the article or not is "as much a question of style as of grammar."[12] Taking into account the additional variation found in the different manuscripts, only occasionally if ever mentioned in the NT grammar books, it would be an easy step to assume that scribal custom should also figure in the list of factors determining the use of the article.[13]

In view of the principles that were able to be identified with respect to personal names using the tools of discourse analysis, there is reason, however, to have some optimism about recognizing the linguistic factors influencing a speaker's choice to use the article with geographical names. In order to reach a full and complete explanation, a range of texts and authors will need to be examined in detail, elucidating patterns and testing the principles that evolve in a variety of situations. This study of geographical names in the book of Acts is presented as one small part of that examination, in the hope that it will in time become a component of a wider and more complete study of the question, which will achieve the all-important goal of "explanatory adequacy."[14]

Modern Greek

It has been contended by present-day scholars who are native Greek speakers that Koine Greek is closer to modern Greek than is often supposed, that the development of the language was such that once Koine usage had been established it then changed relatively little.[15] That being so, it is of interest to

---

12 Sansone, "Towards a New Doctrine," 204, referring to the work of Gildersleeve.

13 Sansone does draw attention to the existence of variant readings concerning the presence of the article in the text of Plato and the need to take account of it in establishing patterns of use ("Towards a New Doctrine," 202).

14 Wallace, *Beyond the Basics*, 246, citing Chomsky.

15 See notably Chrys Caragounis, *The Development of Greek and the New Testament: Morphology, Syntax, Phonology, and Textual Transmission* (Grand Rapids: Baker

know the practice in modern Greek with regard to the article with geographical names. Discussion with a contemporary speaker reveals that Greek today always has the article with names of places.[16] The article is normally used with everything (towns, islands, countries and so on), unless the sentence wants to give some kind of emphasis. The following were given as examples:

> "Here is [arthrous] Athens," but "[arthrous] Patra is nice, but it is not like [anarthrous] Athens."
> "We'll go to [arthrous] Tinos," but "We went to all the islands, Tinos, Mykonos, Paros [all anarthrous]."

According to my correspondent, this last sentence, in a more formal way, would have actually included the articles before each of the names. Thus, omission of the article is sometimes perceived by present-day Greeks as a sign of laziness in oral discourse. So, although in the question "Are you living in Athens" the city is often anarthrous, it would be considered more "correct" to use the article.

This picture tends to suggest that the presence of the article with names of places could have been the expected usage even in New Testament Greek, and that anarthrous names were not the rule. It is a pattern that can be borne in mind and tested in the examination of place names in Acts.

The text of Acts

Variant readings

As Hemer pointed out, in order to establish patterns of use with regard to the article before place names, "it is essential to search the documents at first hand."[17] In consulting actual documents, as opposed to dictionaries or, for that matter, grammars, it is also essential to search texts that actually existed, rather than a hybrid reconstruction such as is found in an eclectic edition.

Academic, 2006).

[16] Personal communication with Andreas Andreopoulos, Senior Lecturer in Orthodox Christianity, University of Winchester, UK. Caragounis makes no specific mention of geographical names in his extensive investigation.

[17] Hemer, *Hellenistic History*, 241.

For questions of discourse features, a hypothetical text cannot serve as a proper basis for analysis—inevitably, for the editors of the current edition of the Greek New Testament[18] made their choices at each point of variant reading without the benefit of the information yielded by discourse analysis of the language. Furthermore, editorial choices are naturally conditioned by presuppositions as to the intended meaning of a given passage, determined by exegetes working on one type of text alone. In order, then, to identify patterns and define criteria with regard to discourse features it is imperative to work from texts that were at some time and in some place in use.[19]

Now, it is true that for the book of Acts the current Greek New Testament largely transmits the text of one manuscript, Codex Vaticanus (B03), which is usually though not always supported by Codex Sinaiticus (א01). Both manuscripts are representatives of what is known as the Alexandrian type of text, which has dominated the Greek editions (and therefore translations and commentaries) since the end of the nineteenth century. However, there were other forms of Acts circulating at least as early as the Alexandrian text. These texts are found among the earliest papyri of the third century, and were used as the basis for all such early versions as the Latin, Syriac, Aramaic and Middle Egyptian (i.e. before they were standardised and aligned with the by then dominant Alexandrian text from the fourth century onwards). These alternative states of text are commonly and collectively referred to as the "Western" text, although the diversity of places in which this has been located since the label was first assigned in the eighteenth century, from Palestine to Middle Egypt to Gaul, shows that it was far from being a local text belonging to the West. Nor was it derived from a homogenous recension as the Alexandrian text was, but rather it is a text characterized by a freedom of editorial activity such as is not commonly found in manuscripts after 200 C.E.

[18] The two current editions adopt the same text, the difference between them being the information supplied in the critical apparatus: Barbara and Kurt Aland et al., eds., *Novum Testamentum Graece* (27th ed.; Stuttgart: Deutsche Bibelgesellschaft, 1993); *The Greek New Testament* (4th ed.; Stuttgart: Deutsche Bibelgesellschaft/ United Bible Societies, 1993).

[19] Sansone makes this point regarding the text of Plato's work ("Towards a New Doctrine," 194).

Among the earliest Greek manuscripts, one stands out as having a text that is the most distinct from the Alexandrian text, namely, Codex Bezae (D05, c. 400), which differs in over 25% of the text. Codex Bezae appears to have conserved in a fossilized form a Greek text known from documentary evidence to have existed at least in the mid second century. Internal evidence suggests that this date should be moved back to the first century. A detailed comparison of Codex Bezae with Codex Vaticanus has shown that most of the variant readings arose through deliberate editorial activity. Specifically, unlike the familiar Alexandrian text of Acts, the Bezan text presents a critical evaluation of the apostles, including Paul, pointing out their weaknesses and mistakes as they gradually came to terms with the reality of Jesus's teaching; moreover, the narrator speaks from an internal Jewish perspective.[20] These two factors mean that at numerous points the interpretation of the text is dependent on the narrator's perceived purpose and the particular message he wished to communicate. The relevance of this will be apparent in considering some of the occurrences of geographical names and will be highlighted at the appropriate places.

Occurrences of place names

For the purposes of this study, the texts of B03 and D05 were both used, the text of the former being always shared by ℵ01 with respect to the article before place names, except once at 28:16.

In the Appendix, all the place names that occur in the book of Acts are noted except Jerusalem to which there is an exceptional number of references that would overload the table. The name of Jerusalem is nevertheless considered in the analysis (see below). The following points should be noted:

- D05 is lacunose for 8:29b–10:14a, 21:3–10 and 22:29a–28:31.
- Where an occurrence is found in only one of the manuscripts under consideration, this is indicated beside the reference in column 1.

---

[20] For a detailed presentation of the texts of the book of Acts and the significance of the variant readings see the "Introduction" in successive volumes of Josep Rius-Camps and Jenny Read-Heimerdinger, *The Message of Acts in Codex Bezae: A Comparison with the Alexandrian Tradition* (4 vols.; JSNTSup 257/LNTS 302, 365, 415; London: T. & T. Clark 2002–2009).

- Columns 3 and 4 indicate the presence or absence of the article, with the variant readings indicated as they arise.
- In Column 5, the nature of the geographical entity is noted.
- Entries in italics are found in direct speech.

While the references to places are given in the Appendix for the whole of Acts, discussion will focus on the passages that are extant in Codex Bezae. When variant readings are cited, words present in one text and absent in the other are indicated with a solid underline.

Observations

Countries

The classification of territories as distinct countries in the ancient world poses difficulties, in part because borders fluctuated and in part because dominant powers tended to absorb countries into their empires. Concerning places named in Acts, only a small number can be properly treated as countries within the context of the references to them; other countries that had been made into Roman provinces will be treated separately as "regions."

Israel

The name of Israel is included in this study for the sake of completeness, but in actual fact, when Israel is mentioned in Acts it is always in the sense of a nation rather than a geographical location (× 9; + 1 B03 [D05 lac]; + 1 D05). All the references are found in chapters 2–10. In the majority of occurrences, the people are spelt out in one form or another, as the "sons" or the "people" or the "house" of Israel and at those places no article is used before Ἰσραήλ. That the absence of the article is not simply due to the presence of a dependent genitive[21] is demonstrated by the supplementary occurrence in D05 at 4:8, where Peter addresses the assembled gathering of authorities as "rulers of the people and elders of Israel" (Ἄρχοντες τοῦ λαοῦ καὶ πρεσβύτεροι τοῦ Ἰσραήλ). Here, the elders are addressed as specific people and not as a fixed

[21] The same point was made with reference to names of persons (Heimerdinger, *The Bezan Text*, 139).

group such as is represented by the sons or the house or the people of Israel. It would seem therefore to be the stereotypical nature of the phrase that brings about the omission of the article before Israel.[22]

There is only one other mention of Israel, at 5:31 in the course of Peter's response to the Sanhedrin as he speaks of God lifting up Jesus "to give repentance to Israel" (τῷ Ἰσραήλ). This one example provides insufficient data to develop detailed analysis, but the reference nevertheless serves as a useful point of comparison, for it is also arthrous. The presence of the article could be explained again by the fact that Israel is not mentioned within a stereotypical phrase.

Egypt

The country of Egypt is mentioned first in the list of countries represented at Pentecost (2:9) and then 11 times (+ 1 D05; + 1 B03) by Stephen in the course of his defense to the Sanhedrin (7:2b–53). With one exception at 7:11 and another at 7:36 B03, the name is always anarthrous, even when mentioned twice in close succession (e.g., 7:10a, b, 34a, b). Now, it could be said that the very repetition of the name, which occurs in two clusters (7:9–17, 34–40), is a way of highlighting the country and drawing attention to its significance for the history of the Jewish people, and that this may account for the omission of the article. The reason, though, for the exceptional presence of the article is not so easy to account for. A feature for the reference at 7:11 is that Egypt is mentioned in association with Canaan, as two countries jointly affected by a famine: ἐφ' ὅλην τὴν Αἴγυπτον καὶ Χανάαν. That one article is used for both countries is less clear in the D05 text where the genitive case is used: ἐφ' ὅλης τῆς Αἰγύπτου καὶ Χανάαν, but insofar as Χανάαν is an indeclinable Semitic name it is indeed possible. This is the only time in Stephen's speech when Egypt is mentioned alongside another country (though see the discussion of 7:36 below) and it is thus not being highlighted in the way that one would expect in the other occurrences.

[22] Comparison may be made with stereotypical phrases associated with names of persons, such as "the baptism of John" or "the name of Jesus," where the name is typically anarthrous (Heimerdinger, *The Bezan Text*, 137).

At 7:36, only a few witnesses share B03's arthrous reference to Egypt (ἐν τῇ Αἰγύπτῳ, C04 36 453 *pc*). Here, Egypt is mentioned by Stephen as one place where Moses performed signs and wonders, together with the Red Sea and the desert. The reading of γῇ for τῇ in all the other witnesses including D05[23] suggests that the B03 reading is a secondary one, though that does not make the article an "error." On the contrary, it can be assumed that for the scribe of B03 the article had its place. In fact, this is the only mention of Egypt alongside other places apart from 7:11 (see above), though unlike the previous occasion the other places are not countries comparable with Egypt nor are they linked together; furthermore, within the narrative each one of them is of particular significance. Nevertheless, it is perhaps the mention of other places that justifies the presence of the article before Egypt in B03.

Other countries in Stephen's speech

In addition to Israel and Egypt, the following countries are also mentioned by Stephen: at 7:11, Canaan is joined with Egypt which carries the article; at 7:29, Midian is cited in the phrase ἐν γῇ Μαδιάμ, which is typically anarthrous (compare Egypt at 7:36 D05); and at 7:43, Babylon is referred to in an adapted quotation of Amos 5:27, modified differently according to the manuscripts. In most witnesses, Stephen records Amos as prophesying that God will remove the Israelites "beyond Babylon" (μετοικιῶ ὑμᾶς ἐπέκεινα Βαβυλῶνος;) where D05 and part of the Old Latin tradition reads "to the regions of Babylon" (ἐπὶ τὰ μέρη Βαβυλῶνος), a chorographic genitive. Amos 5:27 LXX says: μετοικιῶ ὑμᾶς ἐπέκεινα Δαμασκοῦ, which corresponds to Babylonia geographically if not textually. In any case, Babylon like Damascus is salient information because it is entirely new and unexpected in the context in which it was spoken.

---

[23] Most mss read ἐν γῇ Αἰγύπτῳ; D05, with a range of support, has ἐν γῇ Αἰγύπτου. The majority reading could have been the source of the B03 variant, the unusual adjectival use of Αἰγύπτος being substituted with the substantival form and the article (in uncial writing, the two letters Γ and Τ are easily confused). The Latin page of Codex Bezae reads *in αegypto*, which suggests that the exemplar did not have γῇ but τῇ.

In short, although the article is read before none of these countries, the absence of the article can be accounted for by the nature of the construction, except at 7:43 B03 where salience could be the reason for its absence.

Italy

The two isolated references to Italy are arthrous (18:2; 27:6). On both occasions, the country is mentioned in an indirect way: Aquila had arrived recently in Corinth from Italy; the centurion accompanying Paul to Rome found a boat in Myra going to Italy.

Greece

"Hellas" is named as a country only once at 20:2, the narrator more usually naming cities or the specific region of Achaia. Paul is said to go to Greece (ἦλθεν εἰς τὴν Ἑλλάδα, 20:2) in accordance with the plan he made in Ephesus to visit Achaia after Macedonia (see 19:21). His arrival in Greece is presented as non-salient in so far as it was an intended visit and the reference is arthrous.

Regions mentioned in Acts 1–5

The regions are discussed in the order of their first occurrence in Acts. For ease of reference, they are divided into those names that occur in the first part of the book up to Acts 5, and those that occur principally with reference to Paul's journeys (Acts 13–28) although some of the names are first mentioned earlier. Names of minor importance for the narrative are listed in brackets and discussed under the heading of the more prominent name with which they are associated.

Judaea (Cappadocia)

The name of the province of Judaea is found five times on its own (+ 1 D05; + 2 B03 [D05 lac]), and three times more (+ 1 B03 [D05 lac]) times in conjunction with one or more other regions (Samaria/Galilee, see below). When Judaea is mentioned on its own, it is always arthrous except for once at 10:37a D05. Whereas all the other references to Judaea are made by the narrator, the reference at 10:37a is made by Peter in his speech to the people gathered in the house of Cornelius in Caesarea. As Peter struggles to piece together his first ever explanation of the gospel for a Gentile audience, he begins by presenting Jesus and his ministry as intended initially and primarily for Israel (10:36). In this context, whilst pointing out that Jesus came from Galilee (10:37b, ἀπὸ τῆς Γαλιλαίας), he highlights his activity as having taken place throughout Judaea (10:37a, καθ' ὅλης (τῆς, B03) Ἰουδαίας), in other words and even more emphatically, "the country of the Jews and Jerusalem" (10:39). The significance of this highlighting is that it underscores Peter's belief that Jesus had come for the Jews first and foremost. Galilee, in comparison, is no more than background information of secondary interest, especially in D05 where the mention of Galilee is made in a new sentence conjoined with γάρ (ἀρξάμενος γὰρ ἀπὸ τῆς Γαλιλαίας). In B03, on the other hand, Galilee is mentioned in the same sentence as Judaea, the two areas being on a par with one another.

When Judaea is referred to in association with other regions, the presence of the article varies, and there is also another variant reading between B03 and D05 (8:1). The very first mention of Judaea in the book of Acts is spoken by Jesus at 1:8 in conjunction with a reference to Samaria. Despite being a first mention of either region, the names are arthrous with one article for the two names: ἐν πάσῃ τῇ Ἰουδαίᾳ καὶ Σαμαρείᾳ.[24] The same is true of the narrator's reference to "the regions of Judaea and Samaria" at 8:1, where D05 omits the article. The D05 reading could be seen as an example of what Gildersleeve calls the "chorographic genitive," which he noted was generally anarthrous (compare Babylon, 7.43 D05 above).[25]

At 2:9, Judaea is mentioned in a series of regions and countries from where people were present at Pentecost. The whole series needs to be considered:

> οἱ κατοικοῦντες τὴν Μεσοποταμίαν Ἰουδαίαν τε (omit D05) καὶ Καππαδοκίαν Πόντον καὶ τὴν Ἀσίαν Φρυγίαν τε (omit D05) καὶ Παμφυλίαν, Αἴγυπτον τε (omit B03) καὶ τὰ μέρη τῆς Λιβύης τῆς κατὰ Κυρήνην

[24] D05 omits the repetition of the preposition ἐν.
[25] Gildersleeve, *Syntax*, 2:§553.

Nine regions or countries from Mesopotamia to Libya are seemingly divided into groups, but there is considerable disagreement among commentators and grammarians as to where the divisions occur.[26] An important part of the problem is understanding to what extent the narrator intended the list of 2:9–11 to be references to literal places of the time, or how far the account at this point is written, on the contrary, in a non-literal, theological or symbolical register.[27] In any case, in so far as the first three (Mesopotamia, Judaea and Cappadocia) can be considered to form one unit, especially with the particle τε in B03, the article before Mesopotamia could be construed as including Judaea and Cappadocia, too. On the other hand, it may be the nature of Mesopotamia, like that of Asia in its broader sense (see below), that determines the presence of the article before these two names.

Cappadocia is not mentioned by name again in Acts.

Samaria, Galilee

Samaria is mentioned six times (+ 1 B03 [D05 lac]), twice in combination with Judaea as mentioned above and once with Phoenicia (discussed below). On the three occasions the name appears on its own (8:5, 9, 14), it is arthrous. At 8:5, the name of Samaria is taken up from 8:1 in an episode involving Philip, being now distinguished from Judaea (compare 8:1). It is understood as the name of the capital city according to a few manuscripts (P[74] ℵ01 A02 B03 1175 *pc*) but most witnesses understand the city Philip visited to be an unnamed place in the district of Samaria, an understanding confirmed by the indeterminate reference to "that city" at 8:8.

It is worth noting that the article is maintained despite the fact that Samaria comes into focus on its own for the first time in Acts 8:5, and is of considerable narrative significance as the first place the gospel is taken to outside Jerusalem and Judaea. While 8:5 and 8:9 present examples of a postpositive genitive, this is probably not relevant to the presence of the article since the first is

[26] See Charles K. Barrett, *A Critical and Exegetical Commentary on the Acts of the Apostles* (2 vols.; ICC; Edinburgh: T. & T. Clark, 1994, 1998), 1:120. See also Rius-Camps and Read-Heimerdinger, *The Message of Acts*, 1:157, 162–64.

[27] The interpretation of the Pentecost scene as a non-literal event on one level is discussed in Rius-Camps and Read-Heimerdinger, *The Message of Acts*, 1:152–64.

a partitive genitive and the second appositional. In so far as the episode involving Philip is linked retrospectively with οὖν (at 8:4) to 8:1, it could be said that the mention of Samaria at 8:5 and 8:9 is anaphoric, as it is also at the third instance, 8:14, but that, too, is irrelevant in B03 since the first mention of Samaria at 8:1 B03 (discussed with reference to Judaea above) in any case has the article.

Galilee occurs once in association with Judaea and Samaria (9:31 [D05 lac]) and once on its own at 10:37a. Both references are arthrous. The narrator's mention of Galilee between Judaea and Samaria at 9:31 echoes the references to the two places at 1:8 and 8:1 (see section on Judaea above) and again there is one article for the three names.

Mesopotamia (Libya)

Mesopotamia, being more an extensive land area than a distinct country in the first century CE, heads the series of regions and countries from where people were present at Pentecost (2:9; see above). However this list is interpreted, Mesopotamia is one of the three names in the enumeration to have the article (together with Asia and Libya).[28] Leaving Libya aside as a special case as discussed below, it may be relevant that both Mesopotamia and Asia are the only two large land areas in the list rather than specific provinces (taking Asia in the wider sense in this case, see below where Asia is discussed in more detail).

The only other reference to Mesopotamia in Acts (7:2) is spoken by Stephen at the outset of his narration of the history of Israel, and is also arthrous.

Libya only occurs in the list of 2:9. The article can be accounted for by the identifying specification that follows: τὰ μέρη τῆς Λιβύης τῆς κατὰ Κυρήνην.

---

[28] Contrast Gildersleeve, *Syntax*, 2:§550, who notes with reference to Asia that the article is only omitted "when three or at least two grand divisions are named together."

Other regions of 2:9

The regions listed at 2:9 not already discussed above are Pontus, Phrygia, Pamphylia and Cyrene, all anarthrous. Of those, Pamphylia figures at several places in the course of Paul's journeys and is discussed more specifically below. Pontus comes after a group of three places possibly linked with one article (on Judaea, see above); it is connected to the mention of Asia (arthrous) with καί. It is possible that Phrygia and Pamphylia, which follow next, are being used adjectivally to mean regions within Asia in the wider sense than the Roman province of Asia (see below). Alternatively, as was suggested above, the article before Asia could be due to its nature as a large land area (see above, and compare Mesopotamia, which is always arthrous in Acts). This explanation has the advantage of providing a single reason for the article before Asia and Mesopotamia. The absence of the article before the other places may be connected with the fact that they appear in a list, a factor that Gildersleeve noted as affecting the presence of the article, but a reason still needs to be found in that case for the articular names of Mesopotamia and Asia.[29]

Regions principally mentioned with reference to Paul's journeys

Once the church is established in Jerusalem, the disciples begin to move beyond the borders of Judaea, and the Greek-speaking Jews, together with their regions and cities, start to play a major role in the narrative. Their importance becomes most apparent once Paul becomes an active participant as a Jesus-believing disciple. The regions mentioned in connection with the stages of Paul's mission are discussed in this section in the order of their first occurrence (after the list of 2:9 in the case of Asia and Pamphylia, see above).

Asia

Asia is mentioned nine times (+ 1 B03; + 2 D05; + 1 B03 [D05 lac]), first at 6:9 after appearing in the list of 2:9. The name is usually arthrous, even

[29] Gildersleeve, *Syntax*, 2:§568.

when the country is referred to for the first time in the context (see 2:9; 16:6; 19:1 D05; 20:3 D05, 16; 27:2 B03). The article is also retained when the region is set in contrast to Jerusalem at 19:1 D05: Θέλοντος δὲ τοῦ Παύλοθ κατὰ τὴν ἰδίαν βουλὴν πορεύεσθαι εἰς Ἱεροσόλυμα εἶπεν αὐτῷ τὸ πνεῦμα ὑποστρέφειν εἰς τὴν Ἀσίαν. The reason for the article seems to be that Paul had already indicated when he was last in Asia (specifically in Ephesus, as in 20:16) that he would return if God was willing (18:21). So Asia represents the direction both expected and intended for Paul and, as will be seen with reference to Syria and Macedonia at 20:3 (IV.3.e below), this factor apparently plays a part in the retention of the article before names of places.

The persistence of the article suggests that it is the default way of referring to Asia and it makes the anarthrous references of particular interest. Asia is mentioned without the article at 6:9 B03 (D05 omits the mention); 19:26 D05 (B03 arthrous), 27 B03 (D05 arthrous). At 6:9, it is a question of people who began to argue with Stephen, people who were from Cilicia and, according to all manuscripts except A02 and D05/d5, from Asia. Neither region has the article. It could be that the narrator is highlighting Cilicia as being of special importance for this is the first mention of the province from where Paul originated and his later role in the story concerning Stephen (see 7:58; 8:1) suggests he would have been among those Jews from Cilicia disputing with Stephen. Asia, too, will later emerge as the place from where the fiercest Jewish opponents of Paul as a Jesus-believer came (see 21:27); pointing out their presence here anticipates the part they will continue to play in opposing the attitudes of Jewish Jesus-believers to the Temple (6:13–14; compare 21:28). If the unexpected absence of the article before Cilicia and Asia at 6:9 does indeed have a highlighting function, it can be assumed that the addressee of the narrative would have had an interest in, and understanding of, this aspect of the conflict between believers and non-believers.[30]

[30] If, as is claimed for the audience of the Bezan text (see Rius-Camps and Read-Heimerdinger, *The Message of Acts*, 1:40; 2:3–4; 3:3–4; 4:3–4), the addressee was Theophilus the High Priest of 37–41 C.E., then his identity accounts for the attention drawn to the people involved in disputes over the attitude of Jesus-believers to the Temple.

At 19:26, 27 the references to Asia made by Demetrius in his address to the Ephesian craftsmen could be seen as salient according to the articulation of the narrative. At 19:26, he speaks of the harm caused by Paul not only in Ephesus but also in the whole of Asia. In D05, an adverbial καί underlines how the damage has spread beyond Ephesus and throughout Asia, and the attention focused on Asia is reinforced by the absence of the article: οὐ μόνον Ἐφέσου ἀλλὰ <u>καὶ</u> σχεδὸν πάσης Ἀσίας. At 19:27, "the whole of Asia" is mentioned alongside the "inhabited world" as personifications of the worshippers of Artemis. B03 (alone) omits the article before both places; the first omission could have arisen through homoioteleuton (ΟΛΗΗΑCΙΑ) and the second then could be a means to balance the two phrases. Alternatively, both omissions could be a way of highlighting the wide extent of the worship of the goddess of Ephesus.

Cilicia

The first occurrence of Cilicia at 6:9, where it is anarthrous, is discussed above. The province always has the article at the three other occurrences in the portions of the text extant in D05 (15:23, 41; 22:3), as also at 27:5 (D05 lac). Once, however, at 23:34 (D05 lac) the mention is anarthrous. Here, the name is seen from the point of view of the governor Felix as he learns that Paul is from there. As such, the reference provides new, salient information, which accounts for the absence of the article.

Phoenicia

When Phoenicia is mentioned in Acts it is anarthrous at 11:19 and also 21:2; at 15:3, in contrast, it is arthrous. At the first mention, when Phoenicia appears at the head of a group of places including Cyprus and Antioch, it is very much salient information since this is the first time that Jesus-believers are reported to have travelled to these territories, a fact that the narrator draws attention to with the preposition ἕως. At 15:3, the regions of Phoenicia and Samaria are mentioned for the first time in the new context, but they are mentioned as places that inevitably had to be travelled through in order to reach the destination of Jerusalem (see 15:4) since the road went through them. As such, they are not highlighted and the article is retained.

At 21:2, Phoenicia is again mentioned for the first time in a new context. Here the information is more than part of an inevitable itinerary. Paul and his companions had to look for a suitable ship for the final sea crossing, being fortunate to find one that was going to Phoenicia, which was one alternative among others along the Syrian coast.

Pamphylia, Pisidia, Lycaonia

After the list of 2:9, the region of Pamphylia is first mentioned again at 13:13 as the area of the mainland at which Paul and his companions arrived on leaving Cyprus, with particular reference to the town of Perga, εἰς Πέργην τῆς Παμφυλίας. Here, it is Perga that is in focus, Pamphylia being the region that serves to identify it. In that respect, the reference is similar to that of 27:5, where it is a question of crossing the "open sea off Cilicia and Pamphylia" (κατὰ τὴν Κιλικίαν καὶ Παμφυλίαν).

At the one remaining mention of Pamphylia at 14:24, the article is present in B03 but not in D05. The region is mentioned in the course of the description of Paul's return journey to Antioch at the end of the first phase of his mission (14:21–27). A series of towns and regions along the way are referred to, all of them except the town of Attalia (14:25) having appeared previously in the account of the outward travel. After naming the three towns of Lystra, Iconium and Antioch (of Pisidia), the narrator then has the travellers go through the regions of first Pisidia and then Pamphylia, where they stop in the town of Perga. B03 has the article for both regions, unlike D05 which only has the article for Pisidia. That Pisidia should be arthrous can be explained by the geographical situation, for the last town they stopped in, Antioch, belonged to the province of Pisidia. After finishing their business in the church there, they travelled through the province, not as a new place but as one in which they were already present. Arriving in Pamphylia, on the other hand, is a new stage where a significant stop is made in Perga to "speak the word" for the first time in the town. D05 marks the development at 14:24 with the connective δέ and presents Pamphylia anarthrously, whereas B03 continues the narrative with καί and has the article before Pamphylia.

The other region mentioned during the course of this first phase of Paul's mission is Lycaonia. It is arthrous at the single occurrence at 14:6, where it arises with reference to two cities, Lystra and Derbe, which are introduced into the narrative here for the first time.

Syria

Syria is mentioned five times in Acts, with the article except at 20:3 D05 and 21:3 (D05 lac). The first occurrence of the name is at 15:23, where it occurs alongside Antioch and Cilicia in the address of the letter from Jerusalem to the churches in those regions. In those circumstances, the places are known and familiar entities and the article is unsurprising. At 15:41, where Syria is mentioned again arthrously and again together with Cilicia (the article is repeated in D05), the reference is anaphoric, relating as it does to the places named in the letter. The same is not true at the two other places where the reference is arthrous. At 18:18 and 20:3a B03, it is a question of Paul sailing to Syria (εἰς τὴν Συρίαν), where there is no preparation or warning that he would do so. Syria, however, is the destination of a sea journey that will take Paul back to familiar territory, which is where he was ultimately heading (Antioch, 18:22b–23a, or Jerusalem, 20:22; 21:15). So to say that, after spending extended time in Corinth/Greece, Paul set off for Syria is the equivalent of saying that "he went back home," which could be an expected move. A Jewish plot caused him to change his plans on the second occasion (20:3) and he decided to go through Macedonia instead (διὰ Μακεδονία). The unexpected mention of Macedonia and the contrast with the intended destination of Syria accounts for the omission of the article.

At 20:3 D05, though, there is no article before Syria. In the opening verses of Acts 20, D05 presents the events leading up to Paul's departure from Greece somewhat differently compared with most other manuscripts.[31] In D05, it is the plot of the Jews that causes Paul to want to sail for Syria (εἰς Συρίαν), as opposed to staying in Greece where he had arrived some three months earlier (εἰς τὴν Ἑλλάδα, 20:2). The timing of his decision to leave for Syria is thus presented as unexpected, prompted by the threat posed by the plot against him (though it is evident from his correspondence with the Corinthians that he had long intended to go from Corinth to Jerusalem; see

[31] For details, see Rius-Camps and Read-Heimerdinger, *The Message of Acts*, 4:83–84.

2 Cor 1:15–16). His decision is countered by the intervention of the Holy Spirit, who instructs him to return through Macedonia instead. Within the narrative of Acts according to D05, Macedonia would be an expected place to which to direct Paul for it has been clear since 19:1 D05, through a series of readings absent from most other manuscripts, that the divine plan was for Paul to be heading for Rome at this point but Paul's own plan was first to pay a last visit to Jerusalem. He had arrived in Macedonia (εἰς Μακεδονίαν, 20:1) on his way to Italy from Ephesus and then had headed south to Greece. The Spirit's direction to go back to Macedonia is thus both anaphoric and, within the Bezan articulation of the narrative, expected as the place intended by God for Paul to be.

When Paul's final arrival in Syria after the sea journey is recorded at 21:3 (D05 lac), Syria is once more anarthrous. The omission of the article is surprising in that Syria has long been established as the final destination of Paul's sea journey. It could be a tactic on the part of the narrator to highlight the arrival of Paul and his company after a long and eventful journey. As far as the narrator of the D05 text is concerned, and assuming that Syria is similarly anarthrous in that text (the Greek page of D05 is missing at this point), it is also possible that a contrast is being underlined with the island of Cyprus as the place that Paul ignored in his determination to get to Jerusalem. This point is developed with reference to Cyprus (see below).

Macedonia

The country of Macedonia is first mentioned in direct speech by a Macedonian man who, in a vision, called to Paul in Troas to go over to his country to help his people (16:9). The name is anarthrous, reflecting the salience of the country in the context of Paul being asked to go to a country that had apparently not figured in his plans hitherto, although there had been divine prompting to keep him moving westwards (see 16:6–7). According to the Bezan text, Paul shared his vision with his companions who included the narrator; they deduced that "the Lord was calling us to evangelize the people in Macedonia (ἐν τῃ Μακεδονίᾳ," 16:10b D05). The presence of the article could be explained by the fact that the reference is anaphoric, although from the point of view of the group who speak, it is a first mention and new information. It is perhaps more satisfactory to view the article as the default usage since that is the case for most other countries examined. When the country is mentioned for the third time in this context (16:12), it is the capital city of Philippi that is in focus, and Macedonia is once more arthrous.

Macedonia becomes topical again in the narrative at the point when Paul, then in Ephesus, is beginning to plan his final journey back to Jerusalem to deliver the collection from the Gentiles. In 19:21, Paul takes the decision to go to Macedonia and Achaia first, before travelling to Jerusalem; D05 reads the article before both countries, so treating them as distinct, but in B03 one article is used with respect to the two countries. Grouping them together in that way accounts for the absence of the article in B03 before Macedonia, when it is singled out in the following sentence (19:22) as the country to where Paul sent Timothy and Erastus ahead of him. In contrast, D05 retains the article, simply picking up the reference to Macedonia from the previous sentence, as the first place Paul planned to travel to.

Trouble in the city prevented Paul from leaving Ephesus immediately—when he did finally get away, it was to Macedonia that he went (20:1), the name being anarthrous without variant. The absence of the article is surprising in as much as Macedonia was the expected destination once Paul left Ephesus, given his careful advance planning (cf. 19:21–22). However, since making his plans, fierce opposition had arisen against Paul and other believers and was so intense that as soon as the uproar had quieted down Paul left Ephesus. First, though, as the narrator comments, he was at pains to meet with the disciples in the city and to talk with them at length. Ephesus is thus clearly in focus at the point when Paul is about to travel on, both from a negative point of view because of the extreme hostility and from a positive one because of the care Paul had for the disciples there. In that sense, then, Macedonia represents a switch of focus and a new area of activity (20:2), throughout the entire region according to D05 (πάντα τὰ μέρη ἐκεῖνα).[32]

[32] It is probable that Paul's extensive talks not only in Ephesus (20:1) but in Macedonia as well (20:2) were restricted to an audience of disciples, with the likely topic of the collection of money to be taken to Jerusalem, especially in the Bezan text where the verb παρακαλέω is twice replaced with more specific verbs of instructing (παρακελεύω) and forcefully urging (χράομαι λόγῳ πολλῷ; see Rius-Camps and Read-Heimerdinger, *The Message of Acts*, 4:82–83, 85–87).

The mention of Macedonia in 20:3 and the variant reading involving the use of the article are discussed in relation to Syria above.

Mysia, Bithynia, Thessaly

Toward the beginning of the second phase of Paul's mission, a number of regions are mentioned that Paul and Silas either passed through or attempted to go to. Following the intervention of the Holy Spirit to stop them from speaking the word (of God to anyone, D05) in Asia (16:6), they arrived at the border of Mysia to the northwest of Asia from where they wanted to go east into Bithynia (16:7). This time it was the spirit of Jesus who prevented them and so they headed south to Troas (16:8). The two references to Mysia, like Asia, are arthrous, as is also Bithynia in B03; in D05 the latter is anarthrous. With the article, Bithynia is not highlighted, as though it were a possible, expected step to go from Mysia to neighbouring Bithynia; indeed, B03 says that Paul and Silas attempted to go there: ἐπείραζον εἰς τὴν Βιθυνίαν πορευθῆναι. The Bezan text expresses it as a wish rather than an actual attempt: ἤθελαν εἰς Βιθυνίαν πορευθῆναι. Bearing in mind that the narrator of the Bezan text presents Paul as using tactics to delay the time when he would carry out God's purpose for him to go west to Rome, and given the three successive measures of divine intervention in 16:5–10 to keep him moving in that direction, his desire to turn east instead of west when he arrives at the border of Mysia is particularly significant for it underlines his resistance to God's leading.

An additional intervention to prevent Paul from speaking the word to a region that would take him away from Rome is recorded in D05. It occurs after the brethren helped him escape from the opposition against him in Thessalonica and Berea (17:1–14). Having taken him to the coast (south of these towns), they took him as far as Athens, sailing past Thessaly as the Bezan text reports (παρῆλθεν τὴν Θεσσαλίαν, 17:15 D05), since he was not allowed to proclaim the word there. The name is arthrous, the region remaining in the background as one that was bypassed.

Achaia

The four mentions of the Roman province of Achaia are arthrous, all of them isolated references (18:2 D05, 12; 27; 19:21).

Mountains

The only mountain mentioned in Acts is Sinai (7:30, 38), prefixed each time with the arthrous noun ὄρος.

Islands

A number of islands are mentioned in Acts, all of them in the course of Paul's journeys.

Cyprus

Cyprus is the only island to appear prior to the account of Paul's journeys, at 11:19 where the name is anarthrous, sandwiched between the region of Phoenicia and the city of Antioch. The exceptional interest of the place as one where the gospel was taken for the first time outside Judaea, Galilee and Samaria has been discussed with reference to Phoenicia above. The reference to Cyprus is also anarthrous at 13:4 and 15:39. At 13:4, the mention of the island is quite unanticipated at this point; moreover Cyprus will acquire considerable importance as symbolizing the first place across the sea to where the gospel was taken, representing a departure from the mainland of Judaea, Galilee, Samaria and Syria, an "exodus" from Judaism. There is, therefore, every reason to highlight it.

At 15:39, likewise, Cyprus is salient information as the place Barnabas chose to go to with Mark after his disagreement with Paul. It is important to note that in the Bezan text, the narrator presents this choice as evidence that it was Barnabas with Mark, and not Paul, who was in harmony with the divine plan, going back to the point of departure for the mission to the Gentiles (compare 13:4) while Paul is presented as continuing to be interested in developing his relationship with Jews.[33] It will eventually be made clear that the attention Paul devoted to his own people in giving them priority over the Gentiles was in contradiction with the orders of Jesus (see 22:17–21). As an integral expression of Paul's concern with the salvation of the Jews, he will travel to

---

[33] See Rius-Camps and Read-Heimerdinger, *The Message of Acts*, 3:passim, but esp. 3:230–41.

Jerusalem before going to Rome in order to personally deliver the collection from the Gentiles (20:3—21:17). His insistence on accomplishing this mission is presented by the narrator of Codex Bezae as being in contradiction with the guidance of the Holy Spirit, and his subsequent arrest as a direct consequence of his disobedience.[34]

The lasting symbolism of Cyprus as the place where the mission to the Gentiles was to have begun is seen in the remaining two references to the island, first at the point when Paul is about to complete his sea journey en route to Jerusalem (21:3 [D05 lac]) and then again as he leaves Sidon on his final voyage to Rome (27:4 [D05 lac]). Both references are arthrous, the importance of the island in the narrative having long been established but its significance for Paul remaining in the background on both occasions. As Paul's ship approaches Syria, the narrator comments that Cyprus was sighted, as could be expected, but was "left to port" (21:3). Although in terms of the account of the journey the comment is superfluous, it allows the narrator (of the Bezan text, at least) to make the point that the place where the mission to the Gentiles was begun was being ignored by Paul as he persisted with his goal of reaching Jerusalem and attempting to convince the Jews about Jesus. The reference to Cyprus could be the factor that causes Syria in this context to be named without the article, so establishing an unfavourable comparison (see above). In contrast, when Paul is at last on his way to Rome, safe under the protection of a Roman guard to ensure that he reaches the destination God intended for him, the ship sails close to Cyprus, keeping under its lee for protection (27:4).[35]

Other islands on Paul's journeys

Two more islands are mentioned in the course of the account of Paul's final journey to Jerusalem: Cos and Rhodes (21:1). Both references are arthrous in B03; the same is true of the island of Crete mentioned during the narrative of Paul's journey as a prisoner to Rome (27:1–28:14 [D05 lac]). The omission of the article before Cos and Rhodes in D05 may have arisen because both were also the names of cities as well as of islands, and when cities are mentioned for

---

[34] Ibid., 4:168–70, 257–68.

[35] See the discussion of this point in ibid., 4:384.

the first time in Acts they are typically anarthrous (see below). This is seen in the comparable references at 20:15 to Chios and Samos, again names of both islands and cities, but seemingly thought of as the latter here since the names are anarthrous in all manuscripts.

Cities

The use of the article with the names of cities is considerably more complex than with the names of other geographical locations. Some preliminary observations allow a general pattern of the use of the article with cities to be determined with relative ease, but there are many places where the usual pattern is not followed; there are, furthermore, a number of variant readings. In order to investigate the variation thoroughly, it would be essential to carry out a detailed investigation of the intention of the narrator at each point and of the particular articulation of the narrative in the distinct texts of the manuscripts. Such an enquiry is beyond the scope of this current study, so this section will be limited to noting some general points and examining the special case of Jerusalem.

Cities in general

When a city is mentioned for the first time in an episode it is almost always anarthrous. At subsequent mentions within the same episode, the article is then frequently present. Examples may be seen at 9:2 (D05 lac), 3 (D05 lac) – Damascus; 13:6, 13 – Paphos; 13:13, 14 – Perga; 17:15, 16; 18:1 – Athens; 18:19, 21; 18:24, 26 D05 – Ephesus; 20:15, 27 – Miletus. From this it may be concluded that the article is present by default and that its omission reflects the salience of a town when it is mentioned for the first time. In that respect, the pattern of the article with the names of cities is similar to that noted with the names of persons.

There are, however, several exceptions where the first mention is arthrous (17:1 – Amphipolis; 18:2 – Rome; 20:13 – Assos; 20:16 – Ephesus; 26:12 – Damascus). And many more which are anarthrous although anaphoric. These could be the starting point for further study.

Jerusalem

The numerous references to Jerusalem (× 47 D05; × 41 B03)[36] have not been included in the Appendix because they would have unduly overloaded the list since, whether the Hebrew derived form Ἰερουσαλήμ or the Hellenistic spelling Ἱεροσόλυμα is used, the occurrences are always anarthrous with one exception at 5:28 (τὴν Ἰερουσαλήμ).[37] This is an unexpected pattern in view of what has been established regarding other cities; it may be suggested that it is the special nature of Jerusalem that produces the unusual absence of the article, for the city was not only the religious center of Judaism but also a geographical location in its own right, and furthermore of central significance to the development of the narrative as the focus of attention moves progressively away from Jerusalem towards the west, even when the action continues to return there.

It is instructive to consider the context at 5:28: Jerusalem is mentioned in direct speech by a member of the Sanhedrin (the priest D05 or the high priest B03) as he interrogates the apostles about their teaching regarding Jesus in the Temple which they had earlier been forbidden to continue (see 4:18). He objects that they have "filled Jerusalem" with their teaching. Within his work, Luke uses the Hebrew-derived spelling of Jerusalem to refer to the city as the center of Jewish worship and life,[38] of which the Sanhedrin represents the supreme authority. As such, it is typically attributed to speakers who assigned significance to Jerusalem for this very reason. Moreover, since this appearance of the apostles before the Sanhedrin takes place in the locality of Jerusalem, the reference in this case is to the immediate environment. Thus, it is as if the speakers were saying "you have filled Jerusalem here with your teaching."

---

[36] At the majority of references to Jerusalem in the text of Acts extant in Codex Bezae (up to 22:29a), the same spelling is found without variant. There are four places of variant reading and six additional mentions of the city in D05, as follows: Ἰερουσαλήμ: 2:42 D05; 8:1b D05, 14 D05; 11:2 B03; 15:2a D05, 4 D05; 20:22 B03; Ἱεροσόλυμα: 8:14 B03; 11:2 D05; 15:4 B03; 18:21 D05; 19:1 D05; 20:22 D05, 23 D05. After 22:29b, there are 13 further references to the city by name in the extant manuscripts, always anarthrous as in the earlier parts of the book.

[37] The single exception in Acts is noted by many of the standard grammars, see e.g., BDR, §261.

[38] For a study of this question, see Read-Heimerdinger, *The Bezan Text*, 311–44.

This is the only occurrence of Jerusalem with this kind of immediate and direct relevance. A comparable mention of Jerusalem is made by a speaker while he is in the city in 4:16 where Gamaliel addresses the Sanhedrin precisely on the occasion which will conclude with the apostles being forbidden to utter the name of Jesus again. There, however, Gamaliel refers to everyone living in Jerusalem (πᾶσιν τοῖς κατοικοῦσιν Ἰερουσαλήμ) having heard about the apostles' healing activity where it is the people rather than the city that is in focus. On one other occasion, Jerusalem is mentioned in a similar context to that of 5:28, where it was reported to the chiliarch that "all of Jerusalem is in confusion" (21:31, ὅλη συγχύννεται Ἰερουσαλήμ) but there the reference is indirect, made anonymously via the narrator.

The possibility that the absence of the article before Jerusalem indicates a first mention is not borne out by the evidence. On the contrary, some occurrences of the name arise in quick succession within the same episode, even within the same sentence, and with the same spelling (e.g., 1:12a, 12b; 8:26, 27; 21:11, 12, 13). Some of the references do, it is true, involve a contrast, one that is made all the sharper by a change of spelling because of the distinct connotations associated with each form of the name that allows the narrator to make use of the distinction as a tool to evaluate his characters' attachment to Jerusalem as a spiritual center (e.g., when Paul is in Caesarea he is warned that it is in the religious institution of Ἰερουσαλήμ [21:11, 12, 13] that he will meet hostility, and not in the city of Ἱεροσόλυμα where he initially arrives [21:15, 17]).

It would appear, then, that references to Jerusalem are normally anarthrous, and that the presence of the article depends on a speaker-hearer context of immediacy in both a local and a temporal sense.

Conclusion

In his analysis of the article with nouns in general in Plato, Sansone concluded that "study of the phenomenon [the article] requires the application of semantic, syntactic, pragmatic, psychological, and even historical categories."[39]

[39] Sansone, "Towards a New Doctrine," 205.

The analysis carried out here of the article with geographical names bears out that conclusion.

As an overall pattern it has been seen that place names are generally arthrous, with the three exceptions of Israel, Egypt and Jerusalem. In the case of Israel, it was noted that the name is not strictly a geographical name in Acts but an ethnic one; most of the references involve a stereotypical phrase, which is always anarthrous. The context of the references to Egypt, chiefly Stephen's speech where Egypt is of special significance for his history of Israel, may account for the almost consistent omission of the article. As for Jerusalem, the pattern of the article is different from that observed with other cities; it may be again surmised that the significance of the city within the context of the narrative is what causes this difference. Comparison with other writers, including ones outside the Bible, could serve to verify the supposition.

The first mention of a place does not bring about the omission of the article, except for cities where it happens with some regularity. The idea that grammatical constraints (for example, an oblique case or preposition) dictate whether the article should be used or not is not substantiated. There are a number of places, notably regions whatever their size or history or significance for the story, that are only referred to with the article even at the first mention. When references are anarthrous, it can generally be seen that the place is being highlighted because of its significance for an active participant at that point in the narrative. So while the default presence of the article with geographical names is similar to what has been noticed with names of persons, and the overall reason for omitting the article is salience in both cases, the nature of the salience within the scheme of the discourse varies. In the case of places, it is not so much that the place is important for the articulation of the narrative or speech but rather for the activity of a character within the story.

Bibliography

Barrett, Charles Kingsley. *A Critical and Exegetical Commentary on the Acts of the Apostles*. 2 vols. International Critical Commentary. Edinburgh: T. & T. Clark, 1994, 1998.

Blass Friedrich W., Albert Debrunner and Friedrich Rehkopf. *Grammatik des neutestamentlichen Griechisch*. 15th ed. Göttingen: Vandenhoeck & Ruprecht, 1979.

Caragounis, Chrys. *The Development of Greek and the New Testament: Morphology, Syntax, Phonology, and Textual Transmission.* Grand Rapids: Baker Academic, 2006.

Gildersleeve, Basil L. "On the Article with Proper Names." *American Journal of Philology* 11 (1890): 483–87.

———. *Syntax of Classical Greek from Homer to Demosthenes.* 2 vols. New York: American Book Company, 1900–1911.

———. "Problems in Greek Syntax: II. The Article." *American Journal of Philology* 23 (1902): 9–11.

Heimerdinger, Jenny, and Stephen H. Levinsohn. "The Use of the Definite Article before Names of People in the Greek Text of Acts with Particular Reference to Codex Bezae." *Filologia Neotestamentaria* 5 (1992): 15–44.

Hemer, Colin J. *The Book of Acts in the Setting of Hellenistic History.* Edited by Conrad H. Gempf; Tübingen: J. C. B. Mohr, 1989.

Levinsohn, Stephen H. *Discourse Features of New Testament Greek.* 2nd ed. Dallas: Summer Institute of Linguistics, 2000.

Porter, Stanley E. *Idioms of New Testament Greek.* Biblical Languages: Greek 2. Sheffield: JSOT Press, 1992.

Read-Heimerdinger, Jenny. *The Bezan Text of Acts: A Contribution of Discourse Analysis to Textual Criticism.* Journal for the Study of the New Testament Supplement Series 236. Sheffield: Sheffield Academic Press, 2002.

Rius-Camps, Josep and Jenny Read-Heimerdinger. *The Message of Acts in Codex Bezae: A Comparison with the Alexandrian Tradition.* 4 vols. Journal for the Study of the New Testament Supplement Series 257/Library of New Testament Studies 302, 365, 415. London : T. & T. Clark, 2002–2009.

Robertson, A. T. *A Grammar of the Greek New Testament in the Light of Historical Research.* 4th ed. Nashville: Broadman, 1934.

Sansone, David. "Towards a New Doctrine of the Article." *Classical Philology* 88 (1993): 191–205.

Wallace, Daniel B. *Greek Grammar Beyond the Basics: An Exegetical Syntax of the New Testament.* Grand Rapids: Zondervan, 1996.

Winer, Georg Benedikt. *A Treatise on the Grammar of New Testament Greek Regarded as a Sure Basis for New Testament Exegesis.* 3rd ed. Translated by W. F. Moulton. Edinburgh: T. & T. Clark, 1882.

Appendix

Place Names in Acts, Showing the Use of the Article

Appendix to: The Use of the Article Before Names of Places: Patterns of Use in the Book of Acts

Jenny Read-Heimerdinger

Reference	Place Name	Arthrous	Anarthrous	Type of place
1:8	Ἰουδαία καὶ Σαμαρία	√ single for pair		regions
2:9	Μεσοποταμία	√		region
	Ἰουδαία		√	region
	Καππαδοκία		√	region
	Πόντος		√	region
	Ἀσία	√		country/region
	Φρυγία		√	region
	Παμφυλία		√	region
	Αἴγυπτος		√	country
	Λιβύη	√		region
	Κυρήνη		√	region/city
2:36	Ἰσραήλ		√	country; house of
4:8 D05	Ἰσραήλ	√		country; elders of
4:10	Ἰσραήλ		√	country; people of

Reference	Place Name	Arthrous	Anarthrous	Type of place
4:27	Ἰσραήλ		√	country; people of
5:21	Ἰσραήλ		√	country; sons of
5:31	Ἰσραήλ	√		country; repentance to
6:9	Κιλικία		√	region
6.9 B03	Ἀσία		√	region
7:2	Μεσοποτάμια	√		region
7:2	Χαρράν		√	city
7:4	Χαρράν		√	city
7:9	Αἴγυπτος		√	country
7:10 x 2	Αἴγυπτος		√	country
7:11	Αἴγυπτος	√		country
7:11	Χαναάν		√	country
7:12	Αἴγυπτος		√	country
7:15 D05	Αἴγυπτος		√	country
7:16a	Συχέμ (Συχέν D05)		√	city (person D05)
7:16b	Συχέμ	√		city
7:17	Αἴγυπτος		√	country
7:18 B03	Αἴγυπτος		√	country
7:23	Ἰσραήλ		√	country; sons of
7:29	Μαδιάμ		√	region
7:30	Σινᾶ		√	mountain
7:34 x 2	Αἴγυπτος		√	country
7:36	Αἴγυπτος		√	country
7:37	Ἰσραήλ		√	country; sons of
7:38	Σινᾶ		√	mountain
7:39	Αἴγυπτος		√	country
7:40	Αἴγυπτος		√	country

Reference	Place Name	Arthrous	Anarthrous	Type of place
7:42	Ἰσραήλ		√	country; house of
7:43	Βαβυλών		√	country
8:1	Ἰουδαία καὶ Σαμαρία	B03 single for pair	D05	regions
8:5	Σαμαρία	√		region
8:9	Σαμαρία	√		region
8:14	Σαμαρία	√		region
8:26	Γάζα		√	city
8:40	Ἄζωτος		√	city
8:40	Καισάρεια		√	city
9:2 D lac	Δαμασκός		√	city
9:3 D lac	Δαμασκός	√		city
9:8 D lac	Δαμασκός		√	city
9:10 D lac	Δαμασκός		√	city
9:15 D lac	Ἰσραήλ		√	country; sons of
9:22 D lac	Δαμασκός		√	city
9:28 D lac	Δαμασκός		√	city
9:30 D lac	Καισάρεια		√	city
9:30 D lac	Ταρσός		√	city
9:31 D lac	Ἰουδαία καὶ Γαλιλαία καὶ Σαμαρία	√ single for three		regions
9:32 D lac	Λύδδα		√	city
9:35 D lac	Λύδδα		√	city
9:35 D lac	Σαρόν	√		region
9:36 D lac	Ἰόππη		√	city
9:38 D lac	Λύδδα		√	city
9:38 D lac	Ἰόππη	√		city
9:42 D lac	Ἰόππη	√		city
9:43 D lac	Ἰόππη		√	city
10:1 D lac	Καισάρεια		√	city

Reference	Place Name	Arthrous	Anarthrous	Type of place
10:5 D lac	Ἰόππη		√	city
10:8 D lac	Ἰόππη	√		city
10:23	Ἰόππη		√	city
10:24	Καισάρεια	B03	D05	city
10:25	Καισάρεια	√		city
10:32	Ἰόππη		√	city
10:36	Ἰσραήλ		√	country; sons of
10:37a	Ἰουδαία	B03	D05	city
10:37b	Γαλιλαία	√		region
10:38	Ναζαρέθ		√	city
11:1	Ἰουδαία	√		region
11:5	Ἰόππη		√	city
11:11	Καισάρεια		√	city
11:13	Ἰόππη		√	city
11:19	Φοινίκη καὶ Κύπρος καὶ Ἀντιόχεια		√	region, island, city
11:20	Ἀντιόχεια		√	city
11:22	Ἀντιόχεια	D05	B03	city
11:25	Ταρσός		√	city
11:26 x 2	Ἀντιόχεια		√	city
11:27	Ἀντιόχεια		√	city
11:29	Ἰουδαία	√		region
12:1 D05	Ἰουδαία	√		region
12:19	Ἰουδαία	√		region
12:19	Καισάρεια		√	city
13:1	Ἀντιόχεια		√	city
13:4	Σελεύκεια		√	city
13:4	Κύπρος		√	island
13:5	Σαλαμίς	D05	B03	city
13:6	Πάφος		√	city

Reference	Place Name	Arthrous	Anarthrous	Type of place
13:13	Πάφος	√		city
13:13	Πέργη		√	city
13:13	Παμφυλία	√		region
13:14	Πέργη	√		city
13:14	Ἀντιόχεια		√	city
13:14	Πισιδία	√		region
13:51	Ἰκόνιος		√	city
14:1	Ἰκόνιος		√	city
14:6	Λυκαονία	√		region
14:6	Λύστρα καὶ Δέρβη		√	city
14:7 D05	Λύστρα		√	city
14:19	Ἰκόνιος καὶ Ἀντιόχεια		√	city
14:20	Δέρβη		√	city
14:21	Λύστρα	B03	D05	city
14:21	Ἰκόνιος καὶ Ἀντιόχεια		√	city
14:24	Πισιδία	√		region
14:24	Παμφυλία	B03	D05	region
14:25	Πέργη		√	city
14:25	Ἀττάλεια		√	city
14:26	Ἀντιόχεια		√	city
15.1	Ἰουδαία	√		region
15:3	Φοινίκη καὶ Σαμαρία	√ single for pair		regions
15:23	Ἀντιόχεια καὶ Συρία καὶ Κιλικία	√ single for three		city, regions
15:30	Ἀντιόχεια		√	city
15:35	Ἀντιόχεια		√	city
15:38	Παμφυλία		√	region
15:39	Κύπρος		√	island

Reference	Place Name	Arthrous	Anarthrous	Type of place
15:41	Συρία καὶ Κιλικία	√		regions
16:1	Δέρβη καὶ Λύστρα		√	cities
16:2	Λύστρα καὶ Ἰκόνιος		√	cities
16:6	Ἀσία	√		region
16:7	Μυσία	√		region
16:7	Βιθύνια	B03	D05	region
16:8	Μυσία	√		region
16:8	Τρῳάς		√	city
16:9	Μακεδονία		√	region
16:10 D05	Μακεδονία	√		region
16:11	Τρῳάς		√	city
16:11	Σαμοθράκη		√	city
16:11	Νεάπολις		√	city
16:12	Φιλίπποι		√	city
16:12	Μακεδονία	√		region
17:1	Ἀμφίπολις	√		city
17:1	Ἀπολλονία	B03	D05	city
17:1	Θεσσαλονίκη		√	city
17:10	Βέροια		√	city
17:11	Θεσσαλονίκη	D05	B03	city
17:13	Θεσσαλονίκη	B03	D05	city
17:15	Ἀθῆναι		√	city
17:15 D05	Θεσσαλία	√		region
17:16	Ἀθῆναι	√		city
18:1	Ἀθῆναι	√		city
18:1	Κόρινθος		√	city
18:2	Ἰταλία	√		country
18:2	Ῥώμη	√		city
18:2 D05	Ἀχαία	√		region

Reference	Place Name	Arthrous	Anarthrous	Type of place
18:12	Ἀχαία	√		region
18:18	Συρία	√		region
18:18	Κενχρεαί		√	city
18:19	Ἔφεσος		√	city
18:21	Ἔφεσος	√		city
18:22	Καισάρεια		√	city
18:22	Ἀντιόχεια		√	city
18:24	Ἔφεσος		√	city
18:26 D05	Ἔφεσος	√		city
18:27 D05	Κόρινθος		√	city
18:27	Ἀχαία	√		region
19:1 D05	Ἀσία	√		region
19:1 B03	Κόρινθος		√	city
19:1	Ἔφεσος		√	city
19:10	Ἀσία	√		region
19:17	Ἔφεσος		√	city
19:21	Μακεδονία καὶ Ἀχαία	√ (single for pair, B03)		regions
19:21	Ῥώμη		√	city
19:22	Μακεδονία	D05	B03	region
19:22	Ἀσία	√		region
19:26	Ἔφεσος		√	city
19:26	Ἀσία	B03	D05	region
19:27	Ἀσία	D05	B03	region
20:1	Μακεδονία		√	region
20:2	Ἑλλάς	√		country
20:3a	Συρία	B03	D05	region
20:3b	Μακεδονία	D05	B03	region
20:4 D05	Ἀσία	√		region
20:5	Τρωάς		√	city
20:6	Φιλίπποι		√	city
20:6	Τρωάς	B03	D05	city

Reference	Place Name	Arthrous	Anarthrous	Type of place
20:13	Ἄσσος	√		city
20:14	Ἄσσος	√		city
20:14	Μιτυλήνη	√	√	city
20:15	Χίος		√	island/city
20:15	Σάμος		√	island/city
20:15 D05	Τρωγυλία		√	city
20:15	Μίλητος		√	city
20:16	Ἔφεσος	√		city
20:16	Ἀσία	√		region
20:17	Μίλητος	√		city
20:17	Ἔφεσος		√	city
20:18	Ἀσία	√		region
21:01	Κός	B03	D05	island/city
21:1	Ῥόδος	B03	D05	island/city
21:1	Πάταρα		√	city
21:1 D05	Μύρα		√	city
21:2	Φοινίκη		√	region
21:3 D lac	Κύπρος	√		island
21:3 D lac	Συρία		√	region
21:3 D lac	Τύρος		√	city
21:7 D lac	Τύρος		√	city
21:7 D lac	Πτολεμαΐς		√	city
21:8 D lac	Καισάρεια		√	city
21:10 D lac	Ἰουδαία	√		region
21:16	Καισάρεια		√	city
21:27	Ἀσία	√		region
22:3	Ταρσός		√	city
22:3	Κιλιλία	√		region
22:5	Δαμασκός		√	city
22:6	Δαμασκός	B03	D05	city
22:10	Δαμασκός		√	city
22:11 D lac	Δαμασκός		√	city

Reference	Place Name	Arthrous	Anarthrous	Type of place
23:11 D lac	Ῥώμη		√	city
23:23 D lac	Καισάρεια		√	city
23:31 D lac	Ἀντιπατρίς	√		region
23:33 D lac	Καισάρεια	√		city
23:34 D lac	Κιλικία		√	region
25:1 D lac	Καισάρεια		√	city
25:4 D lac	Καισάρεια		√	city
25:6 D lac	Καισάρεια		√	city
25:13 D lac	Καισάρεια		√	city
26:12 D lac	Δαμασκός	√		city
26:20 D lac	Δαμασκός		√	city
26:20 D lac	Ἰουδαία	√		region
27:2 D lac	Ἀσία	√		region
27:3 D lac	Σιδών		√	city
27:4 D lac	Κύπρος	√		island
27:5 D lac	Κιλικία καὶ Παμφιλία	√ single for two		regions
27:5 D lac	Μύρα		√	city
27:5 D lac	Λυκία	√		region
27:6 D lac	Ἰταλία	√		country
27:7 D lac	Κνίδος	√		city
27:7 D lac	Κρήτη	√		island
27:7 D lac	Σαλμώνη		√	city
27:8 D lac	Λασαία		√	city
27:12 D lac	Φοίνικα		√	city
27:12 D lac	Κρήτη	√		island
27:13 D lac	Κρήτη	√		island
27:17 D lac	Σύρτις	√		area of quicksand
27:21 D lac	Κρήτη	√		island
27:27 D lac	Ἀδρίας	√		sea
28:12 D lac	Συρακούσα		√	city

Reference	Place Name	Arthrous	Anarthrous	Type of place
28:13 D lac	Ῥήγιος		√	city
28:13 D lac	Ποτιόλοι		√	city
28:14 D lac	Ῥώμη	√		city
28:16 D lac	Ῥώμη	א01	B03	city

Author Index

Scripture Index

Ezekiel

John

Acts

www.ingramcontent.com/pod-product-compliance
Lightning Source LLC
LaVergne TN
LVHW080412220926
848584LV00029B/308
9781577995203